Exploring the Basic Income Guarantee

Series Editor

Karl Widerquist
Associate Professor, SFS-Qatar
Georgetown University
Doha, Qatar

Basic income is one of the most innovative, powerful, straightforward, and controversial proposals for addressing poverty and growing inequalities. A Basic Income Guarantee (BIG) is designed to be an unconditional, government-insured guarantee that all citizens will have enough income to meet their basic needs. The concept of basic, or guaranteed, income is a form of social provision and this series examines the arguments for and against it from an interdisciplinary perspective with special focus on the economic and social factors. By systematically connecting abstract philosophical debates over competing principles of BIG to the empirical analysis of concrete policy proposals, this series contributes to the fields of economics, politics, social policy, and philosophy and establishes a theoretical framework for interdisciplinary research. It will bring together international and national scholars and activists to provide a comparative look at the main efforts to date to pass unconditional BIG legislation across regions of the globe and will identify commonalities and differences across countries drawing lessons for advancing social policies in general and BIG policies in particular.

More information about this series at
http://www.springer.com/series/14981

Malcolm Torry

The Feasibility of Citizen's Income

palgrave
macmillan

Malcolm Torry
London, United Kingdom

Exploring the Basic Income Guarantee
ISBN 978-1-137-53077-6   ISBN 978-1-137-53078-3 (eBook)
DOI 10.1057/978-1-137-53078-3

Library of Congress Control Number: 2016940869

© The Editor(s) (if applicable) and The Author(s) 2016
This work is subject to copyright. All rights are solely and exclusively licensed by the Publisher, whether the whole or part of the material is concerned, specifically the rights of translation, reprinting, reuse of illustrations, recitation, broadcasting, reproduction on microfilms or in any other physical way, and transmission or information storage and retrieval, electronic adaptation, computer software, or by similar or dissimilar methodology now known or hereafter developed.
The use of general descriptive names, registered names, trademarks, service marks, etc. in this publication does not imply, even in the absence of a specific statement, that such names are exempt from the relevant protective laws and regulations and therefore free for general use. The publisher, the authors and the editors are safe to assume that the advice and information in this book are believed to be true and accurate at the date of publication. Neither the publisher nor the authors or the editors give a warranty, express or implied, with respect to the material contained herein or for any errors or omissions that may have been made.

Cover illustration: Tony Eveling / Alamy Stock Photo

Printed on acid-free paper

This Palgrave Macmillan imprint is published by Springer Nature
The registered company is Nature America Inc. New York

Preface

There is no shortage of debate about the desirability and feasibility of the State paying to every citizen an unconditional regular income. Whether we call it a Basic Income, a Citizen's Income, or a Universal Basic Income,[1] increasing numbers of individuals, think tanks, and governments are taking the idea seriously. Successful pilot projects have taken place in Namibia and India[2]; Iran has found itself with something like a Citizen's Income[3]; and Switzerland is soon to hold a referendum on whether to establish a Citizen's Income.[4] In the UK, significant think tanks across the political spectrum are conducting their own research on the idea,[5] and at the 2015 General Election the Green Party had a proposal to plan for a Citizen's Income in its manifesto.[6]

It is essential that the increasingly widespread debate should be well informed. There is already a massive Citizen's Income literature—newspaper and journal articles, website articles, introductions to the subject, reports on pilot projects, and surveys of the state of the debate in different countries and around the world[7]—and the debate is already well informed by detailed studies of aspects of feasibility;[8] but so far we have been lacking a full-length study of a Citizen's Income's feasibility. This book seeks to fill that gap.

Citizen's Income is a global issue. Thirty years ago, the Basic Income European Network (BIEN) brought together individuals from a variety of European countries in which the Citizen's Income proposal was being discussed. By the turn of the millennium, it was clear that the movement was becoming global rather than European, so BIEN became BIEN—the Basic Income Earth Network: a rather clumsy name, but nobody wanted to lose the acronym.[9] This book is designed for that global debate. The main body of each chapter is therefore a general discussion of a particular aspect of a Citizen's Income's feasibility. This general discussion will apply in any country[10] and in any social and economic context. Each chapter also contains a case study which applies the general points made in the body of the chapter to a particular country's situation. While the case studies are necessarily about particular situations, it is hoped that readers will be able to adapt them to their own situations, both in broad outline and in detail. Most of the case studies relate to the UK for three reasons: because that is the situation that I know best; because readers might find it helpful to get to know one particular situation well in order to understand how different feasibilities might relate to each other in practice; and because the UK's current tax and benefits system contains all of the elements that are likely to be found in other country's systems. It would be a pleasure to see similar detailed case studies written for other countries.

I hope that this book will be useful to governments, think tanks, public servants, and others who are thinking about how their countries' tax and benefits systems might better serve a fast-changing world, and who are wondering whether the Citizen's Income proposal that so many people are talking about might be feasible. I also hope that the book will contribute usefully to the existing academic debate on Citizen's Income's desirability and feasibility, and to public education about an idea that is now regularly in the news; and that it will stimulate a major international research effort on the desirability and feasibility of Citizen's Income.

London, UK   Malcolm Torry

Terminology[11]

(Tax and benefits names will be capitalized where they are the names of particular benefits—for instance, the UK's Jobseeker's Allowance, or the USA's Earned Income Tax Credit. Generic types will not be capitalized. So 'income tax' means any tax on income, whereas in a UK context 'Income Tax' means the UK's Income Tax along with its rates, thresholds, and regulations. Technical terms such as Tax Credit and Negative Income Tax might also be capitalized in order to emphasize that these mechanisms have clear technical definitions. Quotation marks around a national benefit's name carry the suggestion that the name does not represent the reality; so in the UK, 'Working Tax Credit' is a means-tested benefit and not a Tax Credit.)

Citizen's Income

A Citizen's Income is an unconditional, nonwithdrawable income paid automatically to every individual as a right of citizenship.

- 'Unconditional' means that the level of the Citizen's Income would vary with someone's age, but there would be no other conditions; so everyone of the same age would receive the same Citizen's Income, whatever their employment status, whatever their family structure, whatever their housing status, and whatever their other income or wealth.
- 'Automatic' means that every individual's Citizen's Income would be paid weekly or monthly, would start at birth, and would stop when they died.

- 'Nonwithdrawable' means that if someone's earned income rose, or their wealth increased, then their Citizen's Income would not change.
- 'Individual' means that Citizen's Incomes would be paid to individuals, and not to couples or households.
- 'As a right of citizenship' means that everybody legally resident in the country would receive a Citizen's Income.[12]

The word 'universal' is sometimes added to the definition: 'a universal, unconditional ...' and so on, but this is not necessary as the income's unconditionality, its nonwithdrawability, and its payment as a right of citizenship between them imply universality.

A Citizen's Income is sometimes called a Basic Income or a Universal Basic Income. Sometimes the words 'guarantee' and 'minimum' are used to describe a Citizen's Income. We shall not use these words in this book because in the UK and some other countries, the words 'guarantee' and 'minimum' have been used to denote means-tested benefits.

Citizen's Income, Citizen's Incomes, a Citizen's Income

The ways in which these different expressions are used are somewhat fluid.

'Citizen's Income', without an article, generally means the idea itself: that is, the proposal that every individual should be paid an unconditional and nonwithdrawable income.

The addition of an indefinite article introduces an ambiguity. 'A Citizen's Income' can mean the same as 'Citizen's Income': that is, the idea itself. The following two sentences therefore mean the same thing: 'Citizen's Income is a brilliant idea', 'A Citizen's Income is a brilliant idea.' When preceded by an indefinite article, 'a Citizen's Income' might also refer to a particular or generic individual's Citizen's Income: 'If a working age adult were to be paid a Citizen's Income then they would be more likely to seek employment.'

If a possessive pronoun precedes 'Citizen's Income', then the reference will be to a particular or generic individual's Citizen's Income: 'Where means-tested benefits remain in place, her Citizen's Income will be taken into account when they are calculated.'

'Citizen's Incomes' in the plural will always refer to the incomes paid to a group of individuals: 'Young people would be paid Citizen's Incomes rather than being given personal tax allowances.' Because all of their

Citizen's Incomes would be the same, it would also be correct to say: 'Young people would be paid a Citizen's Income rather than being given personal tax allowances.'

Citizen's Income Scheme

A Citizen's Income is an unconditional, nonwithdrawable income paid to every individual as a right of citizenship. This definition never changes.

A Citizen's Income *scheme* is constituted by Citizen's Incomes (with rates specified for defined age groups) and by the means of funding the Citizen's Incomes, for instance, specified changes to existing tax and benefits regulations, descriptions of new taxes, or proposals for permanent fund dividends or for money creation.

Universal Benefits

This term always means 'universal within constraints'. For instance: a 'universal' benefit within a particular country means a benefit received by everyone within that country; and a 'universal child benefit' means a benefit received by every child. We call the UK's Winter Fuel Allowance universal because it goes to every citizen who receives a State pension. 'Universal' usually connotes unconditionality, so the UK's Child Benefit and its Winter Fuel Allowance are unconditional. The connection between universality and unconditionality is that if a benefit is unconditional, then there can be no conditions that would cause someone who did not fulfil them to cease to receive the benefit.

Tax Credit and Negative Income Tax

A Tax Credit is an amount of money ascribed to an individual and administered either by the government or by their employer. If earnings are below a defined threshold, then a proportion of the Tax Credit is paid to them, with the proportion depending upon the difference between the threshold and the wage received. If earnings are at the threshold, then no Tax Credit is paid to the employee and no tax is collected. If earnings are above the threshold, then no Tax Credit is paid to the employee and income tax is collected from them. The rate at which the Credit is withdrawn as wages rise below the threshold might be the same as the income tax rate, or it might be different.

A Negative Income Tax is the same as a Tax Credit except that the specification is different. Instead of a defined Tax Credit being ascribed, tax rates are defined. If wages fall below the threshold, then a payment is made equal to the tax rate multiplied by the difference between the wage received and the threshold (hence *negative* income tax). Above the threshold, income tax is charged. The rates above and below might be the same, or they might be different.

Further discussion of Tax Credits and Negative Income Tax can be found in Chap. 6.

Social Insurance, or Contributory, Benefits

In many countries, employees and self-employed individuals pay social insurance contributions, generally in proportion to earned income. Social insurance benefits are paid if a contingency arises—such as retirement, sickness, maternity, or unemployment—and if the defined contribution conditions have been fulfilled. The benefits might be genuinely 'insurance' benefits if contributions are paid into a dedicated fund and if the amounts and durations of benefits are based on actuarial calculations. If there is no dedicated fund, if contributions are credited when no contributions have been paid (for instance, when an individual is caring for young children or is ill), and if benefit levels and durations are not based on actuarial calculations, then the benefits might still be called 'insurance' benefits, but they ought not to be. They might or might not legitimately be called 'contributory' benefits.

Means-Tested Benefits

Means-tested benefits are paid on the basis of a calculation of a household's needs and the means that it has available to meet them. Calculations generally begin with an element for each household member for living costs. Separate amounts for housing and/or heating costs might be added based on actual expenditure. Defined proportions of any earnings and/or income from savings will then be deducted, and the resulting figure will then be paid to a member of the household. Additional tests might be applied, and in particular 'work tests', which require working-age adults to prove that they are seeking or preparing for employment; and because the household is the basis of the benefit calculation, there will generally be a relationship or cohabitation test to determine who is living with whom.

Marginal Deduction Rate

If someone is earning £x and they earn an extra £1, then income tax will be deducted from that £1, social insurance contributions might be deducted from the £1, and if they are receiving means-tested benefits then these will be withdrawn from the extra £1 according to a defined taper. The total withdrawal rate applied to the extra £1 is the '*marginal* deduction rate' because it is on additional income, not on total income.

UK Benefits[13]

Because many of the case studies in this book are based on the UK's benefits system, it might help readers to be aware of the names of some of the benefits available in the UK.

There are a number of contributory benefits, for instance, Contribution-based Jobseeker's Allowance (for the unemployed), Contributory Employment and Support Allowance (for people who are sick or disabled), and Basic State Pension. The first two are time-limited. If these benefits expire, or they are not enough to live on, then the household can claim means-tested benefits.

Means-tested benefits are available both in and out of employment. Working Tax Credits and Child Tax Credits are means-tested benefits paid to households with an adult in employment of at least sixteen hours a week. Income-based Jobseeker's Allowance is paid to someone unemployed, and Income Support to someone not expected to seek employment (e.g., the lone mother of very young children). Income-related Employment Support Allowance is paid to people with disabilities or an illness, and is meant to help them into employment. Pension Credit is a means-tested pension top-up; Housing Benefit is a locally administered means-tested benefit to help with housing costs; and Council Tax Support is a locally regulated and administered benefit to help with local Council Tax. The new 'Universal Credit' (which is neither universal nor a credit) is slowly replacing many of these means-tested benefits.

Some benefits are not contributory and not means-tested, for instance, Child Benefit, Winter Fuel Allowance for people receiving a State pension, and Disability Living Allowance to help with the costs of disability.

The Structure of the Book

The book opens with a chapter that defines a Citizen's Income and then discusses its desirability. The rest of the book, from Chap. 2 onwards, is on the feasibility of Citizen's Income—or rather, feasibilities, in the plural. Much of the content follows a conceptual structure formulated and discussed in two articles by De Wispelaere and Stirton and a chapter by De Wispelaere and Noguera.[14] Chapter 2 introduces the different kinds of feasibility; Chaps. 3 and 4 discuss two different kinds of financial feasibility; Chap. 5 discusses psychological feasibility, Chap. 6 administrative feasibility, Chap. 7 behavioural feasibility, Chap. 8 political feasibility, and Chap. 9 policy process feasibility. Chapter 10 asks how conclusions that we have drawn about feasibility might relate to implementation, and it asks whether the world really works in the way that previous chapters suggest that it does.

Acknowledgements

My acquaintance with the UK's benefits system began over forty years ago when during university holidays I worked in Bexleyheath's Department of Health and Social Security office. I spent several weeks filing National Insurance stamp cards. This was when employers had to buy stamps for their employees and stick them on cards, which were then sent in to form their employees' National Insurance records. My Uncle Norman worked in the office, which is how I got the job. He died some years ago, but before he did we occasionally discussed the state of the benefits system and how to reform it. I am still grateful to him for providing my first close encounter with the UK's benefits system. I am equally grateful to the staff of Brixton's Supplementary Benefit office where I worked for two years following graduation; to Sir Geoffrey Utting, the Department of Health and Social Security's Permanent Secretary, for inviting me to a departmental summer school when I was a curate at the Elephant and Castle, which was then the location of the department's headquarters; and to the staff of that summer school for the serious consideration that they gave to a Citizen's Income's potential for reforming the benefits system.

One of those staff members was Hermione (Mimi) Parker, who invited me to join a small group convened by Peter Ashby at the National Council for Voluntary Organizations. That group became the Basic Income Research Group, and then the Citizen's Income Trust. It has been a pleasure to have been able to serve the Trust as its honorary Director for most of its existence, and I am most grateful to the trustees for granting me that privilege and to successive Bishops of Woolwich for permission to spend some of my time working for the Trust.

It was a pleasure to be able to enhance my understanding of social policy during the two years I spent working for a Master of Science degree in Social Policy and Administration at the London School of Economics (LSE). Professor David Piachaud's supervision of my dissertation on a Citizen's Income's likely effects on labour market activity and on family structure was particularly helpful. It has also been a pleasure to have been a Senior Visiting Fellow at the LSE, and I am grateful to the Social Policy Department, and particularly to Professor Hartley Dean, for that opportunity. Writing this book would not have been possible otherwise.

Some of the case studies in this book employ the microsimulation program EUROMOD. I am most grateful to Professor Holly Sutherland for introducing me to its predecessor, POLIMOD, in 2003, and for her support since then as I have learnt how to use EUROMOD. Gratitude is also due to the staff of the Institute of Social and Economic Research at the University of Essex who have been most helpful, training me to use EUROMOD, answering questions, and publishing the two working papers on which the case studies in this book's third and fourth chapters are based.

Some of the ideas in this book first appeared in papers presented to the Social Policy Association's conferences in Sheffield in 2013 and 2014, to the BIEN (Basic Income Earth Network) conference in Munich in 2012, and to the BIEN conference in Montreal in 2014. I am grateful to conference participants for their useful comments. Discussions following presentations on the feasibility of Citizen's Income for the Cambridge Society for Economic Pluralism, the Warwick University Think Tank Society, the Lancaster University Green Party, and the Merseyside Fabians have also been helpful.

I continue to be grateful to Emily Watt and her colleagues at the Policy Press for their help with my first two books on Citizen's Income: *Money for Everyone* (2013) and *101 Reasons for a Citizen's Income* (2015). In relation to this book, I am most grateful to Karl Widerquist, the series editor, for inviting me to write the book, to Sarah Lawrence, Leila Campoli, and Allison Neuburger at Palgrave Macmillan for their encouragement and help with the project, and to the publisher's referees for some most useful comments. My thanks to Dr Karl Widerquist, Professor Hartley Dean, and Mark Wadsworth for reading an entire draft of the book and making valuable comments, and to Ben Dyson for comments on sections of the draft. Any remaining mistakes and infelicities are of course my responsibility.

I am grateful to colleagues, parish officers, and parishioners in the Parish of East Greenwich, and to my colleagues in the Greenwich Peninsula Chaplaincy for their understanding as I retired early last year in order to pursue my interest in the reform of the benefits system. We very much miss the parish and the Greenwich Peninsula, but being able to devote sufficient time to the Citizen's Income debate without overworking has been life-enhancing. I am most grateful to my wife Rebecca for supporting my decision to retire early, and for her constant support for my work for the Citizen's Income Trust.

I am grateful to the Institute for Social and Economic Research at the University of Essex for permission to reprint material previously published in a working paper,[15] and to the trustees of the Citizen's Income Trust for permission to quote from material previously published by the Trust. All royalties from this book will be donated to the Trust.

Contents

1. Is a Citizen's Income Desirable? ... 1
2. Is a Citizen's Income Feasible? And What Do We Mean by 'Feasible'? ... 25
3. Is a Citizen's Income Financially Feasible? Part One: Fiscal Feasibility ... 39
4. Is a Citizen's Income Financially Feasible? Part Two: Household Financial Feasibility ... 67
5. Is a Citizen's Income Psychologically Feasible? ... 87
6. Is a Citizen's Income Administratively Feasible? ... 119
7. Is a Citizen's Income Behaviourally Feasible? ... 143
8. Is a Citizen's Income Politically Feasible? ... 167

9 Is a Citizen's Income Policy Process Feasible?	195
10 From Feasibility to Implementation	237
Bibliography	247
Index	265

Abbreviations

BI	Basic Income
CI	Citizen's Income
DWP	Department for Work and Pensions
EU	European Union
GLA	Greater London Authority
MIS	Minimum Income Standard
MP	Member of Parliament
NHS	National Health Service
NIC	National Insurance Contribution
NLW	National Living Wage
NMW	National Minimum Wage
OECD	Organization for Economic Co-operation and Development
STP	Single-Tier State Pension
UBI	Universal Basic Income
UK	United Kingdom of Great Britain and Northern Ireland
US	United States (of America)
USA	United States of America

List of Figures

Fig. 3.1	Net income of a single earner aged twenty-five and receiving (a) the National Minimum Wage and a Citizen's Income, and (b) the National Minimum Wage and current benefits	54
Fig. 6.1	Tax Credits/Negative Income Tax. Net income as earned income rises	126
Fig. 6.2	Citizen's Income. Net income as earned income rises	128
Fig. 7.1	The relationship between welfare state regime type and income inequality	151
Fig. 7.2	Utility curves on which utility is equal for different combinations of leisure hours and earned income	157
Fig. 7.3	The budget constraint that relates earned income to hours worked	158
Fig. 7.4	The budget constraint when tangential to a utility curve identifies the maximum utility available	158
Fig. 7.5	Maximum utility obtainable when earned income is taxed or means-tested benefits are withdrawn	159
Fig. 7.6	Net income of a single earner aged 25 or over against hours worked at the National Minimum Wage per week, for the existing benefits system and for a Citizen's Income scheme described in Table 7.3	160
Fig. 7.7	Net income of a single earner aged 25 or over against hours worked at the National Minimum Wage per week, for the existing benefits system and for the Citizen's Income scheme described in Table 7.3, and with a utility curve showing maximum utility under the current system to be equal at both zero and sixteen hours of employment	161

Fig. 7.8	Net income of a single earner aged 25 or over against hours worked at the National Minimum Wage per week, for the existing benefits system and for the Citizen's Income scheme described in Table 7.3, and with a utility curve showing maximum utility under the illustrative Citizen's Income scheme	162
Fig. 8.1	Percent increase in disposable income on the implementation of scheme B by disposable income decile	184
Fig. 8.2	Percent increase in disposable income on the implementation of scheme C by disposable income decile	186

List of Tables

Table 2.1	Typology of feasibilities	27
Table 2.2	A revised typology of feasibilities	30
Table 3.1	Citizen's Income amounts for the illustrative scheme	53
Table 3.2	The money saved by abolishing tax allowances and some means-tested and other benefits	55
Table 3.3	The costs of the illustrative Citizen's Income scheme	56
Table 3.4	UK benefits neither abolished nor altered when the Citizen's Income scheme is implemented	56
Table 3.5	Three illustrative Citizen's Income schemes, with their relationships to existing benefits, levels of Citizen's Incomes, increased tax rates required, and net costs	59
Table 4.1	Three illustrative Citizen's Income schemes, with their relationships to existing benefits, levels of Citizen's Incomes, and losses imposed at the point of implementation	76
Table 4.2	Two Child Citizen's Income schemes, showing the Income Tax rate increases required, and losses imposed on households at the point of implementation	79
Table 4.3	Reductions in inequality and child poverty achieved by the two Child Citizen's Income schemes	79
Table 4.4	Two young adult Citizen's Income schemes, showing the Income Tax rate increases required, and losses imposed on households at the point of implementation	81
Table 6.1	2011 census figures for England and Wales for the economically inactive, between the ages of 16 and 74	136
Table 7.1	Welfare state regimes and their characteristics	149

Table 7.2	Relationships between the ratio of the average net income of those in the highest income decile to the average net income of those in the lowest income decile and countries' welfare regime types	150
Table 7.3	An illustrative Citizen's Income scheme: weekly rates for 2012–13	160
Table 9.1	Criteria for successful implementation of policy proposals. The chart shows how it would be unlikely that Citizen's Income could be implemented for every citizen all at the same time, but that an evolutionary process might make implementation possible	224

Notes

1. See the note on terminology.
2. Sarath Davala, Renana Jhabvala, Soumya Kapoor Mehta and Guy Standing (2014) *Basic Income: A Transformative Policy for India* (London, Bloomsbury); Claudia Haarman and Dirk Haarmann (2007) 'From Survival to Decent Employment: Basic Income Security in Namibia', *Basic Income Studies*, 2 (1), 1–7; Basic Income Grant Coalition (2009) *Making the Difference: The BIG in Namibia: Basic Income Grant Pilot Project, Assessment Report* (Namibia: Basic Income Grant Coalition, Namibia NGO Forum) www.bignam.org/Publications/BIG_Assessment_report_08b.pdf, 23/09/2011.
3. Hamid Tabatabai (2011) 'Iran's economic reforms usher in a de facto Citizen's Income', *Citizen's Income Newsletter*, 2011/1, 1–2; Hamid Tabatabai (2011) 'The Basic Income Road to Reforming Iran's Price Subsidies', *Basic Income Studies*, 6 (1), 1–24.
4. www.businessinsider.com/heres-how-switzerlands-basic-income-initiative-works-2013-11?IR=T; https://en.wikipedia.org/wiki/Swiss_referendums,_2016.
5. At a conference on the 4 March 2015 convened by the Fabian Society and by Bright Blue, both the Fabian Society and the Adam Smith Society announced that they were researching the feasibility of Citizen's Income. At the time of writing, Compass and the Royal Society of Arts were also conducting research on the idea, and the Joseph Rowntree Foundation published a paper by Donald Hirsch: 'Could a "Citizen's Income" work?' (York: Joseph Rowntree Foundation, 4 March 2015) www.jrf.org.uk/publications/could-citizens-income-work.
6. www.greenparty.org.uk/assets/files/manifesto/Green_Party_2015_General_Election_Manifesto.pdf.

7. For instance, Larry Elliott, 'Would a citizen's income be better than our benefits system?' *The Guardian*, 10 August 2014, http://www.theguardian.com/business/2014/aug/10/tax-benefits-citizens-income-self-employment?CMP=twt_gu; *Basic Income Studies*, www.degruyter.com/view/j/bis; Malcolm Torry (2013) *Money for Everyone* (Bristol: Policy Press), and Malcolm Torry (2015) *101 Reasons for a Citizen's Income* (Bristol: Policy Press); Claudia Haarman and Dirk Haarmann (2007) 'From Survival to Decent Employment: Basic Income Security in Namibia', *Basic Income Studies*, 2, (1), 1–7; Sarath Davala, Renana Jhabvala, Soumya Kapoor Mehta and Guy Standing (2014) *Basic Income: A Transformative Policy for India* (London: Bloomsbury); Richard K. Caputo (2012) *Basic Income Guarantee and Politics: International Experiences and Perspectives on the Viability of Income Guarantee* (New York: Palgrave Macmillan).
8. Jürgen De Wispelaere and José Antonio Noguera (2012) 'On the Political Feasibility of Universal Basic Income: An Analytic Framework', pp. 17–38 in Richard Caputo (ed.) *Basic Income Guarantee: International Experiences and Perspectives on the Viability of Income Guarantee* (New York: Palgrave Macmillan); Malcolm Torry (2014) *Research note: A feasible way to implement a Citizen's Income*, Institute for Social and Economic Research Working Paper EM17/14 (Colchester: Institute for Social and Economic Research, University of Essex), www.iser.essex.ac.uk/research/publications/working-papers/euromod/em17-14; Malcolm Torry (2015) *Two feasible ways to implement a revenue neutral Citizen's Income scheme*, Institute for Social and Economic Research Working Paper EM6/15 (Colchester: Institute for Social and Economic Research, University of Essex), www.iser.essex.ac.uk/research/publications/working-papers/euromod/em6-15. These two papers were subsequently published in the *Citizen's Income Newsletter*, 2015/1, 4–9 and 2015/3, 3–11.
9. Guy Standing (2012) 'An Anniversary Note—BIEN's Twenty-fifth', pp. 55–60 in Richard Caputo (ed.) *Basic Income Guarantee: International Experiences and Perspectives on the Viability of Income Guarantee* (New York: Palgrave Macmillan).
10. This book restricts itself to a discussion of the implementation of a Citizen's Income in a single country. Other options would be regional Citizen's Incomes—for instance, a Citizen's Income for the European Union—or a global Citizen's Income. Much of this book's discussion of feasibilities would apply to a regional or global Citizen's Income, but in both cases all of the different feasibilities would be complicated by the requirement for agreements between different national governments. Further research on regional and global Citizen's Incomes would clearly be of interest. On global and regional Citizen's Incomes, see Malcolm Torry (2013) *Money for Everyone* (Bristol: Policy Press), pp. 61–3 and 198–9. On a European Citizen's Income, see an article by Philippe Van Parijs at http://bit.ly/12yKTMU.

11. A more detailed discussion of some of the terminology, and particularly of UK terminology, can be found in Malcolm Torry (2013) *Money for Everyone*, pp. ix–xiii.
12. For a detailed discussion of citizenship, see Malcolm Torry (2013) *Money for Everyone*, pp. 187–209.
13. A very useful guide to the UK's benefits system is the Child Poverty Action Group's *Welfare Benefits and Tax Credits Handbook*, www.cpag.org.uk/bookshop/wbtch.
14. Jürgen De Wispelaere and Lindsay Stirton (2011) 'The administrative efficiency of Basic income', *Policy and Politics*, 39 (1), 115–32; Jürgen De Wispelaere and Lindsay Stirton (2012) 'A Disarmingly Simple Idea? Practical Bottlenecks in Implementing a Universal Basic Income', *International Social Security Review*, 65 (2), 103–121; Jürgen De Wispelaere and José Antonio Noguera (2012) 'On the Political Feasibility of Universal Basic Income: An Analytic Framework', pp. 17–38 in Richard Caputo (ed.) *Basic Income Guarantee: International Experiences and Perspectives on the Viability of Income Guarantee* (New York: Palgrave Macmillan).
15. Malcolm Torry (2015) *Two feasible ways to implement a revenue neutral Citizen's Income scheme*.

CHAPTER 1

Is a Citizen's Income Desirable?

1.1 Introduction

A Citizen's Income is easy to define—which is itself a desirable characteristic. It is an unconditional, nonwithdrawable income paid automatically to every individual as a right of citizenship. Its amount would vary with age, but not in relation to any other conditions; it would be paid automatically, normally once a week or once a month; it would not be withdrawn as earnings, other income, or wealth, increased; it would be paid to each individual, rather than to couples or households; and it would be received by everyone legally resident.[1]

We shall begin with an obvious question: Why start a book on the feasibility of Citizen's Income with a chapter on its desirability? Because if it would not be desirable to establish a Citizen's Income, then I probably ought not to be troubling Palgrave Macmillan to publish this book, and my readers ought not to be troubling themselves to read it. There are plenty of feasible policies that are not desirable. The abolition of a publicly funded police service would be feasible, but it would not be desirable; the repeal of all laws relating to contracts would be feasible, but it would not be desirable; and an income tax rate of 100 % would be feasible, but not many people would think it desirable. These policies would be feasible in theory in the sense that it might be possible for a government to carry them out. They would not be feasible in a democracy in practice because any government that carried them out would become unelectable and would therefore not implement them in the first place;

and in a dictatorship, they might not be feasible in practice because they would cause unmanageable civil unrest.

Here we have already come across one of the complexities with which we shall have to cope throughout this book: feasibility and desirability are interrelated. For a policy to be feasible in anything like the normal public sense of the word, it will need a majority of the population to regard it as potentially desirable; and to be thought desirable, a policy will need to be feasible. This is as true of the detail as it is of the generality. For instance, in Chap. 6, we shall discuss the administrative feasibility of a Citizen's Income. If it were to prove infeasible to administer a Citizen's Income, then we would not think the proposal to be desirable; and the fact that it would be easy to administer a Citizen's Income scheme is one of its most desirable characteristics.

However, because it would be possible for a Citizen's Income to be feasible without it being desirable, the question of its desirability is a real one. The only way to answer that question will be to discover Citizen's Income's characteristics and effects, to ask ourselves which are desirable and which are not, and to see if it might then be possible to come to an overall decision about desirability, although, here again, we shall encounter a problem. When we ask whether a social policy's effects are desirable, we might be asking an absolute question, or we might be asking a relative one: that is, it might be desirable because all of its characteristics and effects are intrinsically desirable, or it might be desirable because in some ways it is more desirable than another policy option. To take an example from another social policy field: An impartial police service is a public good, and it is the kind of public good that it would be both infeasible and undesirable for private individuals or corporations to fund. This means that if we were to ask about the desirability of a publicly funded police service, we would not be comparing a publicly funded service with another viable option. We would in fact be asking about the desirability of a police service. But when we come to a country's tax and benefits systems, we are generally looking at a variety of options rather than only one. If the choice is between unconditional benefits and conditional benefits, then either we shall have to say that both would be desirable, or we shall have to decide that one is more desirable than the other. A policy's desirability would therefore be relative to some other option.

Our task in this chapter will therefore be to study a variety of characteristics and likely effects of a Citizen's Income, to decide in the case of each characteristic and likely effect whether it is either absolutely desirable or more desirable than the characteristics and effects of other viable policy options, and at the end to come to a view as to whether a Citizen's Income would be generally desirable.

The final thing to say in this introduction is that in this book on feasibility, we can only give one chapter to the question of desirability. The desirability of Citizen's Income is a multifaceted question, and to deal in sufficient depth with each of its aspects would not be possible. There are other books available that do that.[2]

1.2 Contested Desirabilities

1.2.1 The Poverty and Unemployment Traps

All developed countries have social security benefits systems of some kind, and many developing countries are creating them. Any one of us might fall on hard times, and if all else fails, then we want a safety net to be available. Only the State can provide a safety net of last resort, so in a democracy, the government will be unable to resist providing such a safety net; and even in undemocratic countries, there will be sufficient public pressure to ensure that some provision is made. Provision might be made by way of compulsory social insurance, with individuals having to pay insurance premiums in order to be protected from a variety of contingencies such as old age, sickness, or unemployment; it might be by way of tax-funded means-tested benefits; or it might be by way of universal benefits—that is, benefits paid to everyone to ensure that everyone is covered, with those who would otherwise manage without them paying more in income tax than they receive in universal benefits.

Unfortunately, what might seem the obvious way of achieving a policy goal might also have unintended consequences. It might at first sight seem sensible to keep control of public expenditure by means-testing benefits. Somebody might be receiving an income from the government because they are not in employment, are sick or disabled, are caring for young children, or are in work and not earning enough to live on. If they then started to earn an income, or their earned income rose, then the government might decide that they no longer needed as much from the public purse and so reduced the level of benefits received. This might appear to be a desirable way to manage a benefits system. However, if someone is in low-paid employment, and on means-tested benefits, and their earnings then increase, they will find their benefits reduced and they might be little better off. They might therefore have little incentive to increase their earned income.[3] This unintended consequence[4] of means-testing is the poverty trap. It keeps people poor. If, on the other hand, someone has no employment and they are on means-tested benefits, then if they find employment, their benefits will be reduced and they will experience additional costs, such as fares to work. They might be no better off. They are in the unemployment trap.[5]

If means-tested benefits were to be wholly or partially replaced by a Citizen's Income, then the effects of the poverty and unemployment traps would be ameliorated because, by definition, someone's Citizen's Income would not be reduced if they started to earn an income or their earnings increased. If someone's means-tested benefits were to be completely replaced by a Citizen's Income, then any additional income might be taxed, but it would not result in benefits being withdrawn. There would therefore be a far greater incentive to seek employment than if they were receiving means-tested benefits, and there would be a greater incentive to increase earnings by working longer hours or by seeking new skills. If only some of someone's means-tested benefits were to be replaced by a Citizen's Income, then they would still experience benefits withdrawal as other income rose, but because they would be on less means-tested benefit than if they were only on means-tested benefit, their other income would have to rise by less than would previously have been the case before they ceased to suffer benefit withdrawal.[6] In both cases, it would be easier for individuals and households to climb out of poverty by increasing their earned income.

A Citizen's Income would not disincentivize employment, skills acquisition, or seeking additional income, in the way that means-tested benefits do, and it would more easily enable individuals and households to earn their way out of poverty. In these respects, a Citizen's Income is more desirable than means-tested benefits.

Social insurance benefits are not the same as means-tested ones, but in practice, they can result in similar effects. Social insurance or contributory benefits are generally time-limited (for instance, to a certain number of months of unemployment or illness), and, once they have run out, an application has to be made for means-tested benefits, at which point the disincentives discussed above will apply. The amounts and lengths of payment of social insurance benefits generally depend on contribution records: that is, the amounts that individuals have contributed. Some people might have more ability to contribute than others; and it might be those who are less able to contribute who will be in most need of benefits, particularly in today's complex world of fluid employment patterns. Again, people can find themselves on means-tested benefits. Because the amounts of contributory social insurance benefits paid out are not calculated in relation to people's needs, and means-tested benefits take needs into account, individuals and households can find themselves on means-tested top-ups. In order to solve these problems, some governments pretend that people have made contributions when they have not, or the benefits paid out bear little relation to amounts contributed—in which case the benefits have ceased to be social insurance benefits and are on their way to becoming universal ones. It might then be best if they were to complete that journey.

The above logical argument has shown that a Citizen's Income could set poorer households free from poverty, whereas means-tested benefits dig them further into it,[7] so a Citizen's Income simply must be more desirable than either means-tested or contributory benefits, but that is not how people necessarily feel about the situation. If an individual who is earning an income is asked whether they think a Citizen's Income or means-tested benefits is the more desirable approach, then they might argue as follows: 'I wish to pay as little tax as possible, so I want public expenditure to be as low as possible consistent with preventing anyone from falling into destitution. If people are poor then they should receive benefits from the government; but if they are not poor then they should not.' To this individual, a Citizen's Income will look less desirable than means-tested benefits. Similarly, someone receiving means-tested benefits might understand those benefits in the way in which they might understand temporary financial assistance from family or friends. When in need, they ask for help and receive it, and when they do not need help, they do not ask for it because other people might need the money more than they do. They might not always need to rely on benefits, and if they were to find themselves able to get by without them, then they would not wish to receive them because other people might need the money. These thought processes rely on deeply embedded presuppositions about how social relationships function, and the fact that means-tested benefits cause poverty and unemployment traps, and that a Citizen's Income would not, does not impinge on the ways in which people's minds work in the real world.

Equally embedded in our thought patterns is the 'less eligibility' presupposition: that an able-bodied unemployed adult is less eligible to receive financial assistance from the State than are disabled people, elderly people, and children. The UK has lived with this assumption since the Elizabethan

Poor Law established 'houses of correction' for able-bodied men who could not find work; and it has lived with the phrase 'less eligibility' since the 1834 revision of the Poor Law.[8] The fact that someone might be unemployed because the only factory in their town has just closed down does not come into it. For any member of society that has lived with the 'less eligibility' presupposition for any length of time, the idea of providing an able-bodied adult with an income for doing nothing meets with immediate rejection. It would not matter that a Citizen's Income would be a far more efficient way of ensuring that everyone had enough to live on than any other method for doing it. What would matter would be the prejudice that anyone unemployed should receive as little as possible, should be made to suffer while receiving benefits, and that conditions of receipt should be as difficult as possible to fulfil. The increasingly onerous workfare and sanctions regimes now afflicting developed countries are the modern 'houses of correction'.[9] A Citizen's Income could not possibly fulfil the same function as punitive means-tested benefits regulations, so in many people's minds, it will remain highly undesirable.

Can we continue to say that a Citizen's Income is more desirable than means-tested benefits when so many people think that it is not? The answer to this question is: potentially, yes, but not before people experience a Citizen's Income. This is a problem to which we shall return fairly frequently in this book because it is also a question about feasibility. If society in general understands Citizen's Income to be less desirable than means-tested benefits, and particularly if legislators feel the same way, then it does not matter how deep the employment market disincentives and the poverty and unemployment traps become, how useful a Citizen's Income would be in ameliorating them, or how possible it might be to fund a Citizen's Income: a Citizen's Income will remain infeasible because it is held to be undesirable.

1.2.2   Household Structure

Because means-tested benefits are calculated on the basis of need, and because needs are generally met within households, means-tested benefits are usually calculated on the basis of the needs and the existing resources of the household rather than on the basis of individual needs and resources. This means that if someone who is unemployed is living with someone in employment, any means-tested benefits will be reduced, either by the amount of earnings coming into the household, or by a proportion of them, depending on how much the government wishes to incentivize the employed person to continue to earn an income.[10] Also, because people living together reap economies of scale (one home rather than two, one heating bill rather than two, etc.), the government pays less in means-tested benefits to two people living together than it would have paid in total to two individuals living separately. For these two reasons, public servants need to know who is living with whom. I once administered means-tested benefits for two years, and working out who was living with whom required us to ask highly personal questions. Both staff and claimants found this process demeaning.

Also, when means-tested benefits are paid, they are calculated on the basis of the household, and they are paid to one member of the household. This means that in a cohabiting couple, one member of the couple has to know the financial details of the other in order to make the claim, and one member of the couple might end up with control of the household's benefits income.[11] In Germany, married couples are assessed together for income tax; in the UK, the two individuals are assessed separately; and in the Republic of Ireland, married couples have the choice. Where income tax is assessed on the basis of the individual, although members of a couple might choose to share their financial details with each other, there is no requirement for them to do so. If two members of a couple are earning incomes, and they are not on means-tested benefits, then they can maintain areas of financial independence from each other, and they can both have an equal stake in financial decision-making. These options might not be available to the couple on means-tested benefits.

Perhaps even more problematic is the way in which a cohabitation rule discourages the formation of permanent relationships. Someone on means-tested benefits might think twice before moving in with someone earning a wage, or with someone on benefits, because they would risk losing their independent income. Such effects are necessarily unquantifiable, but the fact that the disincentive exists at all is surely a serious problem.[12]

None of this applies to contributory benefits, which are based on individual contribution records, but these are generally of limited duration; and it does not apply to universal benefits, such as the unconditional child benefits and pensions that some countries pay. It would not apply to Citizen's Income, which would be paid to individuals and not to households, and which would never be affected by who was living with whom, by who moved in with whom, by a partner's earnings, or by anything else.

It might appear obvious that the way in which Citizen's Income treats households would be far preferable to the way in which means-tested benefits treat them. Couples would keep the economies of scale that they generate by living together; nobody would need to divulge personal information to public servants; and the earned income of one member of a couple would not affect the level of their own Citizen's Income or that of their partner. People currently on means-tested benefits would therefore find a shift towards Citizen's Incomes highly desirable. However, people not receiving means-tested benefits could conceivably see the situation rather differently. If I were not receiving means-tested benefits, then I might want the government to harvest the economies of scale generated by people living together so that less tax revenue needed to be collected, and I might want benefits calculations to take into account household earnings and not just the earnings of the individual claimant, again so that less means-tested benefits needed to be paid out. It is therefore possible that a majority could think means-tested benefits to be more desirable than unconditional ones.

1.2.3 Stigma

Because of the casework approach required by means-tested benefits, because street-level bureaucrats have to enquire into the intimate details of people's lives,[13] and because means-tested benefits are paid to the poor and not to those who are not poor, means-tested benefits carry considerable stigma.[14] Where benefits are paid as food stamps, or the use to which benefits income can be put is controlled in some other way, the stigma is increased, because such bureaucratic control is a statement that someone is incapable of managing their money. It might be objected that employment remuneration is sometimes partially paid in non-cash ways, but if it is, then it is generally to avoid income tax, and not because the employer thinks that the employee is feckless.

Because a Citizen's Income would be paid to everyone, in cash, and because nobody would need to ask recipients anything about anything, there would be absolutely no stigma attached to it. This would suggest that Citizen's Income would be more desirable than means-tested benefits. Individuals and households suffering the stigma attached to means-tested benefits would certainly understand Citizen's Income as more desirable than means-tested benefits, but that does not mean that everybody else would. While they might not wish to admit it, people not receiving means-tested benefits could be perfectly happy for people receiving them to experience stigma as an incentive to get off them.

1.2.4 *Differential Desirabilities*

The situation would appear to be this: Individuals and households receiving means-tested benefits would be likely to see the implementation of a Citizen's Income scheme as highly desirable because it would grant to each individual an unconditional and nonwithdrawable income and would abolish or reduce means-tested benefits. However, as we have seen, many members of society might think means-tested benefits to be more desirable than Citizen's Income. A few people who were not receiving means-tested benefits, but who had either administered them, or could see the damage that they do, might see Citizen's Income as a desirable replacement for means-tested benefits.

On the basis of the argument so far, are we able to say that Citizen's Income is simply desirable? No.

1.3 Uncontested Desirabilities?

1.3.1 *Errors, Fraud, and Administrative Costs*

Social insurance or contributory benefits require the government to keep records of who has contributed what, and to pay benefits on the basis of contribution records. Administrative costs appear to be quite low, until the costs to the employers, or in some countries to independent societies and trades unions, are taken into account. Few errors are made in relation either to contribution records or to the payment of benefits. Fraud is a possibility, because somebody might have lost their job, declared themselves to be unemployed, and then started working in the informal economy; or a doctor might have declared them to be sick and they might be working on their brother's building site and receiving sickness benefit: but fraud levels will typically be quite low, particularly for contributory pensions.

Error rates for means-tested benefits are higher, and fraud levels likewise. Calculations are generally quite complicated because they have to take into account complicated household relationships, complex household financial needs, complex household employment patterns and incomes, and frequent changes in circumstances. Errors can be generated by claimant mistakes, administrative mistakes, or both. Means-tested benefits claimants can pretend not to be living with someone when they are, they can pretend not to have income that they do have, they can pretend to be paying housing costs that they do not have, they can fail to report changes in circumstances, or they can pretend to have more than one identity. Fraud levels can be high.[15]

The amount of Citizen's Income that someone would receive would depend on their age and on nothing else. Contributory pensions and universal and unconditional child benefits experience almost no errors and almost no fraud, and similarly Citizen's Income would attract almost no errors and no fraud.

It costs a lot of money to administer means-tested benefits because everyone's benefits have to be separately calculated and frequent recalculations are required. Household structures need to be researched, earnings and rent levels need to be checked, and every change in circumstances, however minor, can result in recalculation of benefits. Social insurance benefits are easier and cheaper to calculate, and universal unconditional benefits are the cheapest of all. A Citizen's Income would start at an individual's birth, it would adjust automatically with their age, and it would cease at their death. Only if Citizen's Incomes were paid to adults who had not received them as children would new identity checks be required. A government agency to keep track of each individual's contact details and bank account would be the only administration required.

In relation to errors, fraud, and administrative costs, it looks as if Citizen's Income would be unambiguously more desirable than means-tested and contributory benefits. This is probably how most people would see it. However, there is one significant group of people who would be unlikely to see it that way: the public servants whose status and livelihoods depend on the administrative effort required by means-tested benefits. Public servants benefit from administrative complexity, from having to correct errors, and from finding and prosecuting fraud. This is what quite a lot of public servants are paid to do. It is what I was once paid to do. This is not to criticize; it is simply to recognize that we are all self-interested to some extent, and that if our livelihood and our sense of who we are in society depend on the tasks that we undertake for our public employers, then we are unlikely to want policy change to make those tasks redundant. The heads of government departments are in a particularly significant position. Their status, and sometimes their remuneration, might depend on the size and responsibilities of their department. It is often the heads of department that advise government ministers on how policy ought to change, as much by the way that they word options and by the research results that they choose to provide as by explicit lobbying for a particular policy. A head of department will think twice before recommending a policy change that might reduce the size of their department, and will be happy to agree to develop and implement a policy suggestion if it might increase their department's size and responsibilities. It is no surprise that governments find it so hard to reduce administrative costs.

A Citizen's Income, that would need only a small and simple computer system and a small group of administrators for its administration, could look rather less desirable than a tangled muddle of contributory and means-tested benefits. Given that the group of individuals who would find a Citizen's Income less desirable than other kinds of benefits will have a significant say in how benefits policy evolves, and that those many people who might think a Citizen's Income highly desirable (because it would almost eliminate errors, fraud, and administrative costs) will have almost no influence over how policy evolves, the fact that a few public servants might not think Citizen's Income to be desirable is considerably more significant than the fact that a lot of people might think the proposal to be highly desirable.

1.3.2 *Social Cohesion*

Where benefits are either contributory or means-tested, some people will receive them and some will not. People's experiences will be different. So, for instance, if low earners receive means-tested in-work benefits, like the French Family Income Supplement[16] or the UK's Working Tax Credit,[17] then they are subject to high withdrawal rates as earnings rise, and to constant complex means-test calculations, whereas employees not receiving these benefits experience lower withdrawal rates and no means test. This difference in experience constitutes a social fracture. A variety of other institutions can cause social fractures. In some countries, there are two education systems: private and public. The UK's private school system offers smaller class sizes, but perhaps more importantly a set of social relationships that can remain useful throughout someone's career. These are privileges not available to those educated in the public system. It might not be entirely insignificant that institutions that cause social fractures are frequently misnamed. In the UK, private schools are called 'public schools', even though they are as far from being public as it is possible to get; and the new means-tested benefit is called 'Universal Credit', although it is not universal and it is not a credit—which the USA's Earned Income Tax Credit is.[18]

So would a Citizen's Income contribute to social cohesion? Theoretically, yes. Everybody would receive it, so everybody would have the same experience of it.[19] However, the real world might not be so simple. In the UK, Child Benefit is paid for every child. In September 2010, the government announced that Child Benefit would be means-tested for the highest earners. The fact that this was never going to be possible[20] is not the point here. What is significant is that at the Conservative Party conference at which the initiative was announced, a journalist went round the audience with a microphone to ask party members what they thought about means-tested Child Benefit. 'A good idea. The rich don't need it' was the unanimous response. What we were hearing was wealthier members of society seeking ways to differentiate themselves from poorer members of society, in much the same way as wealthier members of society differentiate themselves from poorer members by sending their children to private schools and by taking out private health insurance so that when they have routine operations, they get their own room and do not have to share a ward with everyone else. Nobody wants the extremes of incohesion that create riots, but up to that point a lack of cohesion is entirely acceptable to a substantial proportion of any society.

For someone currently receiving means-tested benefits—which label them as poor—a Citizen's Income would be highly desirable because it would put them in the same category as the rich who would also be receiving it. From the point of view of the poor, increased social cohesion would be an advantage. For the rich, increased social cohesion might look less attractive, and any social policy that might increase it might look less than desirable. In the UK, there used to be 'One Nation' Conservatives. Before the 2015 General Election, the Labour Party took up the 'One Nation' slogan which the Conservatives had ceased to use. Inequality is increasing everywhere, so there will be increasing numbers of people for whom social cohesion does not look very attractive.

1.4 Desirabilities for the Powerful

So far, we do not appear to have discovered a single uncontested desirability related to Citizen's Income. We have recognized that for many members of society, a Citizen's Income might possess a number of desirabilities, but for others—and perhaps for those in the most powerful positions—the proposal might look entirely undesirable.

So the question is this: Might there be aspects of Citizen's Income that *would* make it a desirable proposition for those people who might currently not see it that way?

We have identified public servants as a group that would not view Citizen's Income as a desirable development. However, if it were to be implemented in such a way that means-tested benefits remained in place, and if it were to be implemented gradually, perhaps one single-year cohort at a time, then during the long transition, the number of public servants required would remain much the same, or would drop so slowly that no individual career would be affected. Departmental heads might then see Citizen's Income as a desirable long-term project.

1.4.1 Stability in the Midst of Flexibility

The employment market is becoming increasingly 'flexible'. Zero-hour contracts, short contracts, and employers turning their employees into subcontractors are all mechanisms to enable employers to have labour available when they need it and not when they do not. A global market in goods and services might be a useful way of increasing competition and keeping prices down, but it also increases the cost pressures faced by employers, and ensuring that human labour is used in the most efficient way possible becomes ever more important if a firm is to survive. Increasing automation across the different parts of the world's economy will continue to reduce the availability of low-skill and middle-skill jobs, so none of these pressures is going to go away.[21] The problem with increasing flexibility and complexity in the labour market is that most people rely on their earned income for financial stability.[22] Yes, means-tested in-work benefits do help, where they exist, but changes in earned income have to be reported, administration of changes is often slow and inaccurate, and if overpayments occur, then paying them back can be stressful. Such annual top-ups as the USA's Earned Income Tax Credit assume that household earned incomes remain fairly constant, which is often far from the case.[23]

An important advantage of a Citizen's Income would be that it would never change, it would never need to be adjusted, and there would never be underpayments to be fought over or overpayments to be paid back. It would be a solid floor on which a household could build a financial strategy. Zero-hour contracts (provided that they were not exclusive and not onerous[24]) would become useful elements in an overall strategy that might include self-employment and part-time employment. Employment market flexibility would no longer be the problem that it now is.[25]

One of the difficulties facing employers in our current situation is that for most of their employees the weekly or monthly wage provides the foundation of their household's financial strategy, so for most employees only full-time employment is feasible. This is why most firms' employment strategies are built around the presupposition that full-time employment is the norm, even if a different presupposition might better serve their production methods or service provision. So most jobs are full-time, and in a family with children, the norm is for one partner to be employed full-time and the other full-time, part-time, or not at all, depending on the family's circumstances. A Citizen's Income would make a broader range of employment patterns possible for families because it would matter less if earned income varied more.

Such a changed situation for households would be advantageous for employers, who would no longer be so tied to a full-time employment norm, and would therefore be more able to recruit to more flexible arrangements. Something like a classical market in employment would emerge. This does not happen at the moment because there is too much interfering with it. The fact that most households' subsistence needs require wages to reach a certain level puts an artificial floor under wages; income tax provides upward pressure on wages and thus reduces employment; and means-tested in-work benefits rise as wages and hours fall, which will put some downward pressure on wages and will increase employment, but because the amounts of benefit are unpredictable, the wage effects will be unpredictable and workers will still tend to seek wages that match subsistence needs. None of these mechanisms makes for an efficient employment market, and so each one reduces firms' efficiencies. In the context of a flawed market, we need minimum wage legislation so that employers that try to meet their employees' subsistence needs do not face unfair competition from those that pay less; and in this flawed context, we need adequate means-tested in-work benefits to lift the disposable incomes of families with high subsistence needs. Such benefits are particularly important in cities with high living costs in which their absence would denude the cities' firms of the low- and semi-skilled workers that they need. If every working-age adult were to receive a Citizen's Income, then no longer would a wage need to provide the whole of the household's subsistence income, and fewer households would be receiving means-tested benefits. The employment market would become a lot more efficient. For desirable jobs—'good jobs'—wages might fall because there would be competition for the jobs and no longer would the wage need to provide the whole of a subsistence income; and for less desirable jobs—'lousy jobs'—wages might have to rise in order to attract employees. An important outcome would be fewer lousy jobs and more good ones.[26]

So here at last is an effect of Citizen's Income that would be desirable for everyone, although for different reasons: but that need not be an obstacle, and could be quite helpful. The wealthy—for whom some aspects of Citizen's Income might remain undesirable—might then come to understand a few additional desirabilities: that a Citizen's Income would enable more people to start their own businesses, which would be good for the economy; that a Citizen's Income would encourage employees to seek a job, or to seek new skills so that they could seek better jobs, thus benefiting the economy; and that a Citizen's Income would release public servants from administering regulations that demean both claimants and themselves and free them to spend their time on more useful activity.

1.5   Case Studies

1.5.1   Marginal Deduction Rates in the UK

In the UK, someone on means-tested Working Tax Credit who earns an extra £1 can find themselves paying additional Income Tax and National Insurance Contributions (NICs) and having their Working Tax Credits, Housing Benefit, and Council Tax Support reduced. They can end up just 4p better off. They have suffered a marginal deduction rate of 96%. The new Universal Credit, which is slowly replacing most other means-tested benefits, will result in marginal deduction rates of around 73%, which means that the household will keep 27p of every extra £1 earned.[27] This will be an improvement, but whether it is an incentive to improve one's earned income is a complex question. Compare the situation of people on means-tested benefits with the UK's highest earners. The highest earners pay just 2% of additional income in NICs, compared to lower earners who pay 12%; and the maximum Income Tax rate is 45%. They are not having means-tested benefits withdrawn, so their marginal deduction rate is 47%. They keep 53p out of every extra £1 that they earn. With a Citizen's Income, as soon as they had escaped from means-tested benefits, lower earning members of society would experience a marginal deduction rate of 32%. This would be on the right side of the 47% that wealthier members experience, and 96% is on the wrong side of it.

1.5.2 Reform Proposals in the UK

In 1601, the Poor Law established local administrations to manage poor relief: a tidying up of a wide diversity of existing local provisions. The 1834 revision established workhouses to replace the 'out relief' provided by the 1601 Act. During the early twentieth century, the government implemented non-contributory pensions for poor older people who had not received Poor Relief, and then contributory unemployment insurance; and then during the 1930s depression, benefits subject to a draconian means test were established to provide for families whose contributory Unemployment Benefit had expired.[28] William Beveridge's report in 1942,[29] and subsequent legislation, tidied existing State provisions and numerous Friendly Society insurance schemes into a national scheme for contributory benefits with means-tested top-ups, and for the first time established an unconditional Family Allowance for the second and subsequent children in every family. The rediscovery of in-work poverty during the 1960s led to the establishment of Family Income Supplement[30]—an in-work means-tested benefit—and since then the story has been one of renamings and tinkering.[31]

Before Family Income Supplement was established, the government gave thought to a system of Tax Credits (genuine ones: not what the UK government now calls Tax Credits). Each employee working more than a minimum number of hours would have been granted a credit. Earnings below a threshold would have resulted in no Income Tax being paid and in payment to the employee of a proportion of the Credit based on the amount that earnings fell below the threshold. At the threshold, neither Income Tax nor Tax Credit would have been payable. Above the threshold, Income Tax would have been charged.[32] If the Conservative government had not lost the General Election in 1974, then the UK would have found itself with a Tax Credit scheme. It would not have reduced the number of public servants.

When Family Allowance was extended to the first child in every family and became Child Benefit,[33] the number of public servants would not have decreased.

During the Coalition government of 2010–2015, the Minister for Pensions, Steven Webb, established a Single-Tier State Pension (STP): an increase in the Basic State Pension to the income level to which the current means-tested Pension Credit takes State pension recipients.[34] This is soon to be phased in. The STP will be paid in full to everyone with a thirty-year contributions record, and less will be paid to people with less complete records. The STP will be introduced slowly enough for there to be little reduction in means-tested Pension Credit in the medium term, so in the medium term, there will be little if any reduction in the number of public servants required to administer the State pension system. The STP will be a useful step towards a Citizen's Pension: an unconditional pension for every legal resident. All that will be required is the abandonment of the contributions record condition.

In 1942, Juliet Rhys Williams, a member of William Beveridge's committee, made a counterproposal to his plan for a national scheme of contributory and means-tested benefits. She proposed something that looks very like a Citizen's Income. It would have provided the same benefit to every adult unconditionally (apart from the requirement that able-bodied unemployed adults should accept any employment offered). It would have raised employment incentives, would have reduced means-testing, and would have improved married women's status.[35] In 1982, Juliet Rhys Williams' son, Brandon Rhys Williams MP, made a similar proposal to a parliamentary committee. The committee recommended that the government should work on the proposal.[36] A General Election intervened, and nothing happened. And then in 1994, the Labour Party's Commission on Social Justice suggested that Citizen's Income could be important in a changing world and that it should remain an option.[37] When the Labour Party won the General Election in 1997, the idea was not pursued.

Tax Credits would have happened, Child Benefit happened, and the STP will happen. All of the implemented proposals have shared a number of characteristics. They were developments of existing provisions; there was some public understanding and approval of the proposals; they were for identifiable groups of deserving individuals (and where they were not, they imposed harsh conditions and sanctions); and each change required additional public servants. The one proposal that has not been implemented is Citizen's Income. It would have been a development of the existing universal and unconditional benefit for children, and also of the UK's universal healthcare provision free at the point of use, but a Citizen's Income would be for everyone, and not just for an identifiable group of deserving individuals; and in spite of the many good arguments for Citizen's Income's desirability, there has been little public understanding and little public approval.[38] Perhaps crucially, the establishment of the Citizen's Incomes envisaged by Juliet and Brandon Rhys Williams would have rapidly decreased the number of public servants required.[39] It is perhaps no surprise that Citizen's Income has not happened.

1.5.3 Reasons for Voting for Family Allowance

During the First World War, child allowances were paid to the wives of soldiers at the front, on the basis that it cost more to look after a larger family than a smaller one. In 1924, Eleanor Rathbone published *The Disinherited Family*, which made the same point.[40] William Beveridge was converted to the idea,[41] and when during the Second World War he chaired a committee on the future of social insurance, he wrote child allowances into the preface of the report as a presupposition on which the rest of the report was based.[42] In 1945, the Family Allowance Act was passed with all-party support. Members of Parliament (MPs) had voted for the proposal from diverse motives. Some were concerned about inflation picking up after the war, and could see that Family Allowances would reduce the upward pressure on wages that might result from the higher subsistence needs of larger families; the unconditional nature of the payments was attractive to those who wanted to avoid disincentives in the employment market; by the end of the war, Trades Unions had more women members than they had had before, so Trades Unions found themselves supporting Family Allowance payments to children's mothers; and the war had led to hope for a post-war world less unequal than 1930s Britain, so payments that would increase lower disposable incomes by a greater proportion than they would increase higher incomes, and which would not be removed as earnings increased, were attractive. Diverse motives were not a problem.[43]

The UK found itself with an unconditional and nonwithdrawable income for the second and subsequent children of every family because two political activists[44]—Rathbone and Beveridge—had said and done the right things at the right time and in the right place, and because MPs could find reasons to vote for the proposal.

1.6 Conclusion

Jordan and Richardson suggest that in order for a new policy to be implemented, it has to solve a recognized problem and that there needs to be a clear explanation of how it solves it.[45] In relation to Citizen's Income, we could put it like this: Our society and its economy experience multiple problems, particularly in relation to means-tested benefits. Citizen's Income would contribute to the solution of many of those problems. Hence the desirability of Citizen's Income.

However, some public servants might not see Citizen's Income as a desirable development, but if it were to be implemented slowly, and if means-tested benefits were to be maintained during the transition, then the number of public servants required would diminish very slowly. There will be many other members of society who will have little understanding of Citizen's Income's desirability. However, it should not be impossible to improve understanding of the proposal's desirability. Citizen's Income would be a development of existing universal benefits: and where a country does not possess any universal benefits, the universal franchise would be an important precursor: so although public understanding of the proposal and of its desirability might still be lacking, that can be repaired, particularly if a government decides to educate the public. A particular barrier to understanding Citizen's Income's desirability is the concept of 'less eligibility'. A Citizen's Income is for everybody, which might be a stumbling block for people who would not wish the 'undeserving' to receive it. Citizen's Income could be introduced one age cohort at a time, so that the more 'deserving' cohorts could receive their Citizen's Incomes first (children, older people, not quite such old people, student-age adults), and then working-age adults at the end, enabling the evolving process to provide the necessary educational experience.

Achieving public understanding of Citizen's Income's desirability will be a challenge, but it is not one that cannot be met. There would be many advantages for people with low disposable incomes, so for them Citizen's Income would be desirable. For wealthier individuals, some aspects and effects of Citizen's Income might appear to be less desirable, but some other aspects—particularly its effects on the employment market—might come to be understood as desirable. Other aspects and effects understood as undesirable might then pale into insignificance. Different people might regard Citizen's Income as desirable for different reasons, but that is not a problem.

The important conclusion to draw at the end of this chapter is that everyone can potentially regard a Citizen's Income as desirable. Not only does this provide an essential basis for the consideration of the proposal's feasibility, but Citizen's Income's desirability will itself provide an essential foundation for the other feasibilities.

Notes

1. For a detailed discussion of citizenship, see Malcolm Torry (2013) *Money for Everyone: Why we need a Citizen's Income* (Bristol: Policy Press), pp. 187–209.
2. Malcolm Torry (2013) *Money for Everyone: Why we need a Citizen's Income* (Bristol: Policy Press); Malcolm Torry (2015) *101 Reasons for a Citizen's Income: Arguments for giving everyone some money* (Bristol: Policy Press).
3. Hermione Parker (1989) *Instead of the Dole: An enquiry into integration of the tax and benefit systems* (London: Routledge), pp. 318–30.
4. Stuart Adam, Mike Brewer and Andrew Shephard (2006) *The Poverty Trade-off: Work incentives and income redistribution in Britain* (Bristol: Policy Press/York: Joseph Rowntree Foundation), p. 1.
5. Hermione Parker (1995) *Taxes, Benefits and Family Life: The seven deadly traps* (London: Institute of Economic Affairs), p. 27.
6. Hermione Parker, *Taxes, Benefits and Family Life*, p. 42.
7. Michael O'Brien (2007) *Poverty, Policy and the State* (Bristol: Policy Press), p. 124; Pierre-Carl Michaeu and Arthur van Soest (2008) 'How did the elimination of the US earnings test above the normal retirement age affect labour supply expectations', *Fiscal Studies*, 29 (2), 197–231; Thomas F. Crossley and Sung-Hee Jeon (2007) 'Joint taxation and the labour supply of married women: Evidence from the Canadian tax reform of 1988', *Fiscal Studies*, 28 (3), 343–65.
8. Michael Hill (1990) *Social Security Policy in Britain* (Aldershot: Edward Elgar), p. 16.
9. Joel. F. Handler (2005) 'Myth and ceremony in workfare: rights, contracts, and client satisfaction', *The Journal of Socioeconomics*, 34 (1), 101–124, p 117; Mick Carpenter, Belinda Freda and Stuart Speeden (eds) (2007) *Beyond the workfare state* (Bristol: Policy Press), pp. 5, 6.
10. A.B. Atkinson and Gunnar Viby Mogensen (eds) (1993) *Welfare and Work Incentives* (Oxford: Oxford University Press), p. 191.
11. Jan Pahl (1986) 'Social security, taxation and family financial arrangements', *BIRG Bulletin*, no.5, pp. 2–4; Almaz Zelleke (2008) 'Institutionalizing the Universal Caretaker Through a Basic Income?' *Basic Income Studies*, 3 (3), 1–9.
12. Patricia Morgan (1995) *Farewell to the Family? Public Policy and Family Breakdown in Britain and the USA* (London: Institute of Economic Affairs), pp. 4, 61.
13. Michael Hill (1990) *Social Security Policy in Britain* (Aldershot: Edward Elgar), p. 110; Richard E. Wagner (2007) *Fiscal Sociology and the Theory of Public Finance: An Exploratory Essay* (London: Edward Elgar), p. 196.
14. Erving Goffman (1990) *Stigma: Notes on the management of spoiled identity* (London: Penguin), pp. 13–14; Christian Albrekt Larsen (2006) *The Institutional Logic of Welfare Attitudes* (Aldershot: Ashgate), p. 141.

15. www.gov.uk/government/uploads/system/uploads/attachment_data/file/371459/Statistical_Release.pdf
16. www.cleiss.fr/docs/regimes/regime_france/an_4.html
17. www.gov.uk/working tax-credit/overview
18. www.irs.gov/Credits-&-Deductions/Individuals/Earned-Income-Tax-Credit/EITC,-Earned-Income-Tax-Credit,-Questions-and-Answers
19. Bill Jordan (2010) 'Basic Income and Social Value', *Basic Income Studies*, 5 (2), 1–19.
20. The plan was to reduce the Child Benefit to any household containing a higher-rate taxpayer. The problem was that there is no database that links higher-rate taxpayers with Child Benefit recipients, and to have sought intrusive information about the living arrangements of the country's highest earners was not going to be politically popular. The outcome is an additional question in the tax return, asking taxpayers whether they live in a household that receives Child Benefit. If so, additional tax is charged.
21. Georg Graetz and Guy Michaels (2015) *Robots at Work*, Centre for Economic Performance Discussion Paper no. 1335 (London: London School of Economics), http://cep.lse.ac.uk/pubs/download/dp1335.pdf
22. Guy Standing (2011) *The Precariat: The new dangerous class* (London: Bloomsbury).
23. John Hills (2014) *Good Times, Bad Times: The welfare myth of them and us* (Bristol: Policy Press), pp. 111–32.
24. There are two kinds of zero-hour contracts. Exploitative zero-hour contracts require workers to accept shifts offered at short notice, and not to work for other employers; non-exploitative zero-hour contracts require workers to work shifts offered with reasonable notice but leave them free to refuse shifts offered at short notice, and they do not prevent the worker from working for other employers, and they often allow shifts to be negotiated. In the entertainment and hospitality industries, non-exploitative zero-hour contracts can be useful both to employers and to workers, particularly those who are students or carers.
25. Ursula Huws (1997) *Flexibility and Security: Towards a new European balance* (London: Citizen's Income Trust), pp. 47–50.
26. Maarten Goos and Alan Manning (2007) 'Lousy and Lovely Jobs: The rising polarization of work in Britain', *Review of Economics and Statistics*, 89 (1), 118–33.
27. Richard Murphy and Howard Reed (2013) *Financing the Social State: Towards a full employment economy* (London: Centre for Labour and Social Studies), pp. 25–7.
28. Tony Lynes (2011) 'From Unemployment Insurance to Assistance in interwar Britain', *Journal of Poverty and Social Justice*, 19 (3), 221–33.

29. Sir William Beveridge (1942) *Social Insurance and Allied Services*, Cmd 6404 (London: Her Majesty's Stationery Office).
30. Keith G. Banting (1979) *Poverty, Politics and Policy: Britain in the 1960s* (London: Macmillan), p. 89.
31. For the history of the welfare state in the UK, see Nicholas Barr (1987) *The Economics of the Welfare State* (London: Weidenfeld and Nicholson); Michael Hill (1990) *Social Security Policy in Britain* (Aldershot: Edward Elgar); Pat Thane (2011) 'The making of National Insurance, 1911', *Journal of Poverty and Social and Justice*, 19 (3), 211–19.
32. Her Majesty's Government (1972) *Proposals for a Tax-Credit System*, Cmnd. 5116 (London: Her Majesty's Stationery Office).
33. Tony Atkinson (2011) 'The case for universal child benefit', pp. 79–90 in Alan Walker, Adrian Sinfield and Carol Walker (eds), *Fighting Poverty, Inequality and Injustice: A manifesto inspired by Peter Townsend* (Cambridge: Polity Press), p. 83; A.B. Atkinson, (1969), *Poverty in Britain and the Reform of Social Security* (Cambridge: Cambridge University Press), p. 141; Paul Spicker (2011) *How Social Security Works: An introduction to benefits in Britain* (Bristol: Policy Press), p. 118; John Walley (1986) 'Public support for families with children: A study of British politics', *BIRG Bulletin*, no.5, pp. 8–11.
34. Department for Work and Pensions, *A state pension for the 21st century*, Cm 8053 (London: The Stationery Office).
35. Juliet Rhys Williams (1943) *Something to Look Forward to* (London: MacDonald and Co); H.S. Booker (1946) 'Lady Rhys Williams' Proposals for the Amalgamation of Direct Taxation with Social Insurance', *The Economic Journal*, 56, 230–43, p. 232.
36. House of Commons Treasury and Civil Service Committee Sub-Committee (1982) *The Structure of Personal Income Taxation and Income Support: Minutes of evidence*, HC 331–ix (London: Her Majesty's Stationery Office), p. 423; Brandon Rhys Williams (1989) *Stepping Stones to Independence: National Insurance after 1990* (Aberdeen: Aberdeen University Press); Hermione Parker, *Instead of the Dole: An enquiry into integration of the tax and benefit systems* (London: Routledge), pp. 224–53.
37. Commission on Social Justice (1994) *Social Justice: Strategies for national renewal* (London: Vintage), p. 264.
38. D.V.L. Smith and Associates (1991) *Basic Income: A research report*, prepared for Age Concern England, London, pp. 5, 29.
39. J. Harris (1981) 'Some Aspects of Social Policy in Britain during the Second World War,' pp. 247–62 in W. J. Mommsen, *The Emergence of the Welfare State in Britain and Germany, 1850–1950* (London: Croom Helm), p. 258.

40. Eleanor Rathbone (1986) *The Disinherited Family* (Bristol: Falling Wall Press, first published 1924), pp. 139, 167, 353; John Macnicol (1980) *The Movement for Family Allowances, 1918–1945: A study in social policy development* (London: Heinemann), pp. 5–10, 20–23; Pat Thane (1996) *Foundations of the Welfare State*. 2nd edition (London: Longman), pp. 63–4, 202.
41. William Beveridge, in Eleanor Rathbone (1949) *Family Allowances* (London: George Allen and Unwin) (a new edition of *The Disinherited Family* with an epilogue by William Beveridge), p. 270.
42. Sir William Beveridge (1942) *Social Insurance and Allied Services*, Cmd 6404 (London: Her Majesty's Stationery Office), pp. 7–8.
43. Stuart Adam, Mike Brewer and Andrew Shephard (2006) *The Poverty Trade-off: Work incentives and income redistribution in Britain* (Bristol: Policy Press/York: Joseph Rowntree Foundation), p. 30; J. Harris (1981) 'Some Aspects of Social Policy in Britain during the Second World War', pp. 247–62 in W. J. Mommsen, *The Emergence of the Welfare State in Britain and Germany, 1850–1950* (London: Croom Helm), p. 249; John Macnicol (1980) *The Movement for Family Allowances, 1918–1945: A study in social policy development* (London: Heinemann), pp. 93, 172, 176, 191–3, 202; Pat Thane (1996) *Foundations of the Welfare State.*, 2nd edition (London: Longman), pp. 157–230 in Phoebe Hall, Hilary Land, Roy Parker and Adrian Webb, *Change, Choice and Conflict in Social Policy* (London: Heinemann), pp. 169, 173–9, 195–6, 205, 221.
44. Anna Yeatman (1998) 'Activism and the Policy Process', pp. 16–35 in Anna Yeatman (ed.) *Activism and the Policy Process* (St. Leonards, NSW: Allen and Unwin), pp. 32–5.
45. A.G. Jordan and J.J. Richardson (1987) *British Politics and the Policy Process: An arena approach* (London: Unwin Hyman), p. 239.

CHAPTER 2

Is a Citizen's Income Feasible? And What Do We Mean by 'Feasible'?

2.1 Introduction

'Feasible', according to the Oxford English Dictionary, means 'capable of being done, accomplished or carried out; possible, practicable'.[1] The question that we need to answer is this: 'Is a Citizen's Income feasible?'—by which we mean, presumably: Is it possible that at some point in the future, in some country, or perhaps across some continent, every individual legal resident will receive an unconditional, nonwithdrawable income as a right of citizenship? In the words of the Oxford English Dictionary: Is it 'able to be done or put into practice successfully'?[2] In order to answer this question, we shall need to ask a series of questions. Some of them would need to be answered before a Citizen's Income could be implemented: Would it be possible to administer a payments system that would pay a regular income to every member of a society? Would it be possible to manage the transition from the present benefits system to one based on Citizen's Income? Would it be possible to fund the payments? Would there be any adverse effects on individuals or households? Would politicians be likely to vote for the proposal?—which would require a positive answer to the question: Would the general public, as well as politicians, understand Citizen's Income and approve of the idea? And finally: Would it be possible for

---

Some of the material in this chapter was presented at the BIEN (Basic Income Earth Network) Congress in Munich in 2012, and some of it at the BIEN Congress in Montreal in 2014.

© The Editor(s) (if applicable) and The Author(s) 2016
M. Torry, *The Feasibility of Citizen's Income*,
DOI 10.1057/978-1-137-53078-3_2

Citizen's Income to travel from idea to implementation?—which is a question about the institutions of the policy-making process.

Having asked and answered all of those questions, we shall also have to ask some additional questions if Citizen's Income is to be sustainable after its implementation: Will Citizen's Income achieve the changes promised for it, particularly in the fields of household structure, income security, labour market freedom and flexibility, and social cohesion? And will the general public and legislators continue to understand and approve of Citizen's Income? While these last two questions will need to be asked after implementation, there will need to be some assurance before implementation that when they are asked the responses will be positive, because otherwise implementation will be unlikely to occur.

It might appear that if we can answer all of those questions in general terms, then we will have answered the question as to whether Citizen's Income is feasible. Unfortunately not, for two reasons. A Citizen's Income will always need to be established somewhere. To answer feasibility questions in principle will therefore not carry us very far. Feasibility is always in relation to the context in which we would hope to implement a Citizen's Income. Citizen's Income might be feasible in some places but not in others. Also, no Citizen's Income comes alone. It always comes as part of a Citizen's Income *scheme*. A Citizen's Income scheme specifies the levels of Citizen's Incomes for different age groups; the administrative methods that will be employed; how the scheme will be implemented (all at once, one age group at a time, or in some other way); and the changes that will be made to the tax and benefits systems, and perhaps elsewhere in the economy, to enable the Citizen's Incomes to be funded. Citizen's Income will only be feasible if there is at least one Citizen's Income scheme that is feasible. Citizen's Income schemes are always related to particular contexts: to the particular tax and benefits systems, psychologies, institutions, and administrative mechanisms of particular places: so questions about context and scheme will always be entangled with each other—and we shall only be able to say that Citizen's Income is feasible if we can show that in a particular context at least one Citizen's Income scheme can answer all of our feasibility questions in the affirmative. This is a tall order.

So the task before us is this: To study a variety of feasibilities, and in each case to ask what a feasible Citizen's Income scheme might look like in general; and then to ask whether, in a particular place, there might be at least one Citizen's Income scheme that it would be feasible to implement. If by the end of the book we have discovered just one Citizen's Income scheme that passes all of our different feasibility tests in its own context, then we shall be in a position to declare Citizen's Income feasible—but only in that place. If no such scheme exists, then Citizen's Income is not feasible. But having found just one place in which one feasible scheme can be formulated, we shall of course have learned some lessons, and we shall be in a better position to ask whether Citizen's Income schemes in other places might also be feasible.

2.2 THE DIFFERENT FEASIBILITIES

De Wispelaere and Noguera offer a typology of feasibilities.[3] They suggest that any consideration of feasibility must take account of agency (individuals and institutions that act in the political sphere—with 'political' here broadly defined) and constraints (any factors that might hinder implementation). Agency can be discrete (identifiable individuals and institutions that can act in the political sphere) or diffuse (an amorphous set of actors, perhaps described as 'society', or as sections of it, with 'little or no apparent coordination or collective intention'[4]). Constraints can be prospective ('constraints that affect the probability of a policy being instituted') or retrospective ('constraints that affect both the functioning and resilience of a policy once instituted'[5]). The two distinctions generate the matrix[6] in table 2.1.

'Strategic feasibility' is the feasibility of being able to engage sufficiently powerful political individuals and institutions to ensure that they will advocate and then implement a Citizen's Income. The agents here are discrete: they are identifiable individuals, legislatures, governments, political parties, think tanks, and individual politicians and public servants; and the constraint is prospective: that is, the identifiable agents have to be persuaded to act prior to Citizen's Income's implementation. In this book,

Table 2.1 Typology of feasibilities

	Prospective constraints ('achievability')	*Retrospective constraints ('viability')*
Discrete agency	A. Strategic feasibility	B. Institutional feasibility
Diffuse agency	C. Psychological feasibility	D. Behavioural feasibility

Source: Jürgen De Wispelaere and José Antonio Noguera (2012) 'On the Political Feasibility of Universal Basic Income: An Analytic Framework', pp. 17–38 in Richard Caputo (ed.) *Basic Income Guarantee: International Experiences and Perspectives on the Viability of Income Guarantee* (New York: Palgrave Macmillan), p. 21

I shall divide strategic feasibility into two components: political feasibility and policy process feasibility. Here I use 'political' in the narrower sense of 'political ideology', so that by 'political feasibility' I mean the feasibility of Citizen's Income cohering with the political ideologies of the agents that need to act in order for Citizen's Income to achieve implementation. By 'policy process feasibility' I mean the feasibility of Citizen's Income being able to navigate the policy process from idea to implementation. A country's policy process is constituted by the ways in which ideas travel through institutions, so policy process feasibility requires an understanding of the relationships between institutions as much as an understanding of the institutions themselves.

'Institutional feasibility' is the feasibility of institutions successfully implementing Citizen's Income. I prefer to call this 'administrative feasibility', because it is constituted both by the feasibility of administering the Citizen's Incomes once a scheme has been implemented and by the feasibility of administering the transition. This feasibility is again about identifiable discrete agents, because we need to be able to identify and test the institutions that will manage Citizen's Income's administration, but whether it is purely retrospective is an interesting question. Once Citizen's Income has been implemented, Citizen's Incomes will need to be efficiently paid out, and if they are not, then the policy will become infeasible. Administrative or institutional feasibility is therefore retrospective. But at the same time, the political actors thinking about implementing a Citizen's Income will need to be persuaded of a pre-existing administrative feasibility before they will be willing to act. Administrative feasibility is therefore both a prospective and a retrospective constraint.

'Behavioural feasibility' relates to the changes that individuals and households have been promised and that have persuaded them to support the implementation of a Citizen's Income scheme. If effects on employment patterns, disposable incomes, and relationship and household structures are what people want, and they are what they have been led to expect, then Citizen's Income will be behaviourally feasible. Here we are discussing diffuse actors, and not discrete ones. It is 'people in general' who will experience changes. De Wispelaere and Noguera suggest that this feasibility, too, is retrospective. Yes, it is, because a Citizen's Income's effects will only be felt after implementation; but if prior to implementation there is no existing evidence that the changes promised will be likely to occur, then implementation will be unlikely. Behavioural feasibility is therefore as much a prospective constraint as a retrospective one.

'Psychological feasibility' is similar. Only if the general public come to believe that Citizen's Income is desirable, are we likely to see implementation. The general public is a diffuse actor, so this will be a difficult feasibility to achieve; and it will be particularly difficult because many countries' general publics have internalized a variety of presuppositions that would make implementation of Citizen's Income difficult psychologically. 'If you give people something for nothing then they won't work', 'the rich don't need it', and 'we must target money on the poor' are deeply embedded assumptions, and they are all inimical to the implementation of Citizen's Income. Psychological feasibility is a prospective constraint, because without a major change in public opinion, there might be little chance of policymakers wanting to implement Citizen's Income. However, psychological feasibility is also a retrospective constraint. Only if experience of Citizen's Income embeds in people's minds the new presuppositions that have enabled them to support the implementation of Citizen's Income, will the implementation of Citizen's Income be secure.

But having agreed with De Wispelaere and Noguera that psychological feasibility is a prospective constraint, and that behavioural feasibility is also prospective to some extent, legislative evidence might lead us to revise these decisions. Governments can sometimes lead public opinion, which then falls into line with the new legislation. Anti-smoking legislation and equalities legislation are two examples where legislators have identified a small but increasing shift in public opinion, and new legislation has given to public opinion a shove in the new direction in which it was already moving. So the question then becomes: Is it possible to see and/or create signs that public opinion is moving against some of the public's currently embedded presuppositions and towards rather different ones? If so, then Citizen's Income might become politically and policy process feasible, and might then be implemented, with psychological and behavioural feasibility being left to one side and only tested post-implementation.

I can now slightly amend De Wispelaere's and Noguera's typology as in Table 2.2.

Table 2.2 looks more complete than matrix Table 2.1, but there is still something missing. Citizen's Income will get nowhere near the policy process unless at least one Citizen's Income scheme can be shown to be financially feasible. This will first of all require us to specify the level of Citizen's Income for each age group, and how all of the Citizen's Incomes will be paid for, either by making adjustments to the current tax and benefits systems, by the implementation of new taxes, or in some

Table 2.2 A revised typology of feasibilities

	Prospective constraints ('achievability')	*Retrospective constraints ('viability')*
Discrete agency	Political feasibility Policy process feasibility Administrative feasibility	Administrative feasibility
Diffuse agency	Psychological feasibility? Behavioural feasibility?	Behavioural feasibility Psychological feasibility

other way. Theoretically, almost any Citizen's Income scheme *could* be financially feasible in this 'fiscally feasible' sense because taxes could be increased to pay for it. In one sense, high income tax rates or other high tax rates would not be a problem if someone's Citizen's Income were to compensate them for any increase, but however high the Citizen's Income might be, if income tax rates were to rise by more than about 3%, then anyone who had not previously been receiving means-tested benefits would experience a significant increase in marginal deduction rates (the total amount of money withdrawn on every additional £1 of earnings). This means that for Citizen's Income to be 'fiscally feasible' in a particular context, a Citizen's Income scheme would have to be available that could be paid for by changes in the tax and benefits systems, or by some other specified method, and that would not raise income tax rates by more than about 3%.

However, there is another kind of financial feasibility that any fiscally feasible Citizen's Income scheme would also need to satisfy. I call this 'household financial feasibility'. If a Citizen's Income can be paid for, then it will be financially feasible for the government, but not necessarily for individuals and households. Because of the complexity of many of the benefits systems that Citizen's Income schemes would wholly or partially replace, some households would suffer losses at the point of implementation, and some would experience gains. It is therefore possible that households with low disposable incomes might suffer losses at the point of implementation. For households, a Citizen's Income scheme would only be financially feasible if it did not impose large losses on them at the point of implementation. We should therefore say that a Citizen's Income scheme would only be household financially feasible if it were to impose few losses on households, and negligible losses on households with low disposable incomes.

We can therefore conclude that Citizen's Income will only be financially feasible in a particular context if there is at least one Citizen's Income scheme that is both fiscally feasible and household financially feasible. We might regard financial feasibility as a 'gateway' feasibility, because any other kind of feasibility test will require that the scheme to be tested has already been shown to be financially feasible. This is why fiscal feasibility and household financial feasibility occupy the next two chapters. After that, I shall take the different feasibilities in no particular order. This is because they are all prospective constraints, even if some of them are also retrospective constraints, which means that they will all need to be satisfied if we are to see Citizen's Income implemented.

2.3 Relationships Between Feasibilities

Ivan Steiner has identified three types of group task:

- *Additive*: all group members do the same thing. The outcome is the sum of contributions (as in a tug of war).
- *Conjunctive*: the performance depends on the performance of the least talented. All members' contributions are needed for success, and the links between the elements are often crucial (as in a relay race).
- *Disjunctive*: here accomplishment depends on the performance of the most talented member. The group remains better than that individual because even the best at something does not necessarily know all of the right answers (as in a pub quiz). Here the major requirement is that less talented members of the group should not be able to hold back the most talented member.[7]

We might employ this categorization of group tasks analogically to discuss the relationships between the different kinds of feasibility that we have discussed.

The pre-implementation feasibilities required for the establishment of a Citizen's Income are financial (fiscal and household), administrative, psychological, behavioural, political, and policy process feasibilities. If one of the feasibilities is absent or weak, then it is difficult to see how implementation is likely to be possible. This means that the relationships are not disjunctive. Some of the feasibilities relate to each other (for instance, psychological and policy process feasibilities form a circular, or possibly a spiral, process; and financial feasibility and policy process feasibility are clearly closely related), so here an element of additivity might be present: but generally, the feasibilities are independent of each other,[8] and because they are all required, it would appear that we are looking at conjunctive feasibilities. The order in which the feasibilities are established is important in some cases: for instance, financial and administrative feasibilities and a certain amount of psychological feasibility will need to be in place before political and policy process feasibilities can be constructed. This makes the relay race analogy even more relevant.

The relay race analogy might be relevant in another sense as well. One possibility that we shall find ourselves exploring is the possibility of establishing a Citizen's Income for one age group at a time: perhaps for children, then retired people, then young people, then the pre-retired, and so on. If this approach is taken, then the different feasibility questions will all need to be answered in the affirmative before each individual age group's Citizen's Income can be implemented, which will add to the work required; but at the same time, any behavioural feasibility achieved retrospectively for one age group will contribute to the psychological feasibility of the Citizen's Income proposed for the next, as well as embedding the Citizen's Income that generated it. Thus, the feasibilities of the different implementations might relate to each other in positive ways. On the other hand, if the implementation of one age group's Citizen's Income does not generate the required retrospective behavioural and psychological feasibilities, then that Citizen's Income will be insecure, and it will also be difficult to implement Citizen's Incomes for further age groups.

However closely connected some of the feasibilities might be, in practice as well as in theory, they remain conjunctive. This means that for a Citizen's Income to be established, whether for a whole population or for a single age group, sufficient work will need to be done on all of the feasibilities. None of them can be neglected.

2.4 Case Study

2.4.1 *The Transition from Family Allowance to Child Benefit in the UK*

The UK's unconditional Family Allowance was established after the Second World War. William Beveridge, who chaired the committee established by the government during the war to make recommendations for the reform of social insurance benefits, had wanted an allowance to be paid for every child in the family,[9] but he had only achieved payments for the second and subsequent children. Because the real value of Family Allowance then started to fall, by the early 1960s, a family with someone in full-time employment and with six or more children could have a disposable income below that of a similar family with nobody in employment. This was because the levels of means-tested benefits had largely kept pace with prices, whereas the level of Family Allowance had not.[10] One reason for the situation not being worse than it was was that Child Tax Allowances were being paid. One employee in each family (usually the man in full-time employment) had more of their earned income untaxed if they had children. While this reduced the poverty of many families with children, higher-rate taxpayers benefited more than anyone else (because the Child Tax Allowance increased the amount of their earned income not taxed at the higher rate), and if someone was earning at or close to the tax threshold, and was therefore paying little or no tax, then the additional tax allowances could be of little or no value.[11]

During the mid-1960s, research by Richard Titmuss, Brian Abel-Smith, and Peter Townsend revealed that almost one in five families were on incomes below half average income.[12] The new Child Poverty Action Group argued for higher Family Allowances, for Family Allowance to be paid for every child, including the first,[13] and for the increased cost to be met by abolishing Child Tax Allowances. By 1968, the idea of paying 'Child Benefit' for every child[14] had gained support in the Cabinet, largely because this would reduce the amount of means-tested benefits any family with children was receiving and would therefore increase labour market incentives.[15] A change of government then precipitated a delay, but in 1974 the Labour Party returned to power, and legislation was passed to establish Child Benefit. Again there was a delay. In 1976, Frank Field, who was then Director of the Child Poverty Action Group, received a set of leaked Cabinet minutes which revealed that the government was concerned that to abolish Child Tax Allowances would reduce net incomes for men and would therefore cause higher wage demands, and also to pay increased benefits for children would make it look as if public expenditure had increased (because the UK's national accounts do not record as public expenditure revenue foregone in the form of tax allowances). Field published the minutes in *New Society*.[16] Child Benefit was implemented and Child Tax Allowances were abolished.

Why did Child Benefit happen? The change from Family Allowance to Child Benefit was fiscally feasible because the higher rates and the extension to the first child of every family could be paid for by abolishing Child Tax Allowances. Household financial feasibility was achieved by the higher rates and by the payments for the first child of the family compensating for any loss incurred by the abolition of the Child Tax Allowance. Psychological feasibility was assured because families had already had twenty years' experience of Family Allowance; behavioural feasibility was obtained because the effects expected were the effects that were produced; and administrative feasibility was assured because Child Benefit was simply an extension to the first child in each family of a system that already successfully paid out Family Allowances for the second and subsequent children. There was no problem with political feasibility, in the sense that the abolition of poverty, and achieving greater equality, were Labour Party objectives. Child Benefit reduced poverty, and abolishing the Child Tax Allowance removed a mechanism that had enabled higher earners to benefit more than low earners, and that had enabled people paying Income Tax to benefit more than people earning too little to pay tax.

As we have seen from the above account of how Child Benefit came about, the problem was with policy process feasibility. Cabinet members had been concerned that the abolition of the Child Tax Allowance would encourage inflationary wage demands, and that a quirk in the UK national accounting system (one from which we still suffer) would mean that it would look as if public expenditure had increased when it had not. But Parliament had legislated for Child Benefit, and the embarrassment caused by the leaked minutes precipitated rapid implementation. But the policy process that led to the passing of the Child Benefit legislation, and that after a delay led to implementation, was not simply a government process. Academic research had identified a poverty problem, and Child Benefit as a partial solution; the Child Poverty Action Group had campaigned for Child Benefit, and once the Cabinet minutes had been leaked, its 'Child Benefit Now' campaign was a significant reason for rapid implementation. An increasing number of Trade Union members were women,[17] so Trade Unions were now less likely to support Child Tax Allowances, which tended to benefit men, and were more likely to support Child Benefit, which benefits women. Margaret Herbison MP and Barbara Castle MP provided significant support for Child Benefit in the country as well as in Parliament.[18]

Family Allowance becoming Child Benefit is an instructive process that reveals the importance of all of the different feasibilities—and it also raises another issue to which we shall return at the end of this book. Being able to answer all of the feasibility questions in the affirmative does not guarantee implementation of a policy proposal, and sometimes it is a political accident that achieves that.

2.5 Conclusion

In this second introductory chapter, we have constructed a typology of feasibilities and begun to explore how they might fit together and how we might go about evaluating them in relation to policy proposals. We have recognized that for Citizen's Income to be feasible, we need more than just the general idea to pass all of the feasibility tests in principle; we need at least one particular Citizen's Income scheme to pass all of the tests in the social, economic, and political context of a particular country. This we need to emphasize: that it is in today's context, in a particular place, that a Citizen's Income scheme needs to be fiscally feasible, household financially feasible, psychologically feasible, behaviourally feasible, administratively feasible, politically feasible, and policy process feasible.

However, our case study reveals that the situation is even more complicated than that. Legislating a policy idea, and then implementing it, takes time. As time goes on, the social, economic, and political context will change—so it is in a constantly changing context that the different feasibilities will have to be tested over and over again. This will be the case if a single implementation is envisaged. It will be even more the case if a series of implementations is under consideration, which might happen if the need to generate psychological feasibility requires us to implement Citizen's Income for one age group at a time. In particular, it is through the policy process institutions of today that the first steps towards implementation will need to be taken, and it is in the institutions as they will be tomorrow that the next steps will need to be taken.

This complexity is a major reason for social policy change generally being evolutionary rather than radical, even where radical change is required. Particularly in the benefits field, in which complexity is already endemic, trying to manage the complexities of policy change, and to propel an idea such as Citizen's Income successfully towards implementation, will be a major challenge. But that is not a reason to give up on the possibility. It is a reason for starting as soon as possible.

Notes

1. www.oed.com
2. www.oed.com
3. Jürgen De Wispelaere and Noguera, José Antonio (2012) 'On the Political Feasibility of Universal Basic Income: An Analytic Framework', pp. 17–38 in Richard Caputo (ed.) *Basic Income Guarantee: International Experiences and Perspectives on the Viability of Income Guarantee* (New York: Palgrave Macmillan), pp. 18–21.
4. Jürgen De Wispelaere and Noguera, José Antonio (2012) 'On the Political Feasibility of Universal Basic Income: An Analytic Framework', p. 19.
5. Jürgen De Wispelaere and Noguera, José Antonio (2012) 'On the Political Feasibility of Universal Basic Income: An Analytic Framework', p. 20.
6. Jürgen De Wispelaere and Noguera, José Antonio (2012) 'On the Political Feasibility of Universal Basic Income: An Analytic Framework', p. 21.
7. Ivan D. Steiner (1972) *Group Process and Productivity* (New York: Academic Press).
8. Cf. Francesca Pasquali (2012) *Virtuous Imbalance: Political Philosophy between Desirability and Feasibility* (Farnham: Ashgate), p. 60, on the importance of keeping ideological considerations separate from other feasibilities. Not to maintain the separation limits 'normative work to the domain of the practically relevant options' (p. 188) and therefore constrains it unnecessarily. The relationship is similar to that between science and technology. To limit science to the immediately practicable would deprive technology of scientific developments that later on find technological uses.
9. Sir William Beveridge (1942) *Social Insurance and Allied Services*, Cmd 6404 (London: Her Majesty's Stationery Office), pp. 7–8.
10. A.B. Atkinson (1969) *Poverty in Britain and the Reform of Social Security* (Cambridge: Cambridge University Press), p. 24.
11. Peter Townsend (1979) *Poverty in the United Kingdom* (Harmondsworth: Penguin), p. 151; Keith G. Banting (1979) *Poverty, Politics and Policy: Britain in the 1960s* (London: Macmillan), p. 95. The problem had to some extent been ameliorated by Family Allowance being taxed as earned income and by a 'clawback' mechanism that reduced the Child Tax Allowance by an amount for each child for whom Family Allowance was in payment. In 1974–5, a Child Tax Allowance of £240 was reduced by £52 for each child for whom Family Allowance was paid. (Nicholas Barr and Fiona Coulter (1991) 'Social Security: Solution or Problem?', pp. 274–337 in John Hills (ed.), *The State of Welfare: The Welfare State in Britain since 1974* (Oxford: Clarendon Press), pp. 279–80.) The significance of this seemingly insignificant piece of history is that it marked the first direct

relationship between the tax and benefits systems. (Keith G. Banting (1979) *Poverty, Politics and Policy: Britain in the 1960s* (London: Macmillan), p. 66.)

12. Brian Abel-Smith and Peter Townsend (1966) *The Poor and the Poorest: A new analysis of the Ministry of Labour's Family Expenditure Surveys of 1953–54 and 1960* (London: Bell); Richard Titmuss (1962) *Income Distribution and Social Change* (London: Allen and Unwin).
13. Michael Hill (1990) *Social Security Policy in Britain* (London: Edward Elgar), p. 41.
14. On Peter Townsend's contribution to this debate, see Tony Atkinson (2011) 'The case for universal child benefit', pp. 79–90 in Alan Walker, Adrian Sinfield and Carol Walker (eds), *Fighting Poverty, Inequality and Injustice: A manifesto inspired by Peter Townsend* (Cambridge: Polity Press), p. 83.
15. A.B. Atkinson (1969) *Poverty in Britain and the Reform of Social Security*, p. 141.
16. Paul Spicker (2011) *How Social Security Works: An Introduction to Benefits in Britain* (Bristol: Policy Press), p. 118. Before his death, Malcolm Wicks MP admitted to being the young civil servant who leaked the minutes.
17. Nicholas Barr and Fiona Coulter (1991) 'Social Security: Solution of Problem', p. 291. See also the film *Made in Dagenham* (2010) on the campaign for equal pay for equal work.
18. John Walley (1986) 'Public support for families with children: A study of British politics', *BIRG Bulletin*, no. 5, pp. 8–11; Keith G. Banting (1979) *Poverty, Politics and Policy*, pp. 102–103; Paul Spicker, *How Social Security Works*, p. 119; Nicholas Barr and Fiona Coulter, 'Social Security: Solution or Problem?', pp. 279–80.

CHAPTER 3

Is a Citizen's Income Financially Feasible? Part One: Fiscal Feasibility

3.1 Introduction

Whether a Citizen's Income is fiscally feasible—that is, whether a country can afford to pay for a Citizen's Income—depends on two factors: (a) the amounts of Citizen's Income paid to each individual; and (b) the revenue available to pay for those amounts.

Before we begin, we need to distinguish between a Citizen's Income and a Citizen's Income scheme. A Citizen's Income is an unconditional, nonwithdrawable income for every individual as a right of citizenship. A Citizen's Income scheme is a Citizen's Income, with the levels payable to each age group specified, along with a detailed plan to meet the cost.

3.2 The Level of the Citizen's Income

Most Citizen's Income schemes envisage the payment of different amounts to people of different ages: a standard amount for working-age adults, less to children (usually payable to the main carer), an amount between the child amount and the working-age adult amount for young people or young adults (variously defined), and more for elderly people (a Citizen's Pension).

The two questions as to how large the Citizen's Income should be, and how the scheme should be paid for, are intimately connected. Rarely will a decision be made about the levels to be paid in the absence of some understanding of how much revenue will be required to enable the government to pay the Citizen's Incomes and of how that revenue will be obtained. A common approach is to peg the levels of Citizen's Incomes to the levels of existing benefits, or to the values of existing tax allowances. This has obvious advantages. To peg Citizen's Income levels to the levels of existing benefits enables those benefits to be turned into Citizen's Incomes by removing their conditionalities. This makes transition from an existing benefits system to a system based on a Citizen's Income fairly easy to achieve. Similarly, the level of a Citizen's Income might be pegged to the value of a tax allowance. (A personal income tax allowance is an amount of earned or other income that is not taxed, so the value of the allowance is the amount of the allowance multiplied by the basic rate of tax.) If the Citizen's Income is pegged to the value of the personal allowance, and is established at the same time as the personal allowance is abolished, then for any adult earning more than the allowance, the cost of the lost allowance will be equal to the new Citizen's Income. The individual will suffer neither a loss nor a gain at the point of implementation, and their Citizen's Income will not require additional public revenue.

3.3 Revenue Neutrality and Strict Revenue Neutrality

Whether or not the levels of Citizen's Incomes for different age groups are chosen with an eye to the ways in which they will be funded, to give to every individual citizen an unconditional, nonwithdrawable income will be expensive, and the money will have to be found from somewhere.

Two definitions will help us to understand the different ways in which Citizen's Incomes might be paid for:

- A scheme for any new social security benefit is 'revenue neutral' if it can be funded by reducing existing benefits, increasing the rates at which existing taxes are collected, and reducing tax allowances.
- A scheme for any new social security benefit is 'strictly revenue neutral' if it can be funded by reducing existing benefits, increasing the rates at which income taxes are collected, and reducing personal tax allowances—that is, those allowances that apply to each individual by virtue of their earning an income.

The difference between the two is that a revenue neutral scheme can be paid for by reducing such tax allowances as those for pension contributions, mortgage payments, and other expenditures—that is, by no longer allowing various expenditures to reduce the amount of income tax paid, whereas a *strictly* revenue neutral scheme cannot be funded by reducing such allowances. It might be argued that the difference between 'strictly revenue neutral' and 'revenue neutral' is relatively small, but because there *is* a difference between allowances relating to income and allowances relating to expenditure, and because some organizations and individuals involved in the Citizen's Income debate believe the difference to be significant,[1] we need to treat revenue neutral schemes and strictly revenue neutral schemes separately.

These definitions suggest that there are three different kinds of Citizen's Income scheme:

- A 'strictly revenue neutral' scheme would be paid for by reducing means-tested and other benefits, increasing income tax rates, and/or adjusting personal income tax allowances.
- A 'revenue neutral' scheme would be paid for by reducing means-tested and other benefits, increasing income tax rates, adjusting personal income tax allowances, and/or adjusting a variety of other income, wealth, and expenditure tax rates and allowances.
- A scheme that was neither revenue neutral nor strictly revenue neutral would be entirely or partially paid for by the government implementing new forms of taxation, creating new money, or by some other method.

There are arguments for all of these types of Citizen's Income scheme.

Strict revenue neutrality recognizes that there is a close connection between personal income tax allowances, income tax rates, and social security benefits,[2] because they are all essential building blocks of individuals' and households' income maintenance strategies and they all affect every individual's disposable income:

1. *Social security benefits*: No developed country can provide sufficient income for all of its citizens without relying to some extent on publicly funded benefits for contingencies of various kinds. The levels at which benefits are paid, and the regulations that govern them, will have a direct impact on individuals' and households' disposable incomes.
2. *Personal income tax allowances*: Benefits and other public services have to be paid for, so governments have to implement tax systems.

One way of ensuring that those with higher incomes pay more than those with lower incomes is to charge tax on earned and other income. Any income tax system has to set a personal allowance for every individual: a level of earned income on which tax will not be charged. The allowance might be set at zero, but it still needs to be set; and the level of the allowance will have a direct impact on individuals' and households' disposable incomes.
3. *Income tax rates*: Tax rates on taxable income have to be specified, and the structure of tax rates (for instance, whether higher rates apply to higher incomes) will have a direct impact on individuals' and households' disposable incomes.

Other factors will of course affect the amount of revenue that a government collects and the levels of disposable income that individuals and households experience, but these three factors will usually be the main determinants of the way in which an individual's or a household's disposable income relates to earned and other income.[3]

If a Citizen's Income is to be seen as an essential building block of a country's income maintenance structure, then it will need to replace, either partially or entirely, existing elements of that structure. Strict revenue neutrality will ensure that the Citizen's Income will be seen as an essential element in a country's income maintenance structure.

Revenue neutrality, as opposed to strict revenue neutrality, makes changes elsewhere in the existing tax system in order to fund a Citizen's Income, as well as adjusting existing benefits, personal tax allowances, and income tax rates. For example, most developed countries employ consumption taxes as well as income taxes to raise public funds. If a Citizen's Income were to be implemented without adjusting either existing benefits or income tax allowances or rates, then it would increase people's ability to consume. There might therefore be an argument for paying for it by increasing consumption taxes.

There is also an argument for Citizen's Income schemes that are *neither revenue neutral nor strictly revenue neutral*. We fund all manner of public provision by a wide variety of taxes that bear no clear relationship to the public goods provided. Defence, the courts, and publicly funded education are paid for out of government revenues, and those revenues have resulted from a wide variety of corporate and individual taxes and from government borrowing. A Citizen's Income would be a public good, in much the same way as publicly funded education, so there is no reason not to fund it in the same way. If a government faces new challenges—for instance, staging the Olympic Games, or an increasing school-age population—then it will increase existing taxes, instigate new borrowing, or establish new taxes. A Citizen's Income would constitute a new funding challenge, so new taxation would be entirely legitimate, as would be consideration of additional means of supplying the necessary funds by creating new money, or by establishing a sovereign wealth fund and applying the dividend payments to a Citizen's Income scheme.

3.4 Additional Funding

If it is decided that a Citizen's Income scheme is not to be funded purely from within the current tax and benefits system, then a number of options are available.

3.4.1 A Financial Transaction Tax

If you buy shares on the New York Stock Exchange, then a Stock Transfer Tax has to be paid. (The tax rate varies with the price of the shares: for instance, $0.0125 on each share up to a value of $5, and $0.025 on a share valued between $5 and $10.)[4] If you buy shares on the London Stock Exchange, then in some circumstances a tax of 0.5% of the purchase price can be payable.[5] In France, the rate is 0.2%, but only on the shares of certain large companies.[6] Tax rates at these levels do not appear to disincentivize trading on these stock exchanges.

At the moment, no such taxes apply to currency trading. Currency is traded for two main reasons: to facilitate trade between countries with different currencies, and to make a profit by speculating on exchange rate movements. Currency traded for the first reason can benefit the economy, but currency trading of the second kind can destabilize currency markets. This is why in 1972 James Tobin suggested a 1% tax on all currency trading. This would restrict the amount of 'short-term financial roundtrip excursions into another currency',[7] and would probably have little effect on currency exchange for the purpose of trade in goods and services between countries. A tax at 1% might just possibly discourage currency trading in the countries that apply a Tobin tax and thus cause transactions to move to jurisdictions where a Tobin tax is not charged, so perhaps a rate of 0.5% would be preferable, as we know that that rate does not discourage share trading on the London Stock Exchange. The ideal situation would be a global tax, because that would eliminate the possibility of transactions moving to untaxed markets. Similar new taxes on other kinds of financial transaction would also be possible, of course, and some of them would be suitable for the funding of a Citizen's Income.

3.4.2 Land Value Tax

Most taxes distort markets. This can be a useful effect of taxation. We tax some goods, such as tobacco and alcohol, in order to raise their prices and thus discourage their use. But there are some things that we do not wish to discourage, and one of those is productive human labour. We pay for labour in order to get things done, and we sell our labour in order to be able to afford the goods and services that we need; so in relation to both supply and demand, labour is beneficial, and society ought to encourage it. Perversely, we tax it, which discourages it. One of the reasons that we tax it is that income taxation is one of the few reliable methods for redistribution from those with more money to those with less money. Too much inequality is bad for society,[8] so it is socially useful to impose a progressive tax system on earned income: that is, a system that taxes higher incomes at higher rates, and lower incomes at lower rates.[9] An additional reason for taxing labour is that it is a tax that is relatively easy to collect if governments implement Pay As You Earn schemes that collect tax before individuals receive their employment income. In this case, the advantages of taxing income outweigh the disadvantage of distorting the market in labour, but the disadvantage is still potentially significant.

The only kind of tax that does not distort markets is a tax that cannot alter the tax base: that is, the commodity that is being taxed. Apart from changes made to the landmass by coastal erosion, land reclamation, and national boundary changes, the amount of land in a country is fixed; and however much the value of land is taxed, the amount of land will not change. Taxing land might affect the distribution of ownership—because it might encourage individuals and corporate bodies that own land that they are not using to dispose of it—but the same amount of land will still be available and taxable.[10]

There is of course a question as to how land should be valued in order to tax it, and several options are available—rental value, sale value, and development value, for instance, with estimates being made where land is not actively let, for sale, or being developed. There is a complexity here that does not apply to consumption taxes or to income tax, where the tax base already has a clear monetary value, but such problems aside, there is no reason why a Land Value Tax should not be considered for the funding of Citizen's Income.

3.4.3 Money Creation

A government creating money—whether by printing bank notes, or by the central bank increasing the balance in the government's account—might once have sounded like a bad idea, because there is a danger that creating additional money will increase inflation. However, in the years following the recent global financial crisis, the central banks of the USA, UK, and EU have used their power to create money to stimulate spending and economic growth. Through 'quantitative easing', central banks have used newly created money to buy government bonds[11] from the financial markets. In theory, this should inflate bond and share prices, making those with significant investments feel wealthier and encouraging them to spend more, leading to a 'trickle down' effect that benefits the whole economy. In practice, however, there is a strong argument that the effect has been to enrich the already wealthy while doing little for economic growth and employment. Quantitative easing as currently practised has been an ineffective way of distributing newly created money into the economy.

One way of enabling a higher proportion of newly created money to enter the real economy of goods and services would be to give it to members of the public.[12] Even if every legal resident received the same amount—which would be the only way to administer such one-off payments—this would not be a Citizen's Income, because the intervals between payments, and the amounts of payments, would vary. The effects would therefore be closer to those of Alaska's Permanent Fund Dividend, which is a varying annual payment.[13] However, such an equal payment to every individual would benefit the real economy, it would to some extent reduce poverty, it would contribute to social cohesion, and it would be a useful step along the way to a Citizen's Income.

Perhaps a more significant possibility than that of governments creating additional money in the context of a financial crisis is that of changing the source of money in normal circumstances. The majority of money is created not by governments but by privately owned banks. If I borrow money from a bank, then the bank alters the electronic digits related to my bank account number. The bank has simply created the money that it has lent to me. It will then collect interest on that money; and when the money is paid back, the bank will again alter the electronic digits, and the money will disappear. Much of the money created by the banks buys assets that are in limited supply, such as houses, and it therefore creates price bubbles; too little of it is employed as investment in the productive economy; and if the loans are not repaid, then lending stops and a recession is the result. Interest on public and private debt transfers money from the poor to the rich and so increases inequality, and the payment of interest requires climate-changing economic growth, but attempting to reduce the level of debt reduces spending, reduces the amount of money in the economy, and can lead to recession.

Jackson and Dyson argue that banks should be prevented from creating money, and that an independent body should be charged with creating money and spending it into the economy as government spending, tax reductions, direct payments to citizens, or lending to banks on condition that the money is lent to productive businesses. 'The monetary system, being man-made and little more than a collection of rules and computer systems, is easy to fix, once the political will is there and opposition from vested interests is overcome.'[14]

But how much money should governments create? Geoff Crocker has pointed out the increasing gap between the value of production (Gross Domestic Product: GDP) and the total value of wages. This means that wage income is no longer sufficient to absorb the goods and services produced by an economy, so domestic debt has to be employed to fund consumption. Increasing debt is unsustainable, so regular financial crises are inevitable. A solution would be for governments to fill the gap between the value of production and the value of earned incomes by paying newly created money in equal amounts to every citizen. This would release the real economy from artificial financial constraint, and deliver sound finances built on productivity advances. It would also greatly enhance social cohesion.[15]

If payments were weekly or monthly, and if the amounts remained the same or similar from year to year (which would be possible, because the gap between GDP and the value of wages slowly increases), then a Citizen's Income would be the result.[16]

Such ideas as this would once have been regarded as irrational and irrelevant. No longer.[17]

In some ways, the situation relating to money creation mirrors the one facing tax and benefits systems in developed countries. Both have evolved over time, both exhibit complexities, both are tangled up with a wide variety of other aspects of societies and economies, and genuine reform of both is resisted because the transitions look difficult and the effects of change are difficult to predict. It is precisely these aspects of the two situations that make it so difficult to generate the necessary political will to create the necessary change. Both fields would benefit from wide-ranging consultation exercises. In both cases, the international effects of making the recommended changes would be important matters for discussion, as would be the details of the transitions that would need to be managed between current situations and the future situations envisaged.

3.4.4 Dividends

Since 1977, the State of Alaska has received royalties from oil extraction in Prudhoe Bay, and about 20% of those royalties have been used to establish the Alaska Permanent Fund. This pays an annual dividend, a proportion of which funds an annual distribution of money equally to every Alaskan citizen.[18] Because the distribution is paid annually, and because it varies with the profits made by the Permanent Fund, the dividend payment bears some of the characteristics of a Citizen's Income (the equal payment to every citizen, and its regularity) but not others (it varies in amount, and it is paid annually and not monthly or weekly). Its effects on behaviour are therefore somewhat different from those that we would expect from a Citizen's Income. The payments have resulted in increased employment, reduced inflation, and decreased inequality, thus mirroring some of the effects that we would expect from a Citizen's Income, but the annual nature of the payments means that they are used for larger occasional purchases, whereas a Citizen's Income would contribute to weekly or monthly income and would therefore be spent on the purchases made on a weekly or monthly basis.[19]

Alaska is not the only state or country with a sovereign wealth fund, but it is the only one that distributes some of the dividend equally to its citizens. Others could do so. A further possibility is that payments to citizens could be made monthly rather than annually, and that in years with higher dividends, some of the dividend could be reapplied to the fund so that in years with lower dividends, additional payments could be made, thus smoothing the amounts received by citizens. In this way, a Citizen's Income could be paid and families' regular monthly incomes could be increased.[20]

3.4.5 Redirected Subsidy Funding

The majority of Iran's population is now receiving a Citizen's Income of about £43 per person once every two months. (The income is calculated on the basis of the individual, but is paid to the head of the household.) This transfer programme resulted from a government plan to reduce subsidies on basic foodstuffs, electricity, natural gas, petrol, and diesel, and to protect the poor from the increasing prices on these goods by implementing a means-tested benefit; but public unrest related to the implementation of the means test resulted in the test being abandoned and to the money being given to everyone (although the government is now attempting to persuade wealthier households to decline the payments).[21]

A similar approach was taken during a Citizen's Income pilot project in India. For a period of eighteen months, thousands of men, women, and children in urban, rural, and tribal communities in India were given a monthly unconditional income in place of India's flawed subsidized food and guaranteed employment schemes. In the randomly selected pilot communities, equal cash payments replaced the subsidy system; control communities retained the subsidy system and did not receive equal cash payments; and the different outcomes in relation to a number of factors were carefully evaluated during the project and at the end. The communities that received the Citizen's Income instead of the subsidized food programme experienced improvements in housing, electricity and water supply, sanitation, nutrition, health, healthcare, school attendance, school performance (especially for girls of secondary school age), and economic activity. By the end of the project, 'many more households in the basic income villages had increased their earned incomes than was the case in the control villages, and many fewer had experienced a fall in earned income than in the control villages'.[22] In the pilot villages, child and teenage labour shifted from wage labour to own account work on family farms and to increased school attendance; bonded labour decreased as debts were paid off; and the purchase of such assets as sewing machines facilitated an increase in own account economic activity. Women's status was enhanced by their new financial independence, and the elderly and the disabled experienced improved status and living conditions. If India were to reallocate the money currently spent on food subsidy schemes to a Citizen's Income, then the whole of India would be able to benefit from the changes experienced in the pilot project communities.[23]

In both India and Iran, the redirection of funds from subsidy programmes to a Citizen's Income, or to something like one, has proved beneficial. Other countries that subsidize foodstuffs, fuel, and other commodities would benefit from making the same change.

3.5 Calculating the Cost of Citizen's Incomes in Order to Specify the Changes Required to Fund Them

3.5.1 *Strictly Revenue Neutral and Revenue Neutral Schemes*

For Citizen's Income schemes that would fund Citizen's Incomes entirely from within the current tax and benefits system, two methods are available for calculating the cost of the Citizen's Incomes and the changes that would be required in existing taxes and benefits.

3.5.1.1 *National Statistics*

A country's national accounts, population statistics, and other national statistics can be used to calculate the cost of giving to every member of the population a Citizen's Income, the money saved by abolishing tax allowances and means-tested and other benefits, and the additional revenue that would be collected if tax rates were raised. The net cost of the Citizen's Income scheme is then the total cost of the Citizen's Incomes less (a) the money saved by abolishing allowances and benefits and (b) the additional tax revenue collected. If a revenue neutral scheme is required, then an arithmetic trial-and-error process can reduce the net cost to zero.

If means-tested benefits are retained rather than abolished, and the amounts of means-tested benefits received by households are reduced by taking into account households' Citizen's Incomes when the means-tested benefits are calculated, then the amount saved by reducing means-tested benefits will be different for each household. A method that uses the national accounts to calculate the net cost of a Citizen's Income scheme would not be able to calculate the total saving in means-tested benefits that would result from every household on means-tested benefits having its means-tested benefits reduced, so using national statistics to calculate the net costs of Citizen's Income schemes is only appropriate when each existing means-tested benefit is abolished completely or retained in its present form.

An inescapable complexity is that if a Citizen's Income replaces a variety of means-tested benefits, and other means-tested benefits are retained, then a method that employs the national accounts will only generate an accurate net cost for the Citizen's Income scheme if the retained means-tested benefits are calculated in exactly the same way as they were before the scheme's implementation. In practice, the calculation of any retained means-tested benefits would take into account households' Citizen's Incomes, whereas before implementation of the scheme, they would have taken into account the means-tested benefits that have now been abolished. The difference between the cost of a retained means-tested benefit before and after the implementation of the Citizen's Income scheme will be different for every household, and the total difference across the population could be either a saving or an additional cost, depending on how the retained means-tested benefit is calculated both before and after the scheme's implementation. Aggregated national figures are all that are available if national statistics are employed to calculate the net cost of a Citizen's Income scheme, so an assumption has to be made that any change in the total cost of a retained means-tested benefit will be zero. This might or might not be accurate.

3.5.1.2 Microsimulation
Microsimulation undertakes calculations at the level of the household rather than at the national level. A survey of individual and household data relating to wages, benefits, other income, income tax, and social security contributions paid is carried out, preferably for a random sample of at least 0.1% of the country's population. A computer program then uses the income and expenditure information collected to calculate each individual's and each household's disposable income. Tax rates, tax allowances, benefits levels, and other variables can then be changed in the program—and, importantly, entire new benefits can be created—and the program can then be run again to generate a new set of individual and household disposable incomes. An increase in a household's disposable income represents an increase in public expenditure, and a decrease represents a saving; so the total of all of the new disposable incomes, minus the total of all of the original disposable incomes, represents the net cost of the Citizen's Income scheme for the population sample in relation to the time period assumed by the microsimulation program. If the program uses monthly tax and benefits levels, then for an annual figure for the sample, the net cost is multiplied by twelve; and to obtain a total net cost for the

population as a whole, the sample net cost is multiplied by the ratio of the population size to the sample size.

As well as enabling new benefits to be created and their regulations and levels to be specified, the computer program enables the regulations of existing benefits to be amended, and, in particular, enables households' Citizen's Incomes to be taken into account when existing household means-tested benefits are recalculated on the implementation of a Citizen's Income scheme. This means that this method—unlike the method that employs national statistics—can cope with means-tested benefits being retained and recalculated on the implementation of a Citizen's Income scheme.

Microsimulation is thus the more flexible of the two methods; but unfortunately, neither of the two methods can model contributions to the funding of Citizen's Incomes achieved by altering the detail of tax allowances relating to expenditures. Take, for example, the UK tax allowance that enables the money spent on private pension contributions to be regarded as non-taxable income. For anyone paying only the basic rate of Income Tax, the saving in Income Tax will be the money spent on pension contributions multiplied by the basic rate of tax. For anyone paying a higher rate, the saving will be the money spent on pension contributions multiplied by the higher rate. A proposal might be made to reduce the tax relief to the basic rate for everyone. The Income Tax calculation for any individual paying the higher rate of tax would provide the information that would enable us to calculate the additional tax that they would have to pay and that would therefore be available to fund Citizen's Incomes, but this amount will depend on individual circumstances, so no aggregate figure will be available. Neither is the information available in the Family Resources Survey data employed by microsimulation programs. An estimate of the total amount of additional revenue can be made, but it might not be accurate.[24]

3.5.2 *Calculating the Costs of Citizen's Income Schemes That Are Neither Strictly Revenue Neutral nor Revenue Neutral*

Because the Citizen's Income to be paid to an individual of a particular age is totally specified by the level of Citizen's Income for people of that age, the total cost of Citizen's Incomes for a population is easy to calculate from national statistics tables that list the number of members of a population in each relevant age bracket.

If money creation is to be used to pay for the Citizen's Income scheme, then the government will need to create an amount of money to match the cost of the scheme. If the dividends of a permanent fund are to be used, without subsidy from elsewhere, then the government will need to take a view on the likely average dividends over a period of years, and fix the levels of Citizen's Incomes accordingly. Similarly, if redirected subsidies are to be used, then the Citizen's Incomes will need to be paid at levels that deliver a total cost equal to the funds currently spent on the subsidies. If additional taxes are to be used, then trial and error will be required, with Citizen's Incomes set at levels that will cost an amount equal to the minimum that the new taxes will generate, until experience of the new taxes enables a more accurate long-term estimate of receipts to be made.

3.6 Acceptable Tax Rates

'Fiscally feasible', or 'affordable', can imply (a) revenue neutrality, (b) strict revenue neutrality, or (c) neither—with (c) requiring additional taxation, money creation, or revenue sources, to be specified. Any government considering the establishment of a Citizen's Income scheme will need to decide what it means by 'affordable' if it is to discuss whether Citizen's Income might be financially feasible.

In practice, an additional condition will need to be satisfied. A revenue neutral or strictly revenue neutral Citizen's Income scheme with high levels of Citizen's Incomes will require high income tax rates. Even though such a scheme would be 'financially feasible' in the sense that it could be paid for, it would not be 'financially feasible' in the normal public meaning of the term. Thus, a Citizen's Income scheme designed for Japan that would raise the basic rate of income tax on the first 1,200,000 yen per annum (approximately £6400) by 5% might therefore not be regarded as financially feasible even though the increased tax revenue would pay for the Citizen's Income.[25] The public might be content to be charged slightly higher rates of tax if the increase is designed to fund a public good of which the public might generally approve, but even then the rise will need to be kept to a minimum.

But would higher tax rates matter if the overall effect of a Citizen's Income scheme with higher income tax rates and a working-age adult Citizen's Income of higher value than the value of the abolished personal tax allowance would be to impose negligible household losses? Yes, tax rates do matter. Income tax rates are a psychological as well as a financial issue,[26] and to raise them by more than say 3% would probably make a scheme impossible to implement, however irrational that psychological factor might be.

3.7 Case Study

3.7.1 Would a Revenue Neutral Citizen's Income Scheme Be Financially Feasible in the UK?

As described above, there are two different ways to calculate the net cost of a Citizen's Income scheme.

3.7.2 National Statistics

In 2006, the Citizen's Income Trust used the UK's national statistics to research the financial feasibility of a Citizen's Income scheme with Citizen's Income levels pegged to levels of means-tested Income Support, Income-based Jobseeker's Allowance, and Pension Credit. The research results were submitted as evidence to a parliamentary enquiry, and subsequently published. The research was updated in 2013.[27]

In the 2013 version, Citizen's Income rates were set as in table 3.1.

While these Citizen's Incomes are not large, Fig. 3.1, which shows net income for a single working-age adult living alone, reveals that if they worked between two and fourteen hours per week on the National Minimum Wage, then with a Citizen's Income they would experience a lower marginal deduction rate (total withdrawal rate for additional income) than with a Personal Tax Allowance and means-tested benefits.

Table 3.1 Citizen's Income amounts for the illustrative scheme

Age		Weekly rates for 2012–13 (£)
0–15	56.25	Current Income Support rate for 16–24-year-olds
16–24	56.25	Current Income Support rate for 16–24-year-olds
25–64	71.00	Current Income Support rate aged 25 plus
65 plus	142.70	Pensions Credit rate

Source: Citizen's Income Trust (2013) *Citizen's Income: A brief introduction* (London: Citizen's Income Trust), p. 7

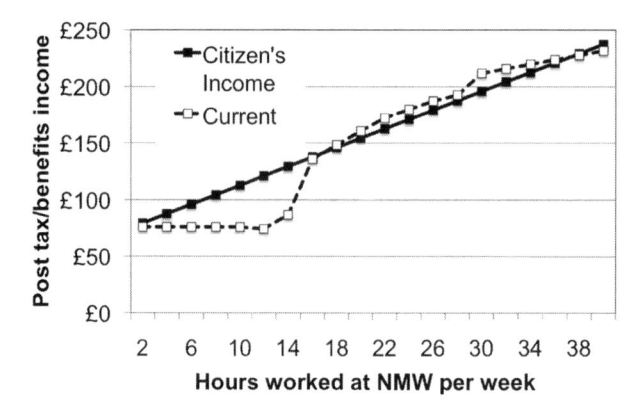

Fig. 3.1 Net income of a single earner aged twenty-five and receiving (a) the National Minimum Wage and a Citizen's Income, and (b) the National Minimum Wage and current benefits (Source: Citizen's Income Trust (2013) *Citizen's Income: A brief introduction* (London: Citizen's Income Trust), p. 7)

This difference represents a substantial increase in incentive to seek employment.

The scheme assumes a basic rate of tax on earned income of 32% (20% Income Tax plus 12% Employee's NICs), with higher and additional rates as at present on higher earnings. Rates of 20% are assumed for pension and investment income; and the scheme assumes that tax relief for pension contributions will be restricted to 20%, which is the rate of Income Tax deducted from pensions in payment.

Running costs are estimated at 1%, which is the cost of administering non-means-tested benefits such as Child Benefit and the state pension.

Table 3.2 shows that the abolition of tax allowances and some means-tested benefits would save £272 billion per annum, and Table 3.3 shows that the Citizen's Incomes would cost £276 billion per annum.

The total cost of the proposed scheme is approximately the same as the total cost of benefits and tax reliefs and allowances that would be replaced, that is, around £275 billion per year in 2012–13.

Table 3.4 shows the benefits that would be left in place and calculated as they are now.

We can see from Tables 3.2 and 3.3 that Citizen's Incomes could be paid for by abolishing the Personal Tax Allowance and means-tested benefits (apart from Housing Benefit and Council Tax Benefit) and by restricting tax relief on pension contributions to 20%. Because the restriction of tax

Table 3.2 The money saved by abolishing tax allowances and some means-tested and other benefits

	Cost, £ billion per annum	Notes
Children		
Child benefit	12	
Child tax credits	<u>22</u>	
	34	
Working age		
Key benefits (income support, etc.)	27	(1)
Working tax credits	7	
Personal Allowances (Income Tax)	68	(2)
National Insurance	23	(2)
Higher rate tax relief on pension contributions	10	(3)
Student grants and student loan write-offs	<u>3</u>	(4)
	138	
Pensioners		
State Retirement Pension and SERPS, S2P, etc.	82	
Pensions Credit and Minimum Income Guarantee	<u>8</u>	
	90	(5)
Running costs		
DWP administration costs	8	
HMRC—Tax Credit administration and Tax Credits written off	<u>2</u>	
	<u>10</u>	
Total	<u>272</u>	

Source: Citizen's Income Trust (2013) *Citizen's Income: A brief introduction* (London: Citizen's Income Trust), pp. 9–10. Sources: Department for Work and Pensions (DWP), *Annual Report 2011-12* (pages 210 onwards); HM Revenue & Customs, *Annual Report 2011-12* (pp. 11 and 95); HM Revenue & Customs Table 1–5 (updated December 2012)

Notes

1. A working-age claimant can receive a maximum of one 'key benefit'. These include Income Support, Jobseeker's Allowance, Employment and Support Allowance, Carer's Allowance, Incapacity Benefit (up to Income Support rates), Statutory Maternity Pay, Statutory Sick Pay, and Bereavement Benefits
2. No longer required, as the Citizen's Income will act as a reimbursement of all Income Tax and Employee's NICs paid on the first £11,569 earnings per year (or the first £18,510 of investment income)
3. The total cost of income and NIC reliefs for pension contributions is over £40 billion a year. Half the value of the tax relief accrues to higher and additional rate taxpayers. We assume that if income tax relief is restricted to the basic rate, this would reduce the cost by a quarter of that (£10 billion)
4. Students from low-income households still receive modest grants. We estimate the cost of the interest subsidy and write-offs at 10% of the total student loans outstanding of £28 billion
5. Under the current pension system, pensioners receive their accrued state pension entitlement and are then 'topped up' to the Pensions Credit rate. With a Citizen's Pension, each pensioner receives £142.70 automatically and would then be 'topped up' to their previous accrued state pension entitlement if higher. The total cost of either scheme would be much the same. One third of the 40% of pensioners currently entitled to Pension Credit do not claim it, and if they did, then current state pensions would cost £92 billion rather than £90 billion (www.gov.uk/docs/single-tier-pension-impact-assessment.pdf, p. 4, no. 4, §2; DWP, *Income Related Benefits: Estimates of Take-up in 2009–10*, 2012). We therefore estimate the cost of entitlements above £142.70 to be £15 billion (see Table 3.3)

Table 3.3 The costs of the illustrative Citizen's Income scheme

Age	Census 2011	Citizen's Income, £ per week	Cost, £ billion per annum
0–15	11.9 million	56.25	35
16–24	7.5 million	56.25	22
25–64	33.4 million	71.00	124
65 and over	10.4 million	142.70	77
State pension entitlements in excess of £142.70			15
Cost of Citizen's Incomes and pension entitlements			273
Running costs (1%)			3
Total annual cost			276

Source: Citizen's Income Trust (2013) *Citizen's Income: A brief introduction* (London: Citizen's Income Trust), p. 8

Table 3.4 UK benefits neither abolished nor altered when the Citizen's Income scheme is implemented

	Cost, £ billion per annum	Notes
Disability-related benefits		
Severe Disablement	1	
Industrial Injuries	1	
Attendance Allowance	6	
Disability Living Allowance	14	
Incapacity Benefit	1	(1)
	23	
Housing-related benefits		
Housing Benefit	18	
Council Tax Benefit	5	
Rent Rebates	6	
	29	
Other old-age benefits		
Over 75s TV licence and Winter Fuel Allowance	3	
Age-related personal allowances	3	
	6	(2)
Total	58	

Source: Citizen's Income Trust (2013) *Citizen's Income: A brief introduction* (London: Citizen's Income Trust), p. 10

Notes

1. Incapacity Benefit is a 'key benefit' paid at slightly higher rates than Income Support rates. We have split the total payments into a basic amount of £71 and an extra amount relating to disability
2. It would be possible to replace these by increasing the Citizen's Pension rate by £10 per week

relief to the lowest rate of income tax is not an income-based tax, the scheme is revenue neutral rather than strictly revenue neutral. Without the restriction of tax relief on pension contributions, there would have been a funding gap of at least £10 billion per annum. The published scheme also estimated administrative savings of £5 billion per annum and assumed this saving when calculating the net cost of the scheme. Even if this estimate is accurate, administrative savings are not intimately connected to a Citizen's Income scheme in the same way that changes in personal tax allowances and means-tested and other benefits are. So yet again, this scheme would be revenue neutral rather than strictly revenue neutral.

It is possible to estimate the net cost of this Citizen's Income scheme because means-tested benefits are either retained in their current form or they are abolished. If they had been retained and the amounts paid to households recalculated to take into account the Citizen's Incomes received, then it would not have been possible to provide some of the values required in Table 3.2, and the method could not have been used to calculate the scheme's net cost.

3.7.3 A Microsimulation Method Employed to Estimate the Net Costs of Three Strictly Revenue Neutral Citizen's Income Schemes

In 2014, three strictly revenue neutral schemes were tested using the EUROMOD microsimulation program developed by the Institute for Social and Economic Research at the University of Essex.[28,29,30]

One of the schemes, scheme A, is very similar to the scheme above, with a Citizen's Income for working-age adults of £71.70 per week; another, scheme B, is a scheme with a lower Citizen's Income of £50 per week; and a third scheme, scheme C, sets Citizen's Income levels according to the Minimum Income Standards (MIS) recommended by the University of York.[31] The first and third schemes abolish means-tested benefits (apart from Housing Benefit and Council Tax Support), whereas the second scheme retains the current benefits structure and takes households' Citizens' Incomes into account when means-tested benefits are calculated. Characteristics that apply to the schemes are as follows:

- NICs above the Upper Earnings Threshold are raised from 2% to 12%, and the Lower Earnings Limit is reduced to zero. This has the effect of making NICs payable at 12% on all earned income. This seems to

me to be an entirely legitimate change to make. The ethos of a flat-rate benefit such as Citizen's Income is consistent with both progressive tax systems and flat-rate tax systems,[32] but not with regressive tax systems.
- Income Tax Personal Allowances are set at zero.
- The schemes are strictly revenue neutral. The net cost of each scheme is at or below £2 billion per annum.
- Estimates of administrative savings are conservative, and conservative administrative savings are assumed not to compromise strict revenue neutrality. In the first and third schemes, means-tested benefits are abolished (apart from Housing Benefit and Council Tax Benefit[33]). Given that current Department for Work and Pensions (DWP) running costs are £8 billion per annum, we can assume savings of £4 billion per annum. For the schemes that do not abolish means-tested benefits, large numbers of households will no longer be receiving means-tested benefits, but the means-tested structure will need to stay in place. So in the case of scheme B, I assume a saving of £1 billion per annum.

Table 3.5 summarizes the characteristics of the schemes and the results of the simulations.[34]

3.7.4 A Comparison: A Citizen's Income Scheme for Catalonia

Microsimulation using income tax data for Catalonia has shown that it is possible to pay a Citizen's Income of €7968 per annum to every adult and of one-fifth of that to every child (under eighteen years old).[35] The Citizen's Incomes would replace any other benefits of lesser quantity, but if existing cash benefits were of a higher amount, then the difference would be paid (a process equivalent to retaining existing means-tested benefits, as in scheme B above: although given the high value of the Citizen's Income, it must be doubtful whether many households would require additional benefits). The Citizen's Incomes would be paid for by removing the preferential treatment of savings income in income tax calculations, and by removing income tax allowances. So again, the funding mechanism is broadly the same as for the UK proposals above.

The microsimulation also shows that funding such a substantial Citizen's Income would require the rate of income tax to rise to 49.57% (if a flat tax system were to be introduced), and would also require additional funding of €3.5 billion,[36] as well as the removal of tax allowances. The level of the Citizen's Income and the funding package look very similar to scheme C above.

Table 3.5 Three illustrative Citizen's Income schemes, with their relationships to existing benefits, levels of Citizen's Incomes, increased tax rates required, and net costs

	Scheme A	Scheme B	Scheme C
Relationship of Citizen's Income to means-tested benefits	Citizen's Incomes replace means-tested benefits except for Housing Benefit and Council Tax Benefit. Child Benefit and State Pension are no longer paid	Means-tested benefits are left in place and the Citizen's Income is taken into account when means-tested benefits are calculated. Basic State Pension and Child Benefit are still paid	Citizen's Incomes replace means-tested benefits except for Housing Benefit and Council Tax Benefit. Child Benefit and State Pension are no longer paid
Citizen's Income levels, £ per week			
Citizen's Pension	145.40	30 (+ Basic State Pension)	120
Working-age adult CI	71.70	50	160
Young adult CI	56.80	40	120
Child CI	56.80	20 (+ Child Benefit)	80
Income Tax rate increase required for strict revenue neutrality	5%	3%	28%
Income Tax, basic rate (on £0–42,010)	25%	23%	48%
Income Tax, higher rate (on £42,010–150,000)	45%	43%	68%
Income Tax top rate (on £150,000+)	50%	48%	73%
NIC changes	NICs above the Upper Earnings Threshold are raised from 2% to 12% and the Lower Earnings Limit is reduced to zero		
Administrative saving assumed	£4bn	£1bn	£4bn
Net cost of scheme	£1.8bn	–£1.9bn	–£0.47

Source: Malcolm Torry (2015) *Two feasible ways to implement a revenue neutral Citizen's Income scheme*, Institute for Social and Economic Research Working Paper EM6/15 (Colchester: Institute for Social and Economic Research, University of Essex), www.iser.essex.ac.uk/research/publications/working-papers/euromod/em6-15, p. 6

3.8 Conclusion

We have discovered that whether a Citizen's Income is financially feasible is a complex question, and answers to the question will be different in different countries. Countries with subsidy programmes would be able to redirect the funds spent on them, and countries with sovereign wealth funds could use the dividends to fund Citizen's Incomes. Current expenditure on subsidy programmes, and the levels of dividends paid out by permanent funds, might determine the levels at which Citizen's Incomes could be paid.

If these funding routes were not available, then tax allowances and/or existing benefits would need to be reduced, tax rates would need to rise, new taxes would need to be established, or new money would need to be created. All of these funding methods are legitimate possibilities that governments would need to consider. If tax rates were to be raised, then governments would need to discover the extent to which increased tax rates would be acceptable.

Decisions about funding methods, and decisions about the levels at which Citizen's Incomes would be paid, belong together. In each country, a different set of funding options would be available, so different levels of Citizen's Income would be feasible.

The conclusion that we can draw from the argument of this chapter, and from the examples quoted, is that a Citizen's Income is financially feasible in any country with a subsidy programme, a permanent fund, an existing tax and benefits system, the ability to create its own money, or the option of establishing new taxes. There will therefore be few countries, if any, for which a Citizen's Income would not be financially feasible.

As for the three schemes for the UK tested in the case study, they are all strictly revenue neutral, and in that sense, they are all financially feasible. The Catalonian scheme might be financially feasible, but it would not be revenue neutral. However, if a Citizen's Income scheme is to be 'financially feasible' in the normal public sense of the term, then only a minor increase in Income Tax rates can be permitted. If 3% were to be agreed as the maximum viable increase, then scheme B would be financially feasible, scheme A would be dubiously financially feasible, and scheme C would only be financially feasible if the requirement for (strict) revenue neutrality were to be abandoned and new taxation or money creation were to be employed to fund the Citizen's Incomes rather than increased Income Tax rates. The Catalonian scheme would only be financially feasible if more additional funding than the proposed €3.5 billion were to become available so that the proposed income tax rate could be considerably reduced.

NOTES

1. Donald Hirsch (2015) *Could a 'Citizen's Income' work?* (York: Joseph Rowntree Foundation), p. 33. www.jrf.org.uk/publications/could-citizens-income-work
2. Donald Hirsch (2015) *Could a 'Citizen's Income' work?* p. 33.
3. It might be thought that this description of the essential income maintenance structure leaves no room for a Citizen's Income. However, once the principle of a personal tax allowance is admitted, there is no reason not to turn it into a cash payment of the same value (i.e., the amount of the allowance multiplied by the tax rate) and then applying income tax rates to all earned income. Similarly, once the provision of benefits is recognized as an essential element of an income maintenance structure, there is no reason not to reduce to zero the taper rate by which existing means-tested benefits are withdrawn as earnings rise.
4. www.tax.ny.gov/bus/stock/stktridx.htm
5. www.gov.uk/tax-buy-shares
6. www.lseg.com/markets-products-and-services/post-trade-services/unavista/regulation/french-financial-transaction-tax-ftt-overview
7. James Tobin (1978) 'A Proposal for International Monetary Reform', *Eastern Economic Journal*, 4 (3–4), 153–59, p. 155. The Mirrlees Review of the UK's tax system recommended instead a 'financial activity tax' that would be less likely to penalize currency exchange required for trade in goods and services: Stuart Adam et al. (2011) *Tax by Design: The Mirrlees Review* (Oxford: Oxford University Press), pp. 151–3, 195–215.
8. Richard Wilkinson and Kate Pickett (2010) *The Spirit Level: Why Equality is Better for Everyone*, 2nd edition (London: Penguin Books); Danny Dorling (2012) *Equality* (Oxford: New Internationalist), pp. 13–40. At a seminar at the London School of Economics on the 18 March 2015, Lane Kenworthy and Timothy Smeeding presented evidence that shows that in affluent nations, there is a strong negative correlation between top-end inequality and median income growth (paper forthcoming).
9. Thomas Piketty (2014) *Capital in the Twenty-first Century* (Cambridge, Massachusetts: The Belknap Press of Harvard University), pp. 493–514.
10. Henry George (1889) *Progress and Poverty* (London: Kegan Paul, Trench and Co.), pp. 290–334.
11. www.bankofengland.co.uk/monetarypolicy/pages/qe/default.aspx
12. Larry Elliott (2014) 'Quantitative easing: giving cash to the public would have been more effective', *The Guardian*, 29 October 2014, www.theguardian.com/business/economics-blog/2014/oct/29/quantitative-easing-policy-stimulus-janet-yellen-ecb; Dwight Murphey (2009) 'A "Classical Liberal" Rethinks the Market System: Invitation to an Intellectual Odyssey', *The Journal of Social, Political, and Economic Studies*, 34 (3),

347–55; Dwight Murphey (2011) 'Capitalism's Deepening Crisis: The Imperative of Monetary Reconstruction', *The Journal of Social, Political, and Economic Studies*, 36 (3), 277–300, p. 296.
13. Almaz Zelleke (2012) 'Basic Income and the Alaska Model: Limits of the resource dividend model for the implementation of an Unconditional Basic Income', pp. 141–68 in Karl Widerquist and Michael Howard (eds), *Alaska's Permanent Fund Dividend: Examining its suitability as a model* (New York: Palgrave Macmillan), p. 150.
14. Andrew Jackson and Ben Dyson (2012) *Modernising Money: Why our monetary system is broken, and how it can be fixed* (London: Positive Money), p. 283. Parts of this section repeat a review of *Modernising Money* in the *Citizen's Income Newsletter*, issue 2 for 2015, 13–14.
15. Geoff Crocker (2012) 'Why Austerity is the Wrong Answer to Debt: A Call for a New Paradigm', *Citizen's Income Newsletter*, issue 3 for 2012, pp. 13–16, p. 16.
16. Nicolaus Tideman and Kwok Ping Tsang (2010) 'Seigniorage as a Source for a Basic Income Guarantee', *Basic Income Studies*, 5 (2), 1–6.
17. www.theguardian.com/business/economics-blog/2015/may/21/now-the-bank-of-england-needs-to-deliver-qe-for-the-people; Josh Ryan-Collins, Tony Greenham, Richard Werner and Andrew Jackson (2011) *Where does Money come from? A guide to the UK monetary and banking system* (London: New Economics Foundation); Michael McLeay, Amar Radia and Ryland Thomas (2014) 'Money Creation in the Modern Economy', *Quarterly Bulletin*, 1st quarter, 2014 (London: Bank of England), www.bankofengland.co.uk/publications/Documents/quarterlybulletin/2014/qb14q1prereleasemoneycreation.pdf
18. Karl Widerquist and Michael Howard (2012) *Alaska's Permanent Fund Dividend: Examining its suitability as a model* (New York: Palgrave Macmillan).
19. Scott Goldsmith (2012) 'The Economic and Social Impacts of the Permanent Fund Dividend on Alaska', pp. 49–63 in Karl Widerquist and Michael W. Howard (eds) *Alaska's Permanent Fund Dividend* (New York: Palgrave Macmillan); Karl Widerquist (2010) 'Lessons of the Alaska Dividend', *Citizen's Income Newsletter*, issue 3 for 2010, pp. 13–15.
20. Stewart Lansley (2015) *Tackling the Power of Capital: The role of social wealth funds*, Thinkpiece no. 81 (London: Compass).
21. Hamid Tabatabai (2011) 'Iran's economic reforms usher in a de facto Citizen's Income', *Citizen's Income Newsletter*, issue 1 for 2011, pp. 1–2; Hamid Tabatabai (2011) 'The Basic Income Road to Reforming Iran's Price Subsidies', *Basic Income Studies*, 6 (1), 1–24; Hamid Tabatabai (2012) 'Iran: A Bumpy Road toward Basic Income', pp. 285–300 in Richard Caputo (ed.) *Basic Income Guarantee and Politics: International*

Experiences and perspectives on the viability of Income Guarantee (New York: Palgrave Macmillan), p. 295; Turquoise Partners (2014) *Iran Investment Monthly* (Iran: Turquoise Partners), April 2014.
22. Sarath Davala, Renana Jhabvala, Soumya Kapoor Mehta and Guy Standing (2015) *Basic Income: A transformative policy for India* (London: Bloomsbury), p. 139.
23. Part of this section appeared first as a review of Sarath Davala, Renana Jhabvala, Soumya Kapoor Mehta and Guy Standing (2015) *Basic Income: A transformative policy for India* (London: Bloomsbury), in the *Citizen's Income Newsletter*, issue 2 for 2015.
24. See the first part of the case study below. Before the UK's 2015 General Election the Labour Party suggested that tax relief on pension contributions should be reduced to the basic rate and the proceeds used to increase the education budget.
25. Shinji Murakami (2014) 'The Financial Feasibility of Basic Income and the Idea of a Refundable Tax Credit in Japan', pp. 219–45 in Yannick Vanderborght and Toru Yamamori (eds) *Basic Income in Japan: Prospects for a radical idea in a transforming welfare state* (New York: Palgrave Macmillan), pp. 227, 235.
26. Donald Hirsch (2015) *Could a 'Citizen's Income' work?* pp. 25–8.
27. *Benefits Simplification*, HC 463, vol I (London: The Stationary Office), July 2007, paragraphs 51, 55, 148, 176, 262, 381. www.publications.parliament.uk/pa/cm200607/cmselect/cmworpen/463/46302.htm. The Citizen's Income Trust's evidence to the Department of Work and Pensions can be found in the second volume on page Ev 84 at www.publications.parliament.uk/pa/cm200607/cmselect/cmworpen/463/463ii.pdf. The Trust subsequently published the scheme in 2007 in its booklet *Citizen's Income: A brief introduction* (London: Citizen's Income Trust). In 2013, the figures were updated to 2012–13 values and the booklet was republished in 2013. The author and the Citizen's Income Trust are grateful to Philip Vince (now deceased) and to Mark Wadsworth for their work on the figures published in *Citizen's Income: A brief introduction* (London: Citizen's Income Trust) in 2007; and to Mark Wadsworth for updating the figures in preparation for the 2013 edition of the booklet.
28. This case study uses EUROMOD version G2.0++. The contribution of all past and current members of the EUROMOD consortium is gratefully acknowledged. The process of extending and updating EUROMOD is financially supported by the Directorate General for Employment, Social Affairs and Inclusion of the European Commission [Progress grant no. VS/2011/0445]. The UK Family Resources Survey data was made available by the Department of Work and Pensions via the UK Data Archive.

29. Parts of this case study were first published in a EUROMOD working paper, Malcolm Torry (2015) *Two feasible ways to implement a revenue neutral Citizen's Income scheme*, Institute for Social and Economic Research Working Paper EM6/15 (Colchester: Institute for Social and Economic Research, University of Essex), www.iser.essex.ac.uk/research/publications/working-papers/euromod/em6–15, and subsequently as an article in the *Citizen's Income Newsletter*, issue 3 for 2015. The Institute for Social and Economic Research's permission to reprint material from the working paper is gratefully acknowledged.

30. The most recent tax and benefits regulations available in EUROMOD version G2.0++ are those for 2013–14, and the most recent Family Resource Survey data is for 2009, uprated to 2013 values. It is therefore not currently possible to simulate Citizen's Income schemes for more recent periods. 'The factors that are used to update monetary variables (parameter sheet *Uprate_uk*) from the mid-point of the data year (October 2009) to the mid-point of the policy years applying on June 30th (that is, October 2010 to October 2013) are shown in Annex 1 of the EUROMOD UK country report. No other updating adjustments are employed. Thus the distribution of characteristics (such as employment status and demographic variables), as well as the distribution of each income source that is not simulated, remain as they were in 2009/10' (Paola De Agostini and Holly Sutherland (2014) *Euromod Country Report: United Kingdom 2009–2013* (Colchester: Institute for Social and Economic Research, Essex University)).

31. Minimum Income Standards for 2013 can be found at www.jrf.org.uk/site/files/jrf/images/MIS-2013-figure2.jpg. Deciding the levels of Citizen's Incomes that would match the MIS is not a simple matter as MIS levels are calculated for households, whereas Citizen's Incomes are paid to individuals. The weekly MIS levels for 2013 are as follows (excluding rent and childcare): single working-age person, £200.64; pensioner couple, £241.25; couple and two children, £471.16; lone parent and one child, £284.57. Citizen's Incomes based on the smaller assessment units would be higher than Citizen's Incomes based on the larger units. I have chosen to be guided by the larger units. I have set the young person's Citizen's Income rate halfway between the adult and child rates.

32. A.B. Atkinson (1995) *Public Economics in Action: The Basic Income/Flat Tax Proposal* (Oxford: Clarendon Press).

33. In 2013–14, Council Tax Benefit was centrally regulated. Under the government's localization agenda, its replacement, Council Tax Support, is locally regulated as well as locally administered. This means that every borough in the country can now invent its own regulations, and, in particular, its own taper rate. It will be far from easy to include Council Tax Support in future tax and benefits simulations.

34. The method is as follows: A new set of benefits is created in the UK country system in EUROMOD—a Citizen's Pension (CP) for over sixty-five-year-olds, a Citizen's Income (CI) for adults aged between twenty-five and sixty-four, a young person's Citizen's Income (CIY) for adults aged between sixteen and twenty-four, and a Child Citizen's Income (CIC) for children aged between zero and fifteen. In the definitions of constants, levels are set for these Citizen's Incomes, and all Personal Tax Allowances are set at zero. So that the additional taxable income is taxed at the basic rate, and not at the higher rate, the first tax threshold is changed from 32,010 to 42,010. The National Insurance Contribution (NIC) Lower Earnings Limit is set to zero, and the NIC rate above the Upper Earnings Limit is set to 12% (to match the rate below the limit). For the first scheme, Working Tax Credit, Child Tax Credit, Income Support, Income-Related ESA, Pension Credit, and Income-based Jobseeker's Allowance are no longer added to the total for means-tested benefits. Incapacity Benefit, Contributory ESA, and Child Benefit are removed from non-means-tested benefits (except that in scheme B, Child Benefit is left in payment). For all schemes, the Citizen's Income total is added to non-means-tested benefits, and for the second scheme, Citizen's Incomes are added to the means applied to means-tested benefits. The state pension is no longer added to the pensions total in schemes A and C (as the Citizen's Pension has already been added to the non-means-tested benefits total). Where benefits are no longer in payment, they are removed from the tax base. Simulations of the 2013 system and the system being tested generate two lists of household disposable incomes for the entire Family Resource Survey sample. These then generate a list of gains (negative gains are losses), and the total of the gains gives the net cost of the scheme for the sample. To convert EUROMOD's monthly figures to annual figures, and the sample size to the total population, a multiplier of (12 × 64.1m/57,381) = 13.4 gives the cost in £ms for the UK population. A process of trial and error adjusts the Income Tax rates until the net cost minus the assumed administrative saving is below £2 billion per annum.
35. Jordi Arcarons, Daniel Raventos Pañella and Lluís Torrens Mèlich (2014) 'Feasibility of Financing a Basic Income', *Basic Income Studies*, 9 (1–2), 79–93.
36. Microsimulation results show that an additional €7 billion would be required on top of the additional tax revenue. The authors estimate that €3.5 billion of this would come from money saved by the reductions in other benefits resulting from payment of the Citizen's Incomes, but because the Catalonian microsimulation method employs only tax data and not benefits data, it is not possible to provide an accurate figure.

CHAPTER 4

Is a Citizen's Income Financially Feasible? Part Two: Household Financial Feasibility

4.1 Introduction

As in the last chapter, we again need to distinguish between a Citizen's Income and a Citizen's Income scheme. A Citizen's Income is an unconditional, nonwithdrawable income for every individual as a right of citizenship. A Citizen's Income scheme specifies the levels at which a Citizen's Income will be paid to members of each age group, and also the way in which the Citizen's Income will be funded by altering current benefits, tax allowances, and/or tax rates, by the government creating money, by the redirection of funding for subsidies, by using permanent fund dividend payments, or by implementing new taxes.

Chapter 3 tackled the question: Is a Citizen's Income financially feasible in the sense that it could be paid for, one way or another? I called this 'fiscal feasibility', because it relates to whether a Citizen's Income is feasible for a government to implement. In this chapter, we shall tackle a rather different kind of financial feasibility: that is, whether a Citizen's Income scheme would be financially feasible for individuals and households. The question that needs to be answered is this: Could a Citizen's Income scheme be implemented without imposing unacceptable losses on households? A particular Citizen's Income scheme could be financially feasible for a government to implement, but we probably ought not to regard it as financially feasible if at the point of implementation the changes made to the existing tax and benefits systems to fund it would impose unacceptable losses on low-income households. We can envisage a situation in which reductions in tax allowances and existing benefits, and increases in tax rates, would impose losses greater than the total that a household would receive in Citizen's Incomes paid to its individual members. Higher earning households can often absorb losses, although existing financial commitments can mean that the level of losses that can be comfortably sustained might not be very high. Low-income households can rarely absorb losses of any amount. To be feasible, a Citizen's Income scheme will need to avoid losses for low-income households and will need to avoid significant losses for any households. I shall call this second kind of financial feasibility 'household financial feasibility'.

It could well be said that it is entirely unfair on the Citizen's Income proposal to suggest that its feasibility requires household financial feasibility, because if replacing a complicated largely means-tested system imposes losses on households, then it is the means-tested system that is at fault and not the Citizen's Income. The Citizen's Income itself could not be more fair or transparent because it would provide the same income to everyone of the same age, and it would be paid for through progressive taxation. But that is not the point. As Majone suggests,

> the transition from a non-efficient to an efficient situation need not be efficient, since some members of the community will probably be damaged by it and compensation may be politically infeasible.[1]

Whether or not the situation is fair to the Citizen's Income proposal, if households would suffer losses at the point of implementation of a Citizen's Income scheme, then that would quite rightly count against the feasibility of the scheme. Such losses therefore need to be kept to a minimum.

I have called this kind of financial feasibility '*household* financial feasibility'. Financial losses are experienced both by households and by individuals within households. It is individuals who receive earned incomes and many other kinds of income, so gain or loss tends to be an individual experience; and within households, income is not necessarily equitably shared, so the amounts that individuals receive might be more relevant than the amount that the household receives. However, we can assume that in most cases income is pooled within households, at least to some extent,[2] so if one member gains and another loses, then the household might be better off, and that might be a more significant fact than that one member of the household has suffered a loss in disposable income.

I have therefore decided to construct this chapter around the gains and losses that would be experienced by households on the implementation of a Citizen's Income scheme. A similar chapter could have been written on the basis of gains and losses experienced by individuals.

(Another point to make about households is that they are of different sizes, so the absolute gain or loss that a household experiences at the point of implementation of a Citizen's Income might not be particularly relevant. What will matter will be the percentage gains and losses.)

A Citizen's Income scheme will only be financially feasible in the sense of household financial feasibility if it imposes almost no losses on low-income households at the point of implementation, and if it imposes only acceptable losses on higher-income households. Putting together the two different kinds of financial feasibility, a Citizen's Income will be simply 'financially feasible' if (a) it is fiscally feasible, and (b) at the point of implementation it imposes almost no losses on low-income households, and only acceptable losses on higher-income households.

4.2 The Sources of Household Income Losses

In some cases, the damage to household budgets might not relate to income, but rather to increased costs. In the case of the Iranian and Indian schemes discussed in Chap. 3, the reduction in subsidies on food and fuel will impose higher prices. If a country were to implement a Citizen's Income scheme by reducing subsidies, and if the additional costs of purchasing food and fuel were greater in total than the total amount of households' Citizen's Incomes, then households would suffer financial loss and the scheme might not be household financially feasible.

Similarly, if a government creates new money in order to fund Citizen's Incomes, then if inflation rises (although there is no reason to assume that it will) and the rise in prices costs a household a greater amount of money than the total of their Citizen's Incomes, then that household will have suffered a financial loss. New taxes on carbon use might cause fuel prices to increase, and a financial transaction tax could cause the prices of imported goods to rise. In both cases, if a household's Citizen's Incomes were to add up to less than the increases in prices, then financial loss would be the result.

For Citizen's Incomes funded by making adjustments to existing tax and benefits systems, any damage to household budgets would be because of additional tax payments and/or the loss or reduction of benefits payments. The Citizen's Incomes would, of course, enhance household income, but if increases in tax payments and reductions in income from other benefits were to add up to more than a household's Citizen's Incomes, then that household would suffer a financial loss.

One source of such losses will be the different ways in which a Citizen's Income and means-tested benefits treat households. People living together generate economies of scale (because they are only paying for one home and the associated fuel and other costs). When a government pays either in-work or out-of-work means-tested benefits, it generally pays less to a couple than it would pay in total to two individuals living separately. This is because the government wishes to reap the economies of scale rather than leave them with the couple. A Citizen's Income would be paid to every individual, regardless of their personal relationships, so if two people decided to live together, then their Citizen's Incomes would not change (although any means-tested benefits to which they remained entitled would of course do so). If a revenue neutral Citizen's Income scheme were to be implemented, then couples in receipt of means-tested benefits would generally find themselves better off, and, because in a revenue neutral scheme, total gains must equal total losses, individuals living alone would tend to be worse off at the point of implementation.

4.3　Coping with Losses?

Are losses at the point of implementation a problem?

Let us take as an example a Citizen's Income scheme funded by increasing tax rates and reducing tax allowances and existing benefits. If the total of such losses for a household were to be greater than the total of Citizen's Incomes paid to members of that household, then a net loss would occur. However, another change might also have occurred. If a proportion of that household's income before the implementation of the Citizen's Income scheme had consisted of means-tested benefits, then before implementation of the scheme, any additional earnings will have been reduced by the tax rate and by withdrawal of those benefits. The total withdrawal rate, calculated by adding the tax rate to the benefits withdrawal rate, can be quite high.[3] On the implementation of the Citizen's Income scheme, either means-tested benefits would no longer be paid, in which case the only withdrawal rate would be the tax rate; or means-tested benefits would still be received, but their amounts would be lower and a smaller proportion of the household budget would consist of means-tested benefits, so it would take less of an increase in earnings to reach the earnings range within which the only withdrawal rate would be the tax rate. In either case, the household would be more able to lift itself out of poverty by earning additional income. Poverty is not just about the absolute amount of money coming into a household; it could also be defined as an inability to climb out of poverty.[4] So we might be able to say that one family could be better off than another if it had a lower income but also a lower marginal deduction rate (i.e., a lower total withdrawal rate: 'marginal' because it would apply to additional income rather than to total income).

However, it would still be difficult for a low-income household if it suddenly found itself a lot worse off, even if it could then keep more of every additional £1 of earned income than it could before. If a Citizen's Income scheme were to impose losses on low-income households at the point of implementation, then there would be a problem, so we would need to avoid as many of those losses as possible.

4.4   Calculating Losses

Losses are experienced by households, so here we cannot use national statistics as we did when calculating the net cost of a Citizen's Income scheme as a whole. This leaves us with two methods: employing the tax and benefit regulations to calculate the gain or loss that ought to be experienced by a typical household, and microsimulation.

4.4.1   *The Typical Household Method*

There is no such thing as a typical household, of course; but what we can do is list a variety of typical households by specifying the values of a number of variables: single or couple, number and ages of children, housing tenure, earnings levels, and so on. However large the set of typical households that we construct, there will of course be numerous households that do not fit any of them (three generational households are often difficult to fit into categories; shared houses containing couples and single adults can be difficult to define, especially when couple relationships are flexible; and a woman and two men, or a man and two women, living together in a household can mean lots of different things). But still, to construct a wide diversity of household types, and to work out for each of them whether they would be likely to suffer losses on the implementation of a particular Citizen's Income scheme, might at least give some indication as to whether the scheme would be household financially feasible.

Take the simplest example: a working-age adult living alone. For each earned income level, from zero to a (somewhat arbitrary) high income, applying the current tax and benefit regulations will generate a disposable income for each earned income level. A second calculation can then be done by applying the new tax and benefit regulations that would accompany a Citizen's Income scheme, and then adding the working-age adult Citizen's Income. The calculation generates a second set of disposable incomes that can then be compared with the first set to determine the gain or loss at each earnings level.

Complications occur in countries with means-tested benefits related to housing costs. For each earnings level, a range of calculations will need to be done for each of a range of rent levels. Further complications relate to households containing more than one employed adult, as for each of one individual's earnings levels, a separate calculation will have to be undertaken for each of the other individual's earnings levels. If all of a country's tax and benefits calculations are based on a household's aggregated earnings, then this step is not required; but in most countries, the calculations of at least some benefits and/or taxes relate to individual earned income, and here the complication would apply.

If a researcher is particularly interested in the way in which a particular Citizen's Income scheme would affect the disposable income of a particular typical household in which the number and ages of children, earnings levels, and housing costs are already closely specified, then this method can be useful. As a guide to whether a particular Citizen's Income scheme would impose a high number of unacceptable losses across particular earnings deciles it is less useful. It would often not be clear to what proportion of households a particular household specification might apply, and so even if calculations were to generate expected gains and losses for a wide variety of household types, no overall picture of gains and losses would be delivered.

4.4.2 *Microsimulation*

In Chap. 3, I described how microsimulation programs can generate a list of gains and losses in disposable incomes for a large sample of the population, and how by summing that list we can gain an accurate estimate of the net cost of a Citizen's Income scheme. In this chapter, we are interested in the list of gains and losses itself. For each household in the sample, the program generates a gain or loss. This can then be turned into a percentage of the household's original disposable income. We can then order the list of households to generate the results in which we are interested. Suppose that we want to know how many households in the lowest disposable income decile (the lowest tenth of disposable incomes) suffer losses in disposable income greater than 5% on the implementation of a Citizen's Income scheme. The households can first be ordered according to original disposable income, and the bottom tenth of the list selected; and then that selected list can be reordered according to the magnitude of gains and losses. The number of losses over 5% can then be counted, and the number turned into a percentage of the size of the sample. This gives for the population as a whole the percentage of losses over 5% for households in the lowest disposable income decile.

Microsimulation programs can also provide a certain amount of detail if that is required. Suppose that a handful of households with low disposable incomes experience massive losses. The program's output will generally enable the particular circumstances of a household's individuals to be studied in order to provide an explanation for the losses.

Clearly, we shall be particularly interested in the losses that would be experienced by low-income households, but household financial feasibility also requires that no losses will be experienced as unacceptable. A particular Citizen's Income scheme might impose no losses at all on low-income households, but if it were to impose large losses on households elsewhere in the earnings range, then it might still not be financially feasible in the way in which either the public or a government would understand that term. For household financial feasibility, we require minimal losses in the lowest disposable income decile, and only acceptable losses higher up the income range.

There is one problem with the method described. A household of two parents and three children with twice the disposable income of a household containing just one adult will not be as well-off as that individual adult. For the purposes of this exercise, I have ignored the different sizes of households. More detailed research, employing household weights so that the disposable incomes of households of different sizes could be more relevantly compared, would constitute a further research project.[5] But for the time being, we shall treat all households with the lowest tenth of disposable incomes as low-income households, knowing that by doing this, we shall at least be capturing the households, large or small, with the very lowest incomes.

In spite of the problems, we are fortunate that modern microsimulation methods enable us to produce the results that they do, and as far as I know, they offer the only way of providing those results.

4.5 Redistribution

It might be true that when it comes to gains and losses, we are primarily interested in what is happening to individual households, but it is also true that policymakers are sometimes interested in the overall redistributive effects of Citizen's Income schemes. A politician on the left of the political spectrum might wish to see a significant redistribution from rich to poor, whereas a politician further to the right might wish to see only slight redistribution, and possibly none at all. (Few politicians will argue for redistribution from poor to rich, even if that might be the effect of some of their policies.) Here we are asking about aggregated gains and losses, and we are again fortunate that microsimulation programs can deliver the required information.

But however interesting the graphs showing redistribution might be to politicians, and possibly to members of the public, we need to take care that we do not allow them to displace careful evaluation of the gains and losses that would be experienced by individual households. We can envisage a revenue neutral Citizen's Income scheme that would produce both large gains and large losses among households in the lowest disposable income decile, but that would generate an aggregate gain for the decile as a whole. This would appear as a redistribution from rich to poor on a graph that showed the gains and losses of income deciles, but such a scheme would not be household financially feasible and so would not be financially feasible.

4.6 Case Studies

4.6.1 How Easily Could a Household Make Good Any Losses Experienced on the Implementation of a Citizen's Income Scheme?

Citizen's Incomes of different levels, and paid for by different adjustments to tax allowances, tax rates, and means-tested and contributory benefits, would deliver different patterns of gains and losses. Losses are always difficult for households to cope with, in particular where households have low incomes. However, the implementation of a Citizen's Income scheme in the UK would make coping with losses easier than it would be for many households currently receiving means-tested benefits, including any on the new Universal Credit.

If we assume a household loss of £10 per week, a Universal Credit taper rate of 65% (on after-tax income), NICs of 12%, and Income Tax at 20%, then additional earnings of about £42 per week will be required to deliver the necessary additional £10 of net income. With a Citizen's Income, the situation would be very different. The Citizen's Income would not be withdrawn, but Income Tax at 20% and NICs at 12% would be payable on the additional earned income. A household loss of £10 per week could be made up by earning an additional £14.70 per week. It would therefore be far easier for a household to make up losses at the point of implementation of a Citizen's Income scheme than it is in relation to losses imposed by changes in current means-tested benefits regulations.

4.6.2 Would a Citizen's Income for the UK Be Household Financially Feasible in the Sense That It Would Not Impose Unacceptable Losses?

4.6.2.1 The Typical Household Method

Take the simplest UK household in 2013–14: a single adult living alone and earning £30,000 per annum. The Personal Allowance was £9440, and the basic rate of tax 20% on earned income up to £32,010. Tax payable would have been £4112. The annual Primary Threshold for NICs was £7752, and the rate 12% above that level, so NICs of £2670 were payable. Net income would have been £23,218. No Working Tax Credit would have been payable.

If a Citizen's Income of £50 per week were to have replaced the Income Tax Allowance and the NIC Primary Threshold, then Income Tax and NICs would have been payable on all earned income: £6000 and £3600, respectively. Net earnings would therefore have been £20,400. A Citizen's Income of £50 per week works out at approximately £2600 per annum, giving a total net income of £23,200. This individual would have experienced a small loss.

4.6.2.2 Microsimulation of Three Citizen's Income Schemes

In Chap. 3, I described a microsimulation exercise that calculated the Income Tax rate increases that would be required to pay for three different strictly revenue neutral Citizen's Income schemes.[6,7] Here I evaluate the gains and losses related to the same three schemes.

Table 4.1 summarizes the characteristics of the schemes and the results of the simulations.[8]

In relation to schemes A and C, while it is true that the high losses imposed on households at the point of implementation are the result of the complexity of the current tax and benefits scheme, and not of the Citizen's Income schemes, such losses would make the schemes impossible to implement. So while all three schemes would be revenue neutral

Table 4.1 Three illustrative Citizen's Income schemes, with their relationships to existing benefits, levels of Citizen's Incomes, and losses imposed at the point of implementation

	Scheme A	Scheme B	Scheme C
Relationship of Citizen's Income to means-tested benefits	Citizen's Incomes replace means-tested benefits except for Housing Benefit and Council Tax Benefit. Child Benefit and State Pension are no longer paid	Means-tested benefits are left in place and the Citizen's Income is taken into account when means-tested benefits are calculated. Basic State Pension and Child Benefit are still paid	Citizen's Incomes replace means-tested benefits except for Housing Benefit and Council Tax Benefit. Child Benefit and State Pension are no longer paid
Citizen's Income levels, £ per week			
Citizen's Pension	145.40	30 (+ Basic State Pension)	120
Working-age adult CI	71.70	50	160
Young adult CI	56.80	40	120
Child CI	56.80	20 (+ Child Benefit)	80
Proportion of households in the lowest disposable income decile experiencing losses of over 10% at the point of implementation	28.03%	1.5% (and 4.37% with losses over 5%)	29.0%
Proportion of all households experiencing losses of over 10% at the point of implementation	15.2%	1.24% (and 15.2% with losses over 5%)	30.2%

Source: Malcolm Torry (2015) *Two feasible ways to implement a revenue neutral Citizen's Income scheme*, Institute for Social and Economic Research Working Paper EM6/15 (Colchester: Institute for Social and Economic Research, University of Essex), www.iser.essex.ac.uk/research/publications/working-papers/euromod/em6-15, p. 6

in the strictest sense, the only scheme that would be household financially feasible, and therefore financially feasible, would be scheme B. Note that this is the scheme that retains means-tested benefits and recalculates them to take into account households' Citizen's Incomes. It is the retention of the means-tested benefits that reduces almost to zero the losses that would be experienced by low-income households.

4.6.2.3   A Comparison: A Citizen's Income Scheme for Catalonia

Microsimulation of the Catalonian proposal for a Citizen's Income of €7968 per annum for every adult and of one-fifth of that for every child (under eighteen years old) described in Chap. 3 shows that all non-taxpayers would gain, 55% of individual taxpayers would gain, 87% of taxpaying households with children would gain, the first 40% of taxpayers would experience net gains, and the richest 10% would contribute almost 80% of the new tax revenue.[9] Only the wealthiest 1% of the population would lose significantly.

However, once we study the detail, it becomes clear that substantial gains among the lowest earners are being paid for partly by losses among the middle range of taxpayers. A total of 22% of the fifth earnings decile would experience losses averaging €559 per annum, and 58.3% of the sixth earnings decile would experience losses averaging €942 per annum. The fact that the Gini coefficient would be reduced by 0.12 might be less relevant than the high rate of losses among some mid-range earners.

4.6.3   A 'One Step at a Time' Method for Implementing Citizen's Income

Just as it is possible to test the fiscal and household financial feasibilities of schemes that would implement Citizen's Incomes for every member of a population, here we test both kinds of financial feasibility for two early stages of a scheme that would implement Citizen's Income one step at a time.

In the UK, there is a tradition of cautious and piecemeal change to the benefits system. This has its disadvantages, particularly when the current system no longer fits the society, economy, and employment market that it needs to serve; but the advantage is that new approaches can be tested out without causing too much disruption to administrative systems or to household budgets. Let us assume that the arguments for Citizen's Income are understood by policymakers, and that only the psychological difficulties relating to the transition from the current system to one based on a Citizen's Income stand in the way of implementation. In this situation, it could be useful to have asked about the financial feasibility of taking the first steps towards a universal unconditional and nonwithdrawable income for every citizen.

Clearly, a possible method would be to start with children and young people, say up to the age of eighteen, and then as they grow into adulthood to allow them to keep their Citizen's Incomes. If at the same time the new STP were to be turned into a genuine Citizen's Pension, then it would take about fifty years to implement the Citizen's Income (a period that could be shortened by thirteen years if a pre-retirement unconditional and nonwithdrawable income were to be paid to everyone over the age of fifty-five).

As for the Citizen's Income schemes that we have already discussed, we assume that Income Tax rises above 3% would be difficult both psychologically and politically.

4.6.3.1 The First Step: Raising Child Benefit for Children Up to the Age of Fifteen

The first step would apply to children up to their sixteenth birthday, and would equalize the Child Benefit paid for every child.

Here, the only other change required would be to increase NICs by 4% above the Upper Earnings Limit.[10] Income Tax Personal Allowances and tax thresholds could remain as they are.

The results for two different rates are as shown in Table 4.2.

Scheme b fulfils our criteria, but the Income Tax rate for scheme a is too high.

However, as we can see from Table 4.3, the number of children in poverty would be reduced by a tenth if a single Child Benefit rate of £40 were to apply to children under the age of sixteen, and to raise Child Benefit to £56.80 would reduce by a quarter the number of children in poverty. Such reductions in child poverty would in themselves be an excellent reason for raising Child Benefit immediately to a single rate of £40, and then to £56.80. For such a virtuous purpose, increasing Income Tax rates by 4.5% might be acceptable.

The modest rise in NICs, and bearable rises in Income Tax rates, would in either case suggest financial feasibility for such a worthwhile outcome. To establish such a Citizen's Income for children would be a useful first

Table 4.2 Two Child Citizen's Income schemes, showing the Income Tax rate increases required, and losses imposed on households at the point of implementation

	Scheme a	Scheme b
Child Citizen's Income (increased CB) £ per week for every child up to the age of 15	56.80	40
Income Tax rate increase required for strict revenue neutrality	4.5%	2.5%
Income Tax, basic rate	24.5%	22.5%
Income Tax, higher rate	44.5%	42.5%
Income Tax, top rate	49.5%	47.5%
Proportion of households in the lowest disposable income decile experiencing losses of over 10% at the point of implementation	0%	0%
Proportion of households in the lowest disposable income decile experiencing losses of over 5% at the point of implementation	0.04%	0%
Proportion of all households experiencing losses of over 10% at the point of implementation	0.52%	0.03%
Proportion of all households experiencing losses of over 5% at the point of implementation	5.72%	1.88%
Administrative saving assumed	£0bn	£0bn
Net cost of scheme	£0.34bn	−£0.43bn

Source: Malcolm Torry (2015) *Two feasible ways to implement a revenue neutral Citizen's Income scheme*, Institute for Social and Economic Research Working Paper EM6/15 (Colchester: Institute for Social and Economic Research, University of Essex), www.iser.essex.ac.uk/research/publications/working-papers/euromod/em6-15, p. 9

Table 4.3 Reductions in inequality and child poverty achieved by the two Child Citizen's Income schemes

	2013 base system	Child Benefit raised to £56.80	Child Benefit raised to £40
Gini coefficient for disposable income	0.30	0.28	0.29
Children in poverty	12.16%	9.18%	10.84%
% reduction of children in poverty		24.5%	10.85%

Source: Malcolm Torry (2015) *Two feasible ways to implement a revenue neutral Citizen's Income scheme*, Institute for Social and Economic Research Working Paper EM6/15 (Colchester: Institute for Social and Economic Research, University of Essex), www.iser.essex.ac.uk/research/publications/working-papers/euromod/em6-15, p. 10

step on the road to a Citizen's Income for every age group, and one that could be achieved with public acceptance simply because children are universally regarded as a deserving demographic group.

4.6.3.2 The Second Step: Implementing a Young Adult Citizen's Income of £56.80 or £40 per Week for Young Adults Between Their Sixteenth and Their Nineteenth Birthdays

(Such a Young adult Citizen's Income could be paid to the main carer until the eighteenth birthday, and then transferred to the young adult, or a staged transfer could occur.)

The only other change required would be to increase NICs, in this case by 6 % above the Upper Earnings Limit.[11] Income Tax Personal Allowances and tax thresholds could remain as they are, except that for those young adults now receiving a Citizen's Income, all earnings would be taxed, thus enabling their Citizen's Incomes to be paid for as they grew older.

Results are as shown in Table 4.4.

Either of the two relatively modest proposals would not raise Income Tax rates, could generate savings (which would be useful), and would begin to sort out the income maintenance of a demographic group that is currently ill-served by a patchwork of provisions that makes little sense and that does not provide the kind of flexibility needed during a period that is inevitably one of transitions.

4.6.3.3 Discussion of Both of the Above Steps Taken Together
Comparing the two schemes b and d with scheme B above shows that the increases in NICs above the Upper Earnings Limit and in Income Tax rates required by scheme B are generated by the Citizen's Incomes granted to children and young adults, and that the working-age adult Citizen's Incomes are effectively paid for by the loss of the Income Tax Personal Allowance, as we would rather expect.

If both the increased Child Benefit and the Young adult's Citizen's Income were to be implemented, then NICs would be at 12 % on all earned income. The recipient year groups would not receive Income Tax Personal Allowances, and as they grew older, they would continue to receive Citizen's Incomes (while everyone older than them would not be receiving Citizen's Incomes and would retain their Personal Allowances). The means-tested benefits structure would still be in place, and we would be well on the way to implementing scheme B (but with a genuine Child Citizen's Income, rather than a combination of Child Benefit and Child

Table 4.4 Two young adult Citizen's Income schemes, showing the Income Tax rate increases required, and losses imposed on households at the point of implementation

	Scheme c	Scheme d
Young adult Citizen's Income, £ per week	56.80	40
Income Tax rate increase required for strict revenue neutrality	0% (i.e., no increase would be required)	0% (i.e., no increase would be required)
Income Tax, basic rate	20%	20%
Income Tax, higher rate	40%	40%
Income Tax, top rate	45%	45%
Proportion of households in the lowest disposable income decile experiencing losses of over 10% at the point of implementation	0.23%	0.52%
Proportion of households in the lowest disposable income decile experiencing losses of over 5% at the point of implementation	0.39%	0.52%
Proportion of all households experiencing losses of over 10% at the point of implementation	0.39%	0.82%
Proportion of all households experiencing losses of over 5% at the point of implementation	1.63%	2.71%
Administrative saving assumed	£0bn	£0bn
Net cost of scheme	−£0.6bn	−£2.65bn

Source: Malcolm Torry (2015) *Two feasible ways to implement a revenue neutral Citizen's Income scheme*, Institute for Social and Economic Research Working Paper EM6/15 (Colchester: Institute for Social and Economic Research, University of Essex), www.iser.essex.ac.uk/research/publications/working-papers/euromod/em6-15, p. 11

Citizen's Income). Gradual increases in the Citizen's Income rates for children and young adults would be both affordable and acceptable, enabling a Citizen's Income of £56.80 to be paid to all adults. Further rises might be acceptable. Because of the gradual nature of the implementation, nobody would ever need to suffer the modest losses in disposable income that would occur if scheme B were to be implemented in its entirety all in one go.

4.7 Conclusion

In order to be financially feasible, a Citizen's Income scheme would need to be both fiscally feasible and household financially feasible: that is, it would need to be affordable as a whole, and it would need to impose no unacceptable losses on households at the point of implementation. For any household not right at the bottom of the earnings range and receiving means-tested benefits before the implementation of the Citizen's Income scheme, a small loss would be acceptable, because the lower marginal deduction rates delivered by the scheme would enable it to earn sufficient to cover the loss more easily than would be the case under the present system; but it is still true that almost no losses should be imposed on households with the lowest disposable incomes. I say almost no losses, because there will always be the occasional household with unusual characteristics that will generate losses whatever kind of Citizen's Income scheme is implemented. (Particularly interesting are the sample households that generate negative disposable incomes under the present system, the Citizen's Income scheme, or both.) Very small numbers of losses can be handled by the households themselves or by transitional provisions, but the aim must still be to avoid any losses at all among households with the lowest disposable incomes.

Given that in a strictly revenue neutral scheme, aggregate losses must equal aggregate gains, ensuring minimal losses among households with the lowest disposable incomes will mean that most losses will appear further up the income range. There will inevitably be some redistribution from the highest income decile to the lowest income decile (and therefore also from the highest earnings decile to the lowest earnings decile). Nobody should regard this as a problem. Any government so minded, of course, would be able to implement a revenue neutral Citizen's Income scheme that delivered the pattern of redistribution that it required. Directing redistribution mainly towards those deciles just above the lowest might be politically attractive.

In his book *Inequality*, Tony Atkinson makes a number of proposals for reducing inequality: a more progressive Income Tax, Child Benefit paid at a substantial rate, an EU-wide Child Basic Income, and a Participation Income that looks as if it has been modelled as a Citizen's Income.[12] It is perhaps no surprise that Atkinson's agenda and the content of this paper are similar; and equally no surprise that the steps that both Atkinson and this paper envisage would be steps towards a Citizen's Income.

We need a new approach to tax and benefits in the UK, and a Citizen's Income offers precisely what we require. Increasingly, objections are not to the principle of a Citizen's Income, but to its feasibility. In Chap. 3 and in this chapter, I have shown that it is perfectly possible to construct a financially feasible Citizen's Income scheme. Schemes A and C and the

Catalonian scheme would be neither fiscally nor household financially feasible in the short term, although as longer-term goals, they could be useful; but scheme B would be both fiscally and household financially feasible from the point of implementation.

A widespread debate about both the principle and the detail is now required. My recommendation would be that the debate should initially restrict itself to strictly revenue neutral schemes that do not propose large increases in Income Tax rates, and that the schemes considered should impose very few losses on low-income households. Scheme B would be a good place to start. Two tracks towards implementation could then be studied: implementation of the entire scheme all in one go, and implementation one step at a time, starting with a Child Citizen's Income and a Young adult's Citizen's Income.

The difficulties facing our current tax and benefits systems, and the importance of fashioning a benefits system that will better serve our society and our economy, suggest that the government, think tanks, and academic institutions should now be applying substantial research and policy analysis resources to the subject; and the many good arguments for a Citizen's Income,[13] along with the results of these two chapters, suggest that a considerable proportion of that effort should be spent on fashioning a tax and benefits system based on a financially feasible Citizen's Income.

But of course the kind of modelling work that I have described in this chapter and in the previous one will never be enough on its own. All it can do is provide the information that enables policymakers to take a number of options off the agenda. It can never ensure that other options remain on the agenda. As Greenberger, Crenson, and Crissey put it in their study of the computer modelling of policy options:

> Although the domain of knowledge in the policy process seems to have been expanding, the expansion may be more apparent than real. There is no evidence that the domain of politics has really contracted.[14]

But that is to simplify the problem. Modelling is itself a political act because if a computer program is to be used to model reform options, then the choice of the options to be modelled, and the detailed regulation and benefit changes that the researcher chooses to implement in the program, will be political choices (but no more political of course than the choices behind the structure and regulations of the current benefits system). To this extent, the modelling might be accused of being partisan: that is, of favouring particular options before the debate has begun. A somewhat different interpretation is to view the choice of schemes to be modelled as contributions to an ongoing debate.[15] If widespread debate occurs on the basis of the modelling of a variety of different Citizen's Income schemes, and that debate then influences further modelling work, then that will be a sign that modelling is being used to promote debate and not to close it down.[16]

What we require is holistic research into the feasibility of Citizen's Income: that is, research that builds relationships between different kinds of research into different kinds of feasibility. In the context of this chapter, that means that research into financial feasibility must remain constantly in touch with research into psychological feasibility, behavioural feasibility, administrative feasibility, political feasibility, and policy process feasibility. This might create a somewhat complex research process, but it will be one that might deliver a robust conclusion about Citizen's Income's feasibility.

NOTES

1. Gian Domenico Majone (1989) *Evidence, Argument, and Persuasion in the Policy Process* (New Haven: Yale University Press), p. 77.
2. Jan Pahl (1983) 'The allocation of money and structuring of inequality within marriage', *Sociological Review*, 31 (2), 237–62; Laura Adelman, Sue Middleton, and Karl Ashworth (1999) *Intra-household distribution of poverty and social exclusion: Evidence from the 1999 PSE Survey of Britain*, Working paper no 23 (Loughborough: Centre for Research in Social Policy); Jan Pahl (1986) 'Social security, taxation and family financial arrangements', *BIRG Bulletin*, no 5, 2–4.
3. In the UK, it can be as high as 96%: Richard Murphy and Howard Reed (2013) *Financing the Social State: Towards a full employment economy* (London: Centre for Labour and Social Studies), pp. 25–7.
4. For Ruth Lister's suggestion that poverty is better defined in terms of dynamic processes than in terms of static measurements, see Ruth Lister (2004) *Poverty* (Cambridge: Polity Press), pp. 94–7, 145–6, 178–83.
5. Malcolm Torry (2014) *Research note: A feasible way to implement a Citizen's Income*, Institute for Social and Economic Research Working Paper EM17/14 (Colchester: Institute for Social and Economic Research, University of Essex), www.iser.essex.ac.uk/research/publications/working-papers/euromod/em17-14, pp. 3–4.
6. This case study uses EUROMOD version G2.0++. The contribution of all past and current members of the EUROMOD consortium is gratefully acknowledged. The process of extending and updating EUROMOD is

financially supported by the Directorate General for Employment, Social Affairs and Inclusion of the European Commission [Progress grant no. VS/2011/0445]. The UK Family Resources Survey data was made available by the DWP via the UK Data Archive.
7. Parts of this case study were first published in a EUROMOD working paper, *Two feasible ways to implement a revenue neutral Citizen's Income scheme* (2015) Institute for Social and Economic Research Working Paper EM6/15 (Colchester: Institute for Social and Economic Research, University of Essex), www.iser.essex.ac.uk/research/publications/working-papers/euromod/em6-15, and subsequently as an article in the *Citizen's Income Newsletter*, issue 3 for 2015. The Institute for Social and Economic Research's permission to reprint material from the working paper is gratefully acknowledged.
8. The method is as follows: A new set of benefits is created in the UK country system in EUROMOD: a Citizen's Pension (CP) for over sixty-five-year-olds, a Citizen's Income (CI) for adults aged between twenty-five and sixty-four, a young person's Citizen's Income (CIY) for adults aged between sixteen and twenty-four, and a Child Citizen's Income (CIC) for children aged between zero and fifteen. In the definitions of constants, levels are set for these Citizen's Incomes, and all Personal Tax Allowances are set at zero. So that the additional taxable income is taxed at the basic rate, and not at the higher rate, the first tax threshold is changed from 32,010 to 42,010. The NIC Lower Earnings Limit is set to zero, and the NIC rate above the Upper Earnings Limit is set to 12% (to match the rate below the limit). For schemes A and C, Working Tax Credit, Child Tax Credit, Income Support, Income-Related ESA, Pension Credit, and Income-based Jobseeker's Allowance are no longer added to the total for means-tested benefits. For all schemes, Incapacity Benefit, Contributory ESA, and Child Benefit are removed from non-means-tested benefits (except that in scheme B, Child Benefit is left in payment), the Citizen's Income total is added to non-means-tested benefits, and for scheme B, Citizen's Incomes are added to the means applied to means-tested benefits. The state pension is no longer added to the pensions total in schemes A and C (as the Citizen's Pension has already been added to the non-means-tested benefits total). Where benefits are no longer in payment, they are removed from the tax base. Simulations of the 2013 system and the system being tested generate two lists of household disposable incomes for the entire Family Resource Survey sample. These then generate a list of gains (negative gains are losses), and the total of the gains gives the net cost of the scheme for the sample. To convert EUROMOD's monthly figures to annual figures, and the sample size to the total population, a multiplier of $(12 \times 64.1 \text{ m}/57,381) = 13.4$ gives the cost in £ms for the UK population. A process of trial and error

adjusts the Income Tax rates until the net cost minus the assumed administrative saving is below £2 billion per annum. The initial disposable incomes are then ordered, the bottom 10% are selected, and the percentage gains are evaluated. The process is then repeated for all households.
9. Jordi Arcarons, Daniel Raventos Pañella and Lluís Torrens Mèlich (2014) 'Feasibility of Financing a Basic Income', *Basic Income Studies*, 9 (1–2), 79–93.
10. Purely for the purpose of modelling the net cost, we eliminate Child Benefit for sixteen- to nineteen-year-olds by adjusting the definition of a dependent child both in the current system and in the system with raised Child Benefit.
11. The results are modelled by removing Child Benefit for everyone aged sixteen and above, and instead paying a Young adult Citizen's Income. In this case, the results are extracted from simulations of individual rather than household disposable incomes. As above, the removal of Child Benefit over the age of sixteen is achieved by adjusting the definition of a dependent child.
12. Anthony B. Atkinson (2015) *Inequality* (Cambridge, Massachusetts: Harvard University Press), pp. 303–4. The text offers some pointers towards social participation conditions for receipt of the Participation Income, but no such conditions are mentioned in the text relating to the results of EUROMOD modelling on p. 297.
13. Malcolm Torry (2013) *Money for Everyone: Why we need a Citizen's Income* (Bristol: Policy Press); Malcolm Torry (2015) *101 Reasons for a Citizen's Income: Arguments for giving everyone some money* (Bristol: Policy Press, Bristol).
14. Martin Greenberger, Matthew A. Crenson and Brian L. Crissey (1976) *Models in the Policy Process: Public decision making in the computer era* (New York: Russell Sage Foundation), p. 23.
15. William H. Dutton and Kenneth L. Kraemer (1985) *Modeling as Negotiating: The political dynamics of computer models in the policy process* (Norwood, NJ: Ablex Publishing Corp), pp. 7, 9.
16. A good example of this process is provided by some recent research papers. Malcolm Torry (2014) *Research note: A feasible way to implement a Citizen's Income* modelled a Citizen's Income scheme; Donald Hirsch (2015) *Could a 'Citizen's Income' work?* (York: Joseph Rowntree Foundation), www.jrf.org.uk/publications/could-citizens-income-work, offered a critique; and Malcolm Torry (2015) *Two feasible ways to implement a revenue neutral Citizen's Income scheme*, Institute for Social and Economic Research Working Paper EM6/15 (Colchester: Institute for Social and Economic Research, University of Essex), www.iser.essex.ac.uk/research/publications/working-papers/euromod/em6-15, took the critique into account.

CHAPTER 5

Is a Citizen's Income Psychologically Feasible?

5.1 Introduction

Would a benefits system based on Citizen's Income be a major shift in policy or merely a minor administrative adjustment? The answer is 'Both'. A revenue neutral scheme would be largely a change in administrative methods: away from income tax personal allowances, means-tested benefits, and social insurance benefits, and towards universal, unconditional, and nonwithdrawable benefits. If the scheme implemented was household financially feasible, then individuals and households would experience little difference in their disposable income at the point of implementation. Later on, they would notice the difference that lower marginal deduction rates were making (if their earnings rose, they would experience an increase in spending power); many households would enjoy greater freedom from bureaucratic control; and every individual would enjoy the efficiency of the Citizen's Income payments, and the financial security that that would create; but at the point of implementation, many people would wonder what all the fuss was about. So yes, Citizen's Income would be a relatively minor change in the way in which a country manages its tax and benefits systems. But it would also be a whole new way of managing a population's income maintenance. For the first time, every individual would regularly receive money into their bank account without having to earn it, without paying any contributions, and without having to submit themselves to means tests, work tests, or any other tests. It is this characteristic of Citizen's Income that thrills some people and perplexes others; and it is this characteristic that will require public understanding and approval before legislators will be prepared to think about implementing a Citizen's Income scheme. Financial feasibility is not enough. Psychological feasibility will be required.

5.2 Psychological Feasibility

De Wispelaere and Noguera define psychological feasibility as

> the legitimation of a policy through securing a broad level of social acceptance among the general public … the challenge of psychological feasibility is to convince the public at large that [Citizen's Income] is a normatively attractive and practically effective policy.[1]

There are two ways of approaching this problem, and each of them understands the term 'psychological feasibility' in a slightly different way:

5.2.1 Hegemonic Moral Discourses

We can recognize, with Antonio Gramsci, that dominant groups within society can exercise 'hegemony'. Gramsci sometimes uses the term to express the process whereby an invading country imposes its culture and laws on an occupied country,[2] but more often as the idea that an interpretation of the world has been imposed on society by a dominant group that benefits from that imposition.[3]

> The functions in question are precisely organisational and connective. The intellectuals are the dominant group's 'deputies'; exercising the subaltern functions of social hegemony and political government. These comprise: 1. The 'spontaneous' consent given by the great masses of the population to the general direction imposed on social life by the dominant fundamental group; this consent is 'historically' caused by the prestige (and consequent confidence) which the dominant group enjoys because of its position and function in the world of production. 2. The apparatus of state coercive power which 'legally' enforces discipline on those groups who do not 'consent' either actively or passively. This apparatus is, however, constituted for the whole of society in anticipation of moments of crisis of command and direction when spontaneous consent has failed.[4]

The transition from the first to the second mechanism for coercion might be illustrated by the increasingly sanctions-dominated character of 'active labour market' policies in European and other countries; but whereas the mechanism through which hegemony is exercised can sometimes be physical or legal force, it will usually be rather more subtle: for instance, via articles in the press—and it will take into account the interests of the classes on which hegemony is imposed.[5] Take the 'scroungers' and the 'strivers v. skivers' language that for thirty years has circulated in the UK press.[6] Politicians rarely use those words, but their speeches will often reference the implied social division. As George Osborne, the UK's Chancellor of the Exchequer, put it in 2012:

> Where is the fairness, we ask, for the shift-worker, leaving home in the dark hours of the early morning, who looks up at the closed blinds of their next-door neighbour sleeping off a life on benefits?[7]

The combination of 'striver' with 'skiver' is now so deeply embedded in the public consciousness that only 'striver' has to be mentioned for 'skiver' to be understood.[8] The language represents a hegemony: in this case, a presupposition that society is divided into two classes of people. It is simply not true that society is divided in this way,[9] but the fiction is a convenient one for the government, because it makes it easier to cut benefit levels; it persuades a large proportion of the public that the government is on their side, thus securing a solid electoral base; it enables everyone in employment to understand themselves as virtuous, and as belonging to society in ways in which those not in employment do not belong; and it enables harsh sanctions to be imposed on people who are unemployed: a strategy that appears to be designed to perpetuate the stated social division in the public mind.

Such 'moral discourses'—'systems of thought that simultaneously take up ideas, ideologies, attitudes, actions, and concepts informing our understandings of self, world, and others'[10]—flow through society and its institutions, significantly influence our ideas and actions, and, to some extent, control them. One factor that prevents any moral discourse from constituting an unchallengeable hegemony is that society is riddled with contradictory moral discourses,[11] so we find ourselves both expressing and acting on entirely contradictory sets of presuppositions. In the UK, a 'strivers and skivers' discourse delivers benefits sanctions, and a solidaristic 'equal citizenship' discourse maintains the National Health Service as a service free at the point of use. The two discourses might be described as 'rights contingent upon contribution' and 'rights an invitation to contribute'.

The hegemony that dominant groups can exercise in society currently ensures the dominance and constant reinforcement of the former,[12] thus ensuring the marginalization of the latter.

So the position that we have reached is that powerful groups within society have the ability to promote the moral discourses that serve their interests, those moral discourses become dominant and can significantly influence our ideas and actions, and alternative discourses, although still available to us, struggle to exert influence.

This understanding of the situation suggests that for Citizen's Income to be psychologically feasible, a solidaristic moral discourse will need to become dominant, which in turn suggests that those groups in society with an interest in maintaining a more divisive moral discourse will need to lose their hegemonic status. The recent major financial crisis has not even dented the current social order or its hegemonic moral discourse, but instead appears to have strengthened them. There would appear to be little chance of a shift in hegemonic moral discourse in the short to medium term. I shall therefore see if by defining psychological feasibility a little differently, we can approach the task in a different way and obtain a psychological feasibility that might contribute to delivering a Citizen's Income scheme.

5.2.2 *Individual and Social Psychologies*

A different way of looking at the situation is to focus first of all on each of our individual psychologies. The way that each of us understands the world is influenced by our upbringing, our genetic inheritance, the social norms that we encounter in the society, institutions and groups to which we relate, and the thinking that we do ourselves: the conceptual connections that we draw, the connections that we reject, and the connections that we change. Our own thought processes will sometimes be conscious, and sometimes unconscious, so we shall sometimes be surprised by the new connections that we draw, reject, or alter.

This understanding of our psychologies suggests that Citizen's Income's psychological feasibility requires that a sufficient number of members of the relevant population come to understand the advantages and acceptability of Citizen's Income, and in particular that a sufficient number of individuals in relevant policy-making positions come to understand them. What is required is a relevant and appropriate social psychological shift, constituted by a sufficient number of individual psychological shifts. What is not required is a change in any hegemonic moral discourse.

In order for the necessary individual psychological shifts to occur, a sufficient number of individuals will need to challenge social norms that are inimical to universal and unconditional benefits at the same time as they

> understand and accommodate the enduring features of the policy-making environment and the ways in which the environment can change to enhance or retard the possibility of policy change.[13]

In most countries, this will not be an easy task. We have lived with contributory and means-tested benefits for a long time—for four hundred years in the UK—so it is difficult not to judge universal and unconditional benefits by criteria based on presuppositions underlying means-testing and social insurance: 'the rich don't need it', 'if people earn more, then their benefits should be reduced', 'people won't work if you just give them the money'. If unconditional benefits are tested using criteria based on these presuppositions, then they inevitably fail the tests. We might argue that it would be just as rational to base criteria on the characteristics of universal benefits and then see if means-tested and social insurance benefits pass the consequent tests,[14] but that is to ignore the fact that we are not entirely rational beings. The fact that something is logical, or that the majority of the evidence supports it, will not necessarily mean that we will believe it. Logical argument and the presentation of evidence are not enough. In order for Citizen's Income to be psychologically feasible for an individual, a conversion experience is required. The penny needs to drop. Deeply held presuppositions need to change, and fears need to be addressed.[15] But even that is not enough. The psychological feasibility of Citizen's Income is not simply about individual psychological feasibilities. It is about psychological feasibility for a sufficient proportion of society, and in particular for the large collection of institutions and individuals that constitutes the policy-making process. After proving financial feasibility, the biggest task facing any individual or institution that wishes to see Citizen's Income implemented will be the achievement of sufficient individual conversions to ensure the relevant social psychological feasibility.

We therefore have two questions to answer: How might individual conversion experiences occur? And how might multiple individual conversion experiences generate a social conversion experience?—that is, how might individual conversions generate a sufficient relevant change in public opinion?

As before, we shall need to discuss the characteristics of different Citizen's Income schemes, as well as the idea of Citizen's Income, because it is always a particular scheme that will need to be implemented; so the task is even more onerous than we might have thought. Not only must the idea of Citizen's Income achieve psychological feasibility, but a particular scheme will also need to achieve it.

There are some public policy fields in which public opinion plays only a small part in policy making,[16] but in the benefits sphere, public opinion matters. This does not mean that every member of a population will need to be enthusiastic about Citizen's Income; it means that for psychological feasibility, a sufficient proportion of the general public will need to be comfortable with the proposal, and that sufficient numbers of individuals and institutions in the policy process will need to be enthusiastic. The task of this chapter is therefore important as well as difficult.

5.3 The Reciprocity Norm

'Reciprocity' can mean a number of different things. It can mean a general sense that we belong together in society and that every member of society should receive what they need and contribute what they can, without specifying the order in which receiving and contributing should occur, or it can be defined as the idea that nobody should receive something until they have contributed. Societies that operate benefits sanctions regimes have shifted towards the latter definition, but because there will be societies at various points along the spectrum defined by the two positions, I shall define reciprocity as a flexible concept that can mean either of the extreme positions or any point between them. I shall also agree with Stuart White when he suggests that the expectation of contribution has to be conditional on society being sufficiently just:

> Where institutions governing economic life are otherwise sufficiently just, e.g., in terms of the availability of opportunities for productive participation and the rewards attached to these opportunities, then those who claim the generous share of the social product available to them under these institutions have an obligation to make a decent productive contribution, suitably proportional and fitting for ability and circumstances, to the community in return. I term this the fair-dues conception of reciprocity.[17]

Wherever our society is on the spectrum of definitions of reciprocity, and wherever we are on it personally, reciprocity will need to be 'fair-dues reciprocity'. If some members of society do not conform to the reciprocity norm, then other members of society are having to contribute more than their fair share and are therefore being exploited by those who are not contributing. 'Civic labour' is therefore required—paid work, care work, and voluntary community activity—in order to create the 'civic minimum' of income and other services that is the right of every citizen.[18] So

> in a context of otherwise sufficiently fair economic arrangements, everyone should do their bit.[19]

Whether this is true of every culture I do not know, but every culture that I know recognizes some version of the reciprocity norm, whether expressed as the work ethic, the contributory principle, or deservingness, depending on where we are on the spectrum of reciprocity definitions.[20] Svallfors[21] and Staerké, Liki, and Scheideggar[22] find that this social norm is not simply an expression of self-interest on the part of taxpayers; it is a deeply held presupposition that undergirds public approval of benefits systems,[23] generates the ubiquitous feeling that 'something for nothing' is wrong, drives the consistent poll findings that most people think that paid employment is the normative route to an income, and underpins the idea that social security benefits should only be paid to those who cannot work and who for some reason deserve to receive them, for instance, through disability. Here deservingness functions as a substitute for reciprocity,[24] and because severe sanctions for current non-contribution can make it psychologically difficult for someone to contribute, being counted as not deserving can make future reciprocity impossible.

Reciprocity provides the strongest legitimation for a benefits system where that system is understood as a redistribution across the lifecycle via social insurance contributions and benefits.[25] The fact that in many social insurance systems—such as that in the UK—the levels of benefits bear little relation to the number or levels of contributions paid in is beside the point. People *feel* that they are getting what they have paid for, even if they are in fact receiving a contingency benefit paid for out of general taxation. The fact that a Citizen's Income would be a more honest way of redistributing income is again beside the point. It is the reciprocity-related psychology that generates the legitimacy of social insurance, and the same psychology is not immediately available to unconditional benefits.

In 2000, Liebig and Mau sent questionnaires to a random sample of 121 German employees and followed them up with interviews based on a series of vignettes:

> We were able to establish that an unconditional granting of a uniform minimum income independent of people's productive contributions runs against the moral intuitions of our respondents. ... People seem to be suspicious of the idea of non-conditionality ... The claim to a share in societal wealth is perceived as unfair if citizens are not willing to cooperate socially and make some kind of effort. Conditionality, therefore, affirms the link between income entitlement and productive contributions and thereby safeguards the reciprocity requirements. ... A uniform and fully unconditional welfare entitlement is not endorsed.[26]

Research in the Netherlands suggests public approval of the idea that

> the government should intervene to reduce inequality in society and should spend adequate amounts for this purpose, and that these government provisions [should] not have unfavourable repercussions in the economic or moral spheres.[27]

Coughlin reports similar research that shows that

> the idea of collective responsibility for assuring minimum standards of employment, health care, income, and other conditions of social and economic well-being has everywhere gained a foothold in popular values and beliefs. And yet the survey evidence suggests a simultaneous tendency supporting individual achievement, mobility, and responsibility for one's own lot.[28]

This suggests that the differences in public opinion in relation to unconditional benefits for different groups in society are the result of different balances between two opposing trends, and perhaps between two opposing moral discourses. The unemployed would be expected to be 'responsible for their own lot', hence the suspicion generated when unconditional benefits for the unemployed are suggested. Children and the elderly cannot always be 'responsible for their own lot', and so are owed a minimum standard of income by society.

5.4 Can Mindsets Be Shifted?

Whatever the cause or causes of the deep psychological barriers to Citizen's Income, at individual and societal levels, the important question to ask in relation to our exploration of the feasibility of Citizen's Income is this: Can mindsets be shifted? Can sufficient individual psychological change deliver the social psychological change that would be required to make Citizen's Income feasible?

My experience of explaining Citizen's Income to intelligent individuals, or to groups of intelligent people, is that at the forefront of people's minds are such understandable presuppositions as 'to reduce poverty we need to give more money to the poor', 'to reduce inequality we need to give more money to the poor', 'if you give more money to the poor then they might not work', and 'the rich don't need benefits'. I might draw the individual or group's attention to existing unconditional benefits, such as the UK's Child Benefit. This gives the same amount of money to every family with the same number of children, *and* it reduces poverty because it provides additional income for families with the lowest incomes, *and* it reduces inequality because it constitutes a higher proportion of total income for those with low incomes than it does for those with high incomes. Child Benefit provides additional income for those with the lowest incomes, but because it is not withdrawn as earned income rises, it does not act as an employment disincentive and so is more likely to encourage additional gainful employment than means-tested benefits are. The wealthy pay more in Income Tax than they receive in Child Benefit, so it hardly matters that they receive Child Benefit; and it is better that they do receive it because to give the benefit to every family with children is administratively efficient, and it removes any possibility of stigma. I might also draw the group's attention to means-tested benefits. These give more to the poor than to the rich, but because the benefits are withdrawn as earnings rise, they prevent families from earning their way out of poverty, and they make it less likely that people will seek gainful employment, and they therefore tend to increase inequality.

When I suggest that the intentions behind the group's presuppositions are better served by Child Benefit than by means-tested benefits, and that a Citizen's Income would also serve those intentions better than means-tested benefits currently do, I can see the penny drop for some of the group's members. They have understood. But by the end of the session, there will still be some members of the group who cannot see beyond the idea that if the poor need more money, then means-testing is the obvious way to make sure that they get the money that they need. At the end of a radio interview in which a similar conversation had occurred, the interviewer remarked: 'Give the money to everyone? I've never heard anything so ridiculous in all my life.' A conversion experience had not occurred.

The presuppositions are so difficult to shake off because we have lived with them for so long. Since Elizabethan times, the UK has operated means tests, with the State giving more to the poor than to the rich and then withdrawing benefits as other income rises. Four centuries ago, this might have been the only option, but in the context of a progressive tax system, unconditional and nonwithdrawable benefits are the administratively efficient way to provide those with low incomes with additional income, and, at the same time, to ensure that they experience no employment disincentives. Unfortunately, whether in small groups, larger groups, or a whole population, the apparently hardwired presupposition in favour of means-testing remains the majority opinion, so individuals conform to it unthinkingly.[29] Moreover, in order to save ourselves intellectual effort, we tend to accept the opinions of such authorities as newspapers and radio show hosts, and our acceptance of the majority opinion becomes even more firmly embedded, particularly when policy change moves in the same direction as public opinion.[30] There is nothing surprising about any of this, and it is here that the understanding of Citizen's Income's psychological feasibility as a combination of individual psychological feasibilities, and the understanding of it as a change in society's moral discourse, comes together: for if the moral discourse were to change, then a lot more people would be susceptible to individual conversion.

The question for us here is this: Is it possible to shift the public mindset sufficiently without the most hegemonic moral discourses changing? Is it possible that sufficient numbers of people will understand that in the context of a progressive tax system, a universal benefit is a more constructive way of targeting money on the poor than means-testing will ever be?—that universal benefits make people more likely to work, and not less?—that the tax system takes far more from the wealthy than they would receive in universal benefits, so that it is not a problem that they would receive the benefits along with everybody else?

Since William James wrote *The Varieties of Religious Experience*, we have known quite a lot about individual conversion experiences, both religious and otherwise[31]; and, more recently, Serge Moscovici has shown how a minority within a group can convert the majority to their viewpoint:

> A minority, which by definition expresses a deviant judgment, a judgment contrary to the norms respected by the social group, convinces some members of the group, who may accept its judgment in private. They will be reluctant to do so publicly, however, either for fear of losing face or to avoid the risk of speaking or acting in a deviant fashion in the presence of others.[32]

If individual but unexpressed conversions then occur, public compliance with the view expressed by the majority can for a long time coexist with an increasing minority thinking differently. Then one act of courage can reveal how opinion is shifting, particularly if the shift required by the majority is not too great.[33] A snowball effect can then occur because

> a consistent minority can exert an influence to the same extent as a consistent majority, and … the former will generally have a greater effect on a deeper level, while the latter often has less, or none, at that level.[34]

Nemeth, Swedlund and Kanki have shown that while the minority needs to propound a consistent position if it is to shift opinion within the group, it also needs to be flexible where it can be if the majority is to be converted to its position, because flexibility in the context of consistency communicates the minority's confidence in its position and makes clearer where it is being consistent.[35] The right balance is essential. Too much flexibility and consistency is lost, which leads to lack of influence; but too little flexibility and dialogue partners will wish to abort the discussion.[36] If a convinced minority can exhibit the right balance between consistency and flexibility, then they will open the minds of members of the majority to a range of alternatives, thus replacing the majority's previous convergent mental processes with divergent thinking that might be willing to take in a variety of views and then judge between them.[37] Two processes are therefore at work. The minority's opinion will directly influence the majority, and at the same time, the minority's flexible consistency encourages the majority to think around the issues and to take seriously the alternatives now on offer.[38] Active, consistent, and flexible minorities can therefore exercise considerable influence.

Moscovici's research related to groups and institutions, and we ought not to assume that a whole society will function in the same way; but our recent experience of a rapid global shift of public opinion towards same-sex marriage suggests that the same process might also occur on a societal level. That particular transition might be informative, particularly in relation to the incremental practical steps by which it occurred. In the USA, Bill Clinton balked at permitting openly homosexual people to serve in the armed forces, and now we have seen an increasing number of States permitting same-sex marriage and a Supreme Court judgement in favour of it. Within just sixty years, the UK has seen the decriminalization of homosexual activity, anti-discrimination legislation, equalities legislation, civil partnerships, and, now, same-sex marriage. Perhaps the most rapid shift has been witnessed in the Republic of Ireland, where in a traditional catholic country, a referendum in 2015 has put same-sex marriage into the constitution. The same process occurred in the UK with equalities legislation more generally. Starting with the Race Discrimination Act in 1965 and the Equal Pay Act in 1970, the UK government has legislated for various equalities when doing so has been somewhat ahead of public opinion. Each legislative step changed public behaviour and propelled an already changing public opinion more quickly along its trajectory, and thus prepared the ground for the next legislative step that would be slightly ahead of public opinion. The public opinion trajectory was always clear, so although it might have looked as though the government was taking a risk, in fact it was not. The same process has been witnessed across much of Europe in relation to smoking in buildings open to the public. Public opinion was beginning to turn, passive smoking was being recognized for the health hazard that it is, and governments have not found it difficult to legislate to prevent smoking in enclosed spaces that are open to the public, including workplaces. While there are still too many people who smoke, and particularly young people, there would be public approval for further restrictions. The Mayor of London recently proposed that smoking should be banned in public parks. There was much approval expressed, and the objections of those still insisting on the freedom to smoke were rather muted. Public opinion can be difficult to gauge,[39] and its future shape can be difficult to predict, but we should never discount the possibility of rapid change.

So what might cause a similar rapid conversion to unconditional benefits among both the general public and policymakers?

5.5 Education

In any developed country, the tax and benefits systems will have evolved over many decades, and they will have reached levels of complexity that make individual and public understanding very difficult to achieve.

Research has shown just how little most people understand even when the questions that they are asked relate to those parts of the tax and benefits systems in which they themselves are involved.[40] In developing countries, a variety of schemes might be in existence: benefits systems, tax systems, subsidy systems, and guaranteed job systems, and they will all be complicated and little understood by the people affected by them.

Is it hopeless to seek to educate even a few individuals, and then the general public, about a subject that even professional benefits advisers find difficult to understand? In the UK, the most recent edition of the Child Poverty Action Group's *Welfare Benefits and Tax Credits Handbook* runs to 1740 pages.[41] Forty years ago, I administered means-tested benefits for two years. During the 1970s, the regulations were in ring binders, and they filled a bookshelf. Now everything is computerized, but if my experience then is anything to go by, staff members will have only a hazy idea about what is in the regulations. Errors are rife.[42] It all adds up to an impression that not even the experts understand the system, so what hope is there that anyone else will understand it?

It might be helpful here to study a policy area that can look as complicated as the benefits system: membership of the EU. Across Europe, we now hear a lot about Euroscepticism. In European, national, and even local elections, political parties that want to take countries out of the EU are doing well in the polls. In the UK, most newspapers are mildly Eurosceptic, and sometimes avidly so. Even though most business leaders, in the UK and elsewhere in Europe, are in favour of their countries staying in the EU, the occasional one who is not is the one who gets the press coverage.[43] In order to appease Conservative Party backbenchers who oppose the UK's membership of the EU, Prime Minister David Cameron is attempting to renegotiate the UK's membership before holding a referendum on whether the UK should stay in. This all makes it look as if the population of the UK is Eurosceptic. It is not. For most of the past twenty-five years, more UK citizens have been in favour of staying in than of leaving, and the number wanting to stay in is increasing.[44]

Is EU membership too complicated a subject for education to be effective? Research has shown that education can be surprisingly effective, both in relation to the principle of membership, and in relation to the detail:

> Europeans' attitudes regarding the vertical allocation of competences in the EU are significantly shaped by the political knowledge that they possess about the correct functioning of some European institutions, and ... they are

more in favour of common EU policies when externalities and economies of scale are present and a redistributive or stabilization function is to be pursued. ... our findings suggest that well-informed citizens are better able to perceive the consequences of alternative policy proposals ... public support for the EU can be influenced by making citizens better informed about the EU. ... raising awareness about the EU can help create greater commitment to European integration among European citizens.[45]

If this is true of EU membership, then there is no reason to think that it would be impossible for appropriate education to achieve greater public understanding of the advantages of unconditional benefits and for a sufficient number of individual conversions to prepare the ground for government action. In every country, the education required will be different, not because the definition of Citizen's Income changes, but because the context in which it will need to be implemented will be different in every case; but it would appear that wherever it takes place, education on the effects of the current benefits system, and on the ways in which unconditional benefits could be an improvement, would influence how people might think about the benefits system, and about the possibility of a shift towards unconditional benefits.

But what kind of education will be helpful in the case of Citizen's Income? De Wispelaere and Noguera suggest that

> carefully framing [Citizen's Income] proposals to avoid triggering negative perceptions, values, and beliefs, and instead trigger positive dispositions, may significantly improve the psychological feasibility of [Citizen's Income]. For instance, framing [Citizen's Income] alternatively as a social heritage, a national dividend, an antipoverty measure, or a citizenship right might produce different levels of social support.[46]

One way to circumvent the negative perceptions attached to the reciprocity norm is to draw attention to Stuart White's suggestion that in order to be fair, a reciprocity requirement has to be conditional on economic arrangements being 'otherwise fair'. This suggests that if they are *not* otherwise fair, then it is as difficult to insist on citizens' duties as it is to sustain citizens' rights.[47]

> Some resources are properly seen as belonging to a common citizens' inheritance fund, and it is implausible that the individual's entitlement to a share of this fund is entirely dependent on a willingness to work.[48]

This is the basis for White's argument for a Citizen's Income: a secure income floor that would establish the civic minimum that would in turn invite a reciprocal obligation.[49] We can therefore conclude that, both in theory and in practice, reciprocity would be served by a Citizen's Income. Whether a public focused on a reciprocity norm would be able to see this connection is an interesting question. For some people, the penny would drop, but for how many?

A further possibility would be to educate the public in the ways in which means-tested benefits disincentivize employment, and in the ways in which a Citizen's Income would not. The contributions that employment makes to meeting society's needs and to household incomes are at the heart of the general public's reciprocity presupposition, so to show how Citizen's Income would positively encourage employment should be at the heart of the educational strategy. To take the UK as an example: Anyone on Housing Benefit, Working Tax Credit, and Child Tax Credit, and paying Income Tax and NICs suffers a marginal deduction rate of 96%. This means that for every extra £1 that they earn, their disposable income goes up by just 4p.[50] When Universal Credit is fully rolled out, that will rise to 24p. Anyone earning over £150,000 per annum keeps 53p out of every extra £1 that they earn. A Citizen's Income would change all of that. But if an enquirer then asks about the detail, we have a problem. Depending on the precise details of the Citizen's Income scheme implemented, someone currently benefitting by only 4p in the £1 would benefit by 68p in the £1 if they were no longer receiving means-tested benefits; or perhaps by say 65p if Income Tax rates had had to rise to pay for Citizen's Incomes; or perhaps they would still be receiving small amounts of means-tested benefits, in which case they might still be receiving only 4p or 24p in the £1, but they would more easily be able to earn their way out of means-testing. Complexity can make communication problematic.

Perhaps the argument that the changes in our society and economy demand a different kind of social security system altogether would be more likely to shift perceptions; or perhaps the argument that a Citizen's Income would deliver labour market flexibility, labour market freedom, social cohesion, freedom from bureaucratic interference, fewer administrative errors, and less fraud would be more likely to shift mindsets in favour of unconditional benefits; or perhaps simply the idea of 'money for everyone'.

Different arguments are going to work for different people, and whether any of them do in practice cause the penny to drop will be largely a matter of personal psychology. This suggests that a diverse set of messages will be required, rather than a single slogan. The necessary education will clearly not be an easy task; but the task is worth the effort, because as the research on people's attitudes towards the EU shows, education can change minds.

5.6 Personal Experience

If a country already has one or more unconditional benefits—whether cash benefits, a universal health care system free at the point of use, or free education available to everyone—then there will be individuals who will understand that in the context of a progressive tax system paying benefits to the rich as well as to the poor is not a problem; that unconditional benefits do not impose the employment market disincentives that means-tested benefits impose; that the poor gain disproportionately from unconditional benefits because equal unconditional benefits constitute a higher proportion of their disposable incomes than they do for the rich; and that for the same reason unconditional benefits reduce inequality. Existing experience of universal provision would be of considerable benefit to any educational effort aimed at shifting presuppositions in the direction of unconditional benefits.

If a country has experienced a successful Citizen's Income pilot study, as Namibia and India have done,[51] then whole communities will have experienced the benefits of Citizen's Income, and those communities will need to be at the heart of any educational strategy; and if a country has some other kind of universal provision—such as Alaska's Permanent Fund Dividend[52]—then it will be relatively easy to shift public opinion in the direction of a more regular and more stable payment. A country with existing experience of something close to a Citizen's Income—as in Iran[53]—will be in an excellent position to hold a public debate if it decides to have one.

If a country has no experience of unconditional benefits, then imagining what they might be like will be more difficult, but it might still be possible to create the necessary public understanding by suggesting an analogy with a universal franchise or equality before the law.

5.7 Implementation One Step at a Time

Fear matters. Both employers and trades unions might fear that they will lose control over employees if every employee is given a Citizen's Income and is therefore less reliant on their weekly or monthly wage. In practice, of course, people would be more likely to seek employment with a Citizen's Income than with the current benefits system because the marginal deduction rates that they suffer would be reduced, making it more worthwhile to earn additional income, but that fact might not reduce the fear that employers and trades unions might experience. Workers themselves might fear tax rises, and might fear that a Citizen's Income could draw in additional migrant workers willing to work for low wages; and there might be a general sense of unease about how the employment market would be affected by a Citizen's Income scheme. Men on means-tested benefits might fear the greater independence that Citizen's Incomes paid to each individual would offer to their wives.[54]

One way of attempting to assuage such fears, and to circumvent the potential psychological infeasibility of a Citizen's Income paid to every legal resident of a country, would be to approach a Citizen's Income by way of evolutionary steps.

One possible approach would be to compare a country's current tax and benefits systems with a Citizen's Income, ask where the differences lie, and then ask which of these differences could usefully be tackled on their own. For instance, an important characteristic of a Citizen's Income is that it is paid to individuals rather than on a couple or household basis; so in countries in which taxation and benefits administration is household based, it could be individualized.[55] Similarly, steps could be taken to reduce the withdrawal rates of means-tested benefits as a preparation for the zero withdrawal rates of a Citizen's Income. A particularly useful step would be to equalize the monetary values of the personal tax allowance and of the benefits paid to individuals not in employment, as this would prepare the way for turning both of them into Citizen's Incomes.[56]

A Participation Income has been suggested, which would require recipients to show evidence of participation in society as a condition of receipt,[57] but see Chap. 6 for reasons not to follow this route. Negative Income Tax and Tax Credit schemes might also look like useful stepping stones. Survey data from Japan suggests that a Negative Income Tax might be a more popular option than Citizen's Income,[58] which might suggest that it would be a feasible first step; but again, Chap. 6 shows that a Negative Income Tax would pose substantial administrative challenges, which would make it difficult to implement. Experience of the complexity of administering a Negative Income Tax would inevitably reduce its popularity, thus putting at risk a future transition to a Citizen's Income scheme.

De Wispelaere and Noguera suggest 'sequential implementation': 'A universal child benefit, a universal basic pension, a guaranteed minimum income for those under the poverty line, and a tax credit for low-income workers might be acceptable, where a direct move toward a full [Citizen's Income] might be opposed.'[59] After discussing Japan's changing labour market, the benefits that a Citizen's Income would offer, and the psychological difficulty that that solution would pose for a workforce imbued with the idea that lifelong loyalty to a company is the route to both company and state welfare provision, Yannick and Sekine also recommend a series of modest steps in the direction of a Citizen's Income.[60] Here a note of caution needs to be sounded. If something that is not a Citizen's Income is described as a step in the direction of one, then public disapproval of conditional aspects of the implemented stage, or of its administrative complexity, will tarnish the image of Citizen's Income, even though a Citizen's Income would avoid those difficulties. An evolutionary approach would be safer if each step was itself a genuine Citizen's Income. The only way in which we could divide up a population in order to pay genuine Citizen's Incomes to different sections of it one at a time would be to divide it by age group: so that is how an evolutionary approach will need to be structured.

De Wispelaere and Noguera locate psychological feasibility as a prospective constraint related to diffuse agency: that is, the general public, or significant sections of it, will need to be persuaded of the advantages of Citizen's Income before implementation will be possible. This would appear to make sense. However, as we have already recognized in Chap. 2, psychological feasibility is also a retrospective constraint, in that a level of public understanding and approval will be required if Citizen's Income's implementation is to become a secure element in our social and economic fabric. But there is also a sense in which psychological feasibility can be both prospective and retrospective at the same time. If a Citizen's Income were to be established for a particular age group, then because that age group's Citizen's Income would affect a lot more people than those actually receiving it—and particularly other family members—a good experience of that first Citizen's Income would generate the psychological feasibility required for the implementation of a Citizen's Income for another age group.

The question then becomes: For which age group would it be easiest to establish a Citizen's Income? If financial feasibilities and administrative feasibility were to be similar for a variety of different age groups, then we would need to ask about differential political, policy process, behavioural, and psychological feasibilities. Psychological feasibility will be crucial, because without a sufficient amount of that, the other feasibilities would not be studied or attempted. Public understanding and approval of a Citizen's Income for a particular age group will therefore be essential, and it is that that will propel the proposal into political and policy process feasibilities. Given the low level of public understanding of the benefits system and of its effects, and of any reform options and their likely effects, psychological feasibility will have to rest on the perceived deservingness of the age group chosen.[61] In most countries, children and the elderly will be at the top of the deservingness list,[62] with working-age adults at the bottom (because it is to them that the 'they won't work' objection will continue to be attached).[63] After children and the elderly, young people, and then the pre-retired, would probably be felt to be the next most deserving groups. Research by Saunders and Pinyopusarek in Australia shows that

> while there is considerable support for mutual obligation, at least for some groups of the unemployed, this does not apply to the older unemployed, those caring for young children, and those with a disability.[64]

Unconditional child benefits already exist, and some countries have Citizen's Pensions: unconditional incomes for people over the State retirement age.[65] Following these existing examples should not be too difficult; and then experience of newly established Citizen's Incomes will create understanding and approval of their effects, which will lay the necessary psychological foundation for the establishment of a Citizen's Income for the next age group, and so on.

Throughout, a strict residency test will be required. An important element of public opinion relating to social security benefits is 'welfare chauvinism'[66] among unskilled workers: the feeling that immigrants should not have access to the country's benefits system. In most countries, it will be important to ensure that the debate about implementing a Citizen's Income remains well insulated from toxic debates about immigration, so that what is being debated is Citizen's Income and not whether immigrants should be able to claim benefits.

So far we have assumed that the causal direction is from public understanding and approval to the possibility of policy change. However, the causal relationship is not in fact as unidirectional as we might have thought. Larsen finds that the structures that characterize the different welfare regimes influence the way the public perceives the poor and the unemployed, which again influences the judgement of deservingness and thereby support for welfare policy.[67]

We are political beings, and 'policy attitudes are influenced by the experienced regime-dependent reality'.[68] We can therefore have some confidence that to roll out a Citizen's Incomes to one age group will shift public opinion in favour of universal benefits, thus laying a sufficient psychological foundation for roll-out to the next age group. Perhaps psychological feasibility might not be as difficult to achieve as we might at first have thought.

5.8 Case Studies

5.8.1 Attitudes to Citizen's Income in Japan

The report of an analysis of the results of a public opinion survey in Japan suggests that variables that influence respondents' attitudes towards Citizen's Income are their age, their health, whether or not they have received public assistance, the level of their household's financial assets, and how they answer the questions 'Do you think that the income gap will increase in the coming five years?' and 'Do you think that it is the government's responsibility to reduce the income gap?'; and there is a particularly strong positive correlation between this last factor and support for Citizen's Income. Gender, marital status, whether or not the respondent has children, educational background, and recognition of widening inequalities appear to have no influence.

Unfortunately, there is a problem with the question asked about Citizen's Income: 'What do you think about the idea that the government covers the minimum necessary cost of living?' The decision was taken to employ this form of words because the term 'Basic Income' is not sufficiently familiar in Japan, but the problem this leaves us with is that the respondent is left to filter the idea of government provision of income through pre-existing understandings of how governments provide citizens with income. Such pre-existing understandings might include means-testing and social insurance, and might not include universal, unconditional, and nonwithdrawable benefits. There must therefore be some doubt as to whether those responding to the survey thought that they were answering a question about Citizen's Income.

It is not insignificant that the results are consistent with results from surveys of the public's attitudes to income redistribution. This suggests that respondents might have been thinking about the redistributive effects of any government redistribution of income, again suggesting that respondents might not have had in mind a Citizen's Income.

But let us suppose for the moment that a sufficient number of the respondents had in mind a Citizen's Income as the mechanism that the government would choose to 'cover the minimum necessary cost of living', that they were aware of the differences between Citizen's Income and other forms of state benefits, and that the Japanese population is not untypical in its attitudes to such issues. We can then conclude that certain groups within society will be easier to persuade of the desirability of Citizen's Income than others, which will be useful information when education strategies are planned.

But perhaps the message that we should take from this Japanese survey is that surveys of public opinion might be helpful, and that the questions that need to be asked need to be carefully framed to ensure that respondents are clear that they are being asked about an unconditional and non-withdrawable income for every individual as a right of citizenship.[69]

5.8.2   Can Attitudes Change in the UK?

The UK's public mindset automatically rejects unconditional benefits: 'The rich don't need it' and 'people won't work' are symptomatic of this rejection, which has roots going back four hundred years. This is why politicians feel a need to express opposition to universal benefits, and why during a speech made on 6 June 2013 the leader of the UK's Labour Party, Ed Miliband MP, said that he wanted to see the unconditional Winter Fuel Allowance means-tested: 'It doesn't make sense to continue sending a cheque every year for Winter Fuel Allowance to the richest pensioners in the country.'[70] It does of course make a lot of sense to send it to every pensioner, because it is efficient to do so, and the wealthy are paying a lot more in Income Tax than they are receiving in Winter Fuel Allowance. The situation is similar with an unconditional National Health Service and unconditional Child Benefit. Compared with other systems, they are both highly efficient, and they serve health and income needs better than any other system possibly could.[71] Nobody wants to see the National Health Service being anything other than unconditionally available and free at the point of use. Child Benefit is now being clawed back from households containing at least one higher-rate taxpayer through the tax system, and those households would now appreciate not having the value of their Child Benefit taken from them, which adds another group to people who appreciate the virtues of unconditional benefits. If every household in the UK were to recognize that the National Health Service and Child Benefit belong in the same category, then there could well be a large silent majority in favour of universal benefits.

The only way to test this would be for the government to argue for turning means-tested benefits into a new universal benefit, and then to make the change, preferably for a group within society that the majority could regard as deserving in some way so that the experiment becomes a test of public appreciation of universal benefits rather than a test of public attitudes towards a demographic group.

There is a precedent. It was a slow and somewhat fraught process, but during the 1970s, Family Allowance for every child except the first in each family became Child Benefit: an unconditional benefit for every child. The mechanism by which the change occurred is that Child Tax Allowances were abolished and Family Allowance was raised in value and extended to the first child in each family. Effectively, a tax allowance became a new universal benefit. Only a minority of the public wanted to replace Family Allowance and the Child Tax Allowance with Child Benefit,[72] but the change was achieved with almost no public opposition.[73] There is therefore no reason for not making similar attempts, and there is every reason to do so.

Groups regarded by the public as deserving, and for whom the government might therefore attempt transitions from tax allowances and means-tested benefits to unconditional and nonwithdrawable benefits, would be the elderly and children, and might then include young adults and pre-retirement working-age adults (perhaps with NIC records functioning initially as a gateway for the latter group, as they will do for the new STP).[74]

My hunch is that we would see the same process as we have seen for same-sex marriage, and that the popularity of the changes for children, the elderly, young adults, and pre-retirement adults would reveal and embed a public opinion already shifting towards an understanding of the advantages of universal, unconditional, and nonwithdrawable benefits. The silent majority will have become conscious of their understanding and approval of change, and might have become vocal about it. The minority, which was willing and able to express the advantages of unconditional and nonwithdrawable benefits, will have converted the rest of society.

5.9 Conclusion

As Ben Baumberg sees it:

> The challenge is ... that a discourse that ignores deservingness will not chime with public attitudes, while a discourse that simply accommodates attitudes will struggle to transform them. The path to a revitalized benefits system that reduces poverty instead seems likely to consist of a series of stages that both respond to public concerns and offer the potential for sequenced change. ... What is needed is a way of deciding (i) where universalism is particularly important for perceptions of deservingness and solidarity; and (ii) what short-term decisions can be taken that allow the greatest space for the future rebuilding of the welfare state.[75]

The argument of this chapter suggests that trying to achieve psychological feasibility for a Citizen's Income scheme that would be implemented for everybody in society at the same time would probably be impossible, but that psychological feasibility might not be impossible to achieve if Citizen's Income were to be implemented one step at a time, and framed as assistance for demographic groups widely considered to be deserving rather than as a handout to the 'deserving' and the 'undeserving' alike. How a policy proposal is framed can have a considerable impact on the feasibility of its implementation.[76] In relation to the staged implementation of Citizen's Income, the understanding and approval generated by each demographic group's Citizen's Income would generate the psychological feasibility required to embed that particular Citizen's Income and also the psychological feasibility required for implementation of the next demographic group's Citizen's Income.

It is helpful to know that minorities with counter-intuitive new ideas are able to convert majorities that are initially committed to deeply entrenched presuppositions. The lesson to learn here is that the minority's educational strategy needs to be both consistent and flexible. In the context of the debate on Citizen's Income, this has to mean that anyone wishing to see serious consideration given to Citizen's Income will need to be consistent about the definition of Citizen's Income, and flexible in relation to the detail of the illustrative Citizen's Income schemes that will inevitably constitute much of the debate.

To implement a consistent but flexible educational strategy in the context of a 'one step at a time' implementation of Citizen's Income would provide an opportunity for existing understanding and approval of unconditional benefits to find its voice and slowly convert individuals and institutions still wedded to means-tested and contributory benefits systems. Recent research reported by Humpage suggests that a substantial reservoir of understanding and approval of unconditional benefits already exists, and that recipients of unconditional benefits believe themselves to be legitimate recipients of payments from the government and those receiving means-tested benefits not to be legitimate recipients.[77] Because

> the public tend to support universal social programmes more than targeted ones because they are visible and proximate to a wider range of citizens[78]

we can hope that new universal benefits, once implemented, would receive public approval, even if before implementation the public might be wary.[79]

Until we implement a Citizen's Income, we cannot be sure how strong the 'policy to opinion' causal direction will be, but the research results discussed in this chapter suggest not only that the verdict could well be favourable, but also that as long as everyone else was receiving them, granting unconditional benefits to the unemployed could be a lot more popular than we might think. The problem is that however much unconditional benefits might become an understood and accepted foundation for the welfare state in the future, there will need to be initial steps in that direction before public understanding and approval have been achieved.

But having said all of that, might we find that public opinion is less significant than we might have thought it to be? As Coughlin suggests,

> where specific policy alternatives are involved, a seemingly broad consensus … often hides a deep indecision concerning the crucial details of the debate, as well as a paucity of knowledge about the precise alternatives under consideration. The impact of public opinion is therefore often less than one might anticipate from a glance at opinion surveys[80];

and as Liebig and Mau point out:

> most social policy innovations have been introduced as contested concepts. The existing justice attitudes are only one factor that could advance or impede new reforms.[81]

In Chaps. 9 and 10, I shall suggest ways in which we might find a Citizen's Income scheme being implemented. Not all of them require widespread public approval of the idea. We might find that a handful of individual conversions among relevant policymakers had been all that was required.[82] If this were to prove the case, then for those few individuals who needed to be persuaded Citizen's Income will have needed to be psychologically feasible. The content of this chapter will therefore always be relevant, although perhaps in relation to the conversion of a small group of people rather than to the conversion of the general public.

Notes

1. Jürgen De Wispelaere and José Antonio Noguera (2012) 'On the Political Feasibility of Universal Basic Income: An Analytic Framework', pp. 17–38 in Richard Caputo (ed.) *Basic Income Guarantee: International Experiences and Perspectives on the Viability of Income Guarantee* (New York: Palgrave Macmillan), p. 27.
2. Antonio Gramsci (1971) *Selections from Prison Notebooks* (London: Lawrence and Wishart, London), pp. 287, 343.
3. Antonio Gramsci, *Selections from Prison Notebooks*, p. 507.
4. Antonio Gramsci, *Selections from Prison Notebooks*, p. 145.
5. Antonio Gramsci, *Selections from Prison Notebooks*, p. 373.
6. Peter Golding and Sue Middleton (1982) *Images of Welfare: Press and Public Attitudes to Poverty* (Oxford: Basil Blackwell), pp. 75, 88, 91; Hartley Dean (2012) *Social Policy*, 2nd edition (Cambridge: Polity), p. 72.
7. The Chancellor of the Chequer, George Osborne, in a speech to the Conservative Party Conference, 2012: www.newstatesman.com/blogs/politics/2012/10/george-osbornes-speech-conservative-conference-full-text
8. www.theguardian.com/politics/2013/jan/09/skivers-v-strivers-argument-pollutes
9. John Hills (2014) *Good Times, Bad Times: The welfare myth of them and us* (Bristol: Policy Press).
10. Thomas A. Schwandt (2005) 'Moral Discourses', encyclopedia article in Sandra Mathison, *Encyclopedia of Evaluation* (London: Sage), https://srmo.sagepub.com/view/encyclopedia-of-evaluation/n350.xml
11. Hartley Dean (2004) 'Popular discourse and the ethical deficiency of "Third Way" conceptions of citizenship', *Citizenship studies*, 8 (1), 65–82.
12. Charles E. Lindblom (1980) *The Policy-making Process*, 2nd edition (Englewood Cliffs, NJ: Prentice Hall), p. 119.
13. Thomas A. Birkland (2005) *An Introduction to the Policy Process*, 2nd edition (Armonk, NY: M.E. Sharpe), p. 49.
14. Malcolm Torry (2014) 'A New Policy World for the Benefits System', *Policy World*, Spring 2014, pp. 12–13.

15. Claus Offe (2013) 'Pathways from Here', pp. 560–63 in Karl Widerquist, José A. Noguera, Yannick Vanderborght, and Jürgen De Wispelaere, *Basic Income: An anthology of contemporary research* (Chichester: Wiley Blackwell), p. 561.
16. Cf. J.J. Richardson (1969) *The Policy-Making Process* (London: Routledge and Kegan Paul), about the Restrictive Trade Practices Act 1956. The general public was largely unaware of the effects of the ways in which trade associations policed resale price maintenance. The motive for change was the UK government's need to make the economy more efficient.
17. Stuart White (2003) *The Civic Minimum: On the Rights and Obligations of Economic Citizenship* (Oxford: Oxford University Press), p. 59.
18. Stuart White (2003) *The Civic Minimum*, pp. 99, 131, 132.
19. Stuart White (2003) *The Civic Minimum*, p. 18.
20. Jürgen De Wispelaere and José Antonio Noguera (2012) 'On the Political Feasibility of Universal Basic Income: An Analytic Framework', pp. 17–38 in Richard Caputo (ed.) *Basic Income Guarantee: International Experiences and Perspectives on the Viability of Income Guarantee* (New York: Palgrave Macmillan), p. 28.
21. Stefan Svallfors (2012) 'Welfare States and Welfare Attitudes', pp. 1–24 in Stefan Svallfors (ed.) *Contested Welfare States: Welfare attitudes in Europe and Beyond* (Stanford, California: Stanford University Press), p. 10.
22. Christian Staerklé, Tiina Likki and Régis Scheidegger (2012) 'A Normative Approach to Welfare Attitudes', pp. 81–118 in Stefan Svallfors (ed.) *Contested Welfare States: Welfare attitudes in Europe and Beyond* (Stanford, California: Stanford University Press), p. 81.
23. Steffen Mau (2003) *The Moral Economy of Welfare States: Britain and Germany compared* (London: Routledge), p. 35.
24. Wim van Oorschot (2006) 'Making the Difference in Social Europe: Deservingness perceptions among citizens of European Welfare States', *Journal of European Social Policy*, 16 (1), 23–42, p. 26.
25. Stefan Liebig and Steffen Mau (2004) 'A Legitimate Guaranteed Minimum Income?' pp. 207–28 in Guy Standing (ed.), *Promoting Income Security as a Right: Europe and North America* (London: Anthem, London), p. 210.
26. Stefan Liebig and Steffen Mau (2004) 'A Legitimate Guaranteed Minimum Income?' p. 224.
27. Wim van Oorschot (2006) 'Welfarism and the multidimensionality of welfare state legitimacy: Evidence from The Netherlands, 2006', *International Journal of Social Welfare*, 21, 71–93, p. 90.
28. Richard M. Coughlin (1980) *Ideology, Public Opinion and Welfare Policy: Attitudes towards taxes and spending in industrialized societies* (Berkeley: Institute of International Studies, University of California), p. 31.

29. Eddy van Avermaet (2001) 'Social Influence in Small Groups', pp. 403–43 in Mike Hewstone and Wolfgang Stroebe (eds), *Introduction to Social Psychology*, 3rd edition (Oxford: Blackwell), pp 408–11; Serge Moscovici (1976) *Social Influence and Social Change* (London: Academic Press), pp. 15–37.
30. Elizabeth Clery, Lucy Lee and Sarah Kunz (2012) *Public attitudes to poverty and welfare, 1983–2011: Analysis using British Social Attitudes data* (York: Joseph Rowntree Foundation), p. 2, www.natcen.ac.uk/media/137637/poverty-and-welfare.pdf
31. William James (2012 / 1902), *The Varieties of Religious Experience: A study in human nature* (Oxford: Oxford University Press), first published 1902; cf. William Sargant (1976) *Battle for the Mind: A physiology of conversion and brain-washing* (London: Heinemann).
32. Serge Moscovici (1980) 'Toward a Theory of Conversion Behavior', pp. 209–39 in Leonard Berkowitz (ed.) *Advances in Experimental Social Psychology*, vol. 13 (New York: Academic Press), p. 211.
33. Serge Moscovici (1976) *Social Influence and Social Change*, Academic Press, London, 1976, p. 81.
34. Serge Moscovici (1980) 'Toward a Theory of Conversion Behavior', pp. 214–16.
35. Charlan Nemeth, Mark Swedlund and Barbara Kanki (1974) 'Patterning of the minority's responses and their influence on the majority', *European Journal of Social Psychology*, 4 (1), pp. 53–64.
36. Eddy van Avermaet (2001) 'Social Influence in Small Groups', pp. 403–43 in Mike Hewstone and Wolfgang Stroebe (eds), *Introduction to Social Psychology*, 3rd edition (Oxford: Blackwell), p. 417.
37. Gabriel Migny (1982) *The Power of Minorities* (London) Academic Press, London, pp. 39, 84–5; Serge Moscovici (1976) *Social Influence and Social Change*, pp. 93, 109.
38. John C. Turner (1991) *Social Influence* (Milton Keynes: Open University Press), p. 100.
39. Andrew Denham and Mark Garnett (1998) *British Think-tanks and the Climate of Opinion* (London: UCL Press), pp. 201–5.
40. D.V.L. Smith and Associates (1991) *Basic Income: A research report* (London: Age Concern England), pp. 5, 29.
41. Child Poverty Action Group (2015) *Welfare Benefits and Tax Credits Handbook, 2015/16* (London: Child Poverty Action Group), www.cpag.org.uk/bookshop/wbtch
42. Department for Work and Pensions (2014) *Fraud and Error in the Benefit System: Estimates, 2013/14*, 2014, www.gov.uk/government/uploads/system/uploads/attachment_data/file/371459/Statistical_Release.pdf
43. It is interesting that on 17 May 2015, a generally EU-friendly UK newspaper, *the Guardian*, headlined a single business leader's call for Britain to

leave the EU, and only much later in the article mentioned the large number of business leaders who disagree with him. www.theguardian.com/politics/2015/may/17/jcb-boss-says-eu-exit-could-lift-burden-of-bureaucracy-on-uk-businesses
44. www.telegraph.co.uk/news/newstopics/eureferendum/11617702/poll.html
45. Floriana Cerniglia and Laura Pagani (2015) 'Political Knowledge and Attitudes towards Centralisation in Europe', *Fiscal Studies*, 36 (2), 215–36, pp. 234–5.
46. Jürgen De Wispelaere and José Antonio Noguera (2012) 'On the Political Feasibility of Universal Basic Income: An Analytic Framework', pp. 17–38 in Richard Caputo (ed.) *Basic Income Guarantee: International Experiences and Perspectives on the Viability of Income Guarantee* (New York: Palgrave Macmillan), p. 29.
47. Stuart White (2003) *The Civic Minimum: On the Rights and Obligations of Economic Citizenship* (Oxford: Oxford University Press), p. 152.
48. Stuart White (2006) 'Reconsidering the Exploitation Objection to Basic Income', *Basic Income Studies*, 1 (2), 1–24, p. 13.
49. Stuart White (2003) *The Civic Minimum*, pp. 155–62.
50. Richard Murphy and Howard Reed (2013) *Financing the Social State: Towards a full employment economy* (London: Centre for Labour and Social Studies), pp. 25–7.
51. Basic Income Grant Coalition (2009) *Making the Difference: The BIG in Namibia: Basic Income Grant Pilot Project, Assessment Report* (Namibia: Basic Income Grant Coalition, Namibia NGO Forum), www.bignam.org/Publications/BIG_Assessment_report_08b.pdf, 23/09/2011; Sarath Davala, Renana Jhabvala, Soumya Kapoor Mehta and Guy Standing (2014) *Basic Income: A Transformative Policy for India* (London: Bloomsbury).
52. Karl Widerquist and Michael W. Howard (eds) (2012) *Alaska's Permanent Fund Dividend: Examining its suitability as a model* (New York: Palgrave Macmillan).
53. Hamid Tabatabai (2012) 'Iran: A Bumpy Road toward Basic Income', pp. 285–300 in Richard Caputo (ed.) *Basic Income Guarantee and Politics: International Experiences and Perspectives on the Viability of Income Guarantee* (New York: Palgrave Macmillan).
54. Claus Offe (2013) 'Pathways from Here', pp. 560–63 in Karl Widerquist, José A. Noguera, Yannick Vanderborght, and Jürgen De Wispelaere, *Basic Income: An anthology of contemporary research* (Chichester: Wiley Blackwell), p. 561.
55. Peter Esam and Richard Berthoud (1991) *Independent Benefits for Men and Women: An enquiry into option for treating husbands and wives as separate units in the assessment of social security* (London: Policy Studies Institute).

56. Bill Jordan, Phil Agulnik, Duncan Burbidge and Stuart Duffin (2000) *Stumbling Towards Basic Income: The prospects for tax-benefit integration* (London: Citizen's Income Trust), p. 65.
57. Tony Atkinson, 'Participation Income' (1993) *Citizen's Income Bulletin*, no. 16, pp. 7–11; A.B. Atkinson, (1996) 'The Case for a Participation Income', *The Political Quarterly*, 67 (1), 67–70.
58. Yannick Vanderborght (2005) 'The Basic Income Guarantee in Europe: The Belgian and Dutch back door strategies', pp. 257–81 in Karl Widerquist, Michael Anthony Lewis and Steven Pressman (eds.) *The Ethics and Economics of the Basic Income Guarantee* (Aldershot: Ashgate), pp. 274–6; Rie Takamatsu and Toshiaki Tachibanaki (2014) 'What Needs to be Considered when Introducing a New Welfare System: Who supports Basic Income in Japan?' pp. 197–218 in Yannick Vanderborght and Toru Yamamori (eds) *Basic Income in Japan: Prospects for a radical idea in a transforming welfare state* (New York: Palgrave Macmillan), p. 205.
59. Jürgen De Wispelaere and José Antonio Noguera (2012) 'On the Political Feasibility of Universal Basic Income: An Analytic Framework', pp. 17–38 in Richard Caputo (ed.) *Basic Income Guarantee: International Experiences and Perspectives on the Viability of Income Guarantee* (New York: Palgrave Macmillan), p. 29.
60. Yannick Vanderborght and Yuki Sekine (2014) 'A Comparative Look at the Feasibility of Basic Income in the Japanese Welfare State', pp. 15–34 in Yannick Vanderborght and Toru Yamamori (eds) *Basic Income in Japan: Prospects for a radical idea in a transforming welfare state* (New York: Palgrave Macmillan), p. 31.
61. Christian Albrekt Larsen (2006) *The Institutional Logic of Welfare Attitudes: How welfare regimes influence public support* (Aldershot: Ashgate), p. 48. Perceived deservingness rises as the group's control over neediness falls, level of need rises, the identity of the group strengthens, the group expresses gratitude, and a future payback can be expected.
62. Richard M. Coughlin (1980) *Ideology, Public Opinion and Welfare Policy*, p. 95; Stefan Svallfors (2012) 'Welfare States and Welfare Attitudes', p. 6.
63. Wim van Oorschot and Bart Meuleman (2012) 'Welfare Performance and Welfare Support', pp. 25–57 in Stefan Svallfors (ed.) *Contested Welfare States: Welfare attitudes in Europe and Beyond* (Stanford, California: Stanford University Press), p. 52.
64. Peter Saunders and Maneerat Pinyopusarek (2001) 'Popularity and Participation: Social security reform in Australia', pp. 143–64 in Erik Schokkaert, *Ethics and Social Security Reform* (Aldershot: Ashgate), p. 161.
65. Denmark and the Netherlands: see Pensions Policy Institute for the National Association of Pension Funds (2014) *Towards a Citizen's Pension*

(London: National Association of Pension Funds), p. 27: www.pensionspolicyinstitute.org.uk/publications/reports/towards-a-citizens-pension. The UK's new STP will be close to a Citizen's Pension.
66. Jan Mewes and Steffen Mau (2012) 'Unraveling Working-class Welfare Chauvinism', pp. 119–57 in Stefan Svallfors (ed.) *Contested Welfare States: Welfare attitudes in Europe and Beyond* (Stanford, California: Stanford University Press), pp. 149–50.
67. Christian Albrekt Larsen (2006) *The Institutional Logic of Welfare Attitudes: How welfare regimes influence public support* (Aldershot: Ashgate), p. 4. Cf. p 109: the higher the degree of means-testing, the more the recipient group will be stigmatized. In each country that he studies, Coughlin traces both welfare state structures and social attitudes to welfare provision back to nineteenth-century elite presuppositions: Richard M. Coughlin (1980) *Ideology, Public Opinion and Welfare Policy*, p. 51.
68. Christian Albrekt Larsen, *The Institutional Logic of Welfare Attitudes*, p. 145.
69. Itaba, Yoshio (2014) 'What Do People Think about Basic Income in Japan?' pp. 171–95 in Yannick Vanderborght and Toru Yamamori (eds) *Basic Income in Japan: Prospects for a radical idea in a transforming welfare state* (New York: Palgrave Macmillan).
70. www.labour.org.uk/one-nation-social-security-reform-miliband-speech#
71. www.commonwealthfund.org/publications/fund-reports/2014/jun/mirror-mirror
72. Richard M. Coughlin (1980) *Ideology, Public Opinion and Welfare Policy*, p. 99.
73. Malcolm Torry (2013) *Money for Everyone: Why we need a Citizen's Income*, Bristol: Policy Press, pp. 22–5.
74. Thirty-nine per cent of workers between the ages of fifty and sixty-four would like to work shorter hours in the same job, and in this age group, 18% are self-employed, 28% are working part-time, and 23% have negotiated flexible working arrangements with their employers (Department for Work and Pensions (2013) *Older Workers Statistical Information Booklet 2013* (London: Department for Work and Pensions), www.gov.uk/government/uploads/system/uploads/attachment_data/file/264899/older-workers-statistical-information-booklet-2013.pdf, p. 15). Alfageme, Pastor, and Viñado suggest that a Citizen's Income would work well with their proposal that throughout the lifecycle, there ought to be opportunities to take periods out of employment paid for by sacrificing pension. This provision could be particularly valuable for pre-retirement working-age adults. See Alfredo Alfageme, Begoña García Pastor and Celia Viñado (2012) 'Temporary exit from employment and Citizen's Income: A reply', *Critical Social Policy*, 32 (4), 716–19. Jay Ginn has suggested that a

Citizen's Income approach would be preferable to their proposed funding mechanism: Jay Ginn (2012) 'Temporary exit from employment: A response', *Critical Social Policy,* 32 (4), 709–15.
75. Ben Baumberg (2012) 'Three ways to defend social security in Britain', *Journal of Poverty and Social Justice,* 20 (2), 149–61, pp. 158–9.
76. T. Alexander Smith (1975) *The Comparative Policy Process* (Santa Barbara, California: Clio Press), pp. 169–71.
77. Louise Humpage (2015) *Policy Change, Public Attitudes and Social Citizenship: Does Neoliberalism Matter?* (Bristol: Policy Press), p. 228.
78. Louise Humpage (2015) *Policy Change, Public Attitudes and Social Citizenship,* p. 240.
79. Louise Humpage (2015) *Policy Change, Public Attitudes and Social Citizenship,* p. 244.
80. Richard M. Coughlin (1980) *Ideology, Public Opinion and Welfare Policy,* p. 161.
81. Stefan Liebig and Steffen Mau (2004) 'A Legitimate Guaranteed Minimum Income?' pp. 210–11.
82. Charles E. Lindblom (1980) *The Policy-making Process,* p. 57.

CHAPTER 6

Is a Citizen's Income Administratively Feasible?

6.1 Introduction

First of all some terminological clarity

De Wispelaere and Noguera employ the term 'institutional feasibility' to mean the feasibility of administering a Citizen's Income. However, what they term 'strategic feasibility' and I term 'policy process feasibility' is about the institutions through which an idea needs to travel in order to achieve implementation; so the term 'institutional feasibility' could equally well apply to both administrative feasibility and policy process feasibility. I propose the term 'administrative feasibility' to express the idea that it would be feasible to administer Citizen's Income. This term does not quite express the breadth of De Wispelaere's and Noguera's use of 'institutional feasibility', which asks about the institutions that would administer a Citizen's Income as well as about the mechanisms that they would employ to administer it, but what matters is that the mechanisms should be available, so administrative feasibility is what matters.[1]

By 'administrative feasibility' I mean (a) the feasibility of administering the transition from current tax and benefits systems to new systems based on Citizen's Incomes; and (b) the feasibility of administering the Citizen's Incomes once the transition has taken place. Implementation will best be debated after a variety of feasibilities have been established, because if a Citizen's Income is not feasible then there is little point in discussing its implementation. However, implementation and ongoing administration are not disconnected, so although in this chapter we shall mainly be discussing the feasibility of administering a Citizen's Income on the assumption that it has been implemented, we shall also have an eye on the feasibility of administering the transition.

But isn't the answer to the question 'Is a Citizen's Income administratively feasible?' a fairly obvious 'yes'? An individual's Citizen's Income would start at birth, would adjust with their age, and would cease when they died. This does not look difficult. In fact, it looks as if it could win the prize for administrative simplicity. We might come to that answer, but first of all we shall need to take seriously the idea that a Citizen's Income scheme would need to be administered, and that the analysis of administrative requirements is an essential component of any attempt to argue for Citizen's Income's feasibility.[2]

6.2 Potential Difficulties

6.2.1 The Construction of a Reliable List of Those Entitled to Citizen's Incomes

First of all, criteria will need to be developed to determine who will be eligible to receive a Citizen's Income. Most countries establish methods for determining who has a right to live in the country, and what rights and obligations those who live there possess. Many countries function with a variety of definitions: citizenship, permanent right to remain, temporary leave to remain, refugee, asylum seeker, European citizenship, lawful permanent resident, and so on. The criteria for belonging to these categories are not always clear, and they can be changed.[3] Any country considering whether to implement a Citizen's Income scheme will need to decide to which categories of individuals Citizen's Incomes will be given. They will also need to decide whether Citizen's Incomes are to be given to citizens living abroad; and any country that has signed treaties relating to social security benefits (whether bilateral treaties, or regional treaties such as those relating to the European Union) will need to pay Citizen's Incomes to residents who are citizens of other countries.

Having decided on the categories of individual to which Citizen's Incomes will be paid, a reliable list of names, ages, and bank account details will need to be constructed. Some countries keep lists of citizens, and of members of other categories of legal residence, and if this is the case then all that will be required will be the collection of bank account details (which will be readily given, but see below on individuals without bank accounts). Where countries do not already possess such lists, there will often be alternative lists that can be easily developed into a full list of people eligible for Citizen's Incomes. In some countries, social security numbers will be a useful starting point; in others, health service numbers; in others, lists of people with driving licences; and in others, lists of passport holders. The combination of such lists could get a country close to a list of legal residents—and where previously privacy concerns have prevented the combination of such lists, the construction of a comprehensive list to facilitate a universal unconditional income might meet with sufficient public approval. A particularly interesting possibility is a country's electoral register. Where voting is compulsory, as in Australia, the electoral register is likely to be relatively complete and accurate; but where it is not, the register will generally be neither complete nor accurate.[4] If the same register were to be used to pay Citizen's Incomes, then it would be in everyone's interest to ensure that it was both accurate and complete, which could only be good for democracy.

In countries that already pay unconditional benefits for children, a further possibility offers itself. If Citizen's Incomes were to be introduced gradually, starting with young people as they come to the end of their child benefit entitlement, the list of child benefit recipients would provide a reliable list for each new annual cohort of Citizen's Income recipients. All that would be required would be to cease paying the income into a parent's bank account and to start paying it instead into the young person's bank account.

Where no useful lists exist, self-registration will be required, along with the necessary identity checks. The construction of such lists in countries without them could be a useful step towards establishing additional citizenship rights, such as the right to vote and a right to healthcare.

While De Wispelaere and Noguera are right to suggest that the construction of a reliable list of Citizen's Income recipients might be a challenge, it would be a challenge that many countries would not find it difficult to meet; and in countries in which the construction of such a list might be more difficult, its construction would be a useful process.[5]

6.2.2 Payment Mechanisms

A second administrative challenge is the potential difficulty of paying Citizen's Incomes to everyone entitled to them. As De Wispelaere and Noguera put it:

> In almost every country a significant part of the population does not have access to a bank account or is too transient to rely on regular postal checks [cheques]. Here again, [Citizen's Income] administrators face hard choices between setting up novel disbursement systems (which incur significant costs and risks of error), combining existing systems without clear indication of how comprehensive the coverage is, or compromising on the target efficiency of [Citizen's Income].[6]

A Citizen's Income pilot project in India that involved 6000 men, women, and children, required every adult to open a bank account during the first few weeks of the project. This part of the project (as well as all of the other aspects of it) was a resounding success, and proved that it is perfectly possible to achieve almost 100 % current account coverage in any country that chooses to implement a Citizen's Income.[7]

In the UK, 98 % of households already have bank accounts into which their Citizen's Incomes could be paid.[8] Two per cent of households use Post Office Card accounts, which are designed purely for the receipt of benefits.

If both the UK and India can achieve close to 100 % bank account coverage, then every other developed and developing country should be able to do so. Sub-Saharan Africa might prove to be a bit more of a challenge, but the rapid spread of mobile phone banking on that continent suggests that even there it would be perfectly possible to provide every individual with the means to receive and manage a Citizen's Income.[9]

6.2.3 Ensuring that Everybody Would Receive Their Citizen's Income

De Wispelaere and Stirton correctly suggest that the two challenges discussed above are 'bottlenecks',[10] in the sense that administration of a Citizen's Income first of all requires a clear and accurate list of recipients, and only if that challenge has been met can the next bottleneck be tackled: the payment mechanism required to ensure that everyone entitled to a Citizen's Income should receive one. Once an implementation plan has successfully negotiated those first two bottlenecks, it can start on the third: a mechanism to ensure that someone who is entitled to receive a Citizen's Income, but is not doing so, should be able to do so. This third challenge is really a combination of the previous two. If a country has met the challenges of providing a robust list of recipients, and of establishing a reliable delivery mechanism, then it will already have met this third challenge. Things do go wrong, of course, and there will always need to be an administrative facility for ensuring that mistakes can be rectified, but this is a requirement for any public service provision, and is not particular to Citizen's Income. No public service could be simpler in conception or in administration than a Citizen's Income, so if anything like an adequate repair mechanism can be provided for any other public service, then a more than adequate one should be possible in relation to the payment of Citizen's Incomes.

Between them, De Wispelaere's and Noguera's three administrative challenges express the administrative requirements for a Citizen's Income. If those challenges can be met, then our verdict must be that a Citizen's Income would be administratively feasible. Those challenges have been met.

6.3 The Administration of Citizen's Income Schemes

However, what needs to be implemented is not just the Citizen's Incomes to which a population would be entitled but the Citizen's Incomes accompanied by the other aspects of the chosen Citizen's Income scheme. Those other aspects might be changes to tax rates and tax allowances, the abolition of existing benefits, the recalculation of existing benefits, the establishment of new taxes, the creation of new money, the collection of permanent fund dividends, and/or the redirection of funds currently spent on subsidy programmes.

In the Indian pilot project, first of all a small project in West Delhi enabled people to choose between access to the subsidized ration shop and a Citizen's Income, and in the larger project residents in the pilot villages were given Citizen's Incomes and left to choose whether to use the subsidized ration shops or not. Use of the ration shops fell, and more food was purchased in the markets and other shops. Nutrition improved. This suggests that shifting funds from providing subsidized food to paying a Citizen's Income would be both feasible and beneficial.[11] Although it has been a bumpy ride, Iran's government has redirected funds previously spent on subsidies into Citizen's Incomes paid to the heads of households.[12] For nearly forty years, citizens of Alaska have been receiving unconditional annual payments funded by dividends from the Alaska Permanent Fund.[13] Quantitative easing is now a fact of life in many of the world's larger economies, it has not resulted in major new inflation, and there is no reason why such new money should not be paid to individuals rather than to the banks once the required delivery mechanism is in place. Financial transaction taxes already exist in relation to share purchase,[14] and there is no reason why other kinds of financial transactions should not be taxed in the same way. Most countries are well used to changing their tax allowances, tax rates, benefits rates, and benefits regulations; to abolishing benefits; and to recalculating individuals' benefits to take into account additional income from other sources.

None of the kinds of Citizen's Income schemes that we discussed in Chap. 3 would include changes that have not already been successfully managed in some context or other; so if it is possible to administer the Citizen's Incomes component of a scheme, then it would also be perfectly possible to administer the scheme as a whole. This suggests that it should also be possible to administer the transition to any Citizen's Income scheme—although as we shall see in Chap. 10, the ability to administer a transition is not the only factor involved in deciding whether the transition is feasible.

6.4 Comparison with the Administrative Requirements of Alternatives to Citizen's Income

There are many alternatives to a Citizen's Income that would offer some of the same advantages. One factor that might help us to decide on their relative feasibilities will be their relative administrative feasibilities. If an alternative can be more easily administered than a Citizen's Income scheme, then that might be a reason to consider its implementation.

6.4.1 Participation Income

Twenty years ago, Tony Atkinson suggested that because 'it will be difficult to secure political support for a Citizen's Income while it remains unconditional on labour market or other activity', a compromise might be required. He thought that political support would be easier to achieve if receipt of an otherwise unconditional and nonwithdrawable income were to be conditional on some kind of participation in society.[15] As Tony Fitzpatrick has put it: such a 'Participation Income' would *require* participation in society, which might be more acceptable to the public and to policymakers than an income that simply invited it.[16]

The 'Participation Income' would be given to people who were ill, disabled, retired, or looking for work, without their having to 'participate' in any other way, but otherwise at least one of a number of participation conditions would need to be met. Employment, self-employment, education, training, voluntary work, and caring for the young, older people, or disabled dependents would all count as participation in society.

What neither Atkinson nor Fitzpatrick factor in is the difficulty of administering a Participation Income. (It is not uncommon for academics to ignore administrative implications. It is less common for those of us who have spent time administering social security benefits to do so.) A casework approach would be required to administer the participation conditions, which would hand to junior civil servants—'street-level bureaucrats'[17]—the kind of discretion that has made claiming means-tested benefits such a demeaning process for both claimants and administrators. Decisions would need to be made about precisely which activities should count as participation in society; and for anyone not employed or retired, mechanisms would need to be constructed to decide whether they were 'participating'. (How much self-employment would count? How much voluntary activity? Caring for whom? How much disability would exempt someone from satisfying a participation condition? etc.) Minimal voluntary activities would no doubt be artificially created to enable people to satisfy a participation condition, and administrators would develop their own criteria to enable them to grant the Participation Income wherever possible. Such 'creative compliance'[18] would quickly undermine any initial public approval based on the idea that the Participation Income should only be paid to people genuinely participating in society. The initial participation conditions would exclude very few citizens, because most people do participate in society in some way or other; and creative compliance would ensure that only a very small number of individuals would not receive the Participation Income. Massive administrative effort would be expended on administering a benefit very like a Citizen's Income, but the difficulties associated with administering the conditions would quickly sour public attitudes. Either the conditions would be quickly abandoned and a Citizen's Income established, or the soured debate would cause the whole plan to be abandoned. It is difficult to predict which would occur.

De Wispelaere and Stirton suggest that 'Participation Income might not be such a great idea after all', because the administrative requirements would be so onerous. Hermione Parker's particularly interesting verdict was that 'a major public education exercise is necessary before voters are likely to adjust their value systems to the problems of post-industrial societies. Fudging the issues could delay this process.'[19]

6.4.2 Tax Credits

(real ones: not what the UK government calls 'tax credits')

A credit is allocated to every individual. If someone is earning nothing, the credit is paid. As earnings rise, the credit is withdrawn. At the point at which the credit is exhausted, income tax starts to be paid.

In Fig. 6.1, the credit is worth £x per week. As earnings rise, the credit is withdrawn, so net income rises more slowly than earned income. At earnings of £y per week (the break-even point), the credit has all been withdrawn. Above this point, income tax is paid.

The graph assumes that the rate at which the credit is withdrawn is the same as the tax rate. If the rates are different, then the slope of line BC is different above and below earnings of £y per week.

6.4.2.1 The Administration of Tax Credits

The Tax Credit can be administered by the government or by the employer. If the government administers the Tax Credit, then the employer must provide regular and accurate earnings information to the government

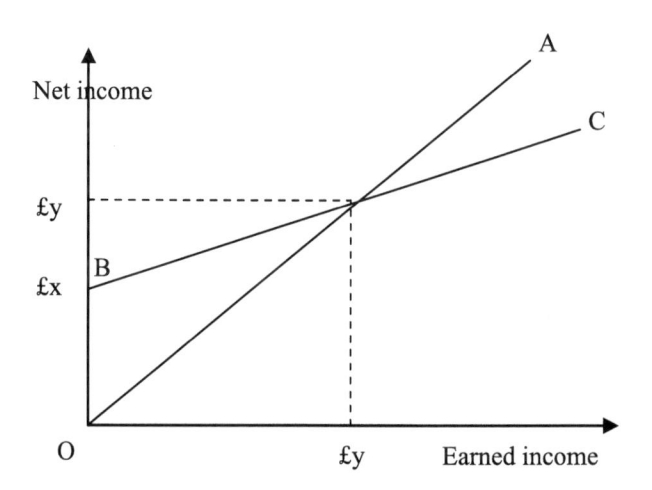

Fig. 6.1 Tax Credits/Negative Income Tax. Net income as earned income rises

(as with the UK's Universal Credit). If the employer administers the Tax Credit, then if someone moves between employers, their Tax Credit administration has to be transferred between employers; and if they have a period of unemployment, then administration of the Tax Credit has to be handed to the government and then on to the new employer. If someone has two employments, then the employers have to decide which of them will administer the Tax Credit; and if someone has occasional other earnings, then their employer needs to be informed so that the Tax Credit can be withdrawn accordingly.

If every working-age adult receives the same Tax Credit, then neither their employer nor the government needs to know any personal details. If people in different circumstances receive different levels of Tax Credit, then their employer and the government will need to know individuals' circumstances in order to allocate the correct credit.

Many income tax systems are cumulative. An annual amount of income is not taxed, so each week, or each month, the employer has to calculate how much tax to deduct so that by the end of the year the correct amount of tax has been deducted. With Tax Credits, the tax system would be non-cumulative. Each week, or each month, the correct amount of the Credit would need to be paid in addition to earnings, or no credit would be paid and earnings would be taxed. A non-cumulative system requires a single tax rate, so anyone paying higher-rate tax would need to pay additional income tax at the end of the tax year.

6.4.3 Negative Income Tax

Income tax deducts money from earnings above an earnings threshold, and a Negative Income Tax pays money to the employee below the threshold, so a Negative Income Tax scheme functions in the same way as a Tax Credit scheme. The only difference is in the specification. For a Tax Credit scheme, the amount to be paid out if there are no earnings is specified, along with a withdrawal rate as earnings rise. For a Negative Income Tax, the threshold is specified along with tax rates above and below the threshold. If the rates above and below the threshold are the same, then for earnings below the threshold, the same amount is paid out for earnings of £z below the threshold as would be collected in tax on earnings of £z above the threshold.

As the system is essentially the same as a Tax Credit scheme, Fig. 6.1 applies. Different rates above and below the threshold would result in the line BC having different slopes above and below earnings of £y per week. Administrative considerations would be the same as for Tax Credits.

6.4.4 Back to a Citizen's Income

A Citizen's Income is an unconditional income paid to every individual by the government, and it is not withdrawn as earnings rise. Tax is paid on all or most earned income. In Fig. 6.2, a Citizen's Income of £x per week is paid to everyone. All earnings are taxed. The line BC shows the net income. (The diagram assumes that a single tax rate is charged on all earnings.)

6.4.4.1 Administration

The government pays a Citizen's Income to every individual, the amount depending only on the person's age. (A different amount would be paid to older people as a Citizen's Pension, and lower amounts to children and young people.) Employers would continue to administer income tax as they do now.

6.4.5 Comparing the Schemes

It will be important to continue to discuss the possibility of a genuine Tax Credits scheme and of a Negative Income Tax because survey data from Japan suggests that a Negative Income Tax could be a more popular

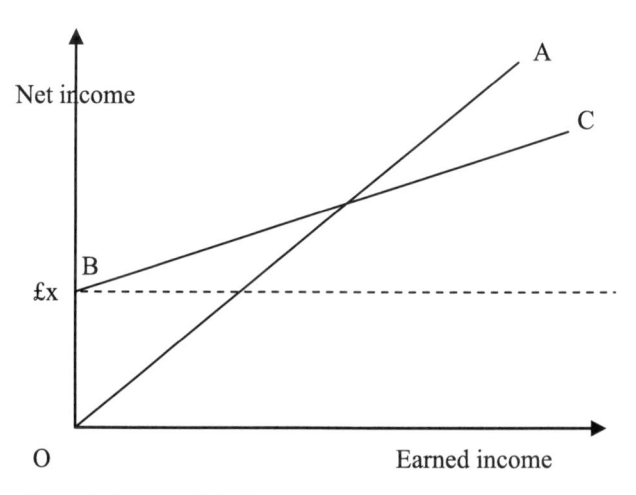

Fig. 6.2 Citizen's Income. Net income as earned income rises

option than Citizen's Income,[20] because a genuine Tax Credits scheme would have been implemented in the UK during the 1970s if the government had not changed at the General Election in 1974,[21] and because a Negative Income Tax could be both affordable and equitable in the UK.[22] However, the Japanese public opinion survey took no account of the difficulty of administering a Negative Income Tax, and Bartlett, Davies, and Hoy took a theoretical approach to the discussion of the equity and affordability of a Negative Income Tax and again took no account of the administrative challenges that would need to be overcome in order to implement the proposal. The UK 1972 Tax Credits proposal became increasingly complex the closer it got to implementation.

A particular problem relating to the Japanese survey was that the questionnaire was not about a genuine Negative Income Tax, as that term is normally understood. It was about a Negative Income Tax only for people in employment.[23] The questionnaire's questions about a Citizen's Income were about a provision for the whole population. It is therefore difficult to draw conclusions from the research about the relative popularities of Citizen's Income and Negative Income Tax.

An underlying difficulty is that members of the general public will usually have little understanding of the administrative complexities associated with both a Negative Income Tax and with Tax Credits, or of the simplicity of a Citizen's Income's administration. A further underlying difficulty is that Tax Credits, Negative Income Tax, and Citizen's Income deliver the same or similar relationships between net income and earned income, so theoretical debate can make a Negative Income Tax or a Tax Credits scheme look very similar to a Citizen's Income, whereas in practice they would be very different. Both a Negative Income Tax and a Tax Credits scheme would be either impossible or very difficult to administer, whereas a Citizen's Income would be very easy to administer. The UK's recent rather difficult experience with 'Universal Credit' (a combined means-tested benefit that is neither universal nor a credit) is a classic case of consultants proposing a benefits system reform without taking sufficient account of the administrative challenges that their proposal would have to face, and of a government and civil service insufficiently in touch with the practicalities of the administration of tax and benefits systems to notice that the proposed reform might be impossible to deliver.

The ability to administer a scheme is crucial. Without qualification we can say that it would be feasible to administer a Citizen's Income scheme, both in terms of administering the transition and in terms of administering the scheme once it was running. We cannot say with confidence that it would be possible to administer any of the other schemes discussed in this chapter.

6.5 Case Studies

6.5.1 The UK's Existing Unconditional Benefits

6.5.1.1 The National Health Service

The UK's NHS provides healthcare to every legal resident free at the point of use. Visits to General Practitioners, hospital stays, operations, visits by District Nurses, and so on, are all free. Small payments are required for spectacles, drugs, and dental care, but these are free to every child up to the age of nineteen, everyone over the age of sixty, and a variety of other categories of people. All of the remaining costs are paid out of general taxation.

Healthcare systems in other countries require insurance premiums or membership fees to be administered, and administrative arrangements to be negotiated between healthcare providers, government agencies, insurance companies, and often employers or trades unions. The UK's NHS largely escapes this administrative burden.

Major advantages of the UK's method of funding healthcare are that it provides a secure source of funds for healthcare providers, nobody is excluded from healthcare, everyone receives the healthcare that they need, nobody receives the healthcare that they do not need, provision can be consistent across the country, those who can afford to pay more are paying more (because they are paying higher amounts of Income Tax), and those who can afford to pay little are paying little. Healthcare providers do not benefit financially by doing more than is necessary, so they are not tempted to undertake unnecessary treatment, thus keeping costs down.

The Washington-based Commonwealth Fund has found that the UK's NHS offers the highest quality of care out of the eleven OECD healthcare systems that it studied, that it is the most efficient, and that is the second cheapest per capita.[24] This is because a healthcare system funded by taxation and free at the point of use provides everyone with the healthcare that they need, it is not tempted to undertake unnecessary treatment, and there are no insurance company shareholders looking for profits.

It is not only social security benefits that are best constructed as unconditional benefits for every member of a population. Other public services might be, too.

6.5.1.2 Child Benefit

The UK's Child Benefit is paid unconditionally for every child living in the UK. It is paid to every child's main carer—usually the mother—who receives a different amount for the first child in the family than for the second and subsequent children. The same amount is paid for every first child, whatever the family's income or other circumstances; and the same amount is paid for every second or subsequent child, whatever the family's income or other circumstances. (In September 2010, the Chancellor of the Exchequer announced that households containing higher-rate taxpayers were to be deprived of their Child Benefit. It proved impossible to administer this change because there is no database that connects higher-rate taxpayers with Child Benefit recipients, so Child Benefit remains an unconditional benefit. A tax on children is now levied on the incomes of higher-rate taxpayers who live in households that receive Child Benefit, but that is a different matter.)

Anyone with a right to live in the UK, and for whom the UK is their main home, receives Child Benefit for any children living with them. A family arriving in the UK might have to wait three months before receiving Child Benefit,[25] but after that they receive Child Benefit in the same way as everyone else. Reciprocal agreements between the UK and some other countries enable families coming to the UK from those countries to receive Child Benefit straight away, and families going to those countries from the UK to receive their similar benefits.

Child Benefit starts when the child is born, and it ends when they are sixteen years old, although it can continue if the child remains in approved full-time education or training. Administration is simple. Changes to contact and bank account details might need to be made occasionally, but otherwise no administrative decisions or actions are required. Annual uprating is computerized. Very few errors occur, and there is almost no fraud.

Child Benefit is the closest UK benefit to a Citizen's Income. It is unconditional and nonwithdrawable, and if it were to be paid at the same rate for every child then it would be a Citizen's Income for children. Experience of Child Benefit suggests that administering a Citizen's Income for every legal resident would not be a problem. The administration of Citizen's

Income would be simple, efficient, and easily computerized, and almost no errors would be made.

6.5.2 The Electoral Register and National Insurance Numbers

The UK already possesses a reliable list of children: the list of Child Benefit recipients, with each entitled child attached to a main carer who receives the money. It is a pity that higher-rate taxpayers living in households that receive Child Benefit now face additional Income Tax, because in order to avoid domestic disharmony—particularly where the children are not those of the higher-rate taxpayer—rather too many women are withdrawing their claims for Child Benefit. This is making the list rather inaccurate for high-earning households. If Child Benefit were to become a Child Citizen's Income, and if there were no longer to be an additional tax charge for higher-rate taxpayers in households in receipt of Child Citizen's Income, then it would not be too difficult to repair the list.

Every sixteen-year-old in the UK is automatically sent a National Insurance Number. A list of recipients of Citizen's Incomes could easily be constructed from the list of National Insurance numbers and the personal and contact details attached to it. Any omissions would be relatively easy to remedy. A small number of young adults, who have dropped out of school, moved house, never been employed, and for some reason are cared for by their parents or other relatives, might never have received a National Insurance Number. The new fact of a National Insurance Number being the gateway to receipt of a Citizen's Income would mean that most of those without National Insurance numbers would soon obtain them.

An intriguing possibility is for the electoral register to be the list of Citizen's Income recipients. Now that individual registration has replaced household registration the list will be more accurate, and if it were to be used for the payment of Citizen's Income, then it would quickly become a lot more complete and a lot more people would vote in elections. Parliament could decide, if it wished, to allow the electoral register to be cross-checked with the list of National Insurance numbers. The British are not keen on identity cards, as the previous Labour administration discovered; but the checking of one existing list against another for the purpose of ensuring an accurate list for the payment of Citizen's Incomes would not be a problem, and might be widely welcomed.

6.5.3 Payment Mechanisms in the UK

We have already noted that in the UK, 98% of households already have bank accounts into which their Citizen's Incomes could be paid,[26] and that 2% of households use Post Office Card accounts, which are designed purely for the receipt of benefits. Some of those households will be the same ones (because some mothers prefer to receive their Child Benefit through Post Office Card accounts, rather than have it go into a household joint bank account), so there will still be some households that have neither a bank account nor a Post Office Card account, and there might be quite a lot of couples with only one bank account. Citizen's Incomes are payable to individuals, not to the household, so every individual should have the option of receiving their Citizen's Income payments into a bank account for which they are the only account holder. Some couples will want their Citizen's Incomes to be paid into a single joint account, and that too should be an option, but each individual should have to make their own choice rather than a single household choice being made. Where a couple has only one account, it would be no problem for one of the partners to start a new bank account or a new Post Office Card account, and the Indian experience shows that obtaining almost 100% coverage of bank accounts is perfectly possible. If a tiny handful of people still fall through the net—probably mainly people without homes and with a variety of other problems—enabling someone to receive their Citizen's Income on their behalf would not be difficult to organize.

But how often should benefits be paid? This is currently a live debate in the UK because until now out-of-work means-tested benefits have been paid fortnightly, means-tested in-work benefits have been paid once every four weeks, and various other benefits have been paid fortnightly or once every four weeks, whereas the new Universal Credit will be paid monthly. (This is because employment income is normally paid monthly, because the monthly benefit payment for people not in work is designed to get their households used to monthly budgeting, and because for the purposes of Universal Credit employers report earnings to Her Majesty's Revenue and Customs (HMRC) monthly, HMRC reports monthly to the Department for Work and Pensions (DWP), and the DWP then pays the household's Universal Credit.)

With a Citizen's Income an interesting possibility presents itself. Existing National Insurance benefits (social insurance benefits designed to cover particular contingencies, mainly for limited periods) and means-tested benefits have default payment periods attached to them because they are already quite complicated and giving claimants discretion over payment periods would complicate them even further. Because everyone's Citizen's Income would be a fixed amount, everyone would be able to choose their own payment period. Even daily payments would be possible, which could be useful for people living with addictions.

In the UK, people without permanent homes can receive benefits through a Post Office Card Account. The same mechanism could apply to their Citizen's Incomes.

While there might be minor problems to solve on the way to implementing a Citizen's Income in the UK, they would be minor problems, and they would not compromise Citizen's Income's feasibility.

6.5.4 Continuing Means-Tested Benefits

Scheme B in Chaps. 3 and 4 envisages the continuation of means-tested benefits, albeit at lower levels because every household's Citizen's Incomes will be taken into account when their means-tested benefits were calculated. There would be no need to change any of the administrative structure. However, an interesting opportunity presents itself. Housing Benefit is administered locally, although regulated nationally, whereas Council Tax Support is both administered and regulated locally. None of this is problem-free, particularly because central government now has no control over total marginal deduction rates,[27] but there are also good reasons for devolving some means-tested benefits to local level. Housing costs vary across the country, rental markets are different in every place, the local Council Tax behaves somewhat differently in every place, and Local Authorities are already involved in services for people with disabilities, so to give to Local Authorities control over disability benefits of all kinds would enable financial and other services to be integrated. A fair central government funding formula would be required, but if this could be achieved, then to localize means-tested benefits as a separate exercise after the establishment of Citizen's Income might be a useful thing to do.

6.5.5 Participation Income: How Many Individuals in England and Wales Would Not Receive It?

(The geographical area under consideration for the case studies above is the UK. Here it is England and Wales because that is the geographical area covered by the census data published by the Office for National Statistics.)

A 'Participation Income' would be paid to any adult 'participating' in society. The list of 'participations' would include employment or self-employment, retirement, absence from work because of sickness or injury, inability to work because of disability, and approved forms of voluntary activity. Students, trainees, those caring for dependents (the young, the elderly, or disabled dependents), and those unemployed but available for work would also be counted as 'participating'.[28]

If we ask: How do we decide whether a particular individual is 'participating' in society, then we need to ask whether they fit into any of these 'participation' categories.

The list raises a few questions: Would an actor receive their Citizen's Income while they were between shows? How much voluntary activity would someone need to be doing for it to count as participation in society? Do we count as 'participants' people who have chosen early retirement? Would someone who chose to give up their employment in order to look after an ageing parent be counted as 'participating' in society? (Would someone need to decide whether the parent needed looking after?) Would a few months spent working without pay in a theatre, in order to gain experience, be counted as qualifying voluntary activity?

Some statistics might be of interest[29]:

In 2011, there were 41,126,540 usual residents in England and Wales between the ages of 16 and 74. Of these, 28,659,869 were economically active, and so would have counted as participating in society.

'Economically inactive' means those without a job, who have not sought work in the last four weeks, and who would not be available to start work during the next two weeks. Table 6.1 shows the number of individuals in each of a number of categories of economic inactivity in England and Wales in 2011.

We shall study each category in turn:

Retired The 'retired' category will include some people who have chosen to retire earlier than the state pension age. Those who retire at the state pension age are counted as participating in society, presumably in recognition of the contribution that they have already made. The same logic would presumably apply to those who retire earlier than the state pension age, although it would of course be possible for the government to determine an arbitrary age below which retirement would preclude someone from receiving a Participation Income if they were not otherwise participating in society.

Table 6.1 2011 census figures for England and Wales for the economically inactive, between the ages of 16 and 74

Retired	5,682,192
Student	2,389,711
Looking after home/family	1,781,530
Permanently sick/disabled	1,714,894
Other	898,344
Total	12,466,671

Source: Table KS601EW, 2011 census data, http://www.ons.gov.uk/ons/rel/census/2011-census/key-statistics-for-local-authorities-in-england-and-wales/rft-table-ks601ew.xls

Students Many part-time students will be employed and so will count as economically active and so as 'participating'. Do we count all economically inactive students as participating in society? Is someone going to decide which courses count as 'participation' and which ones do not? Given that the government supports universities and colleges financially, and encourages the taking of degree and other courses, it would be difficult to argue that people taking those courses were not participating in society.

Looking after home/family In 2010, there were 7.66 million families with dependent children in the UK. If both parents decide to stay at home to care for a large family, then are they both 'participating' in society, or is only one of them doing so? The government counts a child as 'dependent' if it is aged zero to fifteen years, or if it is aged sixteen to eighteen years and is still in full-time education.[30] If a child leaves school at 16 and its parents decide that one of them should remain available to support them as they seek employment and cope with young adulthood, then is that parent 'participating' in society? If someone has a particularly demanding job that involves their home, and their spouse chooses not to be employed outside the home but instead to contribute to the home environment and to the social and other task-related activities that happen in it, then are they participating in society? Many clergy spouses would be in this position, as would the spouses of some public figures.

Permanently sick/disabled In 2006, 71% of people registered disabled were out of work. If someone disabled could work, but chose not to do so, then should we count them as participating in society? And who is going to decide such questions in individual cases?[31] Recent DWP attempts to define robust categories for people sick or disabled, and to determine who belongs in which category, have not met with the kind of public approval that would be required if similar processes were to be used to decide which sick or disabled people should receive a Participation Income without actively participating in society in some other way.

Volunteers Voluntary activity would count as participation in society, as it should. How many hours of volunteering would we believe to be sufficient to qualify for a Participation Income? If any quota of hours were to be agreed, then the Participation Income would become payment for that number of hours of work. Would this reward for voluntary work destroy the very nature of voluntary activity? Would people seek just enough voluntary activity to qualify for a Citizen's Income? And would voluntary organizations adapt to provide the necessary minimum volunteering package required for receipt of a Participation Income?

During 2012–13, 22.7 million people in the UK formally volunteered at least once a year, and 15.1 million volunteered once a month.[32] This suggests that there were 13.4 million monthly volunteers in England and Wales.[33] If we assume that the proportion of monthly volunteers is the same in the 'other economically inactive' category as in the population as a whole (a conservative assumption, as many in the 'other' category will be the non-earning spouses of employed or self-employed individuals, and many of these will be active volunteers), then the number of individuals in the 'other economically inactive' category who are not monthly volunteers will be 682,741, which is 1.2% of the population of England and Wales.[34]

We have seen that working out who should not receive a Participation Income would require a complex set of rules to be used by caseworkers as they decided which economically inactive individuals could be fitted into the 'participation' categories. If we assume that retired people and students were automatically participating, then that would leave four million people to whom caseworkers would need to apply the rules. The idea of employing the notion of 'participation' to determine who should receive an otherwise unconditional income might be appealing politically, but its administration would quickly get bogged down in a morass of regulations, changes of circumstances, and appeals against caseworkers' decisions. If someone leaves university, then after a break of three weeks works for a month carrying pizzas in order to earn some money, and then travels around South America for several months, and for one of those months volunteers with an Argentinian charity, and then returns to the UK, volunteers with a charity for a fortnight, and then finds a temporary job, before going to the Reading Festival, for half of which they are employed serving burgers: I do not envy the civil servant having to sort out for which of those weeks they would receive their Participation Income.

Our somewhat rough and ready calculation suggests that massive administrative effort would be required to exclude about 1.2% of the adult population between sixteen and seventy-four years old from receipt of Participation Income. Those over 74 and all children would receive the Participation Income automatically, so we would be looking at less than 1% of the population of England and Wales being excluded from receipt.

A Participation Income's administration would become such a nightmare, and so few people would not be getting it, that either Participation Income would quickly become a Citizen's Income or people would be so put off by the whole idea that the plan would be simply abandoned.

In his most recent book, Tony Atkinson has reiterated his commitment to Participation Income, but then the accompanying microsimulation appears not to take into account any participation conditions, meaning that what has been modelled is a Citizen's Income.[35] The fact that the microsimulation program cannot cope with participation conditions suggests that civil servants would not be able to cope with them either.

6.6 Conclusion

Tax Credits, Negative Income Tax, and Citizen's Income all generate the same net income diagram, so all three schemes would reduce marginal deduction rates (the total rate of withdrawal of additional income), would incentivize employment, and would enable families more easily to earn their way out of poverty. The differences between the schemes are administrative, and it is not difficult to see that Citizen's Income is the simplest to administer, and that it avoids all of the problems relating to the administration of Negative Income Tax and Tax Credits. Citizen's Income also offers greater flexibility of payment period, because a Citizen's Income could easily have individualized payment periods (anything from daily to monthly, or even annually if required), whereas Tax Credits would be likely to be restricted to monthly payments and Negative Income Tax to monthly or annual payments[36] (as is the USA's Earned Income Tax Credit—in fact an annual Negative Income Tax, which functions rather like the Alaskan Permanent Fund Dividend).[37]

We have explored the difficulties related to the administration of a Participation Income. A Citizen's Income would avoid all of those difficulties, too. Any challenges that the administration of Citizen's Income might experience would also apply to Tax Credits, Negative Income Tax, and Participation Income. For a Citizen's Income, the challenges are real, but they are by no means insuperable, as we have seen. The conclusion to draw is that Citizen's Income is administratively feasible, but that Negative Income Tax, Tax Credits, and Participation Income might not be.

In relation to the UK, an examination of the three schemes studied in Chaps. 3 and 4 reveals an interesting administrative fact about scheme B. Because all existing benefits are left in place, this scheme could be implemented both easily and quickly. All that would be required would be for the Citizen's Incomes to be paid, Income Tax Personal Allowances and the National Insurance Contributions Lower Earnings Limit to be reduced to zero, Income Tax rates to be adjusted, National Insurance Contributions to be collected at 12% on all earned income, and means-tested benefits to be recalculated—which would be easy to do as every household's Citizen's Incomes would be of entirely predictable amounts. If ever a UK government were to be looking for a Citizen's Income scheme that could be implemented almost overnight, then scheme B would be an obvious candidate.

While it might be true that a Citizen's Income of £50 per week for working-age adults would not be the subsistence-level Citizen's Income that many advocates would like to see, the fact that scheme B would be so easy to implement means that it has a major advantage over more generous schemes.[38] To implement a small Citizen's Income that would not abolish means-tested benefits, but that could then grow, might well be a 'low road' to Citizen's Income rather than a 'high road',[39] but at least it would be preferable to asking for a larger Citizen's Income that might never be implemented.

A final suggestion from Herbert Gans[40]: that if a Citizen's Income is to be implemented, then we should call it a Negative Income Tax, because that name might be the more acceptable of the two. The argument against doing this is that Negative Income Tax and Citizen's Income are administratively very different. The argument for doing it is that they would have the same effects on net disposable incomes, and so in the most important respect they are in fact identical. I would hesitate to contribute to the long history of the misnaming benefits, but I can see that the ploy might be psychologically helpful.

Notes

1. Jürgen De Wispelaere and José Antonio Noguera (2012) 'On the Political Feasibility of Universal Basic Income: An Analytic Framework', pp. 17–38 in Richard Caputo (ed.) *Basic Income Guarantee: International Experiences and Perspectives on the Viability of Income Guarantee* (New York: Palgrave Macmillan), pp. 24–7.
2. Jürgen De Wispelaere and Lindsay Stirton (2011) 'The Administrative Efficiency of Basic Income', *Policy and Politics*, 39 (1), 115–32, pp. 126, 128.
3. www.gov.uk/check-british-citizen; www.gov.uk/long-residence/eligibility; www.gov.uk/claim-asylum; http://www.uscis.gov/us-citizenship; www.uscis.gov/tools/glossary/lawful-permanent-resident-lpr; www.expatica.com/de/visas-and-permits/A-guide-to-German-citizenship-and-permanent-visas_108795.html
4. The Electoral Commission (2014) *The quality of the 2014 electoral registers in Great Britain: Research into the last registers produced under the household registration system* (London: The Electoral Commission). The UK has now changed to an individual registration system, which might produce a more accurate register, but perhaps also a less complete one. See also Bill Jordan (1989) *The Common Good: Citizenship, morality and self-interest* (Oxford: Basil Blackwell), p. 124.
5. Jürgen De Wispelaere and José Antonio Noguera (2012) 'On the Political Feasibility of Universal Basic Income', p. 26.
6. Jürgen De Wispelaere and José Antonio Noguera (2012) 'On the Political Feasibility of Universal Basic Income', p. 26.
7. Sarath Davala, Renana Jhabvala, Soumya Kapoor Mehta and Guy Standing (2014) *Basic Income: A Transformative Policy for India* (London: Bloomsbury), p. 38. The research team achieved bank accounts in 98% of households.
8. Department for Work and Pensions (2014) *Family Resources Survey, 2012–13* (London: Department for Work and Pensions), https://www.gov.uk/government/collections/family-resources-surveyDOUBLEHYPHEN2
9. http://news.bbc.co.uk/1/hi/8194241.stm
10. Jürgen De Wispelaere and Lindsay Stirton (2012) 'A Disarmingly Simple Idea? Practical Bottlenecks in Implementing a Universal Basic Income', *International Social Security Review*, 65 (2), 103–21, p. 105.
11. Sarath Davala, Renana Jhabvala, Soumya Kapoor Mehta and Guy Standing (2014) *Basic Income: A Transformative Policy for India*, pp. 32, 91.
12. Hamid Tabatabai (2012) 'Iran: A Bumpy Road toward Basic Income', pp. 285–300 in Richard Caputo (ed.) *Basic Income Guarantee and Politics: International Experiences and perspectives on the viability of Income Guarantee* (New York: Palgrave Macmillan), p. 290.

13. Karl Widerquist and Michael Howard (2012) *Alaska's Permanent Fund Dividend: Examining its suitability as a model* (New York: Palgrave Macmillan).
14. www.tax.ny.gov/bus/stock/stktridx.htm; www.gov.uk/tax-buy-shares
15. Tony Atkinson, 'Participation Income' (1993) *Citizen's Income Bulletin*, no 16, pp. 7–11; A.B. Atkinson (1996) 'The Case for a Participation Income', *The Political Quarterly*, 67 (1), pp. 67–70.
16. Tony Fitzpatrick (1999) *Freedom and Security: An introduction to the Basic Income debate* (Basingstoke: Macmillan), pp. 101, 111–22; cf. Stuart White (2003) *The Civic Minimum: On the rights and obligations of economic citizenship* (Oxford: Oxford University Press), pp. 170–75.
17. Michael Lipsky (1980) *Street-level bureaucracy: dilemmas of the individual in public services* (New York: Russell Sage Foundation).
18. Jurgen De Wispelaere and Lindsay Stirton (2008) 'Why Participation Income Might Not Be Such a Great Idea After All', *Citizen's Income Newsletter*, issue 3 for 2008, pp. 3–8; cf. Jürgen De Wispelaere and José Antonio Noguera, 'On the Political Feasibility of Universal Basic Income', pp. 25–6.
19. Hermione Parker (1994) 'Citizen's Income', *Citizen's Income Bulletin*, no 17, 4–12, p. 9.
20. Rie Takamatsu and Toshiaki Tachibanaki (2014) 'What Needs to be Considered when Introducing a New Welfare System: Who supports Basic Income in Japan?' pp. 197–218 in Yannick Vanderborght and Toru Yamamori (eds) *Basic Income in Japan: Prospects for a radical idea in a transforming welfare state* (New York: Palgrave Macmillan), p. 205.
21. Malcolm Torry (2013) *Money for Everyone: Why we need a Citizen's Income* (Bristol: Policy Press), pp. 29–32.
22. Randall Bartlett, James Davies, and Michael Hoy (2005) 'Can a Negative Income Tax System for the United Kingdom be Both Equitable and Affordable?' pp. 293–315 in Karl Widerquist, Michael Anthony Lewis and Steven Pressman (eds.) *The Ethics and Economics of the Basic Income Guarantee* (Aldershot: Ashgate).
23. Rie Takamatsu and Toshiaki Tachibanaki, 'What Needs to be Considered when Introducing a New Welfare System: Who supports Basic Income in Japan?', p. 201.
24. www.commonwealthfund.org/publications/fund-reports/2014/jun/mirror-mirror
25. www.gov.uk/child-benefit-move-to-uk
26. Department for Work and Pensions (2014) *Family Resources Survey, 2012–13* (London: Department for Work and Pensions), https://www.gov.uk/government/collections/family-resources-surveyDOUBLEHYPHEN2
27. Geoff Fimister and Michael Hill (1993) 'Delegating Implementation Problems: Social security, housing and community care in Britain',

pp. 110–29 in Michael Hill (ed.), *New Agendas in the Study of the Policy Process* (New York and London: Harvester Wheatsheaf), pp. 114, 128.
28. A.B. Atkinson (1996) 'The Case for a Participation Income', *The Political Quarterly*, 67 (1), 67–70, p. 69.
29. 2011 census data, table no. KS601EW.
30. www.statistics.gov.uk/hub/population/families/families-children-and-young-people
31. A total of 2,546,000 people with disabilities were out of work: Richard Berthoud (2006) *The Employment Rates of Disabled People*, Department for Work and Pensions Research report no. 298 (London: Department for Work and Pensions).
32. www.ncvo.org.uk/about-us/media-centre/briefings/431-uk-charity-sector-briefing
33. The estimated populations of the four constituent countries of the UK in mid-2012 were 53.5 million people in England, 5.3 million in Scotland, 3.1 million in Wales, and 1.8 million in Northern Ireland. So if there were 15.1 million monthly volunteers in the UK, we can assume (15.1 × (53.5 + 3.1))/63.7 = 13.4 million in England and Wales. www.ons.gov.uk/ons/rel/pop-estimate/population-estimates-for-ukDOUBLE-HYPHENengland-and-walesDOUBLEHYPHENscotland-and-northern-ireland/mid-2011-and-mid-2012/index.html
34. A total of 13.4 million monthly volunteers is 13.4/56.6 = 24% of the population of England and Wales. Let us conservatively assume the same proportion of the 'other' category, so 76% of 898,344 are economically inactive and not volunteers = 0.76 × 898,344 = 682,741. This is 682,741/56.6 m = 1.2% of the population of England and Wales.
35. Anthony B. Atkinson (2015) *Inequality*, Harvard University Press, Cambridge, Massachusetts, 2015, p. 295.
36. Pertti Honkanen (2014) 'Basic Income and Negative Income Tax: A comparison with a simulation model', *Basic Income Studies*, 9 (1–2), 119–35.
37. For a discussion of the differences between Negative Income Tax and Citizen's Income in a US context, see Troy Camplin (2013) 'BIG and the Negative Income Tax', pp. 97–122 in Guinevere Liberty Nell (ed.), *Basic Income and the Free Market: Austrian Economics and the Potential for Efficient Redistribution* (New York: Palgrave Macmillan).
38. Jason Burke Murphy (2010) 'Baby Steps: Basic Income and the need for incremental organizational development', *Basic Income Studies*, 5 (2), 1–13.
39. Bill Jordan (2012) 'The Low Road to Basic Income? Tax-Benefit Integration in the UK', *Journal of Social Policy*, 41 (1), 1–17.
40. Herbert J. Gans (2014) 'Basic Income: A remedy for a sick labor market?' *Challenge*, 57 (2), 80–90.

CHAPTER 7

Is a Citizen's Income Behaviourally Feasible?

7.1 Introduction

All that is required for this test to be passed is for households' situations to improve after implementation. As De Wispelaere and Noguera put it:

> For a [Citizen's Income] to be behaviourally feasible, it must neither produce perverse or counterproductive effects, nor fail to produce key desired outcomes.[1]

We can theorize the useful effects of the secure financial floor that a Citizen's Income would create, the loss of bureaucratic intrusion in connection with intimate relationships and household activity, the greater ability to turn increased earned income into increased disposable income, an increasing range of options in the employment market, a reduction in administrative complexity, and the advantages of increased social cohesion. Because workers' Citizen's Incomes would continue in a seamless fashion through any changes in employment market status, workers would have an increased ability to leave one job and look for another.[2] This suggests that wages in 'bad jobs' would rise and wages in 'good jobs' might fall, so employers would have an incentive to improve working conditions, training provision, and career progression, and employees would experience better jobs.[3] The fact that there are some problems that a Citizen's Income would not solve is beside the point.

A problem related to behavioural feasibility is that the test can only be passed or failed after the implementation of a Citizen's Income scheme. This will of course have implications for the way in which a Citizen's Income is implemented. The uncertainty related to the consequences of a Citizen's Income scheme for individuals, households, society, and the economy will mean that governments will be hesitant to implement the proposal. This suggests that an evolutionary implementation method could be helpful—provided that at every stage it is a Citizen's Income that is being implemented.

But that still leaves us with a problem. How can we say anything at all about behavioural feasibility before a Citizen's Income scheme has been implemented? In practical terms: How am I going to write this chapter?

A subsidiary problem is this: It will not be just the Citizen's Incomes being paid that will cause behavioural change. A Citizen's Income will never come alone. It will always come along with a funding mechanism: with changes to the existing tax and benefits systems, with new taxes, or with a variety of other funding methods; and these changes too will cause behavioural change in such a way that it will often be difficult to differentiate between behavioural change caused by Citizen's Income and behavioural change caused by the other changes that will accompany its implementation.

Some of the consequential behavioural changes might be a bit of a surprise. In a revenue neutral scheme, individuals' and households' income tax payments will rise. This will not normally affect disposable income because the household will already be receiving a Citizen's Income for each member. However, there would be other effects, and a particularly interesting one could be an increase in the frequency with which people vote in elections. Increasing personal tax allowances, which is what is happening now in the UK and some other countries, has the opposite effect. If we want an engaged democracy, then we need to decrease personal tax allowances and increase income tax payments. A revenue neutral Citizen's Income scheme would achieve this, and so would enhance democratic engagement without it costing anyone anything.[4]

A further problem is that any change in tax and benefits systems can cause two different kinds of behavioural change: forced change, and new possibilities for behaviour that might or might not be chosen. Let us suppose that a government decides to ban restrictive zero-hour contracts and to allow only non-restrictive ones: that is, zero-hour contracts that permit the employee to work for more than one employer, and without penalty to refuse shifts offered at short notice. Employers would find behavioural change forced upon them. They would no longer be able to dismiss employees who worked for a second employer, or for refusing a shift offered at less than say a fortnight's notice. The employee would have no change forced upon them, but they would be able to take advantage of some new freedoms: to work for a second employer, and to commit themselves to educational, leisure, and social activities without the anxiety that their employer might demand their presence at short notice. The implementation of a Citizen's Income would also result in both kinds of behavioural change. Everyone would automatically receive into their bank account a regular weekly or monthly income. This would simply happen, and it would have consequences: mostly good ones. But in the case of Citizen's Income, most of the behavioural change would be of the kind that might or might not be chosen. If a household were to find itself still on small amounts of means-tested benefits, then it might decide to cease to claim them and to run a market stall on Saturdays in order to fill the income gap. The option to abandon means-tested benefits would not have been available to them in the same way before implementation of the Citizen's Income, but now it would be. Or perhaps a single young artist would see if they could live on their Citizen's Income and on sales of their work rather than being employed. In one case, earned income would go up, and in the other it could go either way. The important point is that in both cases there would be new choices to be made. Net income and the ways in which time can be used are both significant factors when someone is evaluating their welfare, and both will need to be taken into account when tax and benefits changes are being evaluated.[5]

What is not required is that we should be able to show that any particular household, or households generally, would be better off financially at the point of implementation. Some might be, and some might not be. What will matter is the new range of choices that they might experience: and one of those new choices might be to earn additional income in order to increase their disposable income. Previous to the implementation of Citizen's Income, an increase in disposable income might have been difficult to achieve because the withdrawal of benefits and the payment of income tax might have made it difficult for a household to turn increased earned income into increased disposable income. For a Citizen's Income to replace all or most of means-testing benefits would change that, and would therefore provide the household with a new choice to make, whether to remain at their present earned income, or to raise their disposable income by seeking new or additional earned income.

In addition to new choices being available in relation to net income and use of time, the implementation of Citizen's Income would also enable new choices to be made about relationships. A father might have decided not to live with the mother of his child because this would have lost the mother her means-tested in-work or out-of-work benefits. Citizen's Incomes would replace a proportion of those means-tested benefits, and living together in the same flat might now be financially advantageous. Such factors can tip relationship decisions one way or the other, and for many families the replacement of means-tested benefits wholly or partially by Citizen's Income would offer a whole new set of choices around the kinds of relationship that might be possible, and the employment patterns that might be viable. A group of people who might benefit substantially from such new choices being available would be children currently living with one parent who might find themselves living with two. A further clear benefit of new advantages for couples living together would be a more efficient employment of a constrained housing stock.

While it might be possible to predict some of the consequences of the changes that will simply happen when a Citizen's Income is implemented, we have seen that the most significant changes for individuals, households, societies, and economies are likely to be those that would result from individuals and households experiencing new sets of choices in relation to family structure and employment pattern. How people will react to the new choices available to them might be difficult to predict. To take the example of labour market activity: If large numbers of people decided not to be gainfully employed, but instead to spend their time surfing,[6] then this might discredit Citizen's Income in the eyes of the public, and the policy would not be behaviourally feasible. Before implementation, we can model the labour market effects, and find that traditional models of labour market behaviour find that labour market participation would increase if means-tested benefits were to be replaced by a Citizen's Income,[7] but we cannot know what choices people would make in practice, so we cannot know for certain whether Citizen's Income would be behaviourally feasible.

7.2 Evidence for Behavioural Feasibility

One possible approach to this dilemma is to seek evidence of what the new sets of choices might be and of how people might react to them. We will not be able to draw any firm conclusions because evidence will have to be gleaned from natural and staged experiments in contexts different from those in which a Citizen's Income scheme would be likely to be implemented, but it will be the best that we can do. It is therefore for such evidence that this chapter will seek, and we shall then draw what tentative conclusions we can.

So far I have only discussed behavioural feasibility in relation to individuals and households. Just as important will be behavioural feasibility in relation to private sector firms, voluntary organizations, and the public sector. These too will experience the consequences of the implementation of Citizen's Income. If Citizen's Income is to be behaviourally feasible, then the consequences for institutions will need to be as good as they will be for individuals and households.

If we can show evidence that a Citizen's Income would be likely to change behaviour in beneficial ways, and that it would offer new sets of choices that households and society's institutions would experience as beneficial, then we shall be able to say that Citizen's Income is probably behaviourally feasible—while at the same time recognizing that only the passage of time would show whether Citizen's Income really was in fact behaviourally feasible in the contexts in which it had been implemented.

7.2.1   *Empirical Evidence from Constructed Experiments*

Empirical evidence[8] for the effects that a Citizen's Income might generate is provided by large pilot projects in Namibia[9] and India,[10] which have revealed the sizeable positive employment market, income, educational, health, and democratic effects of small Citizen's Incomes. In the two large villages of the Namibian pilot project, mean earned income increased by 29% (in addition to the small Citizen's Income), and self-employment income grew by 301%.[11] The extent to which these significant positive effects would be replicated in developed economies is difficult to predict, but we can legitimately conclude that the effects would be positive rather than negative.

A Negative Income Tax (NIT) is not a Citizen's Income,[12] but because the disposable income effects of a NIT and a Citizen's Income are similar, results from NIT experiments can tell us how a Citizen's Income might affect employment market behaviour. NIT experiments in the USA during the 1970s found very little labour market effect. Most of the small employment reduction effect was people between employments taking longer to look for their next job, which suggests that they were looking for the right job rather than just any job; and some of it was women with children working fewer hours each week, which might also be a good thing. We can therefore assume that any employment market effects of a Citizen's Income would be small, and that those that did occur could be beneficial.[13] On the basis of a similar Canadian experiment, we can assume that there would be measurable positive effects on health and on educational achievement.[14] The US and Canadian experiments took place in OECD countries, and the Namibian and Indian projects in developing countries, so it is reasonable to assume that the effects produced by Citizen's Income are related to the characteristics of Citizen's Income and not only to the social and economic contexts of the countries in which the experiments have taken place.

7.2.2 Natural Experiments

Sometimes a country makes a change to its tax and benefits system that enables information to be gathered about the different effects of different systems without anyone having to set up an experiment. Research on New Zealand's replacement of an unconditional family benefit with a means-tested one shows that the change entrenched more families in poverty.[15] This suggests that to switch from a means-tested to an unconditional benefit would release families from entrenched poverty.

In the USA, a rule that withdrew pension benefits from retired people who continued to earn an income was abolished, and research shows that the probability of being gainfully employed went up.[16] Similarly, when Canada reduced the marginal deduction rates experienced by higher earners, and particularly for women who were employed part-time, part-time employment rose by 10% among higher earning women, and did not rise at all among lower earning women.[17] These results suggest that if marginal deduction rates are lowered, then labour market activity increases, and therefore that if a Citizen's Income were to replace or partially replace means-tested benefits, then we would see an increase in labour market activity.

7.2.3 A Global Natural Experiment: Welfare State Regimes[18]

In his *The Three Worlds of Welfare Capitalism*,[19] Gøsta Esping-Andersen scores welfare states for corporatism (the number of large occupationally distinct public pension schemes), étatism (expenditure on pensions for government employees), means-tested poor relief, private pensions (as a proportion of total pensions), private health spending (as a proportion of total healthcare spending), universalism (social security benefits available to every citizen, excluding income-tested schemes), and average benefit equality (the ratio of the legal maximum benefits to the guaranteed minimum income). By combining these scores, each country is then scored for conservatism (corporatism), socialism (i.e., universalism and equality), and liberalism (private provision, with a residual, means-tested welfare state). Esping-Andersen discovers some clear clusters of countries, as we can see in Table 7.1.

The countries listed in the right-hand column are those that score 'strongly' for each of the welfare regime types. The same countries will also score 'medium' or 'low' for the other welfare regime types. Some countries do not score strongly for any particular type: the UK, for example, scores 'low' for conservatism (corporatism), and 'medium' for both liberalism and socialism. This is no surprise. The NHS is 'social democratic/socialist' in character, and a significantly means-tested benefits system is 'liberal'.

Do the welfare regime types correlate with income inequality? The first column in Table 7.2 shows the ratio of the average net income of those in the highest income decile to the average net income of those in the lowest income decile, and the other three columns identify the welfare regime types for which the countries score strongly.

Because Esping-Andersen's figures were published in 1990 and were often drawn from the mid-1980s sources, and the income ratio figures

Table 7.1 Welfare state regimes and their characteristics

Type of welfare regime	Character	Represented by
Social democratic regime/'socialism'	The state is committed to full employment, generous universalist welfare benefits, income redistribution, &c	Denmark, Finland, the Netherlands, Norway, and Sweden
Conservative/corporatist regimes	Occupationally segregated benefits	Germany, France, Austria, Belgium, and Italy
Liberal welfare regimes	Private provision, selective provision, and a residual safety net for the poor	Australia, Canada, Japan, Switzerland, and the USA

Source: This table was constructed by the author from the text of Gøsta Esping-Andersen (1990) *The Three Worlds of Welfare Capitalism* (Cambridge: Polity Press), pp. 26–29, 69–77

Table 7.2 Relationships between the ratio of the average net income of those in the highest income decile to the average net income of those in the lowest income decile and countries' welfare regime types

Country	Ratio	Socialist	Conservative	Liberal
Japan	4.5			X
Finland	5.6	X		
Norway	6.1	X		
Sweden	6.2	X		
Germany	6.9		X	
Austria	6.9		X	
Denmark	8.1	X		
Belgium	8.2		X	
Switzerland	9.0			X
France	9.1		X	
The Netherlands	9.2	X		
Canada	9.4			X
Italy	11.6		X	
Australia	12.5			X
USA	15.9			X

Sources: Income ratios from United Nations (2009) *Human Development Report, 2009* (New York: United Nations), p. 195, table M; regime type scores from Gøsta Esping-Andersen (1990) *The Three Worlds of Welfare Capitalism* (Cambridge: Polity Press), p. 74

are more recent, we need to treat any correlation that we discover with a degree of scepticism; but there is clearly a correlation between welfare regime type and income inequality. The outlier here is Japan, which combines a highly liberal welfare state with an income equality based on a fairly egalitarian original distribution of earned income rather than on any redistribution of initially unequally distributed incomes: a national characteristic at least partly explained by status attaching to someone's position within the company rather than to their earned income. For the other outliers, there are also rational explanations: The Netherlands scores strongly for socialism, but it also scores 'medium' for both liberalism and conservatism; Denmark scores strongly for socialism, but it also scores 'medium' for liberalism; Italy and France score strongly for conservatism, but they also have high 'medium' scores for liberalism; and Switzerland scores strongly for liberalism, but it also scores 'medium' for socialism.

Figure 7.1 represents the correlation that we have discovered.

We can conclude that there is a correlation between high income inequality and more liberal welfare regimes, mid-range income inequality

```
Low inequality      ↑    Socialist / universalistic welfare regimes

                         Conservative / corporatist welfare regimes

High inequality     ↓    Liberal welfare regimes
```

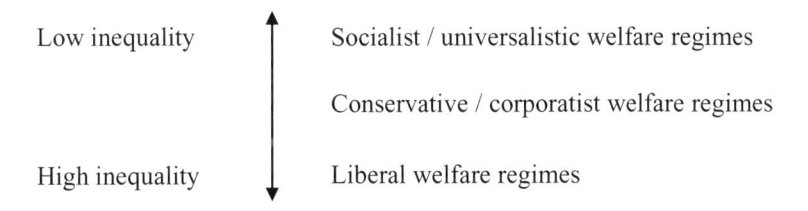

Fig. 7.1 The relationship between welfare state regime type and income inequality

and more conservative welfare regimes, and low income inequality and more socialist, or universalistic, welfare regimes.

The question now becomes one of the directions of causality. Does the income inequality cause the welfare state regime, or vice versa? Given that welfare regime types stem from deep historical roots,[20] unless we can prove otherwise we must assume that to some extent the deep structures of society generate both the welfare state regime and the level of income inequality, and that to some extent the welfare state regime generates the level of income inequality. Because of the differences in marginal deduction rates found in the different welfare state regime types, and therefore of households' ability to increase disposable income by increasing earned income, we can assume that a more liberal regime that means-tests benefits will experience more inequality than one based on social insurance, and much more than one based on universal benefits. The theory explains the results, and in the absence of an alternative theory we can conclude that society's deep historically determined social structures give rise to the kind of welfare state to be found in that society and to its level of income inequality, and also that the welfare state regime reinforces the level of income inequality.

We find confirmation of this conclusion in Geert Hofstede's categorization of national cultures: the result of research among IBM employees in sixty-six countries. Hofstede ranked countries along four spectra: from individuals' tendency to assertiveness to their tendency to more modest behaviour; from individualism to collectivism; from behaviour designed to avoid ambiguity and uncertainty to a more welcoming attitude to uncertainty and ambiguity; and from substantial differences in power between different people in society to lower differences in power, in relation to which each country is ascribed a Power Difference Index (PDI) constructed on the basis of answers to such questions as: How often is there a problem in expressing disagreement with managers?[21] For fifteen countries with developed economies, Hofstede found that the ratio of the average net income of the top net income decile to that of the bottom net income decile correlated closely with the PDI.[22] As Hofstede writes: 'We can take the data as proof that income inequality is larger in high PDI than in low PDI countries',[23] and that taxation exacerbates differences in inequality. 'In higher PDI countries the tax system, rather than reducing the greater income inequalities, in fact increases them.'[24] Of particular interest might be the fact that '43 percent of the variance in PDI can be predicted from the geographical latitude of the country's capital alone ... 51 percent can be predicted from a combination of latitude and population size'.[25] Is the UK's ambiguous position perhaps a result of its northern latitude and the Gulf Stream's creation of a warmer climate uncharacteristic of that latitude?

We therefore have additional support for the proposal that deep social structures are important factors affecting both a country's welfare state regime type and its level of income inequality, and that the welfare state regime type has a direct influence on income inequality. For the purpose of this chapter, we can conclude that to extend the use of universal benefits, and to reduce the amount of means-testing, would shift the welfare state regime type towards the social democratic end of the spectrum, and would therefore reduce income inequality.

Danson, McAlpine, Spicker, and Sullivan survey evidence related to welfare states of different kinds, and draw the following conclusions:

- Universalism is incredibly efficient—the selective element of pension entitlement is more than fifty times more inefficient than the universal element measured in terms of fraud and error alone and without even taking into account the cost of administration.
- In economic terms, universalism is clearly shown to deliver Merit Goods (things we all benefit from) and Public Goods (things that could not be delivered without collective provision) which selectivity simply cannot deliver.
- The economic impact of universalism is much greater than the economic impact of selectivity because of the multiplier profile of expenditure.
- Universalism also creates positive economic stability by mitigating the swings in the business cycle and creating much more economic independence among the population.

- On virtually every possible measure of social and economic success, all league tables are topped by societies with strong universal welfare states.[26]

This is evidence drawn from experience of existing universal benefits. Citizen's Income is a universal benefit. We can confidently expect the same effects to occur.

7.2.4 Combining the Evidence

We have discovered three kinds of evidence for the likely effects of replacing means-tested and other benefits wholly or partly with unconditional benefits: natural experiments, constructed experiments, and a global natural experiment. Constructed experiments suggest that implementing Citizen's Income would cause an increase in economic activity, a particularly significant increase in self-employment, and improved health and educational outcomes, and that the only labour market effects would be people spending longer looking for the next job, and working for fewer hours per week in employment when caring for young children. This last effect would be particularly beneficial for women, and because a Citizen's Income would provide an independent income for many women who do not at the moment have one, the enhanced choices available to women,[27] and a general redistribution of financial resources both generally and within the household, could well generate more understanding and approval of Citizen's Income among women than among men.[28] Natural experiments suggest that labour market activity would rise, and that entrenched poverty would be reduced. The global natural experiment that relates income inequality to welfare state regime type suggests that a shift from means-testing to unconditional benefits would reduce income inequality.

While it would be useful to have available data from additional natural and constructed experiments (for instance, on the relationship between saving and welfare regime type), this chapter already contains a substantial body of evidence for the likely effects of implementing Citizen's Income; so although, strictly speaking, we cannot test for behavioural feasibility before implementation, we can be sufficiently sure that behavioural feasibility would be forthcoming to enable us to approach implementation with confidence.

7.3 Changing Attitudes

An important question, though, is whether a shift towards more universal benefits would in practice result in greater public approval of them. However much other beneficial behavioural effects might follow the implementation of a Citizen's Income scheme, if implementation does not shift public opinion in the direction of universal benefits, there is little chance that the reform will last and little chance than implementation for one age cohort might lead to implementation for another.

Kumlin and Stadelmann-Steffen conclude that policy feedback effects can be significantly affected by a changing political context,[29] and Muuri finds a highly complex picture, in which attitudes to social security benefits can be most negative among people with experience of claiming them, and in which 'the groups who were the most critical were those who should be benefiting the most from the services and allowances of society'.[30] Given that most social security benefits are subject to bureaucratic testing of claimants, perhaps this attitude should not surprise us. However, there *is* evidence that the structure of a welfare state can affect the public's attitude towards it, and of particular interest is the evidence that welfare states characterized by universal benefits tend to have a higher approval rating than welfare states more characterized by contributory benefits, and that welfare states characterized by contributory benefits tend to have a higher approval rating than welfare states more characterized by means-tested benefits.[31]

The evidence that we have collected suggests that not only would the implementation of Citizen's Income generate the beneficial effects required for behavioural feasibility but that such implementation would also deliver the change in public opinion that would be required to embed the change and to prepare the ground for further implementation of universal benefits.

7.4 Case Study

7.4.1 Behavioural Change in the UK

In the UK, behavioural outcomes will, as always, be the result of a variety of factors, among which will be the structure of Income Tax and the extent to which such means-tested benefits as Housing Benefit will still be required. The behavioural outcomes that the UK government and public might wish to see, and the behavioural outcomes that people might wish for themselves, will be diverse. This is not a problem. Lower marginal deduction rates, the individual claimant unit, and simpler administration will offer more choices to individuals and to households, enabling citizens to determine their own behavioural feasibilities and then to ask whether their expectations have been met.

We might think that in order to demonstrate behavioural feasibility we would need to show that a Citizen's Income would work for households in the sense of providing them with an ideal income maintenance system, somehow defined. Such a demonstration would not be possible. Take the case of housing costs. In London, in particular, but also across much of the south-east and elsewhere, housing is becoming unaffordable for large sections of the population, forcing households to live in accommodation too small for their needs, at some distance from their workplaces, and often with too insecure a tenure. An unconditional benefit high enough to enable every household to pay for the accommodation that it needs at the same time as paying other living expenses would be unaffordable without politically unsustainable increases in Income Tax rates. For the time being, Housing Benefit, calculated in relation to both housing costs and ability to pay, will be required; and because it is households that live in houses and flats, Housing Benefit will need to continue to be paid on the basis of the household as the claimant unit, unlike Citizen's Incomes which would be paid equally to every individual of the same age.[32]

Similarly with Council Tax Support. The assistance given to those unable to pay Council Tax (a tax levied by local authorities) because their incomes are too low has now been localized, and although Council Tax is always based on the value of the household's accommodation, Council Tax Support is now differently calculated by every Local Authority. There is no reason in principle why a Citizen's Income could not be paid at a sufficiently high level to enable Council Tax Benefit to be abolished, but the fact that Council Tax is paid by households and not by individuals, and that Council Tax can be of very different amounts for different households, means that for the time being we must view Council Tax Support in the same way as Housing Benefit, as an unfortunate part of the current system which for the time being a Citizen's Income will be unable to do anything about.

However, the partial or complete replacement of other means-tested benefits with a Citizen's Income would make a considerable difference to many households, because it would provide them with new options in relation to employment patterns. Take, for example, a household in which the male adult has been unemployed for more than a year and the female adult is in low-paying employment. Currently, most of the value of the woman's earnings is deducted from the household's means-tested Jobseeker's Allowance; if the man finds a job then much of the value of the woman's earnings will be deducted from the household's Working Tax Credits; and if Universal Credit is implemented then the same will occur. If Jobseeker's Allowance and Tax Credits were to be replaced by a Citizen's Income then, whether her husband was in employment or not, the woman would be able to earn as much as she wished and the household's Citizen's Incomes would not change. The household would therefore be in a radically different position from the situation in which it finds itself now. If their Citizen's Incomes and the woman's earnings were not enough to live on, and Housing Benefit and Council Tax Support were still in payment, then both partners would have a substantial incentive to earn sufficient income to enable the household to escape from means-testing altogether, because with their Citizen's Incomes in payment, it would be easier to turn increased earned income into increased net income than it is now.

All of that can be confidently predicted simply on the basis of the current means-tested benefits regulations and the characteristics of a Citizen's Income. We can also predict that the household—any household—would appreciate the fact that there would be no errors, fraud, criminalization, or stigma attached to their Citizen's Incomes; that, whatever they did, the solid financial floor created by their Citizen's Incomes would never be taken away; that they would never receive letters telling them that they had received too much Citizen's Income and would therefore need to repay it; and that they would never have to fill in a long and complicated form in order to claim their Citizen's Incomes, or to provide evidence of anything other than identity, date of birth, contact details, and details of their bank accounts, which would mean most people not having to supply any information at all for years on end.

7.4.2 *The Greater Utility of Part-Time Employment in the Context of a Citizen's Income*[33]

7.4.2.1 *Utility Curves*[34]

Hours not spent in paid employment ('leisure') are useful to us (they have utility), and consumer goods, and thus earned income, also have utility.

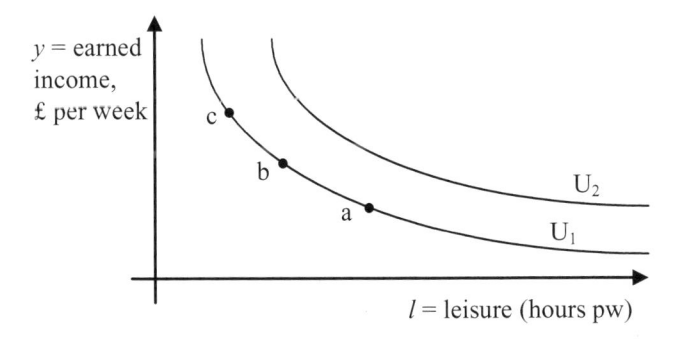

Fig. 7.2 Utility curves on which utility is equal for different combinations of leisure hours and earned income
Source: Malcolm Torry (2008) 'Research note: The utility—or otherwise—of being employed for a few hours a week', *Citizen's Income Newsletter*, issue 1 for 2008, pp. 14–16, p. 14

Each combination of leisure and earned income will yield utility, or satisfaction, which can be pictured as a series of curves, known as utility or indifference curves, as in Fig. 7.2.

If, at the three combinations of leisure and earned income at a, b, and c, we regard ourselves as having equal levels of utility, then we can draw the indifference curve U_1 along which our utility is constant. The curve at U_2 represents a similar series of points of equal utility, all at a higher level of utility than those on U_1.

For a given wage rate w, we can draw a line (a 'budget constraint'), as in Fig. 7.3, showing what our earned income will be for each hour worked, that is, for each hour subtracted from our leisure.

The combinations of earned income and leisure represented by points to the right of the budget line are unobtainable, so our utility will be maximized where a utility curve is at a tangent to the budget constraint (as this is the highest utility available to us under the circumstances), as in Fig. 7.4.

Now suppose that on all earnings up to the amount y_0 tax is charged at rate t, or that means-tested benefits are withdrawn, which has the same effect as taxation: then the wage rate net of tax will be $w(1-t)$ per hour for the first y_0/w hours of employment per week (i.e., between $(168-y_0/w)$ and 168 hours of leisure).

Figure 7.5 shows that the person whose utility was previously maximized at a high number of hours of employment (a low number of hours of

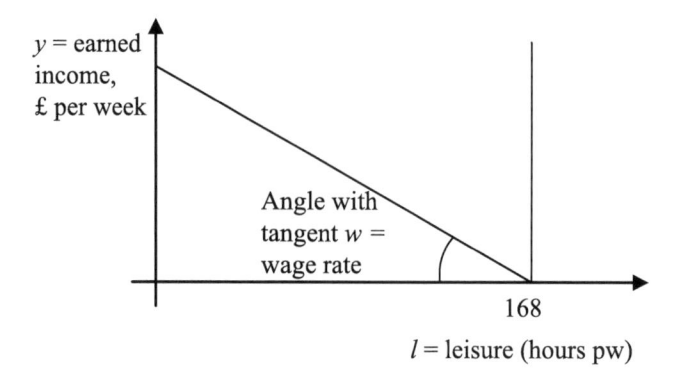

Fig. 7.3 The budget constraint that relates earned income to hours worked
Source: Malcolm Torry (2008) 'Research note: The utility—or otherwise—of being employed for a few hours a week', *Citizen's Income Newsletter*, issue 1 for 2008, pp. 14–16, p. 15

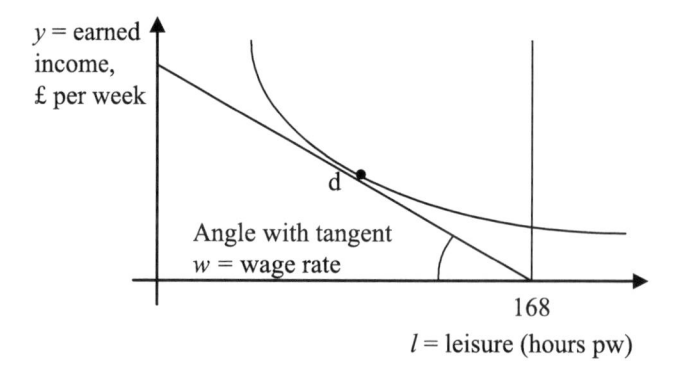

Fig. 7.4 The budget constraint when tangential to a utility curve identifies the maximum utility available
Source: Malcolm Torry (2008) 'Research note: The utility—or otherwise—of being employed for a few hours a week', *Citizen's Income Newsletter*, issue 1 for 2008, pp. 14–16, p. 15

leisure), now has utility maximized at a lower level and at a lower number of hours of employment (a high number of hours of leisure, and possibly at zero hours of employment) as well as at a higher number of hours. The

Key

y = earned income, £ per week

————— The budget constraint that relates earned income to hours worked

————— The budget constraint that relates net income (that is, income after tax has been deducted and benefits have been withdrawn) to hours worked

168-y_0/w   168

l = leisure (hours pw)

Fig. 7.5 Maximum utility obtainable when earned income is taxed or means-tested benefits are withdrawn
Source: Malcolm Torry (2008) 'Research note: The utility—or otherwise—of being employed for a few hours a week', *Citizen's Income Newsletter*, issue 1 for 2008, pp. 14–16, p. 15

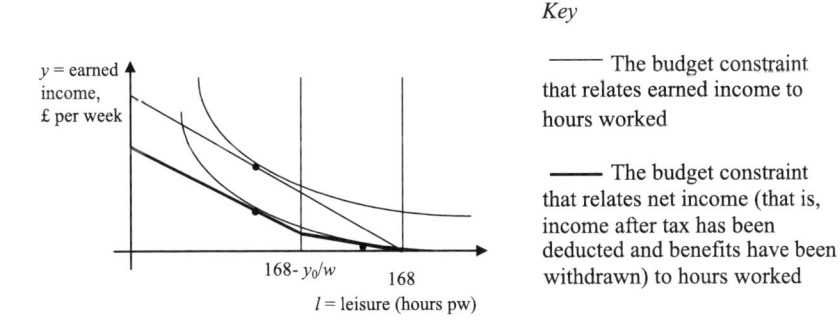

individual might in these circumstances be more likely to choose the lower number of hours of employment.

7.4.2.2 The Effects of the Existing Tax and Benefits System Compared to Those Generated by a Citizen's Income Scheme
In this exercise, we use utility curves to test both the current benefits system and a system based on a Citizen's Income for employment incentives. The Citizen's Income scheme to be tested is outlined in Table 7.3.[35]

Putting housing-related benefits to one side, in 2012–13, the net income of a single earner aged twenty-five or over after Income Tax, National Insurance contributions, Income Support/Jobseeker's Allowance, and Working Tax Credits was as shown by the line marked 'current' in Fig. 7.6. The line marked 'Citizen's Income' shows what net income would have been with a Citizen's Income as described in Table 7.3 replacing means-tested benefits.

The chart clearly reveals a poverty trap, particularly if the person is employed for only a few hours a week. Between zero and twelve hours per week earnings make almost no difference to net income.

The two lines on the graph in Fig. 7.6 represent the employee's budget constraint, and because the horizontal axis is hours worked rather than

Table 7.3 An illustrative Citizen's Income scheme: weekly rates for 2012–13

	Weekly rates for 2012–13	
Citizen's Pension	£145.40	Pension Credit rate
Working-age adult CI	£71.70	Current Income Support rate aged 25 plus
Young adult CI	£56.80	Current Income Support rate for 16–24-year-olds
Child CI	£56.80	Current Income Support rate for 16–24-year-olds

Source: Citizen's Income Trust (2013) *Citizen's Income: A brief introduction* (London: Citizen's Income Trust), p. 7

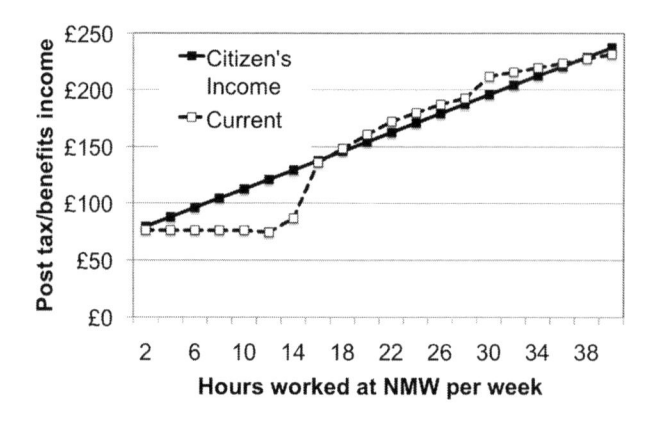

Fig. 7.6 Net income of a single earner aged 25 or over against hours worked at the National Minimum Wage per week, for the existing benefits system and for a Citizen's Income scheme described in Table 7.3
Source: Citizen's Income Trust (2013) *Citizen's Income: A brief introduction* (London: Citizen's Income Trust), p. 7

leisure hours, the budget constraint rises as hours worked increase, rather than falling as leisure hours increase, as in Fig. 7.3. As in Figs. 7.4 and 7.5, notional utility curves can now be drawn—again, reversed (see Fig. 7.7).

If someone has a general preference for leisure rather than for income, then, as Fig. 7.7 shows, utility could be maximized at either or both of zero hours of employment and sixteen hours of employment, and is not much less at any number of hours between zero and sixteen hours. Thus, a poverty trap creates a considerable disincentive to increase the number of hours worked.

With a Citizen's Income, the person employed for only a few hours a week would experience increasing net income as the number of hours

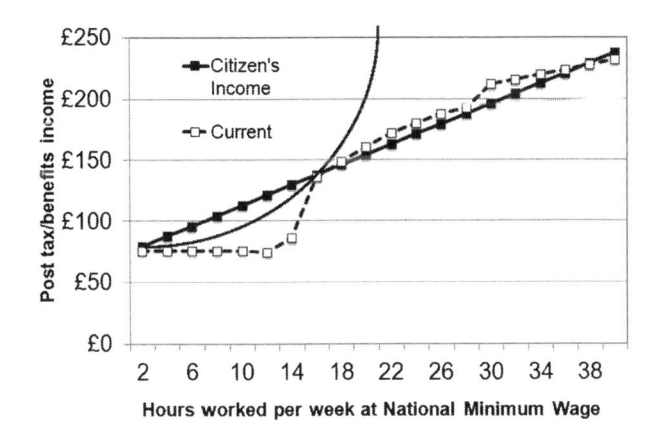

Fig. 7.7 Net income of a single earner aged 25 or over against hours worked at the National Minimum Wage per week, for the existing benefits system and for the Citizen's Income scheme described in Table 7.3, and with a utility curve showing maximum utility under the current system to be equal at both zero and sixteen hours of employment
Source: Malcolm Torry (2008) 'Research note: The utility—or otherwise—of being employed for a few hours a week', *Citizen's Income Newsletter*, issue 1 for 2008, pp. 14–16, p. 16

worked increased. This suggests that there would be an incentive to accept employment of a few hours per week, and also to seek to increase the number of hours of employment: unlike under the present scheme where employment for a few hours a week is unlikely to be attractive, and only increasing hours of employment to more than sixteen hours per week will make much difference to net income.

As Fig. 7.8 shows, whatever the shape of someone's utility curve, they will be able to find an employment level that will match their preferences; and someone with a higher preference for leisure will be able to work for a few hours per week at a higher utility than if they were working zero hours—something impossible under the existing system.

Only the Citizen's Income net income line allows people with *any* shape of utility curve to experience incentives to seek employment of any given number of hours, so the employment options facing most working-age adults will be more diverse under a Citizen's Income scheme than under the current system; and for all of those adults there will always be either the same or more utility to be gained by working more hours.

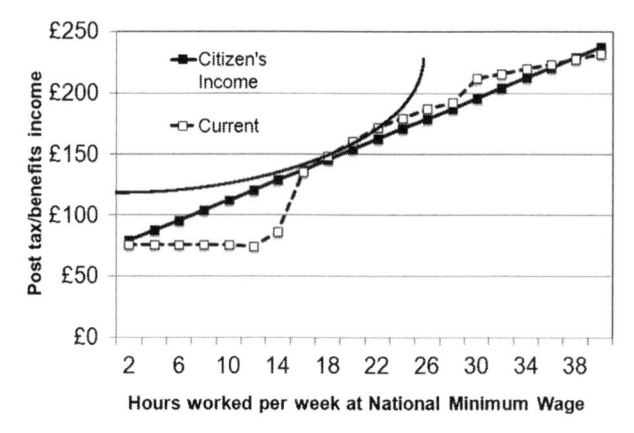

Fig. 7.8 Net income of a single earner aged 25 or over against hours worked at the National Minimum Wage per week, for the existing benefits system and for the Citizen's Income scheme described in Table 7.3, and with a utility curve showing maximum utility under the illustrative Citizen's Income scheme
Source: Malcolm Torry (2008) 'Research note: The utility—or otherwise—of being employed for a few hours a week', *Citizen's Income Newsletter*, issue 1 for 2008, pp. 14–16, p. 16

7.5 Conclusion

We have recognized that in general we cannot prove behavioural feasibility before implementation of a Citizen's Income scheme, but that we can present evidence that strongly suggests that behavioural feasibility would not be difficult to establish following implementation. The same would be true in practice in the UK. The same would also be true if Citizen's Income were to be implemented one step at a time: first a Child Citizen's Income, then a Citizen's Pension, then an unconditional income for young adults, then one for the pre-retired, and finally a Citizen's Income for working-age adults. At each stage—provided that it was a genuine Citizen's Income that had been established—behavioural feasibility would be experienced, would help to embed the already implemented Citizen's Incomes, and would create the psychological feasibility required for the next phase of the implementation strategy. In this sense, psychological and behavioural feasibilities are intimately connected.

A particular point of connection is the way in which the implementation of Citizen's Income might affect the behaviour of the media, and the way in which this would affect the psychological feasibility required by the next stage of Citizen's Income implementation. Research on the UK press published thirty years ago revealed that means-tested benefits and their recipients—viewed as 'scroungers'—were receiving widespread coverage, and that there was plenty of criticism of universal benefits, too.[36] We experience the same situation today. Because Citizen's Income would not pit against the rest of society a group of people that could be classed as undeserving, we could argue that Citizen's Income would not receive negative press coverage; but as a universal benefit it might suffer from negative press coverage of its own. Following the implementation of a Citizen's Income for one age group, we would have to wait to see how the media would behave, and how its behaviour would affect the psychological feasibility of the next stage of implementation.

While psychological and behavioural feasibilities are closely connected, we have dealt with them separately because they are structurally different. Psychological feasibility is the public understanding and approval required before a Citizen's Income can be implemented, and, as we have recognized, it can be created by an implemented Citizen's Income. An important cause of post-event psychological feasibility will have to be behavioural feasibility, that is, practical experience of the beneficial effects promised for Citizen's Income. Such practical experience can only be post-event, but the evidence presented in this chapter can give us considerable confidence that it would occur.

Notes

1. 'Jürgen De Wispelaere and José Antonio Noguera (2012) 'On the Political Feasibility of Universal Basic Income: An Analytic Framework', pp. 17–38 in Richard Caputo (ed.) *Basic Income Guarantee: International Experiences and Perspectives on the Viability of Income Guarantee* (New York: Palgrave Macmillan), p. 29.
2. Yannick Vanderborght (2013) 'The Ambiguities of Basic Income from a Trade Union Perspective', pp. 497–508 in Karl Widerquist, José A. Noguera, Yannick Vanderborght, and Jürgen De Wispelaere, *Basic Income: An anthology of contemporary research* (Chichester: Wiley Blackwell).
3. Wesley J. Pech (2010) 'Behavioral Economics and the Basic Income Guarantee', *Basic Income Studies*, 5 (2), 1–17.
4. Jane Gingrich (2014) 'Structuring the Vote: Welfare institutions and value-based vote choices', pp. 93–112 in Staffan Kumlin and Isabelle Stadelmann-Steffen (eds), *How Welfare States Shape the Democratic Public: Policy*

feedback, participation, voting, and attitudes (Cheltenham: Edward Elgar), p. 109.
5. John Creedy and Nicolas Hérault (2015) 'Decomposing Inequality Changes: Allowing for leisure in the evaluation of tax and transfer policy effects', *Fiscal Studies*, 36 (2), 157–80.
6. Philippe van Parijs (1995) *Real Freedom for All: What (if Anything) Can Justify Capitalism?* (Oxford: Clarendon Press), pp. 2, 89, 96, 133; Brian Barry (1996) 'Surfers' saviour?' *Citizen's Income Bulletin*, no. 22, pp. 2–4.
7. Bernard Michael Gilroy, Anastasia Heimann, and Mark Schopf (2013) 'Basic Income and Labour Supply: The German case,' *Basic Income Studies*, 8 (1), 43–70; A.B. Atkinson (1995) *Public Economics in Action: The Basic Income / Flat Tax Proposal* (Oxford: Clarendon Press), pp. 89–108. On testing for dynamic and static traps in the employment market, see Thierry Laurent and Yannick L'Horty (2005) 'Back to Work Incentives in a Dynamic Perspective: An application to French labor markets', pp. 198–211 in Karl Widerquist, Michael Anthony Lewis and Steven Pressman (eds.) *The Ethics and Economics of the Basic Income Guarantee* (Aldershot: Ashgate).
8. Some of the material in this section first appeared in a Society Central blog post,7May2015,http://societycentral.ac.uk/2015/05/07/citizens-income-the-evidence/.
9. Malcolm Torry (2009) 'Can Unconditional Cash Transfers Work? They Can', a report of a seminar, *Citizen's Income Newsletter*, issue 2 for 2009, pp. 1–3; Claudia Haarman and Dirk Haarman (2007), 'From Survival to Decent Employment: Basic Income Security in Namibia', *Basic Income Studies*, 2 (1), 1–7.
10. Sarath Davala, Renana Jhabvala, Soumya Kapoor Mehta and Guy Standing (2014) *Basic Income: A Transformative Policy for India* (London: Bloomsbury).
11. Basic Income Grant Coalition (2009) *Making the Difference: The BIG in Namibia: Basic Income Grant Pilot Project, Assessment Report* (Namibia: Basic Income Grant Coalition, Namibia NGO Forum), pp. 72–3, www.bignam.org/Publications/BIG_Assessment_report_08b.pdf.
12. See Chap. 6 on the differences
13. Karl Widerquist and Allan Sheahen (2012) 'The United States: The Basic Income Guarantee—Past Experience, Current Proposals', pp. 11–32 in Matthew C. Murray and Carole Pateman, *Basic Income Worldwide: Horizons of Reform* (New York: Palgrave Macmillan), p. 21.
14. Evelyn L. Forget (2012) 'Canada: The Case for Basic Income', pp. 81–101 in Matthew C. Murray and Carole Pateman (eds) *Basic Income Worldwide: Horizons of Reform* (New York: Palgrave Macmillan).
15. Michael O'Brien (2007) *Poverty, Policy and the State* (Bristol: Policy Press), p. 124.

16. Pierre-Carl Michaeu and Arthur van Soest (2008) 'How did the elimination of the US earnings test above the normal retirement age affect labour supply expectations', *Fiscal Studies*, 29 (2), 197–231.
17. Thomas F. Crossley and Sung-Hee Jeon (2007) 'Joint taxation and the labour supply of married women: Evidence from the Canadian tax reform of 1988', *Fiscal Studies*, 28 (3), 343–65.
18. Some of the material in this section appeared in a review article in the *Citizen's Income Newsletter*, issue 1 for 2010, www.citizensincome. org/resources/Newsletter20101.htm, and in a website appendix to Malcolm Torry (2013) *Money for Everyone*, (Bristol: Policy Press) on the Citizen's Income Trust's website: www.citizensincome.org/filelibrary/Money%20for%20Everyone%20appendices/Appendix%20for%20 chapter%2011,%20review%20of%20The%20Spirit%20Level%20-%20 Copy.pdf.
19. Gøsta Esping-Andersen (1990) *The Three Worlds of Welfare Capitalism* (Cambridge: Polity Press).
20. Gøsta Esping-Andersen (1990) *The Three Worlds of Welfare Capitalism* (Cambridge: Polity Press), pp. 1–33, 88–103.
21. Geert Hofstede (1997) *Culture and Organizations: Software of the Mind: intercultural Co-operation and its Importance for Survival* (New York: McGraw-Hill), p. 27.
22. The correlation coefficient is 0.85. Geert Hofstede (1980) *Culture's Consequences: International Differences in Work-Related Values* (Beverly Hills: Sage), p. 148. See also Béla Janky (2012) 'Social solidarity and preferences on welfare institutions across Europe', pp. 209–49 in Marion Ellison (ed.), *Reinventing Social Solidarity Across Europe* (Bristol: Policy Press) on his Redistributive Attitude Index. He constructs an index showing different populations' preferences for increased government expenditure. A similar ranking emerges.
23. Geert Hofstede (1980) *Culture's Consequences: International Differences in Work-Related Values* (Beverly Hills: Sage), p. 147.
24. Geert Hofstede (1980) *Culture's Consequences*, p. 149.
25. Geert Hofstede (1980) *Culture's Consequences*, p. 122.
26. Mike Danson, Paul Spicker, Robin McAlpine, Willie Sullivan (2014) *The Case for Universalism: Assessing the Evidence* (London: The Centre for Labour and Social Studies), p. 4. http://classonline.org.uk/pubs/item/ the-case-for-universalism.
27. Ailsa McKay (2013) 'Crisis, Cuts, Citizenship and a Basic Income: A wicked solution to a wicked problem,' *Basic Income Studies*, 8 (1), 93–104.
28. Estelle James, Alejandra Cox Edwards, and Rebecca Wong (2008) *The Gender Impact of Social Security Reform* (Chicago and London: University of Chicago Press), p. 195.

29. Staffan Kumlin and Isabelle Stadelmann-Steffen (2014) 'How welfare states shape the democratic public: borrowing strength across research communities', pp. 311–25 in Staffan Kumlin and Isabelle Stadelmann-Steffen (eds), *How Welfare States Shape the Democratic Public: Policy feedback, participation, voting, and attitudes* (Cheltenham: Edward Elgar), p. 322.
30. Ana Muuri (2010) 'The impact of the use of the social welfare services or social security benefits on attitudes to social welfare policies', *International Journal of Social Welfare*, 19, 182–193, p. 191.
31. Hans-Jürgen Andress and Thorsten Heien (2001) 'Four Worlds of Welfare State Attitudes? A comparison of Germany, Norway, and the United States', *European Sociological Review*, 17 (4), 337–56, p. 352; Tor George Jakobsen (2011) 'Welfare Attitudes and Social Expenditure: Do Regimes Shape Public Opinion?' *Social Indicators Research*, 101, 323–40, p. 336.
32. Malcolm Torry (2013) *Money for Everyone*, pp. 268–70.
33. A previous version of this part of the case study was published as Malcolm Torry (2008) 'Research note: The utility—or otherwise—of being employed for a few hours a week', *Citizen's Income Newsletter*, issue 1 for 2008, pp. 14–16, and also as a website appendix related to Malcolm Torry (2013) *Money for Everyone*, http://www.citizensincome.org/filelibrary/Money%20for%20Everyone%20appendices/Appendix%20for%20 chapter%2010,%20the%20utility%20of%20part%20time%20employment%20-%20Copy.pdf.
34. A.B. Atkinson and J.S. Flemming, 'Unemployment, social security and incentives' (1978) *Midland Bank Review*, Autumn 1978, pp. 6–16; C.V. Brown and E. Levin (1974) 'The effects of income taxation on overtime: the results of a national survey', *Economic Journal*, 84, 833–48; Angus Deaton and John Muellbauer (1980) *Economics and Consumer Behaviour* (Cambridge: Cambridge University Press), p. 282; Angus Deaton (1992) *Understanding Consumption* (Oxford: Clarendon Press), p. 193; Ronald Shone (1981) *Applications in Intermediate Microeconomics* (Oxford: Martin Robertson), pp. 1–24. For a treatment of demand theory and its lessons for Citizen's Income, see Anne Miller (1986) 'Poverty and adequacy', *BIRG Bulletin*, no. 6, pp. 13–16.
35. For further details of the scheme, see scheme A in Chap. 3.
36. Peter Golding and Sue Middleton (1982) *Images of Welfare: Press and Public Attitudes to Poverty* (Oxford: Basil Blackwell), pp. 75, 88, 91.

CHAPTER 8

Is a Citizen's Income Politically Feasible?

8.1 Introduction

De Wispelaere and Noguera describe as 'political feasibility' the combination of psychological feasibility, behavioural feasibility, institutional feasibility (which I have called administrative feasibility), and strategic feasibility: by which they mean 'political entrepreneurs engaging in all sorts of strategic interventions to build a political coalition enabling the legislation and subsequent implementation of a policy proposal'.[1] In this chapter, I am using 'political feasibility' in a rather more restricted sense, represented by the question: Does Citizen's Income cohere with mainstream political ideologies?

In order to engage with a political process, a policy idea must at least to some extent cohere with the political ideologies of actors in the political sphere. In practical terms, politicians must be able to recognize Citizen's Income as conforming to their own and their parties' deepest convictions and policy commitments. So this chapter asks into which political ideologies Citizen's Income can easily fit. However, politicians recognizing Citizen's Income as consistent with their own and their parties' convictions will not guarantee implementation of the proposal. That requires Citizen's Income to make the journey from idea to implementation, which requires

---

Some of the material in this chapter draws on some of the same sources as Chap. 13 of Malcolm Torry (2013) *Money for Everyone: Why we need a Citizen's Income* (Bristol: Policy Press).

it to negotiate the institutions that together constitute the policy process. We shall tackle the question as to whether Citizen's Income is capable of doing that in Chap. 9.

Having now used 'political feasibility' to refer to just one aspect of De Wispelaere's and Noguera's strategic feasibility, the term is no longer available for the combination of all of the four different feasibilities. This is no problem. If we add financial feasibility to those four, then we are simply discussing 'feasibility' as defined in Chap. 2.

A problem relating to both Chaps. 8 and 9 is that both political ideologies and policy process are highly country-specific. The main body of each of these chapters will therefore have to be in the most general of terms, leaving the reader to work out how Citizen's Income would relate to the political ideologies and the policy process in their own context.

8.2 Citizen's Income's Attraction to a Variety of Common Political Ideologies

Because in most contexts, a Citizen's Income scheme would take several years to negotiate and then to implement, and because for some implementation methods, it might take several decades, the proposal faces a significant challenge. If either in general, or in a particular country, the idea is not compatible with one of the mainstream political ideologies, then maintaining the momentum required for implementation might be difficult if a political party attached to that ideology finds itself in power. To put the situation more positively: It will be a lot easier to implement a Citizen's Income scheme in a country if its political parties can all appreciate the proposal as an attractive policy option. David Purdy suggests that it is

> both necessary and possible to envisage [Citizen's Income] as a central unifying element in a radical political project which transcends any narrowly sectional or partisan affiliation. The transition to a [Citizen's Income] society could not be negotiated and secured without positive support, or at least benevolent neutrality, amongst all the main political parties and currents of opinion.[2]

So our task here is to ask whether Citizen's Income is compatible with *all* of the mainstream political ideologies. I shall study four political ideologies: the New Right, socialism, liberalism, and social democracy. These should not be located on a spectrum, because each of them has their own distinctive political viewpoint, but it is probably fair to say that social democracy stands between the others as a reconciling position.

8.2.1 The New Right

Anthony Giddens defines the 'New Right' (or 'neoliberalism') in terms of

> minimal government, autonomous civil society, market fundamentalism, moral authoritarianism (plus strong economic individuation), a labour market which clears like any other, acceptance of inequality, traditionalist nationalism, the welfare state as a safety net, linear modernization, low ecological consciousness, a realist theory of the international order ... The welfare state is seen as the source of all evils in much the same way capitalism once was by the revolutionary left.[3]

For the New Right, in the words of Margaret Thatcher,

> there is no such thing as society. There is a living tapestry of men and women and people and the beauty of that tapestry and the quality of our lives will depend upon how much each of us is prepared to take responsibility for ourselves and each of us is prepared to turn round and help by our own efforts those who are unfortunate.[4]

The economy is a global market constructed out of contracts between individual actors, and free trade is therefore the route to both national and individual prosperity. Each individual must make the best of their economic potential, and their self-interested effort is what in practice benefits others. Adam Smith is frequently quoted:

> By directing [his] industry in such a manner as its produce may be of greatest value, [the economic actor] intends only his own gain, and he is in this, as in many other cases, led by an invisible hand to promote an end which was no part of his intention.[5]

The New Right's political standpoint is best understood positively as a belief that free markets deliver wealth for all, and negatively that attempts to equalize wealth cause people to be poor and keep them that way. There are both practical and more theoretical arguments. The more theoretical position is that redistribution is theft from the wealthy. The more practical argument is that redistribution requires progressive taxation and/or means-testing, that these deter hard work, and that therefore only limited redistribution can be permitted.[6] All human need is circumstantial, and where someone's need is not their own fault, then friends, family, and neighbours will exercise compassion, and as a last resort, the state will provide for necessities. If someone is in need through their own fault, then it is up to them to change their behaviour.

More positively, each individual has a right to equality before the law, to protection of their person, and to protection of their property, but otherwise all relationships are contracts and so are conditional on people accepting mutual obligations. A minimal state is therefore all that is required, and it must not get in the way of the market; but the practice often denies the theory, because industry and commerce need educated and healthy workers at least as much as they need contract law, so public provision of education and healthcare are still supported in practice.

Because implementing Citizen's Income would mean that earned income would no longer need to provide for the whole of someone's household's subsistence, it would facilitate a free market in labour, which makes the idea attractive to New Right theoreticians. A Citizen's Income would also reduce the disincentives currently imposed on the employment market by means-tested benefits, and so would better enable working-age adults to provide for themselves and their families in the context of a free market economy.

In practice, it is often concerns about 'dependency at the bottom of society'[7] that drive the New Right's interest in a Citizen's Income. Charles Murray suggests that the welfare structure for working-age adults in the USA should be scrapped and replaced with a Negative Income Tax,[8] which would have the same effect on disposable incomes as Citizen's Income. In particular, it would remove the necessity for means-tested benefits, would remove the disincentive to apply for employment opportunities,[9] and would not discourage people from creating their own insurance arrangements or private pensions.

Citizen's Income would appear to cohere well with a New Right political ideology. It would reward hard work, it would encourage self-reliance and private provision, and it would not interfere with the employment market.

8.2.2 Socialism

'Socialism' understands the individual as belonging to society, to which they contribute what they can, and which provides for their needs. As Karl

Marx put it, 'from each according to his ability, to each according to his needs'.[10] At the one extreme we find communism:

> the abolition of private property ... Communism deprives no man of the power to appropriate the products of society; all that it does is to deprive him of the power to subjugate the labour of others by means of such appropriation ... The first step in the revolution by the working class is to raise the proletariat to the position of ruling class, to win the battle of democracy. The proletariat will use its political supremacy to wrest, by degrees, all capital from the bourgeoisie, to centralise all instruments of production in the hands of the State, i.e., of the proletariat organised as the ruling class; and to increase the total of productive forces as rapidly as possible.[11]

One problem, as the Soviet Union and countries in Eastern Europe discovered, is that nationalized industries can make losses, and, if they have a monopoly, they can be inefficient. A further problem is that socialism is ideally ruled by the people and for the people,[12] which suggests that democracy needs to be at the heart of socialism, but democracy frequently delivers governments that are far from being socialist, and State socialism—as in the Soviet Union and Eastern Europe up to 1989—is not always very democratic. The purest form of socialism is now usually found only at local level, in the form of cooperative enterprises that distribute profits to their workers and customers. Such theoretical socialists as Alex Callinicos still hope for a broader socialism, based on this cooperative model, in which 'the working people of the world would co-operate together, rather than being chained to warring nation-states'[13]; but in practice, if we find socialism at all at the level of the nation state, we find it in a somewhat pragmatic form as an essentially free market economy, taxed by a government so that it can provide public services,[14] and sufficiently regulated by the State so that

> people who cannot contribute fully to social production are still entitled to share substantially in its wealth ... in which inequalities of ability and differences of social function do not crystallise into major and persistent social inequalities of wealth and power.[15]

For socialism, Citizen's Income represents social provision for universal needs, leaving differentiated needs to be provided for by individual and other collective effort; and it also represents a transfer of power from capital to labour. As Callinicos puts it:

> The basis of capital's power lies … in its control of production, not in the financial markets. One of the attractions of the idea that every citizen be granted as of right a basic income [Citizen's Income] set, say, at a level that would allow them to meet their socially recognized subsistence needs, is that it could help to emancipate workers from the dictatorship of capital. Such a basic income would radically alter the bargaining power between labour and capital, since potential workers would now be in a position, if they chose, to pursue alternatives to paid employment. Moreover, because all citizens would receive the same basic income (perhaps with adjustments for economic handicaps such as age, disability, and dependent children), its introduction would be an important step towards establishing equality of access to advantage.[16]

In relation to socialism's expectation that every citizen will contribute what they can, Pateman suggests that 'most people do not want to be idle',[17] so they will reciprocate if given a Citizen's Income. One of the important arguments for a Citizen's Income is that it would remove some of the disincentives to employment at the same time as causing the quality of employment to improve so that workers might want it.

Breitenbach et al. argue that a Citizen's Income would reduce inequality, end what they call the 'dull compulsion to labour', and 'end once and for all the pre-eminent place of commodity production under capitalism'.[18] Citizen's Income

> would be an unconditional regular weekly payment made to all adults. Its main purpose would be to reduce the extent of reliance on wage labour as the determinant of individual and household incomes. The existence of the basic income [Citizen's Income] would also reduce the proportional inequality between the highest and the lowest personal and household incomes since it would represent a higher proportional addition to the funds available to low-income recipients. The universal basic income would also perform another important function: it would allow individuals to choose whether to work or not. Initially, basic income would need to be set at a level low enough just to allow a bare existence without income from work for those who wished to live in this way. It seems to us unlikely that many people would actually choose this as a mode of life except for short periods, but the fact that it would be possible to live in this fashion would considerably reduce the monitoring, surveillance and enforcement of regulations on the duty to work that would otherwise be necessary.[19]

A Citizen's Income would encourage more people to work for themselves or in cooperatives, and would provide more people with a genuine choice between part-time and full-time paid employment.[20] Because the Citizen's Income, along with their proposed supplement for care work, would provide those caring for others with a reasonable subsistence income, the 'social economy' that Breitenbach et al. envisage 'can provide a new material base for genuine equality of life between the sexes'.[21] This would be somewhat different from the capitalist society in which we now live, which values by payment the production of commodities (including services bought and sold as commodities) and does not value by payment the care work that people do for one another.

For Breitenbach et al., as for Callinicos, a Citizen's Income is not simply a feasible instrument for promoting a viable socialism under present conditions. They see it as one of a number of proposals that 'contain within them a dynamic' towards a purer socialism in which the Citizen's Income will become 'an equal dividend for all citizens from the wealth they collectively produce'.[22]

8.2.3 Liberalism

For the liberal, individual freedom is the highest priority. As Samuel Brittan puts it: 'It is individuals who feel, exult, despair and rejoice', and statements about group welfare are a shorthand way of referring to such individual effects.[23] The liberal expects the individual to provide for themselves and those dependent on them, but because 'there is nothing inherently right about the pattern of rewards produced by the combination of inheritance and the market' we need 'a framework of rules—including, if necessary, redistributive taxation and transfers—by which a market economy can be induced to serve broader objectives'.[24] Society is therefore a combination of free individuals working together to maintain the conditions for every individual's liberty; and similarly, the global family of nations needs to work together to ensure the maximum freedom of trade between nations. The problem, though, is that global free trade can create hardship for individuals, thus rendering them less than free, so

> the key problem for European economic and social policy is how to obtain the benefits of a flexible US style labour market, without US poverty or US ghettoes.[25]

Means-tested benefits are not a solution to poverty because they trap people in poverty and make the 'ladder of opportunity' rather shaky.

A Citizen's Income would ameliorate the poverty and unemployment traps and would therefore encourage people to seek out new economic opportunities.

> It is positively desirable that people should have a means of subsistence independent of needs [because this would] separate the libertarian, free choice aspects of capitalism from the puritan work ethic.[26]

Burczak points out that a Citizen's Income would reduce the worker's dependence on their earned income, and so would reduce coercion in the employment market; and Weber suggests that the bureaucratic welfare state would be rolled back if a Citizen's Income were to be implemented. Both of these outcomes would increase individual liberty.[27]

Brittan sees a Citizen's Income 'not as a handout, but as a property right', as a 'return on the national capital',[28] and as a

> superior alternative to the minimum wage … Minimum wages represent just that kind of interference with markets which does most harm. … Those most likely to suffer are just the people whom the proponents of minimum wages say they most want to help. They include those on the fringes of the labour market or on the borderline of disablement or other incapacity … and all the others who face a choice between low pay and no pay. Minimum wages are a denial of the human right to sell one's labour to a willing buyer and to make one's own decision about whether or not to take paid work at going rates.[29]

8.2.4 Social Democracy

Social democracy attempts to combine all of equality, liberty, solidarity, and autonomy into a single political ideology, and sees democracy as the appropriate mechanism for creating a just society out of these somewhat diverse principles. As Tony Fitzpatrick puts it:

> Social democracy refers to the attempt to bring capitalist economies under some form of collective control using statist and gradualist reforms that work from within the framework of liberal democracy. Describing the aspirations of the Left it has united both socially-minded liberals and liberal-minded socialists, despite disagreements about the nature, speed and direction of reform that have often divided these groups. … [It is a] synthesis of economic prosperity, political participation, social justice and cultural maturity.[30]

Equality of opportunity is sought so that every individual citizen can experience 'reciprocity, responsibility, ambition and achievement'.[31] A similar route to a similar bundle of ideals was recommended by the UK Labour Party's 1994 Commission on Social Justice, which suggested that the UK

> can be both fairer and more successful: indeed, ... it must be both fair and more successful if it is to be either ... The foundation of a free society is the equal worth of all citizens, expressed most basically in political and civil liberties, equal rights before the law, and so on. ... everyone is entitled, as a right of citizenship, to be able to meet their basic needs for income, shelter and other necessities. ... self-respect and equal citizenship demand more than the meeting of basic needs: they demand opportunities and life chances. That is why we are concerned with the primary distribution of opportunity, as well as its redistribution. ... to achieve the first three conditions of social justice, we must recognise that although not all inequalities are unjust ... unjust inequalities should be reduced and where possible eliminated.[32]

The report goes on to say that economic success requires social justice, that social justice requires economic success, and that

> the case for Citizen's Income is partly moral and partly economic. The moral case rests on the principle of social citizenship ... civil and political rights must go hand in hand with economic and social rights. And just as civil and political rights belong unconditionally to all citizens as individuals, irrespective of need or desert, so all citizens have a right to a share in the social and national product sufficient to make it possible for them to participate fully in the common life of society ... the state is no more entitled to say which citizens have a right to a sufficient share in the common stock to participate fully in the life of the society than to say which citizens have a right to vote or to a fair trial. And in modern conditions that principle can be realised more simply and more completely by a Citizen's Income than by any other mechanism. The economic case rests upon the falling demand for unskilled labour. ... a Citizen's Income ... enables those without saleable skills to take low-paid or casual jobs of some kind, while at the same time receiving an income large enough to enfranchise them, without the stigma of a means test.[33]

8.3 Arguments Against Citizen's Income

The New Right ideology suggests that if someone is in need, then either they should get themselves out of their difficulty, or their family, friends, or neighbours should do so. This means that only a last-resort safety net should be provided. Something for nothing could discourage labour market activity. This attitude was evident during the Conservative Party conference in 2010 when the Chancellor of the Exchequer announced that a household containing a higher-rate taxpayer would be deprived of its Child Benefit. When a television journalist asked members of the audience what they thought of the idea, they said that the wealthy 'don't need it' and that 'the money should be targeted on the poor'.

Socialists might think that during the transition to socialism a Citizen's Income might depress wages, meaning that capitalist profits might rise and workers' share of the product of their labour might be reduced. Esam et al. suggest that a Citizen's Income would be a 'subsidy to wages' in this way. They suggest that 'employers should be compelled to meet the costs of employing the labour from which they derive a benefit', without recognizing that a personal tax allowance also operates as a subsidy to wages, that existing means-tested in-work benefits function as a subsidy that increases as wages fall, and that profits to capital have only a partial relationship to wages. But Esam et al.'s major objection to Citizen's Income is that to pay a Citizen's Income would make 'economic planning' impossible. They would rather see 'selective subsidies to those jobs which met collectively determined needs for employment and for services'. They do not say why that would be incompatible with turning tax allowances into a Citizen's Income. Their final objection is that a Citizen's Income would not entirely solve the problem of inequality, which is true, but is not an argument against Citizen's Income.[34]

Some liberals worry that a Citizen's Income could compromise an individual's autonomy, could be expensive[35] (and thus reduce the freedom experienced by taxpayers), and could be 'underpinned by a negative image of humankind as weak, vulnerable and isolated. The basic thrust of this sentiment is that people cannot cope within the harsh environment of globalized capitalism without state assistance.'[36]

The UK's Labour Party's rather social democratic Commission on Social Justice suggests three 'severe difficulties' with Citizen's Income:

> A change of this magnitude would have to be backed by a broad-based consensus, of which there is, as yet, no sign. In a society with a strong work ethic many people would oppose, as giving 'something for nothing', a scheme deliberately designed to offer unconditional benefits to all … although Citizen's Income is intended to be a means of social inclusion, it could just as easily become a means of social exclusion' [– the report

cites evidence that an unconditional benefit for young people had reduced engagement with education or employment]; ... the tax rates that would be required for funding, and their possible effects.[37]

The Commission recommended a reformed social insurance scheme, and also discussed a Participation Income.[38] However, the report also added:

> It would be unwise, however, to rule out a move towards Citizen's Income in future: if it turns out to be the case that earnings simply cannot provide a stable income for a growing proportion of people, then the notion of some guaranteed income, outside the labour market, could become increasingly attractive. Work incentives might matter less and those who happened to be in employment, knowing that they probably would not remain so throughout their 'working' lives, might be more willing to finance an unconditional payment. Our measures would not preclude a move to Citizen's Income in the future.[39]

We can conclude from this brief summary of arguments against Citizen's Income that the arguments have little to do with the political ideologies themselves, but are in fact rather generic, that is, common across the ideologies, and driven by a number of deeply embedded presuppositions.

The only objection that is not generic in this sense is Esam et al.'s suggestions that a Citizen's Income would reduce a government's ability to plan the economy and would subsidize employers. In response, means-tested benefits are dynamic subsidies, in the sense that the subsidy effect rises as wages fall. A Citizen's Income would provide a static subsidy, which would not rise as wages fell. Therefore the subsidy effect would be reduced. To replace market-skewing means-tested benefits with universal benefits that would not skew the employment market would make economic planning less necessary. But of course, there is no reason why a government should not plan the economy in the context of a Citizen's Income. Similarly, a National Minimum Wage is sometimes offered as an alternative to Citizen's Income in an 'either/or' fashion.[40] There is no reason why a National Minimum Wage should not be implemented alongside a Citizen's Income. They would work very happily together. In the same way, Mitchell and Watts suggest that a government job guarantee scheme would be preferable to a Citizen's Income.[41] There are arguments both for and against a job guarantee (for, in terms of providing everyone with purposeful activity; against, in relation to the difficulties of supervising and administering such schemes, and the ways in which they can displace employment market jobs) but that is not a discussion that we need to have here. Here what needs to be said is that a job guarantee and a Citizen's Income are not mutually exclusive options. They would function perfectly happily together.

8.4 Coalition-Building

De Wispelaere and Noguera rightly suggest that what is required is an enduring coalition of support for Citizen's Income across a variety of significant political actors. The important word here is 'significant':

> Not all instances of expressed support for a policy imply a sustained commitment to promoting this policy. It is one thing for a social or political agent to vocally express a preference in favour of basic income [Citizen's Income], quite a different matter to actively canvass support amongst constituents, party members, or like-minded associations and groups; build a shared platform across political factions; utilize scarce political resources (money, time, and above all political capital) to further the cause; bargain and possibly compromise on other political goals; and so on. Expressed support without either the commitment or the capacity to engage in the necessary political action to build a sustainable coalition around the policy of granting each citizen an unconditional basic income is 'cheap': it seems of little practical worth to basic income advocates.[42]

De Wispelaere and Noguera are particularly wary of the support for Citizen's Income expressed by Green politicians and parties.[43] Green parties rarely find themselves with responsibility for implementing policy ideas, and, when they do, usually in a coalition with other parties, any previous commitment to Citizen's Income can be dislodged by other more immediate policy imperatives.[44] As De Wispelaere and Noguera point out, some kinds of support for Citizen's Income in minority parties can actually be detrimental to the cause, because if a minority party supports a policy, then a more influential party might explicitly condemn it as wrong or impractical in order to distance itself from the minority party.[45] If a centre-right party were to espouse Citizen's Income, then a centre-left party might condemn the policy for giving money to the rich (even though Citizen's Income schemes can easily be designed that would both reduce poverty and increase equality[46]); and if a centre-left party were to espouse Citizen's Income, then a centre-right party might suggest that it would stop people from working (whereas the opposite would be true[47]).

This all leaves us in a rather unusual situation. Every mainstream political ideology, and anyone who espouses any one of the mainstream political ideologies, can in principle support Citizen's Income, not simply as a pragmatic choice ('it can't be worse than what we've got now') but as a choice positively related to any and every mainstream political ideology. Anyone who espouses a mainstream political ideology can of course offer arguments against Citizen's Income, but those arguments will stem from (a) deeply held generic presuppositions, and not their political ideology, and (b) a desire to distance themselves from minority parties that have espoused Citizen's Income and might pose an electoral threat.

Given this situation, how can legislators in mainstream political parties be persuaded to support the implementation of Citizen's Income?

An education programme is clearly required that would (a) educate every member of parliament in the connections between Citizen's Income and their own political ideology; (b) disprove arguments against Citizen's Income, and particularly any that look as if they might relate to a mainstream political ideology; and (c) ignore any support for Citizen's Income given by a minority party, unless that party's electoral success might be electorally helpful to the party of the legislator being educated. Where a country's benefits system is becoming a matter of general concern to members of all parties, then Citizen's Income's administrative feasibility and advantages—which would not normally be a party political issue—should be at the forefront of any educational exercise.

We shall be studying the policy process in detail in the next chapter, but it ought to be stated here that the character of the educational exercise required suggests that think tanks might be particularly significant, particularly if think tanks attached to different political parties find that they can work together on Citizen's Income.

As well as widespread education, also required will be a coalition-building strategy that largely ignores minority political parties and works hard to gain support in mainstream parties. However, one institution that the strategy will also need to include will be trades unions. Citizen's Income would facilitate a more flexible employment market, which might not be good for trade union members; it might enable employees to pursue self-employment as a viable option, thus reducing trade union membership; and it would provide a secure income for every trade union member, which would leave trades unions negotiating over smaller proportions of workers' subsistence incomes, and so would reduce the control that trades unions possess over their members.[48] However, Citizen's Income would be good for trades unions' members because it would provide a secure income floor and would therefore improve workers' negotiating positions[49]; it would give expression to the socialist convictions of many trades unionists; and by increasing the viability of part-time employment, it might bring more people into formal employment and so might increase trade union membership. It is perhaps no surprise that trades unions differ in their attitudes to Citizen's Income.[50]

A slow and patient educational process will clearly be needed to educate trade union officers and members in the advantages of Citizen's Income; and in general, a slow and patient process will be required in relation to all of the political actors that we have discussed in this chapter. The careful choosing of parties and party members to educate might at first sight look like a slower process than seeking political support wherever it can be found, but it could be more effective, and in the end, it could be quicker.[51]

8.5 Case Studies: Political Ideologies in the UK

8.5.1 One Nation Conservatism

During the 1970s, before neoliberal economics took centre stage in the UK's Conservative Party, a significant section of the party identified with a 'one nation' political ideology: the idea that our evolved social structures are stable and valuable, that our differentiated meritocracy works to the benefit of all in society, that those with better life chances have obligations towards those without them, and that a government's task is to fashion society in such a way that everyone has the opportunity to reach their full potential.

A Citizen's Income would signify that we all have a place in society, and it would also enable those better endowed to make the most of their privilege so that all could benefit from their success.

Two 'One Nation' Conservative MPs were at the heart of the Citizen's Income debate between the 1970s and 1980s: Brandon Rhys Williams, and David Howells:

> There is a strong emphasis in policy today on the need for what in the jargon is called 'targeting' of state resources on the most needy. This is a popular approach which at first glance seems to make eminent good sense. Yet beneath the surface of this apparently attractive proposition lurks a frightening void – which we call the poverty trap. The more you relate benefits

to some measure of means (and also, the lower down the income scale you take income taxation), the greater the deterrent to benefit recipients to lift their earnings. ... Here, in the impenetrably complex brew of benefits, thresholds, tax allowances, penalties and disregards, we have the makings of that strange paradox whereby unemployment and labour shortage co-exist, where saving makes you poorer, where a subculture of benefit dependency flourishes. [The solution is] a partial basic income [Citizen's Income] payment for all. (David Howells)[52]

Brandon Rhys Williams' Citizen's Income proposal was a direct descendent of his mother Juliet Rhys Williams' similar scheme designed in opposition to Beveridge's proposals, which she believed to be a 'serious attack upon the will to work ... not only will the idle get as much from the State as will the industrious workers, they will get a great deal more'.[53] Her son Brandon also believed that the inevitable consequence of targeting was 'pauperisation'.[54] He saw a Citizen's Income

> as the basis of a Europe-wide process of reform, underpinning the growth of the great Single Market. Above all, he saw it as a *translucent* process which people would genuinely understand, as against the murky pattern of today.[55]

It would encourage

> thrift, saving and small-scale capital ownership to spread and deepen, so as to create a genuine capital-owning democracy and the 'share economy' – the modern version of One Nation.[56]

It would redistribute income—

> something that people [must] accept because it gives expression to the type of society in which they wish to live[57];

and it would set people free.

> We need liberation for the millions held in dependency on state benefits to take work without committing a crime; liberation for savers to accumulate fortunes and put them to work fruitfully, without the risk of confiscatory taxation; liberation of women, so that they become wholly equal citizens, whether single or married; and liberation for employers from needless, costly paperwork.[58]

Brandon Rhys Williams compared Citizen's Income to Child Benefit, which

> is one of the easiest benefits to administer, and take-up is almost 100 per cent … it is far, far too low. … Child benefit helps all families equally. My answer to those who attack it on the grounds that rich families do not need it, is to say that child benefit does not belong either to the father or to the mother, but is the start of a life-long relationship of obligation and entitlement between the child as junior citizen and the community.[59]

A Citizen's Income is

> about changing attitudes *all the way down the income distribution instead of just at the top*. For there is no reason to suppose that people on low incomes react differently to increased economic incentives than people who are rich.[60]

8.5.2 The Green Party[61]

In a context of limited resources, permanent GDP growth is impossible, and to attempt it will be to impoverish future generations. An 'ecowelfare' position recognizes that members of future generations have rights, and that care work and sustainability will be the marks of an ecologically sustainable future society.[62] A post-productivist position of this kind will need to disconnect subsistence income from production, and will also need to establish an element of income equality and security in order to generate equality of opportunity. A Citizen's Income is thus a natural fit, especially as it would recognize the value of care work and work directed towards sustainability, and would encourage the risk-taking attitude that we shall need in a post-productivist economy.[63]

In March 2014, at its Spring Conference, the Green Party of England and Wales voted to include a Citizen's Income in its manifesto for the forthcoming General Election. Few details were given during the period leading up to the election in May 2015, but the fact that the Green Party had said that it wanted to see a Citizen's Income of £72 per week, and that it wanted to abolish means-tested benefits, suggested that their scheme mirrored the Citizen Income Trust's illustrative scheme that the Work and Pensions Select Committee published as evidence in 2006 and that the Trust then published in 2007 and updated in 2013.[64] There would be no problem with affording this scheme, as the abolition of personal tax allowances, the abolition of means-tested benefits, and the restriction of pension contribution tax relief to the basic rate, would save enough money to pay for the whole of the UK population's Citizen's Incomes, but there would be a problem. A working paper published by the Institute for Social and Economic Research in September 2014 had shown that the scheme would generate significant losses for some low-earning households,[65] for whom their Citizen's Incomes would more than replace the value of their lost personal tax allowances, but would not replace the whole of their abolished Working Tax Credits. Because the Citizen's Income would never be withdrawn, additional earnings would produce more additional disposable income than additional earnings can produce in the context of means-tested benefits, so households suffering small losses at the point of implementation of a Citizen's Income would be able to make them up quite easily by earning a little more; but this was clearly not a total solution, so more work was required.

The immediate cause of the controversy that erupted before the General Election was Andrew Neil's television interview with Natalie Bennett, the Leader of the Green Party.[66] Neil asked a lot of questions about the funding of the Citizen's Income, the Green Party had not published the detail of its funding proposals, and Bennett was left floundering.

The Guardian's Political Editor, Patrick Wintour, then read the Citizen's Income Trust's website, telephoned me for a discussion, and wrote an article that said that the Citizen's Income Trust had said that the Green Party's Citizen's Income scheme would impose losses on low-income families.[67] We had not said that—in fact, we had never commented on the Green Party's scheme, except to note that they intended to develop one for their manifesto, and that they had not published the details; but by noticing the similarities between our illustrative scheme and what the Green Party had so far said about theirs, and by reading the research results relating to household losses at the point of implementation, Wintour had drawn his own perfectly correct conclusion and published it as if it was ours. What he did not emphasize, which he might have done, is that we had proved that it is perfectly feasible to implement a genuine Citizen's Income of £72 a week without imposing losses on low-income households if means-tested benefits are retained and households' Citizen's Incomes are taken into account when their means-tested benefits are calculated.[68]

The controversy was excellent publicity for Citizen's Income, but the question that De Wispelaere and Noguera would quite properly ask is this: Does the Green Party's support for Citizen's Income, and the subsequent controversy, make it more or less difficult for mainstream parties to espouse the idea?

8.5.3 Redistribution

When in 1982 Brandon Rhys Williams MP was asked by the Chair of a parliamentary committee: 'I wonder what degree of redistribution of resources there would be, or is that one of the matters that could be flexible within the system?' He quite correctly responded:

> This is optional. This is why I have not put figures in my paper because you could make the scheme do what you liked. If you want to help people on low wages or low incomes you can tilt the tax and benefit structure in such a way that it is redistributive in certain directions.[69]

Take, for instance, scheme B that we outlined in Chap. 3. On average, it would deliver a modest redistribution from rich to poor, as shown in Fig. 8.1.[70,71]

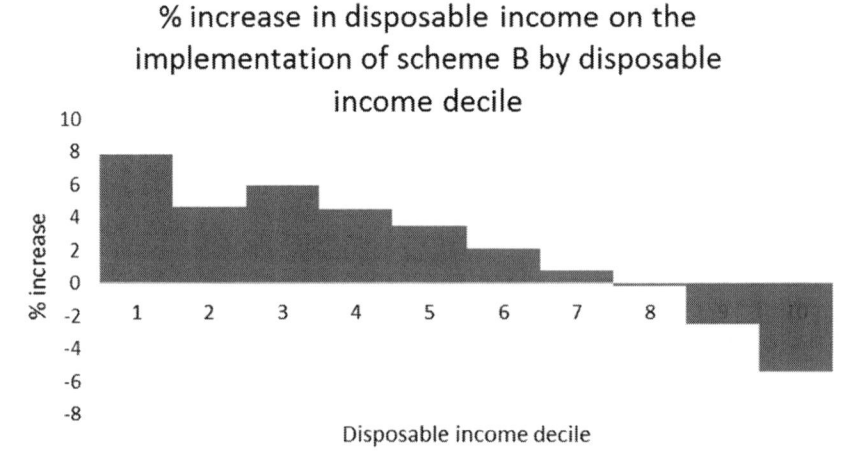

Fig. 8.1 Percent increase in disposable income on the implementation of scheme B by disposable income decile (Source: Malcolm Torry (2015) *Two feasible ways to implement a revenue neutral Citizen's Income scheme*, Institute for Social and Economic Research Working Paper EM6/15 (Colchester: Institute for Social and Economic Research, University of Essex), www.iser.essex.ac.uk/research/publications/working-papers/euromod/em6-15, p. 7.)

Two statistics represent the effects of this scheme:

- The Gini coefficient for disposable income would be reduced from 0.3 to 0.28, representing a reduction in inequality.
- In relation to the income component of poverty, the number of children in poverty[72] would be reduced from 12.16% to 9.19%, that is, by nearly a quarter.

8.5.4 A Long-Term Aim

As we discovered in Chaps. 3 and 4, scheme B would be both fiscally feasible and household financially feasible, and as we pointed out in Chap 6, it would be easy to implement. Scheme C would be rather different. Its more ambitious Citizen's Income rates, based on Minimum Income Standards, and the far higher Income Tax rates required, would suggest an evolutionary approach. However, if ever scheme C were to become attainable, it would have some significantly positive effects.

- The Gini coefficient for disposable income would be reduced from 0.3 to 0.2, representing a substantial reduction in inequality.
- In relation to the income component of poverty, the number of children in poverty would be reduced from 12.16% to 1.60%, that is, it would almost eliminate child poverty.

Redistribution would be largely towards the middle range of incomes, as shown in Fig. 8.2, which could be politically acceptable—although a reduction of 20% in the disposable incomes of the highest disposable income decile might be contentious for some.

Once a scheme such as scheme B had been implemented, it would be a political decision as to whether Citizen's Income rates should be slowly raised in the direction of the Minimum Income Standards, and Income Tax rates raised accordingly. A slow transition would enable disposable income losses to be minimal within any one tax year. Scheme C might at the moment appear to be an unattainable dream, but it might not stay that way.

8.6 Conclusion

Between September 1986 and August 1987, Peter Taylor-Gooby interviewed 101 MPs, and discovered that nearly three-fifths of Conservative MPs wanted Child Benefit to be kept as a universal benefit, and that

% increase in disposable income on the implementation of scheme C by disposable income decile

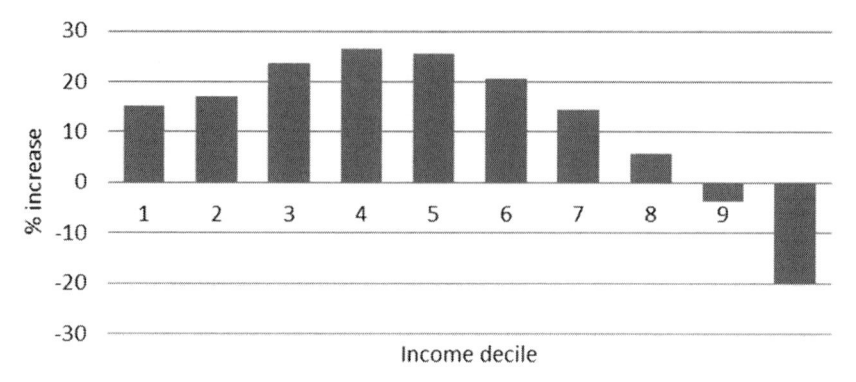

Fig. 8.2 Percent increase in disposable income on the implementation of scheme C by disposable income decile (Source: Malcolm Torry (2015) *Two feasible ways to implement a revenue neutral Citizen's Income scheme*, Institute for Social and Economic Research Working Paper EM6/15 (Colchester: Institute for Social and Economic Research, University of Essex), www.iser.essex.ac.uk/research/publications/working-papers/euromod/em6-15, p. 8.)

Labour MPs were 'strongly opposed to the extension of means-tested benefits, and want universal Child Benefit to stay'.[73] He concluded that MPs would resist a government wishing to cut the value of Child Benefit.

In 2004, the Citizen's Income Trust distributed a questionnaire to all MPs. Seventy-one completed questionnaires and eleven letters were returned. The level of support for a Citizen's Income was considerable. Forty-one respondents were in favour, and only eleven against; and of particular interest was the level of support for a Royal Commission: forty-six in favour, and only sixteen against. (Sir Patrick Cormack MP, one of the respondents, commented in his letter: 'I have long advocated a Royal Commission to look at the Welfare State fifty years on.')

Then in 2007, the Trust distributed a questionnaire to every member of the House of Lords. A total of 134 responses were received. Again the level of support for a Citizen's Income was considerable: seventy-three respondents were in favour and only fourteen against. And this time, support for a Royal Commission on income maintenance was even higher: eighty-three in favour, and only twenty-seven against.[74]

All of this was before the financial crisis of 2008, in the context of which objections to attacks on the level of Child Benefit and on its universality have been muted; but even though its value is now withdrawn through the tax system from households that include a higher-rate taxpayer, it remains universal. There is no reason to think that support for Citizen's Income has declined; although it has to be said that although a substantial proportion of those who returned their questionnaires liked the idea, that was still a small proportion of the House of Commons and the House of Lords.

The question remains: How is a certain level of support for an extension of universal benefits to be turned into something effective? Is ticking a box on a questionnaire the kind of cheap support that De Wispelaere and Noguera were warning about?[75]

The fact that every mainstream ideology can generate arguments for a Citizen's Income, that the positive arguments are closely related to the core positions of the ideologies, that supporters of all of these ideologies have in fact generated positive arguments, and that among the members of the UK's political parties we can find supporters of Citizen's Income[76] will be of little use if expressions of interest cannot be turned into practical political action. The fact that the same arguments against a Citizen's Income are expressed by individuals attached to all of the mainstream political ideologies suggests that arguments against are not closely related to the core positions of mainstream political ideologies, and that arguments against a Citizen's Income are psychological rather than political. This might suggest that political feasibility would be relatively easy to achieve if psychological feasibility had already been achieved; but again, genuine political feasibility means a sufficient number of significant political players putting in hard political work on behalf of Citizen's Income. No doubt an achieved psychological feasibility would facilitate such political work, but it would not be enough to generate it on its own.

So yet again we find ourselves up against the usual presuppositions—'A Citizen's Income would be too expensive', 'We should not pay people to do nothing', 'Rich people do not need it', and 'A Citizen's Income would discourage people from seeking employment'[77]—and up against the requirement for multiple personal conversions, not just conversions to believing a Citizen's Income to be a useful reform option, but conversions that result in political action.

NOTES

1. Jürgen De Wispelaere and José Antonio Noguera (2012) 'On the Political Feasibility of Universal Basic Income: An Analytic Framework', pp. 17–38 in Richard Caputo (ed.) *Basic Income Guarantee: International Experiences and Perspectives on the Viability of Income Guarantee* (New York: Palgrave Macmillan), p. 21.
2. David Purdy (2013) 'Political Strategies for Basic Income', pp. 477–484 in Karl Widerquist, José A. Noguera, Yannick Vanderborght, and Jürgen De Wispelaere, *Basic Income: An anthology of contemporary research* (Chichester: Wiley Blackwell), p. 483.
3. Anthony Giddens (1998) *The Third Way: The Renewal of Social Democracy* (Cambridge: Polity Press), pp. 8, 13.
4. Margaret Thatcher, interview for *Woman's Own*, 31 October 1987, www.margaretthatcher.org/document/106689
5. Adam Smith (1976/1776) *An Inquiry into the Nature and Causes of the Wealth of Nations*, ed. Edwin Cannan (Chicago: University of Chicago Press), first published in 1776, bk. 4, ch. 2, §9.
6. Keith Joseph and Jonathan Sumption (1979) *Equality* (London: John Murray), pp. 19, 23–4, 27.
7. Lawrence Mead (1992) *The New Politics of Poverty: The Non-working Poor in America* (New York: Harper Collins), p. ix.
8. Charles Murray (1984) *Losing Ground: American Social Policy, 1950–1980* (New York: Basic Books), pp. 204, 218, 227, 230; Charles Murray (1996) *Charles Murray and the Underclass: the Developing Debate* (London: Institute of Economic Affairs), pp. 50, 125. (This book contains 'The Emerging British Underclass', first published in 1989, and 'Underclass: The Crisis Deepens', first published in 1994.)
9. See Chap. 6 on the difference between Citizen's Income and Negative Income Tax.
10. Karl Marx (1938/1875) *Critique of the Gotha Programme* (London: Lawrence and Wishart), p. 14 (first published in German in 1875, and in Russian in 1891).
11. Karl Marx and Friedrich Engels (1967/1888) *The Communist Manifesto*, tr. Samuel Moore (Harmondsworth: Penguin), first published 1888, pp. 96, 99, 104.
12. Tony Benn (1974) *Speeches by Tony Benn* (Nottingham: Spokesman Books), p. 165.
13. Alex Callinicos (1983) *The Revolutionary Road to Socialism: What the Socialist Workers Party stands for* (London: Socialist Worker's Party), p. 20.
14. Carole Pateman (2005) 'Another Way Forward: Welfare, Social Reproduction, and a Basic Income', pp. 34–64 in Lawrence Mead and

Christopher Beem (eds), *Welfare Reform and Political Theory* (New York: Russell Sage Foundation), p. 56.
15. Hans Breitenbach, Tom Burden, and David Coates (1990) *Features of a Viable Socialism* (Hemel Hempstead: Harvester Wheatsheaf), p. 22.
16. Alex Callinicos (2003) *An Anti-Capitalist Manifesto* (Cambridge: Polity Press), p. 134.
17. Carole Pateman (2005) 'Another Way Forward: Welfare, Social Reproduction, and a Basic Income', p. 52.
18. Hans Breitenbach, Tom Burden, and David Coates (1990) *Features of a Viable Socialism*, p. 31.
19. Hans Breitenbach, Tom Burden, and David Coates (1990) *Features of a Viable Socialism*, p. 33.
20. Hans Breitenbach, Tom Burden, and David Coates (1990) *Features of a Viable Socialism*, pp. 81–2, 78.
21. Hans Breitenbach, Tom Burden, and David Coates (1990) *Features of a Viable Socialism*, p. 93.
22. Hans Breitenbach, Tom Burden, and David Coates (1990) *Features of a Viable Socialism*, p. 141.
23. Samuel Brittan (1998) *Towards a Humane Individualism* (London: John Stuart Mill Institute), p. 11.
24. Samuel Brittan (1998) *Towards a Humane Individualism*, p. 42.
25. Samuel Brittan and Steven Webb (1990) *Beyond the Welfare State: An Examination of Basic Incomes in a Market Economy* (Aberdeen: Aberdeen University Press), p. 5.
26. Samuel Brittan and Steven Webb (1990) *Beyond the Welfare State: An Examination of Basic Incomes in a Market Economy*, p. 2.
27. Theodore Burczak (2013) 'A Hayekian Case for a Basic Income', pp. 49–64 in Guinevere Liberty Nell (ed.), *Basic Income and the Free Market: Austrian Economics and the Potential for Efficient Redistribution* (New York: Palgrave Macmillan); Cameron Weber (2013) 'Taking Leviathan with a Basic Income', pp. 81–96 in Guinevere Liberty Nell (ed.), *Basic Income and the Free Market: Austrian Economics and the Potential for Efficient Redistribution* (New York: Palgrave Macmillan).
28. Samuel Brittan and Steven Webb (1990) *Beyond the Welfare State: An Examination of Basic Incomes in a Market Economy*, p. 3.
29. Samuel Brittan and Steven Webb (1990) *Beyond the Welfare State: An Examination of Basic Incomes in a Market Economy*, p. 7.
30. Tony Fitzpatrick (2003) *After the new social democracy: Social welfare for the twenty-first century* (Manchester: Manchester University Press), pp. 2, 5.
31. Tony Fitzpatrick (2003) *After the new social democracy*, p. 52.
32. Commission on Social Justice (1994) *Social Justice: Strategies for National Renewal* (London: Vintage), pp. 17–18.

33. Commission on Social Justice (1994) *Social Justice: Strategies for National Renewal*, pp. 261–2.
34. Peter Esam, Robert Good, and Rick Middleton (1985) *Who's to Benefit? A Radical Review of the Social Security System* (London: Verso), p. 53.
35. Stephen Goodwin, 'Liberal Democrats' Conference: Citizen's income plan dropped', *The Independent, Thursday 22nd September 1994:* www.independent.co.uk/news/uk/liberal-democrats-conference-citizens-income-plan-dropped-1450315.html (accessed 21/6/11).
36. Johannes Richardt, 'Basic Income, Low Aspiration', *The Sp!ked Review of Books*, issue 41, January 2011, www.spiked-online.com/index.php/site/reviewofbooks_article/10136/ (accessed 21/6/11).
37. Commission on Social Justice, *Social Justice: Strategies for National Renewal*, Vintage, London, 1994, pp. 262–3.
38. See Chap. 6 on Participation Income.
39. Commission on Social Justice, *Social Justice: Strategies for National Renewal*, Vintage, London, 1994, pp. 263–4.
40. Martin Watts (2010) 'How should Minimum Wages be Set in Australia', *Journal of Industrial Relations*, 52 (2), 131–49.
41. William Mitchell and Martin Watts (2005) 'A Comparison of the Economic Consequences of Basic Income and Job Guarantee Schemes', *Rutgers Journal of Law and Urban Policy*, 2 (1), 64–90; Martin Watts (2011) 'Income v Work Guarantees: A Reconsideration' (Newcastle, Australia: Newcastle University), http://hdl.handle.net/1959.13/934140
42. Jürgen De Wispelaere and José Antonio Noguera (2012) 'On the Political Feasibility of Universal Basic Income: An Analytic Framework', pp. 17–38 in Richard Caputo (ed.) *Basic Income Guarantee: International Experiences and Perspectives on the Viability of Income Guarantee* (New York: Palgrave Macmillan), p. 22.
43. See the UK case study at the end of this chapter for an example of a Green Party espousing Citizen's Income.
44. Pertti Koistinen and Johanna Perkiö (2014) 'Good and Bad Times of Social Innovations: The case of Universal Basic Income in Finland', *Basic Income Studies*, 9 (1–2), 25–57.
45. Jürgen De Wispelaere and José Antonio Noguera (2012) 'On the Political Feasibility of Universal Basic Income: An Analytic Framework', pp. 22–3.
46. Malcolm Torry (2015) *Two feasible ways to implement a revenue neutral Citizen's Income scheme*, Institute for Social and Economic Research Working Paper EM6/15 (Colchester: Institute for Social and Economic Research, University of Essex), p. 7, www.iser.essex.ac.uk/research/publications/working-papers/euromod/em6-15
47. See the second part of the case study in Chap. 7.
48. Yannick Vanderborght (2013) 'The Ambiguities of Basic Income from a Trade Union Perspective', pp. 497–508 in Karl Widerquist, José A.

Noguera, Yannick Vanderborght, and Jürgen De Wispelaere, *Basic Income: An anthology of contemporary research* (Chichester: Wiley Blackwell), pp. 498–9.
49. Yannick Vanderborght, 'The Ambiguities of Basic Income from a Trade Union Perspective', p. 498.
50. Yannick Vanderborght, 'The Ambiguities of Basic Income from a Trade Union Perspective', p. 503.
51. Jürgen De Wispelaere (2015) 'The Struggle for Strategy: On the Politics of the Basic Income Proposal', *Politics*, forthcoming.
52. David Howells MP, in Brandon Rhys Williams (1989) *Stepping Stones to Independence*, edited by Hermione Parker, foreword by David Howells MP (Aberdeen, Aberdeen University Press, for the One Nation Group of Conservative MPs), pp. vii–viii.
53. Juliet Rhys Williams (1943) *Something to Look Forward to* (London: MacDonald and Co.), pp. 141–2, quoted in Brandon Rhys Williams (1989) *Stepping Stones to Independence*, p. 7.
54. Brandon Rhys Williams (1989) *Stepping Stones to Independence*, p. 16.
55. David Howells MP, in Brandon Rhys Williams (1989) *Stepping Stones to Independence*, p. viii.
56. David Howells MP, in Brandon Rhys Williams (1989) *Stepping Stones to Independence*, p. viii.
57. Brandon Rhys Williams, House of Commons, 1/3/1985, quoted in Brandon Rhys Williams (1989) *Stepping Stones to Independence*, p. xiv.
58. Brandon Rhys Williams (1989) *Stepping Stones to Independence*, p. 22.
59. Brandon Rhys Williams (1989) *Stepping Stones to Independence*, p. 28.
60. Brandon Rhys Williams (1989) *Stepping Stones to Independence*, pp. 35–6.
61. Some of the content of this section reflects that of a Policy Press blog post, 'Would a Citizen's Income make some people poorer than they are today?' by Malcolm Torry, https://policypress.wordpress.com/tag/malcolm-torry/
62. Tony Fitzpatrick (2003) *After the new social democracy: Social welfare for the twenty-first century* (Manchester: Manchester University Press), pp. 152, 10.
63. Tony Fitzpatrick (2003) *After the new social democracy: Social welfare for the twenty-first century*, pp. 42, 89.
64. Essentially scheme A in Chap. 3.
65. Malcolm Torry (2014) *Research note: A feasible way to implement a Citizen's Income*, Institute to Social and Economic Research Working Paper EM17/14 (Colchester: Institute for Social and Economic Research, University of Essex), www.iser.essex.ac.uk/research/publications/working-papers/euromod/em17-14, subsequently republished as Malcolm Torry (2015) 'Research note: A feasible way to implement a Citizen's Income', *Citizen's Income Newsletter*, issue 1 for 2015, pp. 4–9. See also

Malcolm Torry (2015) *Two feasible ways to implement a revenue neutral Citizen's Income scheme*, Institute for Social and Economic Research Working Paper EM6/15 (Colchester: Institute for Social and Economic Research, University of Essex), www.iser.essex.ac.uk/research/publications/working-papers/euromod/em6-15, subsequently published as Malcolm Torry (2015) 'Research note: A feasible way to implement a Citizen's Income', *Citizen's Income Newsletter*, issue 1 for 2015, pp. 4-9.
66. www.youtube.com/watch?v=5dFn8RIXOBE&feature=youtu.be
67. www.theguardian.com/politics/2015/jan/27/green-party-citizens-income-policy-hits-poor
68. Malcolm Torry (2014) *Research note: A feasible way to implement a Citizen's Income*, Institute for Social and Economic Research Working Paper EM17/14, Institute for Social and Economic Research (Colchester: UniversityofEssex),www.iser.essex.ac.uk/research/publications/working-papers/euromod/em17-14, subsequently republished as Malcolm Torry (2015) 'Research note: A feasible way to implement a Citizen's Income', *Citizen's Income Newsletter*, issue 1 for 2015, pp. 4-9.
69. House of Commons Treasury and Civil Service Committee Sub-Committee (1982) *The Structure of Personal Income Taxation and Income Support: Minutes of Evidence*, HC 331-ix (London: Her Majesty's Stationery Office), p. 459.
70. The results were obtained using EUROMOD version G2.0++. The contribution of all past and current members of the EUROMOD consortium is gratefully acknowledged. The process of extending and updating EUROMOD is financially supported by the Directorate General for Employment, Social Affairs and Inclusion of the European Commission [Progress grant no. VS/2011/0445]. The UK Family Resources Survey data was made available by the Department of Work and Pensions via the UK Data Archive.
71. Parts of this case study were first published in a EUROMOD working paper, Malcolm Torry (2015) *Two feasible ways to implement a revenue neutral Citizen's Income scheme*, Institute for Social and Economic Research Working Paper EM6/15 (Colchester: Institute for Social and Economic Research, University of Essex), www.iser.essex.ac.uk/research/publications/working-papers/euromod/em6-15. The Institute for Social and Economic Research's permission to reprint material from the working paper is gratefully acknowledged.
72. Children in poverty are those living in households with income below 60% of median income. For detailed discussion of the percentage figures generated by the summary statistics function of EUROMOD, see Paola De Agostini and Holly Sutherland (2014) *Euromod Country Report: United Kingdom 2009-2013* (Colchester: Institute for Social and Economic Research, Essex University), pp. 71-2.

73. Peter Taylor-Gooby (1987) *MPs' Attitudes to Welfare* (Swindon: Economic and Social Research Council), p. 2.
74. Citizen's Income Trust (2007) 'Both the House of Commons and the House of Lords support a Citizen's Income approach to the reform of tax and benefits', *Citizen's Income Newsletter*, issue 1 for 2007, p. 1.
75. Jürgen De Wispelaere and José Antonio Noguera (2012) 'On the Political Feasibility of Universal Basic Income', p. 22.
76. Josh Martin (2015) 'Universal Credit to Basic Income: A Politically Feasible Transition?', unpublished M.Sc. dissertation (London: London School of Economics), p. 30.
77. Malcolm Torry (2013) *Money for Everyone: Why we need a Citizen's Income*, p. 228.

CHAPTER 9

Is a Citizen's Income Policy Process Feasible?

9.1 Introduction

This chapter tackles the second part of what De Wispelaere and Noguera describe as 'strategic feasibility': 'political entrepreneurs engaging in all sorts of strategic interventions to build a political coalition enabling the legislation and subsequent implementation of a policy proposal'.[1] By 'policy process feasibility' I mean the feasibility of Citizen's Income travelling from idea to implementation through the institutions and individuals that together make up the policy process.

As in Chap. 8, we have a problem: The policy process is always highly country-specific. In particular, policy networks function in very different ways in different national contexts.[2] The main body of this chapter will therefore have to be in the most general of terms, leaving the reader to work out how Citizen's Income would relate to the political ideologies and the policy process in their own context. The case studies will study the ways in which various policies either have or have not managed to negotiate their way from idea to implementation in the UK.

A further problem is that the policy process is highly diffused and has very fuzzy boundaries. The media, the general public, and all manner of institutions have roles to play as an idea travels through the process, so policy process feasibility is rarely simply that. Psychological

---

Some of the material in this chapter first appeared in a paper given at the BIEN Congress in June 2014 at Montreal.

feasibility, financial feasibilities, administrative feasibility, and behavioural feasibility are constantly at issue as policy-making institutions and individuals make decisions about whether and how to let policy ideas through the system, so in places, this chapter will return to material that we have discussed in previous chapters, and it will also be longer than the other chapters.

The 'policy process' is a complex network of policy networks and communities,[3] think tanks and other institutional players, the government, Parliament, the civil service, and trades unions, and such self-interested players as computer manufacturers and software writers. A further complexity is that each institutional player is a ferment of informal structures alongside their stated formal structures,[4] that the informal structures in particular change as people come and go,[5] and that growing numbers of political advisors and of civil service appointments from outside the civil service increasingly blur the boundaries between the civil service and other elements of the policy process.[6] Yet another complexity is that as policies travel through the system, they change it, and at the same time, other policies travelling through the policy-making institutions are changing them. The system is highly dynamic, making prediction difficult in the extreme. As Morçöl puts it in terms of complexity theory:

> public policy is an emergent, self-organizational, and dynamic complex system. The relations among the actors of this complex system are nonlinear and its relations with its elements and with other systems are coevolutionary.[7]

It is because of these characteristics of the field that innovation can occur,[8] but these characteristics also mean that policy-making is likely to be evolutionary or incremental. It is easier to make small changes to what exists than to attempt to change what is. The result is path dependency, which means that policy areas, such as benefits policy, find themselves on a path, and that that path is the strongest determinant of any future direction. The outcome is second-best, suboptimal solutions to problems rather than optimal ones.[9]

All of this makes it sound as if it would be impossible for any social policy proposals ever to get from idea to implementation, but sometimes a new policy is implemented, so one of the tasks of this chapter will be to work out the factors that might determine success or failure. Another will be to ask whether one implementation proposal rather than another might help a policy proposal, and in particular Citizen's Income, to get from idea to implementation.

9.2   The Policy Process

I shall take as my guide Michael Hill's *The Public Policy Process*[10]:

> The policy process is a complex and multi-layered one. It is ... a complex political process in which there are many actors: politicians, pressure groups, civil servants, publicly employed professionals, and even sometimes those who see themselves as the passive recipients of policy.[11]

A first step in understanding the policy process in relation to a particular policy proposal is to ask about the geographical location of relevant factors.[12] For instance, are global factors significant, or do we only need to take account of factors relating to the social and economic environment of the UK (which are, of course, influenced by global factors)? To take a different policy proposal: A 'Tobin' tax on currency transactions[13] might be feasible at a very low level in an individual country, but the fact that banking is a global industry, and that currency exchange can occur in numerous financial centres around the world, mean that a Tobin tax in one country at a level that might discourage banks from undertaking currency exchanges in that country would not be feasible. In the case of a Citizen's Income, it might be thought that a relevant geographical factor would be the free movement of labour in Europe. Would a Citizen's Income in one country encourage higher levels of inward migration? The answer to this question is probably 'no' unless the Citizen's Income were to be set at a level higher than current means-tested and universal benefits. The UK already has an unconditional and nonwithdrawable Child Benefit, payable to anyone with the care of children if they ordinarily reside in the UK, they have a right to be there, and they are physically present in the country.[14] Child Benefit is rarely accused of fuelling inward migration. More generally, a Citizen's Income at a level not above that of existing benefits would provide no additional incentive to migrate to the UK, and the same would presumably apply in relation to other countries. This means that while it might have looked as if the social and economic environments in countries other than the one in which a Citizen's Income is to be implemented might be relevant factors, they might not be, and we can concentrate on institutions and processes within a single country.

Crucial to the policy process are the institutions for which ideas and evidence are inputs, and legislation and implementation are outputs. In the case of the UK, in the field of social security benefits, this means ministers, government departments, and Parliament; and in the case of other countries, the institutions in which law-making occurs. Quite often, any one part of a law-making system can block or delay policy change, and all of the parts have to cooperate to enable change to occur.[15] Also essential to the policy process will be a policy community or policy network concerned about a particular issue, or perhaps about a variety of issues. Such networks (interorganizational connections[16] around which information passes)[17] will often be complex, with some members more concerned about one aspect of an issue, and some more concerned about another, and they will overlap with other networks and communities.[18] In relation to Citizen's Income, networks concerned with poverty alleviation, poverty abolition, employment incentives, individual freedom, and the voluntary sector will all be relevant, as will be the already quite well-developed network gathered around the idea of a Citizen's Income.

Hodge and Lowe define a 'policy community' more narrowly as a policy network with a tight-knit group of professionals at its core, and suggest that it can be more effective than an 'issue network' without such a stabilizing element. The example that they offer is that the social work field (with social workers at its core) and the healthcare field (with medical professionals at its core) have managed to exert more control over changing information and communication technology in their fields than has proved possible in the social security field, in which neither practitioners nor claimants have had much influence over the changes in technology imposed on the system. Hodge and Lowe suggest that in general there has been more change in fields with issue networks than in fields with policy communities.[19] This might be true in some areas, such as information and communication technology, but it has surely not been true in relation to the overall structure of provision. In relation to detail, the social security field has seen frequent changes, but it is still operating within the framework established by the Beveridge Report in 1942, whereas social work and healthcare might have seen less change in relation to detail, but they have seen multiple changes in structure. To return to Beveridge: he functioned as the professional core of a policy community, and the result was substantial change (for instance, the implementation of Family Allowances).[20]

But however effective policy networks might be, however well organized they might be,[21] and however adequate the general public's understanding and approval of a policy proposal might be, only if the government, legislators, and relevant public servants[22] (the 'élite'[23] members of the policy network) line up to create the necessary change will the policy change occur.[24] In particular, relevant government departments will need to line up with each other and with other parts of the policy network.[25] If they do all line up behind the proposal, then members of the policy network will exchange research and other resources with each other in order to achieve policy implementation. If they do not all line up, then even the best organized policy community will revert to being a powerless network.[26]

As Hill suggests, institutions relate to institutions, which means that as well as individual proponents of a policy change relating to individuals within the system, it is important that institutions within the policy networks and communities attached to a policy proposal should relate to other institutions.[27] Think tanks are important because they are institutions that can relate to institutions[28] (often by individuals moving between think tanks, legislatures, and government departments).[29] Important to both individual and institutional relationships with a country's government, civil service, and legislative assembly will be a recognition that every actor in the system is to some extent self-interested. Each member of a parliament, each minister, and each civil servant will to some extent be influenced by their own interests; and if supporting a proposal would be clearly against their own interests, then they would be unlikely to support it. So, for instance, civil servants would be unlikely to support proposals that might reduce the size of their departments.[30] They might also be somewhat unenthusiastic about a policy change that might be impossible to implement. Successful implementation of a policy can enhance a civil service career, but impending implementation failure will lead to capable civil servants seeking transfers from the department or section involved, for obvious reasons. Another consequence of the necessarily self-interested nature of political actors is that if a think tank that provides civil servants, government ministers, and legislators with information that is useful to them in the context of their existing interests, then a relationship will be created across which can flow information about reform options in which they might become interested.[31]

What we have said so far about the policy process makes it look as if it might be orderly and rational, but that is generally far from the truth. Hill describes the policy environment as like a soup within which problems (which are socially constructed[32]), policy options (again socially constructed), and political factors[33] (constantly influenced by societal pressures) swirl in unpredictable ways. A particularly important political factor is the number of government departments involved. If, as in the UK, more than one government department is involved in benefits policy, then ministers will follow the prevailing views within their departments, simply because that is the easiest thing to do. The shifting balance of power between the departments will then be an important impediment to rational decision-making.[34] Further factors that compromise the rationality of decision-making are that government departments are constituted as much by informal structures as by formal ones, and that bureaucrats are to some extent professionalized and can therefore maintain considerable areas of freedom for themselves.[35] Gordon, Lewis, and Young go even further:

> The powerful survival of the 'rational system' model is surprising given that its assumptions have been undermined by empirical studies of the policy process … policy-making systems approximate more closely to the 'political model'.[36]

It might occasionally be true that, as Majone suggests,

> people in government achieve their goals by adopting those programs which please voters most, just as entrepreneurs make profits by producing things people want,[37]

but there will be numerous occasions on which government ministers will follow their prejudices rather than attempt to understand what members of the public might think about proposed changes. NHS reform in the UK is a classic case of health ministers taking little notice of either the general public or health service employees.

If either public opinion or government ministers' prejudices are the driving force for change, then it might appear that think tanks would be irrelevant, but this might not be the case. While it is difficult to assess their influence,[38] it might not be marginal because think tanks fulfil a number of useful functions within the policy-making process. Those affiliated to political parties, either formally or informally, enable those parties to undertake research, hold internal debates, and, sometimes, reach a new consensus,[39] out of the glare of the media, which is usually all too ready to describe debate as division and the discussion of options as U-turns. The political process finds it difficult to debate and communicate complexity, and government ministers often do not have the time to do so,[40] whereas think tanks can do that.[41] The problem for think tanks is that they tend to work with a rational model of the policy process, and generally with a 'problem, solution, implementation' model; but, as we have seen, policy-making in the real world is rarely that tidy, and however rational a think tank's proposals, they will remain simply good ideas unless the government of the day can see implementation as advantageous to itself, and getting the idea to implementation as relatively easy.[42] It is all very well asking to test a policy option such as Citizen's Income against the 'do nothing' option, or against other possible options, but that is not how the real world works.[43]

Policy change is generally incremental because that is the only kind that looks feasible within such a complex environment[44]; because we think that we understand the status quo[45]; because incremental change enables learning and useful adaptation to occur[46]; because evidence can only be collected from existing systems; because it is often easier to implement changes to existing systems than to build entirely new systems[47]; because small incremental changes are generally easier for the different parties within a policy network to understand than major system changes; and because political pressures in a variety of directions will often only allow minor policy changes, and will frequently result in a pendulum effect: for instance, between means-testing and universality.[48] Another reason for change generally being incremental in countries with permanent civil services, like the UK, is that civil servants have to serve consecutive ministers with often very different ideological positions, and seeking consensus is the most likely way to avoid turbulence as governments change.[49] (Civil servants achieve the control that they do because ministers have little time available and must therefore rely on civil servants to give regulatory and legislative effect to their ideas.) The media,[50] which is an important and influential component of any policy network, will often not be capable of expressing simply and accurately the smallest policy changes, and nor will public opinion be capable of relating to them,[51] so the media is highly unlikely to be capable of expressing accurately the reasons for major systems changes; so again, consensus and incremental change will be the safest option. The result is 'satisficing': Only a limited number of options are studied, all of them are close to the current system, and genuine system change is off the agenda.[52]

The policy process is often described as a series of steps, for instance:

1. Precise definition of policy objectives;
2. Instruments chosen;
3. Implementation arrangements formulated;
4. Rules for implementation.[53]

whereas in practice 'policy formulation is a piecemeal activity'[54] within which the different theoretical steps merge into each other.[55] Take the example of changes to a benefits system. Theoretically, a government minister will take to the legislative assembly a piece of legislation prepared by civil servants according to instructions given by the minister; the parliament will pass the legislation; and the new policy will then be implemented by civil servants. However, things are rarely as simple as that. For instance, if new computer software is required to implement the benefits changes, then the computer company writing the software will be an interested party, will attempt to influence both the policy and its regulations, and will often succeed in doing so because their statement that computerization would be cheaper or easier if changes were made, or that computerization would be impossible if changes were not made, would be difficult to contradict. The computer company possesses 'expert power' in the situation,[56] even if it is not very expert.

When it comes to the implementation of a new policy, the situation is equally complex, and precisely how the policy is implemented will depend on the characteristics of the policy, on any accompanying regulations, and on the organizations involved in implementation: the relationships between them; their feedback to ministers, parliament, and the civil service; and the ways in which their staff (functioning as 'street-level bureaucrats'[57]) implement the policy and exercise discretion in relation to regulations. A further factor will be public response to implementation.[58]

We can draw some initial conclusions in relation to the policy process feasibility of a Citizen's Income:

- Institutional representation of the policy idea is essential: that is, broadly based think tanks and academic departments actively involved in research, dissemination and education, and perhaps also well-resourced national and regional Citizen's Income organizations functioning as pressure groups[59];
- A policy network or community is required in which institutions and individuals representing the media, community groups, academia, political parties, think tanks, trades unions, employers' organizations, and generally as wide a range of interests as possible relate well to each other, relate consistently to the issues of poverty, the poverty trap, and a Citizen's Income, and together relate to parliament, the government, and the civil service;

- An important task will be to prepare draft legislation, regulations, and implementation strategies, because these will make it clear that some of the complexities related to other policy options would not apply to a Citizen's Income—and, in particular, that computerization would be simple, that institutional arrangements for implementation would be radically simple, and that there would be no street-level bureaucrats to worry about[60];
- Implementation of a Citizen's Income would probably work best if it was incremental: perhaps implementation one demographic group at a time rather than as a single project for the entire age range (and the existence of pilot projects of some kind will be useful to represent the incremental and proven nature of the change envisaged)[61];
- Careful study of current government priorities will be required throughout the process. Current themes of the UK's government are the disaggregation of the public sector (which suggests that the Citizen's Incomes should be managed by a separate agency), explicit standards, output controls, and discipline and parsimony in relation to resources (all easy to achieve with a Citizen's Income)[62];
- Equally important will be an understanding of where a government is open to contributions from pressure groups, and where it is not[63]; and, more generally, where influence might be possible in the relevant policy-making systems[64];
- The proposal will need to be seen to address problems recognized as serious, such as poverty, and the poverty trap;
- The proposal will need to garner government, parliamentary, and civil service support, and this will require public understanding and support—so psychological feasibility will have to have been achieved[65];
- Implementation will need to be, and be seen to be, administratively feasible, both in relation to transition and in relation to ongoing administration;
- The media will need to be actively involved in the policy network, and both this and public understanding will depend on clearly deserving social groups benefiting from the proposed change or changes—which is again an argument for incremental implementation.

Throughout, a tactic that often afflicts the policy process will need to be rejected, and that is compromise.[66] Any compromise over the characteristics of unconditional and nonwithdrawable benefits—for instance, by applying conditions of any kind to their receipt—would destroy the policy proposal, would not deliver the benefits that an unconditional and nonwithdrawable benefit would offer, and would make it more difficult to establish an unconditional and nonwithdrawable benefit for the next demographic group. Commitment to unconditionality and nonwithdrawability by individual and institutional members of relevant policy networks and communities, and their carefully and consistently expressed arguments for these characteristics, will be essential.

Are we asking too much here? We are asking for a rational policy-making process, whereas much of this chapter has suggested that the real policy-making world is political rather than rational, and creates change incrementally and piecemeal. We shall of course to some extent have to conform to the way the world is, and will therefore have to propose a piecemeal and incremental approach to the implementation of Citizen's Income, but at the same time we must continue to emphasize the rationality of Citizen's Income. It might be true, as Robert Gregory suggests, that

> formal techniques of analysis and theory-building—no matter how desirable—are inevitably mediated by processes of political interaction, and are no substitute for them[67]:

but it will also be true that formal techniques of analysis and theory-building will be contributing to the policy process. As Smith and Day put it, the policy process has an obligation to retain at least an element of rationality:

> Although the costs of rational decision-making are high, the costs of failing to explore radical alternatives to existing policies may be even higher.[68]

9.3 Case Study: Policy Change in the UK

The purpose of this case study is to answer the question: What are the factors that in practice determine political decisions made about the UK's income maintenance system (understood as encompassing earned income, investment income, social security benefits, and taxation)?[69] To answer that question might enable us to answer another: Is it possible to evaluate the policy process feasibility of reform options for the income maintenance system that have not so far been implemented?

Study of a number of proposals for reforming the income maintenance system—both those that have succeeded, and those that have failed—should enable us to list the factors that might facilitate a policy's successful negotiation of the policy process. We shall then attempt to draw conclusions relating to the policy process feasibility of the National Minimum Wage (NMW) becoming a National Living Wage (NLW) (defined as a wage 'explicitly tied to the purchasing power deemed necessary ... to provide workers and their families with a basic but acceptable standard of living rather than estimates of what the market can bear without impacting on employment'[70]), and of a Citizen's Income.

9.3.1   Histories and Characteristics

In Chap. 1, I gave brief accounts of policy proposals in the UK, some of which were implemented, and some of which were not. My initial conclusion was that the proposals that were implemented were developments of existing provisions; there was some public understanding and approval of the proposals; they were for identifiable groups of deserving individuals (and where they were not, they imposed harsh conditions and sanctions); and each change required additional public servants.

Here I offer a more detailed discussion of a longer list of proposals—including the NMW and the current Living Wage campaign—in order to test that initial conclusion and to draw further conclusions.

9.3.2   Family Allowance

By the beginning of the Second World War, the payment of an allowance to mothers to help them to care for their children was not a new idea. During the First World War, child allowances had been paid to mothers of soldiers at the front; and child allowances were being paid in addition to wages at the London School of Economics, where William Beveridge, the Director, had been persuaded of the wisdom of the idea[71] by reading Eleanor Rathbone's 1924 *The Disinherited Family*.[72] Rathbone had argued that a worker's wage could be expected to support a small family, but not a large one, so mothers needed an income of their own to enable them to care for their children.[73] When Beveridge was asked to chair a wartime committee to plan for post-war social security benefits, he was not asked to discuss child allowances, so he wrote the idea into the report as a presupposition.[74]

Child allowances were already being paid with Unemployment Benefit, so a worker with a large family could find that when they moved from unemployment to employment, they could be worse off. Not only was this bad for labour market incentives, but employers were also concerned that after the war full employment would create the conditions for unsustainable wage rises, and that the subsistence needs of workers with large families would exacerbate the resulting wage inflation. The only solution to these problems was to provide child allowances both in and out of employment. In 1945, Parliament passed the Family Allowance Act, and the first Family Allowances were paid in 1946. While no allowance was paid for the first child in a family, and the allowance was set lower than Beveridge had wished, an unconditional Family Allowance was implemented because 'little money can be saved by any reasonable income test'.[75]

Family Allowances were an attack on poverty, but they were also an attack on the poverty trap. Because Family Allowances were not means-tested, and were paid whatever the household's employment status, the scheme meant that a worker who moved from Unemployment Benefit to paid employment no longer experienced a drop in net income. Other possible causes for the success of Rathbone's proposal were that the plan had a champion in William Beveridge; there was substantial public approval of the scheme, particularly among women; MPs could support it, because they wanted to keep a lid on wages,[76] because they approved of the scheme's equal treatment of every family, or because they did not wish to be seen to disapprove of a clearly popular measure[77]; trades unions were able to approve (because by the end of the Second World War, there were more women in trades unions than there had been before the war); the civil service was able to approve the plan once a lower allowance than was first intended had been achieved, and presumably because a new department would be needed to administer the Family Allowances; the scheme exhibited clear continuities with previous schemes, both with child allowances paid with Unemployment Benefit and to soldiers' families; the London School of Economics experience was a useful pilot project; administration of the non-means-tested benefit was uncomplicated; the scheme presented no transitional problems; and the benefit's recipients were clearly a deserving social group: that is, children, and the mothers who cared for them. The London School of Economics had functioned as a think tank, and Rathbone, Beveridge and his committee, and the London School of Economics had between them constituted the relevant policy community.

9.3.3 National Insurance and National Assistance

During the Second World War, a committee established by Parliament—which under William Beveridge's chairmanship functioned rather like a modern think tank—produced the report *Social Insurance and Allied Services*,[78] which proposed National Insurance benefits in return for regular National Insurance contributions, and means-tested National Assistance to top up contributory benefits if they were insufficient—for instance, for working-age adults whose contributory Unemployment Benefit had expired, or whose Unemployment Benefit did not provide a high enough income to cover housing costs (Beveridge had intended contributory benefits to be sufficiently high to cover housing costs, but the government set the rates too low for this and more families than originally intended found themselves having to apply for National Assistance).[79] The combination of contributory and means-tested benefits was one that people already knew about, because contributory benefits already existed for some industries, Friendly Societies and other organizations were already paying benefits if contributions conditions were met, and for many households, means-testing was either a difficult memory or a present experience. The plan assumed full employment for households' male breadwinners, and because for all but the largest families a male wage provided more than the benefits system, and for families with children Family Allowances were not withdrawn as earnings increased, no poverty trap was expected to materialize.

In 1946, an Act of Parliament established National Insurance (contributory) Retirement Pensions, Unemployment Benefit, and Sickness Benefit; and in 1948, an Act gave birth to means-tested National Assistance.

The scheme was in continuity with the somewhat chaotic system that had preceded it (elements of which could be regarded as pilot projects); it tackled poverty; it did not generate an appreciable poverty trap; it met with substantial public understanding and approval; it was difficult for MPs of any party to find fault with it; it promised an expansion of the civil service; administration of contributory benefits was relatively simple; it was not thought that there would be many people claiming the more administratively complex National Assistance; and transition into the scheme was undertaken with enthusiasm and relatively little difficulty. While the scheme was universal in coverage, only the contingencies of illness, disability, unemployment, and old-age triggered benefits claims, so in an era of almost full employment, the vast majority of the population had no contact with the scheme apart from their employer fixing the weekly National Insurance stamps onto their cards.

9.3.4 Universal Credit

In 1965, Peter Townsend and Brian Abel-Smith published *The Poor and the Poorest*, which showed that almost one in five families were on incomes below half the average.[80] Many of those families were in work. In 1971, the government responded by implementing the means-tested in-work benefit Family Income Supplement,[81] renamed 'Family Credit' in 1985. Unfortunately, the freezing of Child Benefit[82] and the more generous nature of Family Credit exacerbated an existing poverty trap. The 1997 Labour government renamed Family Credit 'Working Families Tax Credit', and in 2003 replaced it with 'Child Tax Credits' and 'Working Tax Credits' (available for the first time to households without children). The more generous nature of Tax Credits reduced child poverty, but at the same time, it increased the earnings range across which households experienced a poverty trap.[83]

'Universal Credit' is now being implemented—slowly. The plan[84] was put together by the Centre for Social Justice, a think tank established by Iain Duncan Smith, Shadow Secretary of State for Work and Pensions while the Conservative Party was in opposition: so here we have an example of a policy process to which a think tank was crucial, and an example of decisions being made a long way from Parliament.[85] Universal Credit combines in-work and out-of-work means-tested benefits into a single means-tested benefit in order to ease the transition into employment. By reducing the rate at which means-tested benefits are withdrawn,[86]Universal Credit will reduce child poverty and also the depth of the poverty trap, but in doing so, it will increase the earnings range across which households will experience benefits withdrawal. The benefit will therefore embed means-testing at the heart of millions of households' income maintenance strategies, and in particular will make it less worthwhile for second earners to seek employment.

The plan has a champion in Iain Duncan Smith; there is a level of public understanding of the general idea, but not of the detail; the plan is in continuity with previous means-tested benefits; MPs of all parties have been able to support the general idea, whatever they might think about its detail and implementation; the civil service is content to try to make it work; and trades unions have been largely absent from the debate, which is somewhat surprising given that the scheme integrates in-work with out-of-work benefits.[87] Administration of the new benefit requires accurate real-time communication between employers', Her Majesty's Revenue and Customs, and Department for Work and Pensions' computer systems, and because this is proving a problem transition from the existing to the new system is somewhat fraught. This is therefore a case of policy goals being relatively clear but there having been little understanding of the delivery mechanisms required to enable the chosen policy option to be delivered.[88] If the transition fails, then it will be because the scheme was never adequately tested for administrative feasibility. The plan's other characteristics have been no barrier to legislation and attempted implementation.

9.3.5 Child Benefit

I have told the story of how Family Allowance became Child Benefit in Chap. 2.

Child Benefit was an attack on child poverty (because mothers were more likely to spend the Family Allowance on their children than were fathers to spend the value of their child tax allowances on them), and, as we have seen, it was an attack on the poverty trap. The scheme had some significant champions in Barbara Castle and Frank Field; it was in continuity with the highly popular Family Allowance, of which there had been twenty years' experience; the general public, and especially mothers, were in favour; enough MPs had good reasons for voting for Child Benefit; the Child Poverty Action Group functioned as both a think tank and a campaigning organization; and after the scandal of the government's attempt to block implementation, there were plenty of MPs who wanted to see it happen. The civil service was content, and possibly happy, to implement the scheme; trades unions were in favour (women constituted an increasing proportion of members); administration and transition were easy to manage; and again the benefit's recipients were clearly a deserving social group: children, and the mothers who cared for them.

9.3.6 A National Minimum Wage

In spite of the implementation of Family Income Supplement, by the early 1980s, in-work poverty remained a problem.[89] Two solutions vied for attention: a NMW, of which there was already experience in other countries[90]; and an increase in the value of in-work means-tested benefits, which was the policy chosen by the Conservative government when Family Income Supplement became Family Credit. But the problem with that strategy was that because Family Credit was withdrawn as earnings rose, and there was now more to withdraw, the poverty trap was deepened. As proponents of a NMW pointed out, a higher wage would reduce the amount of means-tested benefit required and would therefore reduce the depth of the poverty trap; and as Chris Pond and Steve Winyard pointed out in their *Case for a National Minimum Wage*:

> Even if it were possible to devise a social policy which would compensate for the effects of low wages without stigma and without the problem of the poverty trap, this would not overcome the feelings of injustice and humiliation which are associated with the receipt of low wages.[91]

In 1970, the Trade Union Congress (TUC) suggested a 'guideline' NMW, because there were some trade unionists who wanted to resist government interference in wage-setting; but although during the 1980s this argument was still heard,[92] in 1982 the TUC passed a resolution committing itself to consult with a future Labour government over the establishment of a NMW,[93] and in 1995 the TUC itself published *Arguments for a National Minimum Wage*:

> A National Minimum Wage which raised pay levels in the poorest paid occupations and industries would clearly reduce the extent to which Family Credit currently subsidises low pay.[94]

The 'widespread assumption that raising wages will automatically lead to a loss of jobs'[95] was intuitive: but the counterarguments were increasingly heard: that wage-setting is a political activity[96]; that the wage paid does not necessarily equate to the marginal product of labour[97]; that the impact of a NMW would only increase the total wage bill by about 5 % (because raising the lowest wages to an agreed or statutory minimum would have only a small effect on wage levels above that minimum[98]); that therefore a NMW would lead to very little additional unemployment, if any[99]; that only minor reductions in the return to capital and minor increases in prices would be the result; and that higher wages for the lowest paid would lead to increased consumption of goods and services and would therefore increase demand and thus employment.[100] As for the argument that the government should stay out of wage-setting, the government regulated working conditions, so why not wages?[101]

In 1995, the Confederation of British Industry (CBI) declared itself opposed to a NMW, but by 1997 it was recommending one on the basis that it would create a floor to the market.[102] Crucial to the debate was the expressed view of many business leaders who resented being forced to pay low wages and to reduce investment in both human and physical capital by competitors who reduced their production costs by paying low wages.[103] An additional argument more often thought than expressed was that a general rise in wage rates would put some of the least efficient businesses out of business, thus improving the general efficiency of the industries concerned.

The Labour Party's manifesto for the 1997 General Election included a pledge to establish a NMW, and in 1998 the National Minimum Wage Act was passed. It was implemented in April 1999 with NMW levels set by the new Low Pay Commission at £3.60 per hour for workers aged over twenty-one and £3.00 per hour for workers aged between eighteen and twenty.[104] The Treasury, the Bank of England, the TUC, and the CBI all declared themselves happy with the calculation.[105] In 2003, a new lower rate was established for sixteen- and seventeen-year-olds.[106]

Why did it happen?

The idea was not entirely new. In 1909, the government, with Winston Churchill's enthusiastic support, had established Trades Boards[107] to set minimum wages for particular industries. These later became the Wages Councils; and although these had been abolished by the time of the 1997 election, they provided an important precedent and pilot project. A NMW could therefore be seen as in direct continuity with almost a hundred years of experience of national wage-setting.

The NMW was an attack on poverty, and, as we have seen, it was also an attack on the poverty trap. The Prime Minister and the Cabinet were in favour, so there were plenty of parliamentary champions, but also important was sustained work on the issue by the think tank and campaigning group the Low Pay Unit, and particularly by its Director, Chris Pond, who became a MP in 1997.[108] There was substantial public understanding of the problem of low pay, and of the proposal for a NMW; there were clear arguments for the proposal; and eventually, there was sufficient understanding that evidence did not support the intuitive arguments against it.[109] The legislation established the Low Pay Commission to set NMW levels, an inspectorate to enforce them, and tribunals to hear cases, thus increasing the number of public servants. Administration of the scheme is relatively simple, and implementation was not difficult. Recipients were a clearly deserving group of people: the working poor.

9.3.7 The Campaign for a Living Wage

The Low Pay Commission established by the 1998 National Minimum Wage Act studied a variety of possible levels for the initial NMW, and decided on a relatively low wage that would have only a minor impact on employment. The NMW was never going to be enough to live on, meaning that in-work benefits would continue to be needed. Already in 1996, TELCO (The East London Communities Organization) had brought US-style community organizing to London,[110] and in 2001, the campaign for a Living Wage—a wage level based on a Minimum Income Standard calculated to provide a decent standard of living—became an important activity for what had by then become London Citizens. In 2005, the GLA established its Living Wage Unit to encourage London's employers to pay a Living Wage; and in 2011, the national organization at the heart of community organizing, Citizens UK, gave birth to the Living Wage Foundation, which validates Living Wage employers: that is, employers who pay the Living Wage rates established by the Foundation on the basis of research into Minimum Income Standards by the Centre for Research in Social Policy at Loughborough University[111] and by research into London living costs by the GLA's Living Wage Unit.[112] The number of Living Wage employers continues to grow both because local campaigning has been effective and because a Living Wage makes good business sense. In the early days of mass car production, Henry Ford had more than doubled his workers' wages in order to increase motivation and reduce absenteeism, staff turnover, and training costs. Counterintuitively, doubling the wages saved the company money.[113] Living Wage employers discover similar effects when they increase wages from the NMW to the Living Wage.[114]

When I wrote the first version of this part of the case study for a paper that I presented at the 2014 Social Policy Association Conference, I asked the question: What is the likelihood that we shall see the establishment of a NLW?—that is, a statutory NMW that rises sufficiently to become a statutory NLW? (and in this case, like the Living Wage and unlike the NMW, a higher rate would need to be set for London than for the rest of the country).

I then suggested that one way to tackle this question was to ask the related question: If an NLW were to be established, what would we then say were the causes of its implementation? This was to treat a not yet implemented proposal in the same way as we have treated the implemented proposals studied above. I used the past tense.

The voluntary Living Wage had plenty of champions: the Prime Minister, other party leaders, the Mayor of London, the vast majority of MPs and local councillors, and numerous public, private, voluntary, and religious sector organizations. Initially, it was not clear how much of this support for a voluntary Living Wage would translate into support for a statutory NLW, but public support for NMWs was rising in a variety of OECD countries, the value of NMWs in other OECD countries was rising (apparently without adding to unemployment),[115] and the number of validated Living Wage employers in the UK continued to rise, so increasing numbers of organizations and individuals felt able to support a NLW. Living Wage employers were particularly vociferous in support of a NLW because they were being undercut by firms that were paying only the NMW.

The NLW was an attack on poverty, and also an attack on the poverty trap, for the same reasons that the NMW was an attack on them in 1998. There was substantial experience and public understanding of a NMW, a growing appreciation of the importance of the idea, and increasing awareness that the NMW had made very little difference to employment levels.[116] Research had shown that the NMW had raised the average wage bill by 0.5 %,[117] that in many industries the payment of a Living Wage would increase the wage bill by just 1 %, and that in the lowest-paid sectors' companies, wage bills would rise by about 5 %, but that phased implementation would reduce upfront costs and would enable businesses to adapt.[118] Companies found this to be case. The NLW was in direct continuity with the NMW, and the same mechanisms were employed to enforce it. The legislation permitted transition from the NMW into a NLW over a four-year period, and businesses found that this was sufficient time in which to adjust—and in which to appreciate the higher motivation and lower absenteeism and staff turnover that the policy had delivered. Implementation was enthusiastically handled by the public authorities involved; and the press was behind the change because recipients were a clearly deserving group: the working poor.

A particularly interesting characteristic of the journey towards a NLW was the strong relationship between research and practice. The GLA both researched and paid a Living Wage; and, to take just one example from a London borough: Matthew Pennycook, who had conducted important research on the Living Wage for the think tank the Resolution Foundation, as a Greenwich local councillor was a major influence on the Council becoming a Living Wage employer.

When I wrote the conference paper on which this section of this chapter is based, I then added this: I am not a betting man, but if I were, then I would be willing to put money on a NLW being implemented within ten years. It fulfils all of the criteria for successful legislation and implementation.

As I was revising this part of the Social Policy Association paper for inclusion in this chapter, on 8 July 2015 the Chancellor of the Exchequer announced in his budget statement that by 2020 there would be a 'National Living Wage' of £9 per hour for every employee over twenty-five years of age. This is good news, of a sort. It means that the NMW for the over twenty-five-year-olds will rise to £9 per hour by 2020. However, no higher rate has been set for London, and under twenty-five-year-olds are left with a much lower rate of NMW.[119] Has the Chancellor offered a NLW, or has he not? No, he has not. The Living Wage levels published by the Joseph Rowntree Foundation assume that existing in-work benefits will continue to be paid, but these were reduced in value in the same budget speech in which the 'National Living Wage' was announced. A genuine Living Wage covers every employee, and pays a higher rate for London in view of the higher living costs.[120] So we have yet another example of the UK government misnaming benefits.[121] The rise in the NMW for over twenty-five-year-olds is welcome, but we shall have to wait for a genuine NLW; and, infuriatingly, the Chancellor's employment of the 'Living Wage' terminology for something that is not a Living Wage has sullied the brand and seriously complicated the debate.

The lesson to learn from this episode is that a constant watch will need to be kept on the UK's and every other government to ensure that if and when a Citizen's Income is promised that it really is a Citizen's Income and not something else.

9.3.8 Citizen's Income

> One of the reasons why the rate and intensity of poverty are relatively insensitive to the level of the NMW is that many low paid workers who are in poor households are in families who are in receipt of means-tested benefits. Entitlements to these fall if incomes rise, and rise if incomes fall.[122]

Because means-tested benefits are withdrawn as earnings rise, many families in poverty see only minor differences in disposable income if their earned incomes rise substantially. The structure of the benefits system is therefore an important cause of people's inability to earn their way out of poverty. The non-means-tested Child Benefit does not have this disincentive effect, and so has inspired a long-standing campaign to extend unconditional and nonwithdrawable benefits to working-age adults.

9.3.8.1 Juliet and Brandon Rhys Williams

I have already given partial accounts of the history of the UK debate on Citizen's Income in Chaps. 1 and 8.[123] Here I shall tell the story in more detail in order to draw the conclusions that might be helpful as we discuss the policy process.

In 1942, Juliet Rhys Williams,[124] a member of the commission that issued the report *Social Insurance and Allied Services*[125] and, like Eleanor Rathbone,[126] a policy activist[127]—wrote a minority report which she then expanded and published as *Something to Look Forward To*. She believed that the time-limited nature of the proposed National Insurance benefits, and the fact that National Assistance would be withdrawn as earnings rose, would create too much of a disincentive to seek paid employment, meaning that coercion would be required.[128] She believed that justice required that

> the State owes precisely the same benefits to all of its citizens, and should in no circumstances pay more to one than to another of the same sex and age, except in return for services rendered ... Therefore the same benefits [should be paid] to the employed and healthy as to the idle and sick. ... The prevention of want must be regarded as being the duty of the State to all its citizens and not merely to a favoured few.[129]

For every worker to receive 'the whole benefit of wages (less taxation)',[130] it was essential that benefits should not be withdrawn as earnings rose.

(This did not mean, however, that the income should be entirely unconditional. Although Rhys Williams believed that the nonwithdrawable nature of the benefit would mean that there would always be sufficient incentive to seek employment, she also wanted unemployed workers to have to visit the Labour Exchange and to have to accept any employment offered.[131])

If implemented, Rhys Williams' scheme for nonwithdrawable benefits would have abolished the poverty trap, increased employment incentives, and reduced poverty. It would have been simple to administer, and it would have improved women's status.[132]

Juliet Rhys Williams' scheme was not implemented. Beveridge's scheme achieved immediate public acceptance (it was the scheme that people already knew, although extended and somewhat tidied up), and this left very little social space within which Rhys Williams' scheme could be considered. A further major problem with Rhys Williams' scheme was that it would have 'abolished bureaucrats' and that it therefore 'met with an official wall of silence'.[133]

Forty years later, Juliet Rhys Williams' son, Sir Brandon Rhys Williams, a Conservative MP, gave evidence to the House of Commons Treasury and Civil Service Committee Sub-Committee on a similar scheme for a universal benefit, but this time the proposal was for a benefit entirely unconditional as well as nonwithdrawable:

> Every citizen would be entitled to a personal basic income or PBI. These guaranteed basic incomes would replace virtually all existing benefits and allowances.[134]

The final exchange between Sir Brandon and the committee Chair expressed clearly the scheme's advantages:

> *Chair*: There seem to me to be many benefits of this system.
> *BRW*: There are.
> *C*: Clearly you are expressing them very eloquently. Clearly they would go a long way toward easing the unemployment and poverty traps.
> *BRW*: There would not be any unemployment under these schemes. You would not need to register as unemployed. There would be people who were not in full-time work but they would not need to have themselves labeled as unemployed. If they got an opportunity of work or casual work they could take it and nobody would have to know.
> *C*: Are you saying that the unemployment benefit trap would be virtually eradicated by this?
> *BRW*: Certainly.
> *C*: Also it would be administratively much simpler.
> *BRW*: Yes, it would.
> *C*: I wonder what degree of redistribution of resources there would be or is that one of the matters that could be flexible within the system?
> *BRW*: This is optional. This is why I have not put figures in my paper because you could make the scheme do what you liked. If you want to help people on low wages or low incomes you can tilt the tax and benefit structure in such a way that it is redistributive in certain directions.[135]

The committee recommended that the government should consider an unconditional and nonwithdrawable benefit as a serious option for reform, that more work should be done on the scheme, and that

> meanwhile it is desirable that changes to the present system should be compatible with an eventual move to an integrated structure of tax and social security.[136]

In 1983, a General Election prevented the matter from being taken any further.

9.3.8.2 The Debate Continues

A year later, the Basic Income Research Group was founded, with a brief to promote both research and debate on Basic Income. Ten years later, the organization was renamed the Citizen's Income Trust, and the 'unconditional and nonwithdrawable income for every individual as a right of citizenship'[137] was renamed a Citizen's Income. For thirty years, the Citizen's Income Trust has been a 'pressure group':

> an organisation which seeks to influence the details of a comparatively small range of public policies and which is not a faction of a recognised political party. (Rob Baggott)[138]

The Trust and numerous other organizations, in the UK and around the world, have promoted debate and research and, in many cases, have actively campaigned for the implementation of Citizen's Income; and now in the UK a variety of more broadly based think tanks are working on Citizen's Income.[139]

A Citizen's Income would not be withdrawn as earnings rose, so individuals and households on low earnings would keep all of any additional earnings (minus tax) and would find it much easier than they do now to earn their way out of poverty.[140] A Citizen's Income would therefore be an attack on poverty as well as an attack on the poverty trap.

We already have a Citizen's Income for children in Child Benefit, and we are about to see something like a Citizen's Income for pensioners. The STP planned by the former Minister for Pensions, Steve Webb, will be almost a Citizen's Pension: it will not be withdrawn as earnings or savings rise, although the payment of the maximum pension will be conditional on a complete National Insurance contributions record.[141] The reasons for the likely successful implementation of the STP are similar to those that propelled Family Allowance onto the statute book: it will tackle poverty; it will tackle a poverty trap (in this case the savings trap); it had a ministerial champion; there is sufficient public understanding of the idea; MPs of all parties can support it; there are no intuitive arguments against it; the retention of contributory conditions will mean that no civil service departments will be lost (although there will be some reduction in the numbers of Department for Work and Pensions staff managing means-tested pension top-ups); trades unions will have no problems with the plan; there is clear continuity with the Basic State Pension (which can be regarded as a large pilot project); recipients are clearly a deserving group (the elderly); the plan is administratively feasible; and transition will be relatively simple (as transitional arrangements will be in place for pensioners who have contributed to the State Second Pension, which is to be discontinued). The Pensions Policy Institute[142] has functioned as an effective pensions policy think tank throughout the development of the STP.

A Citizen's Income for every citizen (with the amount varying according to the recipient's age but for no other reason) would be in continuity with Child Benefit and the STP, which could also be regarded as pilot projects, as could be the Citizen's Income pilot projects in Namibia and India which showed such significant results, particularly in relation to economic activity among the lowest earners.[143] A Citizen's Income's administration would be simple; the error rate would be negligible; and the benefit would attract almost no fraud.[144] Transition to a Citizen's Income could, however, be somewhat complex, not because a Citizen's Income would be complex, but because our current system is. The main complexity is that with some possible schemes, some households might experience losses at the point of implementation; but these would be more easily made up by earning additional income than would be possible under the current system because the Citizen's Income would not be withdrawn as earnings rose[145]; and there are schemes that would reduce to almost zero the losses that would be suffered at the point of implementation by maintaining a safety net of means-tested benefits. Because the means-tested benefits still received by households would be of far smaller amounts than they are now, escaping from means-testing by earning additional income would be far more of an option than it is now and would therefore be an attractive option for households to pursue.

As with some of the provisions that we have already discussed, the intuitive counterarguments can all be answered. It is no problem to pay a Citizen's Income to the wealthy, because they pay more in tax than they would receive as their Citizen's Income. People would be more likely to work than they are now, and not less, because the Citizen's Income would not be withdrawn as earnings rose.[146] And there would be additional advantages attached to a Citizen's Income in terms of social cohesion (because everyone would receive a Citizen's Income), household formation (because no longer would officials need to discover the detail of people's personal relationships, as they do now), and employment patterns (because coercion would no longer be required to persuade people to take employment, and part-time and occasional employment would be more feasible than they are now).

The arguments for a Citizen's Income are persuasive. It really is a good idea, and it need not cost an extra penny of public money (although it would be helpful to establish a fund to compensate households that would lose appreciable amounts because of the strange way in which today's system privileges their particular family type).

So let us do as we have done with the Living Wage proposal: that is, in imagination, let us locate ourselves at a time after a Citizen's Income has been established and look back to see the causes of implementation.

To begin with, we shall explore a scenario in which implementation was seriously considered but did not in the end occur[147]:

The Citizen's Income would have tackled both poverty and the poverty trap; it would have been in continuity with Child Benefit and the STP; and they, and time-limited projects in Namibia and India, functioned as pilot projects. Administration would have been simple, and transition would have been possible (and a great deal more possible than the transition into Universal Credit). Trades unions had come round to the idea, because their members would lose less of any negotiated pay rises through benefits withdrawal (although some still worried about the effect on collective bargaining of an unconditional benefit). But there were problems to face: there was little public understanding of Citizen's Income; the press peddled intuitive objections ('People won't work', 'the rich don't need this') rather than discussing the idea's merits or listening to counterarguments to the intuitive objections; no minister was willing to champion the idea in the Cabinet or in Parliament; and the civil service would have suffered substantial cuts because no longer would so many people have been needed to administer means-tested benefits, so it is no surprise that civil servants briefed against the proposal, both to ministers and elsewhere. In the end, although a Citizen's Income could have been implemented by turning tax allowances into cash payments and by removing the tapers attached to means-tested benefits, the Citizen's Income was just too different from what we were used to. We knew where we stood with contributory and means-tested benefits, and transition to a Citizen's Income looked like too much of a leap in the dark.

But another scenario is possible[148]:

After the Chancellor and Prime Minister had failed to fulfil their 2010 promise to means-test Child Benefit (and instead withdrew its value from higher-rate taxpayers through the tax system, thus establishing for the first time a tax on children), and after Steve Webb had established the STP, and we had begun to appreciate the fact that no longer would pensioners be penalized for earning additional income or for saving for their old age, the Secretary of State for Work and Pensions put together a Pre-Retirement Income (PRI) for men and women aged between fifty-five and the state pension age. The plan was to remove personal tax allowances and means-tested and contributory benefits from this group (easy to do), and instead provide them with an unconditional and nonwithdrawable income of the same value as their tax allowance. In order to create a pilot project, volunteers were invited to swap their tax allowances and means-tested and contributory benefits for an unconditional benefit (again, easy to organize). The volunteer scheme was overwhelmed with applications, so legislation for a permanent scheme for everyone in the age range soon followed.

The result of this was that people in the pre-retirement age bracket found themselves able to be more flexible about their employment patterns; and it meant that no longer did they have to sign on regularly but could instead accept occasional employment, and at other times they could offer more time to their communities and families. Administration of the scheme was really simple; and nobody minded much if they lost money on the day it all started, because they soon managed to make it up. Administrative error became a distant memory. Two problems remained: housing costs and Council Tax. Those without sufficient income for their housing costs and Council Tax had to apply for continuing means-tested benefits to help with these, but their increased ability to accept occasional and part-time employment, and the fact that some people took their occupational and private pensions earlier than they might otherwise have done, meant that the number of people in the pre-retirement age bracket receiving means-tested benefits fell rapidly.

So it was not long before students and trainees began to see how useful an unconditional and nonwithdrawable income could be for them. Again a voluntary scheme was tried. Volunteers between the ages of eighteen and twenty-one happily gave up their personal tax allowances and any claim on means-tested benefits, and received an Education and Training Income (ETI)—unconditionally and nonwithdrawably— instead. They then earned what they could to top it up. A nice outcome was that academic results improved, and more young adults sought training places and apprenticeships.

So again it was not long before working-age adults were asking about the rationale for the rather artificial age boundaries to the pre-retirement and young adult schemes; and it was not long before we had a Working Age Income, Child Benefit rose in value and was equalized for every child, the ETI was extended back to sixteen-year-olds; and we found that we had a Citizen's Income for everyone, the amounts differing only in relation to the recipient's age. We have already seen the advantages that we were promised. There is less poverty; the poverty trap has largely disappeared (there is still a problem with housing costs, but that is not the fault of the Citizen's Income); administration is simple (there is hardly any of it, because the Citizen's Income just keeps on coming); we feel much more together as a society; we can negotiate the employment patterns that we want, and the ways in which our household finances are organized; and we wonder why the plan was not tried a lot sooner than it was.

Eventually, of course, the number of public servants needed to run the benefits system fell substantially, but not straight away. Because they no longer needed to police the benefits system, Job Centres were able to model themselves on such successful local job broking and training organizations as Greenwich Local Labour and Business, and public servants were still required for this more satisfying work. Housing costs remained a problem, particularly in London, so a continuing Housing Benefit was still needed, so again public servants were required. The Child Benefit administration was expanded to handle the Citizen's Income scheme, and administration of disability, maternity, and a variety of other contingency benefits continued, but by the end of the transition, the number of public servants administering the benefits system had fallen by three quarters. No compulsory redundancies were required.

Trades unions had started out rather sceptical of the PRI, but so many of their members volunteered for the scheme that their scepticism did not last. The National Union of Students was an enthusiastic supporter of the ETI. Trades unions began to see that a Working Age Income would make it more possible for their members to refuse low wage jobs, and enthusiastic trade union support for the Working Age Income meant that an all-through Citizen's Income became irresistible.

Michael Hill has pointed out that one of the major characteristics of the UK's pensions policy is that it has always been incremental.[149] Successful implementation of a Citizen's Income will probably need to be incremental as well. A consequence of the intuitive arguments against implementing a Citizen's Income being so firmly lodged in the public mind ('The rich don't need it', 'People won't work') is that evidence to the contrary is difficult for most people to even begin to comprehend. As Michael Hill suggests, only evidence that least challenges the status quo, and that conforms to current public opinion, can be received.[150] This means that a new status quo, and a new public opinion, will have to be painstakingly constructed by establishing unconditional and nonwithdrawable benefits on the basis of more easily heard arguments, and on the basis of evidence relating to clearly deserving groups of people.

Julia Unwin, the Chief Executive Officer of the Joseph Rowntree Foundation, would agree with this. On 4 April 2014, she gave a lecture entitled 'Evidence alone won't bring about social change'.[151] She outlined the ingredients required for social change: a sense of crisis, a shared narrative, emotion, vocal supporters, proven solutions, surprising friends, movements of people, and public acceptance. These criteria have much in common with the criteria around which I have structured this case study. In the context of the benefits system, the chronic crises are poverty and the poverty trap; shared narrative, emotional and vocal supporters, movements of people, surprising friends, and public acceptance, between them represent public and parliamentary understanding; and continuity and pilot projects identify proven solutions.

Employing Unwin's criteria: There is certainly a sense of crisis about the benefits system, not least, I suspect, in the Department for Work and Pensions. There is already a shared narrative, and a proven solution, in the sense that Child Benefit is an integral part of our understanding of ourselves as members of society. A STP will fulfil the same function. Emotion, vocal supporters, and movements of people are emerging, both in the UK and around the world. A Citizen's Income has always had surprising friends. What an unconditional and nonwithdrawable income for working-age adults does not have is public acceptance. For one demographic group at a time to receive a Citizen's Income would generate such public acceptance, and thus complete the set of success criteria outlined by Unwin.

9.4 Conclusions

All of the schemes that we have studied in this case study, apart from National Assistance, were designed to reduce both poverty and the poverty trap and because they did so they have generated behavioural feasibility. All of them benefited from some kind of think tank attention, they all claimed some level of continuity with what had gone before, and they could all claim to have been piloted in one way or another. They were all administratively feasible (apart, perhaps, from Universal Credit), and for all of them, transition was a possibility (although perhaps not for Universal Credit). They all had ministerial champions or similar, and reasons for the policies were understood in parliament (which appears from our case study to be the minimum level of political feasibility required). There was sufficient public understanding, and the benefits were for groups believed to be deserving (psychological feasibility). They were all financially feasible, both in terms of fiscal feasibility and in terms of household financial feasibility.

The differences between the schemes that were implemented and those that have not been would appear to be in the areas of public understanding, civil service size and enthusiasm, and recipient group. Juliet and Brandon Rhys Williams' schemes did not have ministerial champions (although this is not a crucial factor, as the implementation of Family Allowance shows); there was insufficient engagement from such significant policy process organizations as trades unions; there was little public understanding of the proposals; and, crucially, they were attempting to encompass the entire population in a single reform, thus precluding the development of a public understanding that a clearly deserving group of people would benefit. While we might regret that this might be a criterion for the success of a scheme, it would appear to be.

We can draw the important conclusion that however good the arguments for a Citizen's Income might be—and they are good—it is probably pointless to pursue the implementation of a Citizen's Income as a single project. The two imaginary scenarios that I have outlined above suggest that a phased implementation could well succeed, and could deliver the public understanding and enthusiasm that would propel the process towards eventual implementation of an unconditional, nonwithdrawable income for every individual as a right of citizenship. An all-at-once approach would deliver financial and administrative feasibilities, but none of the required psychological, behavioural, political, or policy process feasibilities. A phased approach could offer all of them without too much difficulty.

Table 9.1 represents these conclusions in tabular form.

Table 9.1 Criteria for successful implementation of policy proposals. The chart shows how it would be unlikely that Citizen's Income could be implemented for every citizen all at the same time, but that an evolutionary process might make implementation possible

	Tackles poverty	Tackles the poverty trap	Ministerial champion or similar	Public understanding	Reasons for the policy understood in Parliament	Intuitive arguments against proposal answerable	Civil service expansion	Trades Unions	Continuity (path dependency)	Think tank involvement	Pilot project recipients	Deserving recipients	Administratively feasible	Transition feasible	Financially feasible (both fiscal and household)
FA	✓	✓	✓	✓	✓	✓	✓	✓	✓	✓	✓	✓	✓	✓	✓
NI/A	✓	✗	✓	✓	✓	✗	✓	✓	✓	✓	✓	✓	✓	✓	✓
UC	✓	✓	✓	✓	✓	✓	?	?	✓	✓	✗	?	?	?	✓?
CB	✓	✓	✓	✓	✓	✓	✓	✓	✓	✓	✓	✓	✓	✓	✓
NMW	✓	✓	✓	✓	✓	✓	✓	?	✓	✓	✓	?	✓	?	✓
NLW	✓	✓	✓	✓	✓	✓	✗	✓	✓	✓	✓	✓	✓	✓	✓
CI	✓	✓	?	✗	✗	✓	?	?	✓	✓	?	?	✓	✓	✓
STP	✓	✓	✓	✓	✓	✓	?	✓	✓	✓	✓	✓	✓	✓	✓
PRI	✓	✓	✓	✓	✓	✓	?	✓	✓	✓	✓	✓	✓	✓	✓
ETI	✓	✓	✓	✓	✓	✓	?	✓	✓	✓	✓	✓	✓	✓	✓
WAI	✓	✓	✓	✓	✓	✓	?	✓	✓	✓	✓	✓	✓	✓	✓
CI	✓	✓	✓	✓	✓	✓	?	✓	✓	✓	✓	✓	✓	✓	✓

Key:

FA Family Allowance
NI/A National Insurance/National Assistance

UC   Universal Credit
CB   Child Benefit
NMW National Minimum Wage
NLW National Living Wage
CI   Citizen's Income
STP Single-tier State Pension
PRI Pre-Retirement Income
ETI Education and Training Income
WAI Working Age Income
CI   Citizen's Income

Given that the policy process is different in every country, and that policy process feasibility therefore connects differently with the other feasibilities in every country, I have only been able to draw together the different feasibilities in the context of the tax and benefits system of a single country. My readers will need to study the policy processes of their own countries, discover the ways in which policy process feasibility would relate to the other feasibilities, and then work out how to construct an appropriate Citizen's Income implementation method.

Notes

1. Jürgen De Wispelaere and José Antonio Noguera (2012) 'On the Political Feasibility of Universal Basic Income: An Analytic Framework', pp. 17–38 in Richard Caputo (ed.) *Basic Income Guarantee: International Experiences and Perspectives on the Viability of Income Guarantee* (New York: Palgrave Macmillan), p. 21.
2. Robert Presthus (1974) *Elites in the Policy Process* (London: Cambridge University Press), p. 39.
3. Cf. M.J. Smith (1993) 'Policy networks', pp. 56–65 in M.J. Smith, *Pressure, Power and Policy* (Hemel Hempstead: Harvester Wheatsheaf), also at pp. 76–86 in Michael Hill (ed.) *The Policy Process: A reader*, 2nd edition (Hemel Hempstead: Prentice Hall/Harvester Wheatsheaf). Smith locates policy networks on a spectrum between policy communities (stable groups, with few members who frequently interact with government, and who possess substantial resources) and issue groups (changing groups with large numbers of participants, with little contact with government, and with few resources). John Hodge and Stuart Lowe (2009) *Understanding the Policy Process: Analysing welfare policy and practice*, 2nd edition (Bristol: Policy Press), p. 160, makes a similar distinction between 'policy communities' and 'issue networks'. cf. Thomas A. Birkland (2005) *An Introduction to the Policy Process: Theories, concepts, and models of public policy making*, 2nd edition (Armonk, New York: M.E. Sharpe), pp. 97–103: Birkland defines a policy community as 'those actors who are actively involved in policy making in a particular domain', and a policy network as 'the relationships among actors in the policy domain'. Given the different ways in which terminology has been used, I shall use 'policy network' to mean any set of relationships between institutions and individuals involved in a policy discussion, and I shall follow Hudson and Lowe in defining a 'policy community' as a tight-knit network with a professional or some other well-organized core, and an 'issue network' as a loose network without such a coordinating core.

4. Christopher Ham and Michael Hill (1984) *The Policy Process in the Modern Capitalist State* (Brighton: Wheatsheaf Books), p. 124.
5. Nikolaus Zahariadis (1999) 'Ambiguity, Time, and Multiple Streams', pp. 73–93 in Paul A. Sabatier (ed.) *Theories of the Policy Process* (Boulder, Colorado: Westview Press), p. 74.
6. Sonia Exley (2014) 'Think tanks and policy networks in English education', pp. 180–89 in Michael Hill (ed.) *Studying Public Policy: An international approach* (Bristol: Policy Press).
7. Göktuğ Morçöl (2012) *A Complexity Theory for Public Policy* (New York: Routledge), pp. 9, 266.
8. Nikolaus Zahariadis (1999) 'Ambiguity, Time, and Multiple Streams', p. 90.
9. Gian Domenico Majone (1989) *Evidence, Argument, and Persuasion in the Policy Process* (New Haven: Yale University Press), p. 77.
10. Michael Hill (2009) *The Public Policy Process*, 5th edition (Harlow: Pearson/Longman).
11. Michael Hill (2009) *The Public Policy Process*, p. 4.
12. Michael Hill (2009) *The Public Policy Process*, p. 47.
13. Stuart Adam et al. (2011) *Tax by design: The Mirrlees Review* (Oxford: Oxford University Press), pp. 151–3, 195–215.
14. www.hmrc.gov.uk/childbenefit/start/who-qualifies/new-arrivals-uk.htm
15. Michael Hill (2009) *The Public Policy Process*, pp. 68, 73.
16. Bernd Marin and Renate Mayntz (1991) 'Introduction: Studying policy networks', pp. 11–23 in Bernd Marin and Renate Mayntz (eds), *Policy Networks* (Frankfurt am Main: Campus Verlag), p. 16.
17. M.J. Smith (1993) 'Policy networks', pp. 56–65.
18. Michael Hill (2009) *The Public Policy Process*, pp. 58–66.
19. Hodge, John and Stuart Lowe (2009) *Understanding the Policy Process*, pp. 155, 160–1.
20. José Harris (1977) *William Beveridge: A biography* (Oxford: Clarendon Press).
21. Patrick Kenis and Volker Schneider (1991) 'Policy Networks and Policy Analysis', pp. 25–59 in Bernd Marin and Renate Mayntz (eds), *Policy Networks* (Frankfurt am Main: Campus Verlag), p. 48.
22. Xun Wu, M. Ramesh, Michael Howlett and Scott Fritzen (2010) *The Public Policy Primer: Managing the Policy Process* (London and New York: Routledge), pp. 4, 13, 18.
23. Robert Presthus (1974) *Elites in the Policy Process* (London: Cambridge University Press), p. 67.
24. Michael Hill (2009) *The Public Policy Process*, p. 87.
25. Michael Marinetto (1999) *Studies of the Policy Process: A case analysis* (London: Prentice Hall Europe), pp. 10–11.

26. M.J. Smith (1993) 'Policy networks', pp. 56–65.
27. Michael Hill (2009) *The Public Policy Process*, p. 88.
28. Diane Stone (1996) *Capturing the Political Imagination: Think tanks and the policy process* (London: Frank Cass), p. 1.
29. Diane Stone (1996) *Capturing the Political Imagination*, pp. 47–8.
30. Michael Hill (2009) *The Public Policy Process*, pp. 19, 90, 102, 105. Rational choice theory is generally understood as integrated with a particular ideological position, but that does not mean that it cannot be a useful tool for understanding the behaviour of public servants.
31. Robert Presthus (1974) *Elites in the Policy Process*, p. 209. Presthus points out that legislators and ministers will generally think that they are aware of public opinion, so a think tank providing information on public opinion will be less likely to create a relationship than one providing evidence on the likely effects of a policy change.
32. Cf. Sandra M. Anglund (1999) 'American Core Values and Policy Problem Definition', pp. 147–63 in Stuart S. Nagel (ed.) *The Policy Process* (New York: Nova Science Publishers), p. 151.
33. Cf. Martin Minogue (1997) 'Theory and Practice in Public Policy and Administration', pp. 10–29 in Michael Hill (ed) *The Policy Process: A Reader* (London and New York: Prentice Hall/Harvester Wheatsheaf), pp. 12, 15; Robert Gregory (1997) 'Political Rationality or Incrementalism?' pp. 175–91 in Michael Hill (ed) *The Policy Process: A Reader* (London and New York: Prentice Hall/Harvester Wheatsheaf), p. 189.
34. Kaushik Basu (1980) *Revealed Preference of Government* (Cambridge: Cambridge University Press), pp. 44, 86; Michael Marinetto (1999) *Studies of the Policy Process*, p. 7; J.J. Richardson and A.G. Jordan (1979) *Governing Under Pressure: The policy process in a post-parliamentary democracy* (Oxford: Basil Blackwell), p. 28.
35. Christopher Ham and Michael Hill (1984) *The Policy Process in the Modern Capitalist State* (Brighton: Wheatsheaf Books), pp. 124, 146.
36. Ian Gordon, Janet Lewis and Ken Young (1997) 'Perspectives on Policy Analysis', pp. 5–9 in Michael Hill (ed) *The Policy Process: A Reader* (London and New York: Prentice Hall/Harvester Wheatsheaf), pp. 5, 7.
37. Gian Domenico Majone (1989) *Evidence, Argument, and Persuasion in the Policy Process*, p. 76.
38. Donald E. Abelson (2002) *Do Think Tanks Matter? Assessing the impact of public policy institutes* (Montreal and Kingston: McGill-Queen's University Press), pp. 163–4.
39. Alan J. Day (2000) 'Think Tanks in Western Europe', pp. 103–38 in James McGann and R. Kent Weaver (eds), *Think Tanks and Civil Societies: Catalysts for ideas and action* (New Brunswick: Transaction Publishers), p. 132.

40. Nikolaus Zahariadis (1999) 'Ambiguity, Time, and Multiple Streams', pp. 73–93 in Paul A. Sabatier (ed.) *Theories of the Policy Process* (Boulder, Colorado: Westview Press), p. 75.
41. Thomas A. Birkland (2005) *An Introduction to the Policy Process*, pp. 88–9.
42. Andrew Denham and Mark Garnett (1998) *British Think-tanks and the Climate of Opinion*, p. 195.
43. Thomas A. Birkland (2005) *An Introduction to the Policy Process*, p. 191.
44. Michael Hil (2009), *The Public Policy Process*, pp. 156–7, 164; Thomas A. Birkland (2005) *An Introduction to the Policy Process*, p. 213.
45. Gilbert Smith and David May (1997) 'The Artificial Debate between Rationalist and Incrementalist Models of Decision Making', pp. 163–74 in Michael Hill (ed) *The Policy Process: A Reader* (London and New York: Prentice Hall/Harvester Wheatsheaf), p. 166; Richard Rose (2006) 'Inheritance before Choice in Public Policy', pp. 51–64 in Leslie Budd, Julie Charlesworth and Rob Paton, *Making Policy Happen* (London: Routledge), p. 51.
46. Jeremy Richardson (1999) 'Interest Group, Multi-Arena Politics and Policy Change', pp. 65–99 in Stuart S. Nagel (ed.) *The Policy Process* (New York: Nova Science Publishers), p. 67; Richard Rose (2006) 'Inheritance before Choice in Public Policy', p. 57.
47. Michael Hill (2009) *The Public Policy Process*, p. 188.
48. Haim Barkai (1998) *The Evolution of Israel's Social Security System* (Aldershot: Ashgate).
49. Michael Hill (2009) *The Public Policy Process*, p. 186. The permanent civil service's consensual methods have now been somewhat diluted by the presence of increasing numbers of externally recruited civil servants and ministers' political advisers.
50. Michael Hill (2009) *The Public Policy Process*, p. 167.
51. Lawrence R. Jacobs and Robert Y. Shapiro (1999) 'The media Reporting and Distorting of Public Opinion Towards Entitlements', pp. 135–45 in Stuart S. Nagel (ed.) *The Policy Process* (New York: Nova Science Publishers), p. 136.
52. J.J. Richardson and A.G. Jordan (1979) *Governing Under Pressure*, pp. 21–2.
53. Michael Hill (200) *The Public Policy Process*, p. 174.
54. Michael Hill (2009) *The Public Policy Process*, p. 173.
55. Michael Hill (2009) *The Public Policy Process*, p. 191.
56. Michael Hill (2009) *The Public Policy Process*, p. 191; J. R. P. French Jr., and B. H. Raven (1959) 'The Bases of Social Power', pp. 150–67 in D. Cartwright (ed.) *Studies in Social Power* (Ann Arbor, MI: Institute for Social Research), reprinted as pp. 150–67 in D. S. Pugh (1984) *Organization Theory: Selected Readings*, 2nd edition (Harmondsworth: Penguin).

57. Michael Hill (2009) *The Public Policy Process*, p. 299.
58. Michael Hill (2009) *The Public Policy Process*, p. 212.
59. Rob Baggott (2000) *Pressure Groups and the Policy Process* (Sheffield: Sheffield Hallam University), p. 6.
60. Brian Hogwood and Lewis Gunn (1997) 'Why "Perfect" Implementation is Unattainable', pp. 217–25 in Michael Hill (ed) *The Policy Process: A Reader* (London and New York: Prentice Hall/Harvester Wheatsheaf).
61. Malcolm Torry (2013) *Money for Everyone: Why we need a Citizen's Income* (Bristol: Policy Press), pp. 49–52.
62. Michael Hill (2009) *The Public Policy Process*, p. 291.
63. Rob Baggott (2000) *Pressure Groups and the Policy Process*, p. 80.
64. Philip B. Heyman (2008) *Living the Policy Process* (New York: Oxford University Press), pp. 114–17.
65. A point made by John McDonnell MP at a meeting at the House of Commons on the 4 March 2014.
66. J.J. Richardson (1969) *The Policy-Making Process* (London: Routledge and Kegan Paul), p. 107.
67. Gregory, Robert (1997) 'Political Rationality or Incrementalism?' pp. 175–91 in Michael Hill (ed) *The Policy Process: A Reader* (London and New York: Prentice Hall/Harvester Wheatsheaf), p. 189.
68. Gilbert Smith and David May (1997) 'The Artificial Debate between Rationalist and Incrementalist Models of Decision Making', p. 171.
69. Much of the material in this extended case study first appeared in a paper given at the Social Policy Association Conference in Sheffield in July 2014.
70. Matthew Pennycook (2012) *What Price a Living Wage? Understanding the impact of a Living Wage on firm-level wage bills* (London: The Resolution Foundation), pp. 4–5. In 2014, the Greater London Authority (GLA) set the London living wage rate at £9.15 per hour; academics at the Centre for Research in Social Policy at Loughborough University have calculated a separate rate for the rest of the UK, at £7.85 per hour. Both of these rates have gained widespread acceptance. For details of the calculation method used by the GLA, see GLA Economics (2014) *A Fairer London: The 2014 Living Wage in London* (London: GLA Economics Living Wage Unit), www.london.gov.uk/sites/default/files/living-wage-2014.pdf. For details of the calculation method used by Loughborough University's Centre for Research in Social Policy, see Centre for Research in Public Policy (2014) *Working Paper: Uprating the UK Living Wage in 2014* (Loughborough: Centre for Research in Public Policy), www.lboro.ac.uk/research/crsp/mis/thelivingwage/. Both the UK and London living wage rates are explicitly premised on the full take-up of tax credits and other means-tested benefits (such as Housing Benefit and Council Tax Support). If take-up of such entitlements was not factored into living wage calculations, then the

appropriate rates would be far higher. For example, the GLA estimates an hourly London living wage rate of £11.65 if means-tested benefits were to be excluded from the calculations.
71. William Beveridge, in Eleanor Rathbone (1949) *Family Allowances* (London: George Allen and Unwin) (a new edition of *The Disinherited Family* with an epilogue by William Beveridge), p. 270.
72. Eleanor Rathbone (1986 / 1924) *The Disinherited Family* (Bristol: Falling Wall Press), first published in 1924, pp. 139, 167, 353.
73. John Macnicol (1980) *The Movement for Family Allowances, 1918–1945: A study in social policy development* (London: Heinemann), pp. 5–10, 20–23; Pat Thane (1996) *Foundations of the Welfare State*, 2nd edition (London: Longman), pp. 63–4, 202.
74. Another of the presuppositions on which Beveridge based his report was another proposed universal benefit: the National Health Service.
75. Sir William Beveridge (1942) *Social Insurance and Allied Services*, Cmd 6404 (London: Her Majesty's Stationery Office), pp. 154, 157, 163, 177.
76. J. Harris (1981) 'Some Aspects of Social Policy in Britain during the Second World War', pp. 247–62 in W. J. Mommsen, *The Emergence of the Welfare State in Britain and Germany, 1850–1950* (London: Croom Helm), p. 249.
77. Hilary Land (1975) 'The Introduction of Family Allowances: An Act of Historic Justice?' pp. 157–230 in Phoebe Hall, Hilary Land, Roy Parker and Adrian Webb, *Change, Choice and Conflict in Social Policy* (London: Heinemann), pp. 169, 173–9, 195–6, 205, 221, 227.
78. Sir William Beveridge (1942) *Social Insurance and Allied Services*, Cmd 6404 (London: Her Majesty's Stationery Office).
79. A. B. Atkinson (1969) *Poverty in Britain and the Reform of Social Security* (Cambridge: Cambridge University Press), p. 24; Jonathan Bradshaw and Fran Bennett (2011) 'National Insurance: past, present, and future?' *Journal of Poverty and Social Justice*, 19 (3), pp. 207–209; Pat Thane (2011) 'The making of National Insurance, 1911', *Journal of Poverty and Social Justice*, 19 (3), 211–19.
80. Brian Abel-Smith and Peter Townsend (1966) *The Poor and the Poorest: A new analysis of the Ministry of Labour's Family Expenditure Surveys of 1953–54 and 1960* (London: Bell). Also influential was Richard Titmuss (1962) *Income Distribution and Social Change* (London: Allen and Unwin).
81. Keith G. Banting (1979) *Poverty, Politics and Policy: Britain in the 1960s* (London: Macmillan), p. 89.
82. Nicholas Barr and Fiona Coulter (1991) 'Social Security: Solution or Problem?' pp. 274–337 in John Hills (ed.) *The State of Welfare: The Welfare State in Britain since 1974* (Oxford: Clarendon Press), p. 282.
83. Frank Field (2002) *Welfare Titans: How Lloyd George and Gordon Brown compare, and other essays on welfare reform* (London: Civitas), pp. 54, 57.

84. Centre for Social Justice, *Dynamic Benefits: Towards welfare that works* (London: Centre for Social Justice).
85. J.J. Richardson and A.G. Jordan (1979) *Governing Under Pressure*, p. 121; David Marsh (1998) 'The Development of the Policy Networks Approach', pp. 1–17 in David Marsh (ed.), *Comparing Policy Networks* (Buckingham: Open University Press), p. 6.
86. Centre for Social Justice (2009) *Dynamic Benefits: Towards welfare that works* (London: Centre for Social Justice), p. 265; Department for Work and Pensions (2010) *21st Century Welfare*, Cm 7913 (London: The Stationery Office), p. 21; Department for Work and Pensions (2011) *Universal Credit: welfare that works*, Cm 7957 (London: The Stationery Office), p. 13.
87. Working Tax Credits had been distinguished from Child Tax Credits and means-tested out-of-work benefits in an attempt to reduce the stigma attached to means-tested in-work benefits. Universal Credit removes the distinction. See Hartley Dean and Gerry Mitchell (2011) *Wage top-ups and work incentives: The implications of the UK's Working Tax Credit scheme: A preliminary report* (London: London School of Economics); Hartley Dean, 'The Ethical Deficit of the UK's proposed Universal Credit: Pimping the Precariat?' *Political Quarterly*, 83 (2), 353–9.
88. Nikolaus Zahariadis (1999) 'Ambiguity, Time, and Multiple Streams', p. 75.
89. Chris Pond and Steve Winyard (1983) *The Case for a National Minimum Wage* (London: Low Pay Unit), p. 8.
90. Chris Pond and Steve Winyard (1983) *The Case for a National Minimum Wage*, pp. 42–4.
91. Chris Pond and Steve Winyard (1983) *The Case for a National Minimum Wage* (London: Low Pay Unit), p. 24.
92. David Metcalf (1999) *The British National Minimum Wage* (London: Centre for Economic Performance, London School of Economics), p. 2, reports that in 1985 Ron Todd, General Secretary of the TGWU, feared 'that a statutory minimum could be used by employers to undermine trade union organization, negotiation, and collective bargaining'.
93. Chris Pond and Steve Winyard (1983) *The Case for a National Minimum Wage*, pp. 36–7.
94. Trade Union Congress (1995) *Arguments for a National Minimum Wage* (London: Trade Union Congress), p. 19.
95. Chris Pond and Steve Winyard (1983) *The Case for a National Minimum Wage*, p. 51.
96. Paul Edwards and Mark Gilman (1998) *A National Minimum Wage: Stimulus to economic efficiency?* (Warwick: Warwick Business School), Executive Summary.
97. Chris Pond and Steve Winyard (1983) *The Case for a National Minimum Wage*, pp. 17, 51–2.

98. Paul Edwards and Mark Gilman (1998) *A National Minimum Wage: Stimulus to economic efficiency?*; Stephen Bazen (1991) *Introducing a National Minimum Wage in the UK* (Canterbury: University of Kent), pp. 3–4, 11, 17. Cf Trade Union Congress (1995) *Arguments for a National Minimum Wage*, p. 54: 'An increase in the [French National Minimum Wage] improves the relative position of the low paid. Wage differentials are only partially restored. Increases in the [French National Minimum Wage] may reduce young persons' employment by a small amount. There is no effect on adult employment.' And cf. Richard Dickens and Alan Manning (2002) *Has the National Minimum Wage Reduced UK Wages?* (London: Centre for Economic Performance, London School of Economics), p. 9: 'The impact of the NMW on overall wage inequality is rather small, with no detectable impact on earnings at the 10th percentile.'
99. Paul Robson, Shirley Dex, and Frank Wilkinson (1997) *The Costs of a National Statutory Minimum Wage in Britain* (Cambridge: Judge Institute of Management Studies), p. 20.
100. Chris Pond and Steve Winyard (1983) *The Case for a National Minimum Wage*, p. 53; Paul Edwards and Mark Gilman (1998) *A National Minimum Wage: Stimulus to economic efficiency?*; Paul Robson, Shirley Dex, and Frank Wilkinson (1997) *The Costs of a National Statutory Minimum Wage in Britain*, p. 20.
101. Chris Pond and Steve Winyard (1983) *The Case for a National Minimum Wage*, p. 21.
102. David Metcalf (1999) *The British National Minimum Wage* (London: Centre for Economic Performance, London School of Economics), p. 2.
103. Chris Pond and Steve Winyard (1983) *The Case for a National Minimum Wage*, pp. 13, 19. Cf. Trade Union Congress (1995) *Arguments for a National Minimum Wage*, p. 20. The report stated that 86% of employers believed that a National Minimum Wage of £4.10 per week would not raise unemployment levels. On the productivity and efficiency gains related to National Minimum Wages, see Martin Watts (2010) 'How should Minimum Wages be Set in Australia', *Journal of Industrial Relations*, 52 (2), 131–49.
104. Evidence submitted to the Commission had shown that a NMW of £3.20 or £4.20 per hour would raise the wage bill by small amounts, but that a NMW of £4.70 'would produce substantial increases in many employers' costs and possibly some job losses' (Paul Robson, Shirley Dex, and Frank Wilkinson (1997) *The Costs of a National Statutory Minimum Wage in Britain*, p. 19).
105. David Metcalf (1999) *The British National Minimum Wage*, pp. 7, 12.
106. From 1 October 2015, NMW rates are: adult rate, £6.70 per hour; rate for eighteen- to twenty-year-olds, £5.30 per hour; rate for sixteen- to seventeen-year-olds, £3.87 per hour; apprentice rate, £3.30 per hour.

107. Chris Pond and Steve Winyard (1983) *The Case for a National Minimum Wage*, pp. 13, 53.
108. David Metcalf (1999) *The British National Minimum Wage*, p. 1.
109. Chris Pond and Steve Winyard (1983) *The Case for a National Minimum Wage*, p. 51.
110. www.citizensuk.org/about
111. www.livingwage.org.uk/history; www.lboro.ac.uk/research/crsp/mis/thelivingwage
112. In 2014, the GLA set the London living wage rate at £9.15 per hour; academics at the Centre for Research in Social Policy at Loughborough University have calculated a separate rate for the rest of the UK at £7.85 per hour. Both of these rates have gained widespread acceptance. For details of the calculation method used by the GLA, see GLA Economics (2014) *A Fairer London: The 2014 Living Wage in London* (London: GLA Economics Living Wage Unit), www.london.gov.uk/sites/default/files/living-wage-2014.pdf. For details of the calculation method used by Loughborough University's Centre for Research in Social Policy, see Centre for Research in Public Policy (2014) *Working Paper: Uprating the UK Living Wage in 2014* (Loughborough: Centre for Research in Public Policy), www.lboro.ac.uk/research/crsp/mis/thelivingwage/
113. *Ford News*, April 1934, p. 43. www.thehenryford.org/research/henryFord-Quotes.aspx
114. www.livingwage.org.uk/what-are-benefits-accreditation
115. Alan Manning (2014) 'Minimum wages: the economics and the politics', *CentrePiece*, 1 (1), 8–10.
116. James Plunkett, Alex Hurrell, and Conor D'Arcy (2014) *More than a Minimum: The Resolution Foundation Review of the Future of the National Minimum Wage: The Final Report* (London: The Resolution Foundation), p. 25.
117. David Metcalf (1999) *The British National Minimum Wage*, p. 12.
118. Matthew Penycook (2012) *What Price a Living Wage? Understanding the impact of a living wage on firm-level wage bills* (London: The Institute for Public Policy Research and the Resolution Foundation), pp. 2–3.
119. www.gov.uk/government/speeches/chancellor-george-osbornes-summer-budget-2015-speech
120. Both the UK and London living wage rates are explicitly premised on the full take-up of tax credits and other means-tested benefits (such as housing benefit and council tax benefit). If take-up of such entitlements was not factored into living wage calculations, then the appropriate rates would be far higher. For example, the GLA estimates an hourly London living wage rate of £11.65 if means-tested benefits are excluded from the calculations (GLA Economics (2014) *A Fairer London: The 2014 Living*

Wage in London (London: GLA Economics Living Wage Unit), www.london.gov.uk/sites/default/files/living-wage-2014.pdf).
121. Malcolm Torry (2013) *Money for Everyone: Why we need a Citizen's Income*, pp. xii–xiii.
122. Holly Sutherland (2001) *The National Minimum Wage and In-work Poverty* (Cambridge: Department of Applied Economics, University of Cambridge), p. 9.
123. Malcolm Torry (2013) *Money for Everyone: Why we need a Citizen's Income*, pp. 34–6.
124. J. Harris (1981) 'Some Aspects of Social Policy in Britain during the Second World War', pp. 247–262 in W. J. Mommsen, *The Emergence of the Welfare State in Britain and Germany, 1850–1950* (London: Croom Helm), p. 258.
125. Sir William Beveridge (1942) *Social Insurance and Allied Services*, Cmd 6404 (London: Her Majesty's Stationery Office).
126. See Chap. 1.
127. Anna Yeatman (1998) 'Activism and the Policy Process', pp. 16–35 in Anna Yeatman (ed.) *Activism and the Policy Process* (St. Leonards, NSW: Allen and Unwin), pp. 32–5.
128. Juliet Rhys Williams (1943) *Something to Look Forward to* (London: MacDonald and Co.), pp. 13, 45, 139–47.
129. Juliet Rhys Williams (1943) *Something to Look Forward to*, pp. 139, 145.
130. Juliet Rhys Williams (1943) *Something to Look Forward to*, p. 147.
131. Juliet Rhys Williams (1943) *Something to Look Forward to*, p. 167.
132. Juliet Rhys Williams (1943) *Something to Look Forward to*, p. 138.
133. J. Harris (1981) 'Some aspects of social policy in Britain during the Second World War,' p. 258.
134. House of Commons Treasury and Civil Service Committee Sub-Committee (1982) *The Structure of Personal Income Taxation and Income Support: Minutes of Evidence*, HC 331-ix (London: Her Majesty's Stationery Office), p. 423; cf. Brandon Rhys Williams (1989) *Stepping Stones to Independence: National Insurance after 1990* (Aberdeen: Aberdeen University Press); Hermione Parker (1989) *Instead of the Dole: An enquiry into integration of the tax and benefit systems* (London: Routledge), pp. 224–53.
135. House of Commons Treasury and Civil Service Committee Sub-Committee (1982) *The Structure of Personal Income Taxation and Income Support: Minutes of Evidence*, p. 459. The detailed description of the scheme had been prepared by Hermione Parker, Sir Brandon Rhys Williams' research assistant.
136. House of Commons Treasury and Civil Service Committee (1983) *Enquiry into the Structure of Personal Income Taxation and Income Support*, Third Special Report, Session 1982–3, section 13.35, quoted in Hermione Parker (1989) *Instead of the Dole: An enquiry into integration of the tax and benefit systems* (London: Routledge), p. 100.

137. www.citizensincome.org
138. Rob Baggott (2000) *Pressure Groups and the Policy Process*, p. 6.
139. For instance, at a conference in London on 4 March 2015 organized by the Fabian Society and Bright Blue, both the Fabian Society and the Adam Smith Institute announced research projects on Citizen's Income.
140. Malcolm Torry (2013) *Money for Everyone: Why we need a Citizen's Income*, pp. 116–17, 119–20, 131–47; Citizen's Income Trust (2013) *Citizen's Income: A brief introduction* (London: Citizen's Income Trust).
141. Department for Work and Pensions (2011) *A state pension for the 21st century*, Cm 8053 (London: The Stationery Office), pp. 10, 29–35; Malcolm Torry (2013) *Money for Everyone: Why we need a Citizen's Income*, pp. 38–42.
142. www.pensionspolicyinstitute.org.uk/
143. Malcolm Torry (2013) *Money for Everyone: Why we need a Citizen's Income*, pp. 69–75; Malcolm Torry (2013) 'Pilot Projects in India', *Citizen's Income Newsletter*, issue 2 for 2013, pp. 4–5.
144. Malcolm Torry (2013) *Money for Everyone: Why we need a Citizen's Income*, pp. 81–98.
145. Malcolm Torry (2013) *Money for Everyone: Why we need a Citizen's Income*, pp. 245–8.
146. Malcolm Torry (2013) *Money for Everyone: Why we need a Citizen's Income*, pp. 277–8.
147. Malcolm Torry (2013) *Money for Everyone: Why we need a Citizen's Income*, p. 50.
148. Malcolm Torry (2013) *Money for Everyone: Why we need a Citizen's Income*, pp. 51–2.
149. Michael Hill, *The Public Policy Process*, p. 164.
150. Michael Hill, *The Public Policy Process*, p. 159.
151. www.jrf.org.uk/sites/files/jrf/YSJ-Lecture-April-2014.pdf

CHAPTER 10

From Feasibility to Implementation

10.1 Introduction

Having studied Citizen's Income's financial feasibility (both fiscal feasibility and household financial feasibility), psychological feasibility, administrative feasibility, behavioural feasibility, political feasibility, and policy process feasibility, we can now draw a firm conclusion: that Citizen's Income is in principle feasible, and that in any country, it should normally be possible to propose a Citizen's Income scheme that it would be feasible to implement. Both the main content of each of the chapters, and the case studies, enable us to draw further conclusions: that in the UK, a Citizen's Income scheme would be feasible if the scheme chosen were to leave in place existing means-tested benefits and take households' Citizen's Incomes into account when their means-tested benefits were calculated; that such a scheme could meet all of the feasibility criteria if it were to be introduced one demographic group at a time, starting with those believed by the general public to be the most deserving: children, elderly people, the pre-retired, young people—and then, last of all, working-age adults; and that such a scheme could be implemented quickly if political and policy process contingencies enabled psychological and behavioural feasibility tests to be bypassed, as they often have been before in the social security field.

But as we have recognized throughout our discussion, the fact that Citizen's Income is feasible, and the fact that a particular scheme could be shown to be feasible, would be no guarantee that it would happen. There is often a huge difference between satisfying a particular feasibility condition in theory and satisfying it in practice. Some of the feasibilities, once satisfied, would not cause bottlenecks. For instance, any country with a reasonably well-functioning tax and benefits system will take administration of Citizen's Income in its stride if the government decides to implement a scheme. Similarly, the theoretical financial feasibility of a scheme should mean that it would be financially feasible in practice. The difficulties emerge with the other feasibilities. Theoretical satisfaction of psychological, behavioural, political, and policy process feasibilities would be no guarantee that they would be satisfied in practice; and it seems rather improbable that they would all be satisfied at the same time and in the same place. But sometimes a range of feasibilities do line up, enabling new social policies to be implemented; and, as we have seen, new social policies are sometimes implemented without feasibility tests being passed. We therefore need to ask about some additional possibilities.

10.2 Accidents Happen

In the last chapter, we recognized that the policy process is not always entirely rational and orderly. As Conlan, Posner, and Beam suggest, a variety of different 'pathways' through the policy process might be available: the pluralist pathway, in which policy changes by a process of mutual adjustment between different players; a partisan pathway, in which a government with a large majority achieves implementation of a manifesto; an expert pathway, in which policy experts control the agenda; and a symbolic pathway, in which value-laden beliefs appeal to 'common sense'.[1] I would add a fifth option: the accident-strewn pathway. Problems, policy options, and politics constantly flow through the complex policy process, and 'policy windows' occur when the three streams meet, enabling 'policy entrepreneurs' to act.[2] It is not impossible that policy problems, the policy process, and Citizen's Income might converge. It is therefore essential that the results of research on feasible schemes should always be available.

What we might call Citizen's Income accidents have happened. Iran has ended up with something like a Citizen's Income because a new means-tested system collapsed under the weight of public disapproval of the means test and of administrative systems not working. The only immediate solution available was to give the new benefit to every household that applied.[3] We might call this a systemic accident. What we might call relationship accidents happen, too. In relation to the UK, we discovered in Chap. 9 that an unconditional and nonwithdrawable Family Allowance was implemented after the Second World War because William Beveridge was converted to the idea by reading Eleanor Rathbone's *The Disinherited Family*,[4] because he was asked to chair a committee on the future of the country's benefits system, and because when the Family Allowances that he had written into the preface of the report were debated in Parliament, MPs attached to different political ideologies could all find reasons for voting in favour. In this case, a combination of relationship and systemic accidents propelled the idea through the policy process.

If a country's benefits system—say, for instance, the UK's system—were to become completely unmanageable, and attempts to keep it going failed—for instance, if Universal Credit seized up, as the administration of Housing Benefit seized up during the mid-1980s—then might the UK find itself implementing a Citizen's Income by accident, rather as Iran has done?

Perhaps the most difficult issue with which social policy researchers have to grapple is the fact that the policy process is a tangle of relatively predictable and really quite unpredictable elements. As Birkland suggests, this means that

> the likelihood that an issue will rise on the agenda is a function of the issue itself, the actors that get involved, institutional relationships, and, often, random social and political factors that can be explained but cannot be replicated or predicted.[5]

10.3 Paradigm Shifts

In science, culture, philosophy, religion, and, in fact, in any field of human endeavour, paradigm shifts occur: that is, complete shifts in mindset, not just for individuals, but also for whole societies, communities, professions, or academic disciplines. Thomas Kuhn has charted paradigm shifts in the natural sciences. A period during which theories and experimental results appear to be settled and coherent is disturbed by experimental results that no longer cohere with the current theories; a period of turmoil occurs, during which different theoretical options are tried—usually with the majority of the scientific community still fairly wedded to traditional theories, and small but growing numbers of individuals becoming less than satisfied with them. A paradigm shift then occurs, in which a new theory or set of theories manages to explain the new and so far unexplained experimental results, and for most of the community the new theory or set of theories becomes the new norm—although there might still be a small number of individuals still wedded to older ideas. And then the process starts all over again.[6] This is a community or societal conversion process, rather similar to the individual conversions that we discussed in Chap. 5. In the social policy field, a policy monopoly might achieve a closed policy-making world for quite a long period of time, but sufficient disruptive factors—for instance, media attention to social and economic problems—can emerge to cause the equilibrium to break down, creating social space for alternatives, a focus of attention for public debate, policy change, and a new equilibrium. In whatever fields such paradigm shifts occur, 'punctuated equilibria'[7] emerge: that is, repeated cycles of stability, turmoil, and change.

A paradigm shift occurred in the Western world, and to a large extent globally, when during the 1970s what we might call the economic management professions swapped a Keynesian mindset for a monetarist one. The equilibrium had been succeeded by a rather different one.

We have now been living with means-tested benefits for four hundred years. The evidence is stacking up that this is not necessarily a useful paradigm in the current economic and social context. Other paradigms are available, and particularly universal benefits. It would not be impossible for the policy-making community, in one country, throughout a region, or globally, to experience a paradigm shift. Scientific revolutions have generally been preceded by increasing numbers of practitioners trying new theories to see if they might fit the evidence, and we are seeing increasing numbers of individuals and institutions coming to understand the desirability and feasibility of Citizen's Income, and particularly its appropriateness to the societies and economies within which we are now living; and perhaps even more significantly, coming to see that the simplicity of Citizen's Income would suit it to *any* configuration of society and economy that might emerge in the future.

There are two ways to understand the relationship between change and stability in a country's benefits system, or, indeed, in any system. Either we understand change as ubiquitous,[8] social and economic systems as constantly evolving, equilibrium as an exception, and uncertainty as inevitable[9]—which suggests that the simplest possible benefits system is what is required, with as few characteristics as possible connected to social and economic variables, because that is the only kind that will not need to be constantly adjusted as society and the economy change. Or we can see equilibrium as the norm, and understand that it can turn into turbulence when existing solutions no longer work, making space for formerly minority views, one of which might gain traction as increasing numbers of players see the evidence pointing in that direction.[10] On the basis of either understanding, a widespread paradigm shift in favour of universal benefits is by no means impossible.[11] Just like individual conversions, paradigm shifts create possibilities for new connections; and as Kingdon puts it, 'solutions become joined to problems, and both of them are joined to favourable political forces'.[12] However strong the hegemony of such received wisdom as the reciprocity principle,[13] and of deeply embedded prejudices inimical to universal benefits, new connections could rapidly displace them and propel Citizen's Income from idea to implementation. New ideas are perfectly capable of unsettling apparently solid policy configurations and of making space for themselves within the complexities of the policy process.[14] The boundaries of what is politically feasible are not immutable.[15]

Think tanks can be crucial players in this kind of process. In the UK, the Institute for Economic Affairs (IEA) was instrumental in persuading the UK government to privatize public infrastructure and services in a way that previous governments would have thought both crazy and impossible. The IEA propelled an idea from 'lunacy to respectability'.[16] There is no reason why the process should not be repeated with Citizen's Income, which has had a lot more thought and research put into it than many of the rushed privatizations that followed that particular paradigm shift. A 'critical moment'[17] might occur: a coming together of an accelerating paradigm shift and a series of accidents—and a country could find itself with a genuine Citizen's Income and reaping the advantages. Other countries would then quickly follow.

10.4 The Feasibilities

We are now in a position to return to Ivan Steiner's suggestion that there are three types of group task: additive (all group members work together on the same task, and the outcome is the sum of contributions, as in a tug of war); conjunctive (all members' contributions are needed for success, the weakest member's ability is an important factor, and the links between the elements are often crucial, as in a relay race); and disjunctive (where every separate contribution can count, but accomplishment often depends on the performance of the most talented member, as in a pub quiz)[18]; and again we shall apply the categorization to the different kinds of feasibility that we have discussed.

In Chap. 2, I suggested that the feasibilities might be conjunctive—that is, that all of them would need to be fulfilled, and that if just one of them was only weakly satisfied, then implementation of Citizen's Income might not be possible; but now that we have discussed the different feasibilities, and now that we have recognized the possibility of accidents and paradigm shifts, the situation is looking rather more complicated. Perhaps the most interesting piece of evidence is that at least for the time being, Iran has managed to establish something like a Citizen's Income without apparently satisfying any of the feasibilities.[19] To take another example: in the UK, the new combined means-tested benefit called Universal Credit is being implemented without psychological, behavioural, or administrative feasibilities being tested. While it is possible, as we have seen, for post-event behavioural feasibility to generate post-event psychological feasibility, and for a government to move ahead of public opinion if it has good reason to believe that public opinion will move in that direction, to have implemented Universal Credit without testing for administrative feasibility might have been a mistake, but crucially for our argument here, not testing for it did not prevent implementation.

The first major conclusion that I can now draw is that policy process feasibility is the only crucial one, and that the other feasibilities might contribute to the feasibility of implementation but that they are not necessarily essential. The feasibilities are therefore disjunctive. In a pub quiz, the team that wins might have been the one in which all of the members contributed to the score, but it might equally well have been the one in which one knowledgeable member provided all of the answers. In terms of the subject of this book: If a policy proposal can somehow manage to find its way through the policy process from idea to implementation, then that is all that matters. It might do this by a policy community showing how the proposal meets all of the feasibility criteria, and slowly building political support and routes through the policy process; it might be through a rapid social and economic paradigm shift in which government ministers find themselves embroiled; or it might be by a political or policy process accident.

The important practical conclusion to draw is that in whatever way implementation finally occurs—apart from via an Iran-style policy accident—doing the hard work on proving the different feasibilities will be seen to have contributed to implementation and to the success of implementation. When a political accident occurs, or a paradigm shift comes rapidly over the horizon, to have available a Citizen's Income scheme that has already been through the kind of feasibility testing that we have attempted in this book will be quite important.

10.5 One Step at a Time?

A second major conclusion that I can draw is that it would be feasible to implement a Citizen's Income scheme one step at a time: either via a variety of policy changes that we might regard as steps along the way (such as the individualization of benefits, the implementation of a Participation Income, or the reduction of means-tested benefit withdrawal rates), or one age group at a time.

The policy process is complex: no policy-making individual or institution can hope to understand all of the possible effects of a policy change, non-incremental policy options are always difficult to evaluate, and therefore governments understandably prefer incremental change to major systemic change. The history of policy-making is one of incremental trial and error in which policymakers study 'successive limited comparisons' in order to choose successive and often disjointed small shifts from the status quo. They 'muddle through', rather than undertake comprehensive rational policy reviews.[20] Given the practical constraints within which policymakers have to operate, this is an entirely rational approach.

Given that policy process feasibility is the crucial feasibility, and that the policy process is generally incremental, the most useful next step for Citizen's Income research in the UK might be to undertake thorough evaluations of the Citizen's Incomes for children and young adults described in Chap. 4. This would fulfil Majone's condition that

> in the very short run politicians, bureaucrats, interest groups, and private citizens must act within the rules defined by the existing institutional framework[21]:

but he goes on to add:

> In the longer run, however, the rules of the policy game can and do change. Policy actors not only pursue their goals within the limits set by the existing framework; they also strive to change those limits in their favour.[22]

So in the process of implementing steps along the way to a genuine Citizen's Income, it is essential that the goal of implementing an unconditional and nonwithdrawable income for every citizen should remain at the heart of the policy process, as it is that goal that will give momentum and shape to the process. As David Purdy puts it:

> The most realistic prospect for the [Citizen's Income] project is a slow, patient, positional struggle rather than a fast-moving war of maneuver. Its strongest asset in this long haul is the optimistic and expansive view of the future which it brings to bear on the dismal and pressing problems of the present.[23]

So research on the feasibility of establishing Citizen's Incomes for every member of a population should never be neglected. A situation might arise in which a government is seeking a major new direction for tax and benefits policy, because a party's election manifesto has promised that, because the status quo is looking unsustainable and all that incremental change is achieving is yet more problems, or because a new government can only obtain a parliamentary majority if it forms a coalition with minor parties committed to implementing a Citizen's Income scheme.[24] In the UK, scheme B in Chap. 3 would be feasible, and could be implemented almost overnight if required. Further research on scheme B and similar schemes could therefore be highly relevant.

At the same time, research on longer-term options for more substantial Citizen's Incomes ought not to be neglected. Our societies and economies will continue to change, and might change even faster than they do now. The only option for the maintenance of household incomes might one day be a Citizen's Income sufficient to enable every individual to engage in every aspect of the life of society, and we might need new funding methods to achieve that.

We shall therefore continue to need a wide diversity of research and debate on the feasibility of Citizen's Income. My hope is that this book will have contributed in some small way to stimulating that research and debate.

Notes

1. Timothy J. Conlan, Paul L. Posner and David R. Beam (2014) *Pathways of Power: The dynamics of national policy making* (Washington DC: Georgetown University Press), p. 2.
2. Nikolaus Zahariadis (1999) 'Ambiguity, Time, and Multiple Streams', pp. 73–93 in Paul A. Sabatier (ed.) *Theories of the Policy Process* (Boulder, Colorado: Westview Press), pp. 76, 78.

3. Hamid Tabatabai (2012) 'Iran: A Bumpy Road toward Basic Income', pp. 285–300 in Richard Caputo (ed.) *Basic Income Guarantee and Politics: International Experiences and perspectives on the viability of Income Guarantee* (New York: Palgrave Macmillan), p. 290.
4. Eleanor Rathbone (1986/1924) *The Disinherited Family* (Bristol: Falling Wall Press), first published in 1924.
5. Thomas A. Birkland (2005) *An Introduction to the Policy Process*, 2nd edition (Armonk, NT: M.E. Sharpe), p. 134.
6. Thomas Kuhn (1996) *The Structure of Scientific Revolutions*, 3rd edition (Chicago: Chicago University Press).
7. Frank R. Baumgartner and Bryan D. Jones (2002) *Policy Dynamics* (Chicago: Chicago University Press), p. 229.
8. Martin Binder (2010) *Elements of an Evolutionary Theory of Welfare: Assessing welfare when preferences change* (London: Routledge), pp. 4, 12.
9. Göktuğ Morçöl (2012) *A Complexity Theory for Public Policy* (New York: Routledge), pp. 158–9, 263, 266.
10. Thomas A. Birkland (2005) *An Introduction to the Policy Process*, p. 229.
11. Diane Stone (1996) *Capturing the Political Imagination: Think tanks and the policy process* (London: Frank Cass), p. 101.
12. J. W. Kingdon (2011) *Agendas, Alternatives, and Public Policies*, 2nd edition (New York: HarperCollins), p. 20.
13. See Chap. 5. On hegemony, see Antonio Gramsci (1971) *Selections from Prison Notebooks* (London: Lawrence and Wishart), pp. 287, 343, and Hartley Dean (2012) *Social Policy*, 2nd edition (Cambridge: Polity), p. 72.
14. Jeremy Richardson (1999) 'Interest Group, Multi-Arena Politics and Policy Change', pp. 65–99 in Stuart S. Nagel (ed.) *The Policy Process* (New York: Nova Science Publishers), p. 93.
15. Gian Domenico Majone (1989) *Evidence, Argument, and Persuasion in the Policy Process* (New Haven: Yale University Press), p. 94.
16. Diane Stone (1996) *Capturing the Political Imagination*, p. 177.
17. Diane Stone (1996) *Capturing the Political Imagination*, p. 183.
18. Ivan D. Steiner (1972) *Group Process and Productivity* (New York: Academic Press).
19. Hamid Tabatabai (2011) 'Iran's economic reforms usher in a de facto Citizen's Income', *Citizen's Income Newsletter*, issue 1 for 2011, pp. 1–2; Hamid Tabatabai (2011) 'The Basic Income Road to Reforming Iran's Price Subsidies', *Basic Income Studies*, 6 (1), 1–24; Hamid Tabatabai (2012) 'Iran: A Bumpy Road toward Basic Income', pp. 290–5; Turquoise Partners (2014) *Iran Investment Monthly* (Iran: Turquoise Partners), April 2014.
20. Michael Marinetto (1999) *Studies of the Policy Process: A case analysis* (Hemel Hempstead: Prentice Hall Europe), pp. 17–18, 20; C.E. Lindblom

(1959) 'The science of "muddling through"', *Public Administration Review*, 19 (2), 79–88, p. 81; C.E. Lindblom (1964) 'Contexts for Change and Strategy: A reply', *Public Administration Review*, 24 (3), 157–8.
21. Gian Domenico Majone (1989) *Evidence, Argument, and Persuasion in the Policy Process*, p. 95.
22. Gian Domenico Majone (1989) *Evidence, Argument, and Persuasion in the Policy Process*, p. 95.
23. David Purdy (2013) 'Political Strategies for Basic Income', pp. 477–484 in Karl Widerquist, José A. Noguera, Yannick Vanderborght, and Jürgen De Wispelaere, *Basic Income: An anthology of contemporary research* (Chichester: Wiley Blackwell), p. 484.
24. Josh Martin (2015) 'Universal Credit to Basic Income: A Politically Feasible Transition?', unpublished M.Sc. dissertation (London: London School of Economics), p. 30.

Bibliography

A Note on Citizen's Income Trust Publications

*BIRG Bulletin*s are numbered consecutively from 1 to 25. In 1998 the *Bulletin* became the *Citizen's Income Newsletter*, with volumes listed according to year of publication. Each year three editions are published: so *Citizen's Income Newsletter*, issue 2 for 2011, means the second issue of the *Citizen's Income Newsletter* for 2011.

Bibliography

Abel-Smith, Brian, and Peter Townsend. 1966. *The poor and the poorest: A new analysis of the Ministry of Labour's Family Expenditure Surveys of 1953–54 and 1960*. London: Bell.

Abelson, Donald E. 2002. *Do think tanks matter? Assessing the impact of public policy institutes*. Montreal/Kingston: McGill-Queen's University Press.

Adam, Stuart, Mike Brewer, and Andrew Shephard. 2006. *The poverty trade-off: Work incentives and income redistribution in Britain*. Bristol/York: Policy Press/Joseph Rowntree Foundation.

Adam, Stuart, et al. 2011. *Tax by design: The Mirrlees review*. Oxford: Oxford University Press.

Adelman, Laura, Sue Middleton, and Karl Ashworth. 1999. *Intra-household distribution of poverty and social exclusion: Evidence from the 1999 PSE Survey of Britain*, Working paper no 23. Loughborough: Centre for Research in Social Policy.

Alfageme, Alfredo, Begoña García Pastor, and Celia Viñado. 2012. Temporary exit from employment and Citizen's Income: A reply. *Critical Social Policy* November 32(4): 716–719.
Andress, Hans-Jürgen, and Thorsten Heien. 2001. Four worlds of welfare state attitudes? A comparison of Germany, Norway, and the United States. *European Sociological Review* 17(4): 337–356.
Anglund, Sandra M. 1999. American core values and policy problem definition. In *The policy process*, ed. Stuart S. Nagel, 147–163. New York: Nova Science Publishers.
Arcarons, Jordi, Daniel Raventos Pañella, and Lluís Torrens Mèlich. 2014. Feasibility of financing a basic income. *Basic Income Studies* 9(1–2): 79–93.
Atkinson, A.B. 1969. *Poverty in Britain and the reform of social security*. Cambridge: Cambridge University Press.
Atkinson, A.B. 1985. *Income maintenance and social insurance: A survey*, Welfare State Programme, paper no. 5. London: London School of Economics.
Atkinson, Tony. 1993. Participation income. *Citizen's Income Bulletin* 16: 7–11.
Atkinson, A.B. 1995. *Public economics in action: The basic income/flat tax proposal*. Oxford: Clarendon Press.
Atkinson, A.B. 1996. The case for a participation income. *The Political Quarterly* 67(1): 67–70.
Atkinson, Tony. 2011. The case for universal child benefit. In *Fighting poverty, inequality and injustice: A manifesto inspired by Peter Townsend*, ed. Alan Walker, Adrian Sinfield, and Carol Walker, 79–90. Cambridge: Polity Press.
Atkinson, Anthony B. 2015. *Inequality*. Cambridge, MA: Harvard University Press.
Atkinson, A.B., and J.S. Flemming. 1978. Unemployment, social security and incentives. In *Midland Bank review*. London: Midland Bank.
Baggott, Rob. 2000. *Pressure groups and the policy process*. Sheffield: Sheffield Hallam University.
Banting, Keith G. 1979. *Poverty, politics and policy: Britain in the 1960s*. London: Macmillan.
Barkai, Haim. 1998. *The evolution of Israel's social security system*. Aldershot: Ashgate.
Barr, Nicholas. 1987. *The economics of the welfare state*. London: Weidenfeld and Nicolson.
Barr, Nicholas, and Fiona Coulter. 1991. Social security: Solution or problem? In *The state of welfare: The welfare state in Britain since 1974*, ed. John Hills, 274–337. Oxford: Clarendon Press.
Barry, Brian. 1996. Surfers' saviour? *Citizen's Income Bulletin* 22: 2–4.
Bartlett, Randall, James Davies, and Michael Hoy. 2005. Can a negative income tax system for the United Kingdom be both equitable and affordable? In *The ethics and economics of the basic income guarantee*, ed. Karl Widerquist, Michael Anthony Lewis, and Steven Pressman, 293–315. Aldershot: Ashgate.

Basic Income Grant Coalition. 2009. *Making the difference: The BIG in Namibia: Basic Income Grant Pilot Project, Assessment report*. Namibia: Basic Income Grant Coalition, Namibia NGO Forum. www.bignam.org/Publications/BIG_Assessment_report_08b.pdf, 23 Sept 2011.

Basu, Kaushik. 1980. *Revealed preference of government*. Cambridge: Cambridge University Press.

Baumberg, Ben. 2012. Three ways to defend social security in Britain. *Journal of Poverty and Social Justice* 20(2): 149–161.

Baumgartner, Frank R., and Bryan D. Jones. 2002. *Policy dynamics*. Chicago: Chicago University Press.

Bazen, Stephen. 1991. *Introducing a national minimum wage in the UK*. Canterbury: University of Kent.

Beem, Christopher. 2005. Restoring the civic value of care in a post-welfare reform society. In *Welfare reform and political theory*, ed. Lawrence Mead and Christopher Beem, 151–171. New York: Russell Sage Foundation.

Benn, Tony. 1974. *Speeches by Tony Benn*. Nottingham: Spokesman Books.

Benn, Tony. 1988. *Fighting back: Speaking out for socialism in the eighties*. London: Hutchinson.

Berthoud, Richard. 2006. *The employment rates of disabled people*, Department for Work and Pensions Research report no. 298. London: Department for Work and Pensions.

Beveridge, Sir William. 1942. *Social insurance and allied services*, Cmd 6404. London: Her Majesty's Stationery Office.

Beveridge, William. 1949. Epilogue. In *Family allowances*, ed. Eleanor Rathbone, 270. London: George Allen and Unwin, a new edition of *The Disinherited Family*.

Binder, Martin. 2010. *Elements of an evolutionary theory of welfare: Assessing welfare when preferences change*. London: Routledge.

Birkland, Thomas A. 2005. *An introduction to the policy process: Theories, concepts, and models of public policy making*, 2nd ed. Armonk: M.E. Sharpe.

Blair, Tony. 1983. A speech at the Democratic Leadership Forum, 25 Apr 1999, quoted in Alex Callinicos. 1983. *The revolutionary road to socialism: What the Socialist Workers Party stands for*, 45. London: Socialist Worker's Party.

Booker, H.S. 1946. Lady Rhys Williams' proposals for the amalgamation of direct taxation with social insurance. *The Economic Journal* 56: 230–243.

Bradshaw, Jonathan, and Fran Bennett. 2011. National Insurance: Past, present, and future? *Journal of Poverty and Social Justice* 19(3): 207–209.

Breitenbach, Hans, Tom Burden, and David Coates. 1990. *Features of a viable socialism*. Hemel Hempstead: Harvester Wheatsheaf.

Brittan, Samuel. 1998. *Towards a humane individualism*. London: John Stuart Mill Institute.

Brittan, Samuel, and Steven Webb. 1990. *Beyond the welfare state: An examination of basic incomes in a market economy*. Aberdeen: Aberdeen University Press.

Brown, C.V., and E. Levin. 1974. The effects of income taxation on overtime: The results of a national survey. *Economic Journal* 84: 833–848.
Burczak, Theodore. 2013. A Hayekian case for a basic income. In *Basic income and the free market: Austrian economics and the potential for efficient redistribution*, ed. Guinevere Liberty Nell, 49–64. New York: Palgrave Macmillan.
Callinicos, Alex. 1983. *The revolutionary road to socialism: What the Socialist Workers Party stands for*. London: Socialist Worker's Party.
Callinicos, Alex. 2001. *Against the Third Way: An anti-capitalist criticism*. Cambridge: Polity Press.
Callinicos, Alex. 2003. *An anti-capitalist manifesto*. Cambridge: Polity Press.
Camplin, Troy. 2013. BIG and the negative income tax. In *Basic income and the free market: Austrian economics and the potential for efficient redistribution*, ed. Guinevere Liberty Nell, 97–122. New York: Palgrave Macmillan.
Caputo, Richard K. 2012. *Basic income guarantee and politics: International experiences and perspectives on the viability of income guarantee*. New York: Palgrave Macmillan.
Carpenter, Mick, Belinda Freda, and Stuart Speeden (eds.). 2007. *Beyond the workfare state*. Bristol: Policy Press.
Centre for Research in Public Policy. 2014. *Working paper: Uprating the UK Living Wage in 2014*. Loughborough: Centre for Research in Public Policy. www.lboro.ac.uk/research/crsp/mis/thelivingwage/.
Cerniglia, Floriana, and Laura Pagani. 2015. Political knowledge and attitudes towards centralisation in Europe. *Fiscal Studies* 36(2): 215–236.
Child Poverty Action Group. 2015. *Welfare benefits and tax credits handbook, 2015/16*. London: Child Poverty Action Group. www.cpag.org.uk/bookshop/wbtch.
Citizen's Income Trust. 2006. *Citizen's Income: A brief introduction*. London: Citizen's Income Trust, revised and republished in 2013.
Clery, Elizabeth, Lucy Lee, and Sarah Kunz. 2012. *Public attitudes to poverty and welfare, 1983–2011: Analysis using British Social Attitudes data*. York: Joseph Rowntree Foundation. www.natcen.ac.uk/media/137637/poverty-and-welfare.pdf.
Commission on Social Justice. 1994. *Social justice: Strategies for national renewal*. London: Vintage.
Conlan, Timothy J., Paul L. Posner, and David R. Beam. 2014. *Pathways of power: The dynamics of national policy making*. Washington, DC: Georgetown University Press.
Coughlin, Richard M. 1980. *Ideology, public opinion and welfare policy: Attitudes towards taxes and spending in industrialized societies*. Berkeley: Institute of International Studies, University of California.
Creedy, John, and Nicolas Hérault. 2015. Decomposing inequality changes: Allowing for leisure in the evaluation of tax and transfer policy effects. *Fiscal Studies* 36(2): 157–180.

Crocker, Geoff. 2012. Why austerity is the wrong answer to debt: A call for a new paradigm. *Citizen's Income Newsletter*, issue 3: 13–16.
Crossley, Thomas F., and Sung-Hee Jeon. 2007. Joint taxation and the labour supply of married women: Evidence from the Canadian tax reform of 1988. *Fiscal Studies* 28(3): 343–365.
Danson, Mike, Paul Spicker, Robin McAlpine, and Willie Sullivan. 2014. *The case for universalism: Assessing the evidence*. London: The Centre for Labour and Social Studies.
Davala, Sarath, Renana Jhabvala, Soumya Kapoor Mehta, and Guy Standing. 2014. *Basic income: A transformative policy for India*. London: Bloomsbury.
Day, Alan J. 2000. Think tanks in Western Europe. In *Think tanks and civil societies: Catalysts for ideas and action*, ed. James McGann and R. Kent Weaver, 103–138. New Brunswick: Transaction Publishers.
De Agostini, Paola, and Holly Sutherland. 2014. *EUROMOD country report: United Kingdom 2009–2013*. Colchester: Institute for Social and Economic Research, Essex University.
De Wispelaere, Jurgen. 2015. The struggle for strategy: On the politics of the basic income proposal. *Politics* (forthcoming). http://pol.sagepub.com/.
De Wispelaere, Jürgen, and José Antonio Noguera. 2012. On the political feasibility of universal basic income: An analytic framework. In *Basic income guarantee: International experiences and perspectives on the viability of income guarantee*, ed. Richard Caputo, 17–38. New York: Palgrave Macmillan.
De Wispelaere, Jurgen, and Lindsay Stirton. 2008. Why participation income might not be such a great idea after all. *Citizen's Income Newsletter*, issue 3: 3–8.
De Wispelaere, Jürgen, and Lindsay Stirton. 2011. The administrative efficiency of basic income. *Policy and Politics* 39(1): 115–132.
De Wispelaere, Jürgen, and Lindsay Stirton. 2012. A disarmingly simple idea? Practical bottlenecks in implementing a universal basic income. *International Social Security Review* 65(2): 103–121.
Deacon, Alan. 2005. An ethic of mutual responsibility? Toward a fuller justification for conditionality in welfare. In *Welfare reform and political theory*, ed. Lawrence Mead and Christopher Beem, 127–150. New York: Russell Sage Foundation.
Dean, Hartley. 2004. Popular discourse and the ethical deficiency of "Third Way" conceptions of citizenship. *Citizenship Studies* 8(1): 65–82.
Dean, Hartley. 2010. *Understanding human need*. Bristol: Policy Press.
Dean, Hartley. 2012a. The ethical deficit of the UK's proposed Universal Credit: Pimping the precariat? *Political Quarterly* 83(2): 353–359.
Dean, Hartley. 2012b. *Social policy*, 2nd ed. Cambridge: Polity.
Dean, Hartley, and Gerry Mitchell. 2011. *Wage top-ups and work incentives: The implications of the UK's Working Tax Credit scheme: A preliminary report*. London: London School of Economics.

Deaton, Angus. 1992. *Understanding consumption*. Oxford: Clarendon Press.
Deaton, Angus, and John Muellbauer. 1980. *Economics and consumer behaviour*. Cambridge: Cambridge University Press.
Denham, Andrew, and Mark Garnett. 1998. *British think-tanks and the climate of opinion*. London: UCL Press.
Department for Work and Pensions. 2007. *Tax benefit model tables*. London: Department for Work and Pensions. www.dwp.gov.uk/asd/asd1/TBMT_2007.pdf.
Department for Work and Pensions. 2011. *A state pension for the 21st century*, Cm 8053. London: The Stationery Office.
Department for Work and Pensions. 2012. *Annual report 2011-12*. London: Department for Work and Pensions.
Department for Work and Pensions. 2013. *Older workers statistical information booklet 2013*. London: Department for Work and Pensions. www.gov.uk/government/uploads/system/uploads/attachment_data/file/264899/older-workers-statistical-information-booklet-2013.pdf.
Department for Work and Pensions. 2014a. *Family resources survey, 2012-13*. London: Department for Work and Pensions. www.gov.uk/government/collections/family-resources-survey--2.
Department for Work and Pensions. 2014b. *Fraud and error in the benefit system: Estimates, 2013/14*. www.gov.uk/government/uploads/system/uploads/attachment_data/file/371459/Statistical_Release.pdf.
Dickens, Richard, and Alan Manning. 2002. *Has the national minimum wage reduced UK wages?* London: Centre for Economic Performance, London School of Economics.
Dorling, Danny. 2012. *Equality*. Oxford: New Internationalist.
Dutton, William H., and Kenneth L. Kraemer. 1985. *Modeling as negotiating: The political dynamics of computer models in the policy process*. Norwood: Ablex Publishing Corp.
Edwards, Paul, and Mark Gilman. 1998. *A national minimum wage: Stimulus to economic efficiency?* Warwick: Warwick Business School.
Electoral Commission. 2014. *The quality of the 2014 electoral registers in Great Britain: Research into the last registers produced under the household registration system*. London: The Electoral Commission.
Elliott, Larry. 2014. Quantitative easing: Giving cash to the public would have been more effective. *The Guardian*, October 29. www.theguardian.com/business/economics-blog/2014/oct/29/quantitative-easing-policy-stimulus-janet-yellen-ecb.
Esam, Peter, and Richard Berthoud. 1991. *Independent benefits for men and women: An enquiry into option for treating husbands and wives as separate units in the assessment of social security*. London: Policy Studies Institute.
Esam, Peter, Robert Good, and Rick Middleton. 1985. *Who's to benefit? A radical review of the social security system*. London: Verso.

Esping-Andersen, Gøsta. 1990. *The three worlds of welfare capitalism*. Cambridge: Polity Press.
Exley, Sonia. 2014. Think tanks and policy networks in English education. In *Studying public policy: An international approach*, ed. Michael Hill, 180–189. Bristol: Policy Press.
Field, Frank. 2002. *Welfare titans: How Lloyd George and Gordon Brown compare, and other essays on welfare reform*. London: Civitas.
Fitzpatrick, Tony. 1999. *Freedom and security: An introduction to the basic income debate*. Basingstoke: Macmillan.
Fitzpatrick, Tony. 2003. *After the new social democracy: Social welfare for the twenty-first century*. Manchester: Manchester University Press.
Ford News. 1934. April 1934. www.thehenryford.org/research/henryFordQuotes.aspx.
Forget, Evelyn L. 2012. Canada: The case for basic income. In *Basic income worldwide: Horizons of reform*, ed. Matthew C. Murray and Carole Pateman, 81–101. New York: Palgrave Macmillan.
French Jr., J.R.P., and B.H. Raven. 1959. The bases of social power. In *Studies in social power*, ed. D. Cartwright, 150–167. Ann Arbor: Institute for Social Research, reprinted as pp. 150–167 in Pugh, D.S. 1984. *Organization theory: Selected readings*, 2nd ed. Harmondsworth: Penguin.
Galston, William A. 2005. Conditional citizenship. In *Welfare reform and political theory*, ed. Lawrence Mead and Christopher Beem, 110–126. New York: Russell Sage Foundation.
Gans, Herbert J. 2014. Basic income: A remedy for a sick labor market? *Challenge* 57(2): 80–90.
Geoff, Fimister, and Michael Hill. 1993. Delegating implementation problems: Social security, housing and community care in Britain. In *New agendas in the study of the policy process*, ed. Michael Hill, 110–129. New York/London: Harvester Wheatsheaf.
George, Henry. 1889. *Progress and poverty*. London: Kegan Paul, Trench and Co.
Giddens, Anthony. 1998. *The Third Way: The renewal of social democracy*. Cambridge: Polity Press.
Giddens, Anthony. 2000. *The Third Way and its critics*. Cambridge: Polity Press.
Gilroy, Bernard Michael, Anastasia Heimann, and Mark Schopf. 2013. Basic income and labour supply: The German case. *Basic Income Studies* 8(1): 43–70.
Gingrich, Jane. 2014. Structuring the vote: Welfare institutions and value-based vote choices. In *How welfare states shape the democratic public: Policy feedback, participation, voting, and attitudes*, ed. Staffan Kumlin and Isabelle Stadelmann-Steffen, 93–112. Cheltenham: Edward Elgar.
GLA Economics. 2014. *A fairer London: The 2014 living wage in London*. London: GLA Economics Living Wage Unit. www.london.gov.uk/sites/default/files/living-wage-2014.pdf.

Goffman, Erving. 1990. *Stigma: Notes on the management of spoiled identity*. London: Penguin.
Golding, Peter, and Sue Middleton. 1982. *Images of welfare: Press and public attitudes to poverty*. Oxford: Basil Blackwell.
Goldsmith, Scott. 2012. The economic and social impacts of the permanent fund dividend on Alaska. In *Alaska's permanent fund dividend*, ed. Karl Widerquist and Michael W. Howard, 49–63. New York: Palgrave Macmillan.
Goodwin, Stephen. 1994. Liberal Democrats' conference: Citizen's income plan dropped. *The Independent*, September 22. www.independent.co.uk/news/uk/liberal-democrats-conference-citizens-income-plan-dropped-1450315.html. Accessed 21 Jun 2011.
Goos, Maarten, and Alan Manning. 2007. Lousy and lovely jobs: The rising polarization of work in Britain. *Review of Economics and Statistics* 89(1): 118–133.
Gordon, Ian, Janet Lewis, and Ken Young. 1997. Perspectives on policy analysis. In *The policy process: A reader*, ed. Michael Hill, 5–9. London/New York: Prentice Hall/Harvester Wheatsheaf.
Graetz, Georg, and Guy Michaels. 2015. *Robots at work*, Centre for Economic Performance discussion paper no. 1335. London: London School of Economics. http://cep.lse.ac.uk/pubs/download/dp1335.pdf.
Gramsci, Antonio. 1971. *Selections from prison notebooks*. London: Lawrence and Wishart.
Greenberger, Martin, Matthew A. Crenson, and Brian L. Crissey. 1976. *Models in the policy process: Public decision making in the computer era*. New York: Russell Sage Foundation.
Gregory, Robert. 1997. Political rationality or incrementalism? In *The policy process: A reader*, ed. Michael Hill, 175–191. London/New York: Prentice Hall/Harvester Wheatsheaf.
Haarman, Claudia, and Dirk Haarmann. 2007. From survival to decent employment: Basic income security in Namibia. *Basic Income Studies* 2(1): 1–7.
Ham, Christopher, and Michael Hill. 1984. *The policy process in the modern capitalist state*. Brighton: Wheatsheaf Books.
Handler, Joel F. 2005. Myth and ceremony in workfare: Rights, contracts, and client satisfaction. *The Journal of Socioeconomics* 34(1): 101–124.
Harris, José. 1977. *William Beveridge: A biography*. Oxford: Clarendon Press.
Harris, J. 1981. Some aspects of social policy in Britain during the Second World War. In *The emergence of the welfare state in Britain and Germany, 1850–1950*, ed. W.J. Mommsen, 247–262. London: Croom Helm.
Her Majesty's Government. 1972. *Proposals for a tax-credit system*, Cmnd. 5116. London: Her Majesty's Stationery Office.
Heyman, Philip B. 2008. *Living the policy process*. New York: Oxford University Press.
Hill, Michael. 2009. *The public policy process*, 5th ed. Harlow: Pearson/Longman.
Hills, John. 2014. *Good times, bad times: The welfare myth of them and us*. Bristol: Policy Press.

Hirsch, Donald. 2015. *Could a 'Citizen's Income' work?* York: Joseph Rowntree Foundation. www.jrf.org.uk/publications/could-citizens-income-work.

HM Revenue & Customs. 2012. *Annual report 2011–12*. London: Her Majesty's Revenue and Customs.

Hodge, John, and Stuart Lowe. 2009. *Understanding the policy process: Analysing welfare policy and practice*, 2nd ed. Bristol: Policy Press.

Hofstede, Geert. 1997. *Culture and organizations: Software of the mind: Intercultural Co-operation and its importance for survival*. New York: McGraw-Hill.

Hogwood, Brian, and Lewis Gunn. 1997. Why "perfect" implementation is unattainable. In *The policy process: A reader*, ed. Michael Hill, 217–225. London/New York: Prentice Hall/Harvester Wheatsheaf.

Honkanen, Pertti. 2014. Basic income and negative income tax: A comparison with a simulation model. *Basic Income Studies* 9(1–2): 119–135.

House of Commons Treasury and Civil Service Committee Sub-Committee. 1982. *The structure of personal income taxation and income support: Minutes of evidence*, HC 331-ix. London: Her Majesty's Stationery Office.

House of Commons Work and Pensions Committee. 2007. *Benefits simplification*, HC 463, vol. I. The Stationery Office: London. www.publications.parliament.uk/pa/cm200607/cmselect/cmworpen/463/46302.htm, and HC 463, vol. II. London: The Stationery Office. www.publications.parliament.uk/pa/cm200607/cmselect/cmworpen/463/463ii.pdf.

Humpage, Louise. 2015. *Policy change, public attitudes and social citizenship: Does neoliberalism matter?* Bristol: Policy Press.

Huws, Ursula. 1997. *Flexibility and security: Towards a new European balance*. London: Citizen's Income Trust.

Itaba, Yoshio. 2014. What do people think about basic income in Japan? In *Basic income in Japan: Prospects for a radical idea in a transforming welfare state*, ed. Yannick Vanderborght and Toru Yamamori, 171–195. New York: Palgrave Macmillan.

Jackson, Andrew, and Ben Dyson. 2012. *Modernising money: Why our monetary system is broken, and how it can be fixed*. London: Positive Money.

Jacobs, Lawrence R., and Robert Y. Shapiro. 1999. The media reporting and distorting of public opinion towards entitlements. In *The policy process*, ed. Stuart S. Nagel, 135–145. New York: Nova Science Publishers.

Jakobsen, Tor George. 2011. Welfare attitudes and social expenditure: Do regimes shape public opinion? *Social Indicators Research* 101: 323–340.

James, William. 2012/1902. *The varieties of religious experience: A study in human nature*. Oxford: Oxford University Press, first published 1902.

James, Estelle, Alejandra Cox Edwards, and Rebecca Wong. 2008. *The gender impact of social security reform*. Chicago/London: University of Chicago Press.

Janky, Béla. 2012. Social solidarity and preferences on welfare institutions across Europe. In *Reinventing social solidarity across Europe*, ed. Marion Ellison, 209–249. Bristol: Policy Press.

Jordan, Bill. 1998. *The new politics of welfare*. London: Sage.
Jordan, Bill. 2010. Basic income and social value. *Basic Income Studies* 5(2): 1–19.
Jordan, Bill. 2012. The low road to basic income? Tax-benefit integration in the UK. *Journal of Social Policy* 41(1): 1–17.
Jordan, A.G., and J.J. Richardson. 1987. *British politics and the policy process: An arena approach*. London: Unwin Hyman.
Jordan, Bill, Phil Agulnik, Duncan Burbidge, and Stuart Duffin. 2000. *Stumbling towards basic income: The prospects for tax-benefit integration*. London: Citizen's Income Trust.
Joseph, Keith, and Jonathan Sumption. 1979. *Equality*. London: John Murray.
Joseph Rowntree Foundation. 2013. *Minimum income standards*. York: Joseph Rowntree Foundation. www.jrf.org.uk/site/files/jrf/images/MIS-2013-figure2.jpg.
Kenis, Patrick, and Volker Schneider. 1991. Policy networks and policy analysis. In *Policy networks*, ed. Bernd Marin and Renate Mayntz, 25–59. Frankfurt am Main: Campus Verlag.
King, Desmond. 2005. Making people work: Democratic consequences of workfare. In *Welfare reform and political theory*, ed. Lawrence Mead and Christopher Beem, 65–81. New York: Russell Sage Foundation.
Kingdon, J.W. 2011. *Agendas, alternatives, and public policies*, 2nd ed. New York: HarperCollins.
Koistinen, Pertti, and Johanna Perkiö. 2014. Good and bad times of social innovations: The case of universal basic income in Finland. *Basic Income Studies* 9(1–2): 25–57.
Kumlin, Staffan, and Isabelle Stadelmann-Steffen. 2014. How welfare states shape the democratic public: Borrowing strength across research communities. In *How welfare states shape the democratic public: Policy feedback, participation, voting, and attitudes*, ed. Staffan Kumlin and Isabelle Stadelmann-Steffen, 311–325. Cheltenham: Edward Elgar.
Land, Hilary. 1975. The introduction of family allowances: An act of historic justice? In *Change, choice and conflict in social policy*, ed. Phoebe Hall, Hilary Land, Roy Parker, and Adrian Webb, 157–230. London: Heinemann.
Lansley, Stewart. 2015. *Tackling the power of capital: The role of social wealth funds*, Thinkpiece no. 81. London: Compass.
Larsen, Christian Albrekt. 2006. *The institutional logic of welfare attitudes*. Aldershot: Ashgate.
Liebig, Stefan, and Steffen Mau. 2004. A legitimate guaranteed minimum income? In *Promoting income security as a right: Europe and North America*, ed. Guy Standing, 207–228. London: Anthem.
Lindblom, C.E. 1959. The science of "muddling through". *Public Administration Review* 19(2): 79–88.

Lindblom, C.E. 1964. Contexts for change and strategy: A reply. *Public Administration Review* 24(3): 157–158.
Lindblom, Charles E. 1980. *The policy-making process*, 2nd ed. Englewood Cliffs: Prentice Hall.
Lipsky, Michael. 1980. *Street-level bureaucracy: Dilemmas of the individual in public services*. New York: Russell Sage Foundation.
Lister, Ruth. 2004. *Poverty*. Cambridge: Polity Press.
Lynes, Tony. 2011. From unemployment insurance to assistance in interwar Britain. *Journal of Poverty and Social Justice* 19(3): 221–233.
Macnicol, John. 1980. *The movement for family allowances, 1918–1945: A study in social policy development*. London: Heinemann.
Majone, Gian Domenico. 1989. *Evidence, argument, and persuasion in the policy process*. New Haven: Yale University Press.
Manning, Alan. 2014. Minimum wages: The economics and the politics. *CentrePiece* 1(1): 8–10.
Marin, Bernd, and Renate Mayntz. 1991. Introduction: Studying policy networks. In *Policy networks*, ed. Bernd Marin and Renate Mayntz, 11–23. Frankfurt am Main: Campus Verlag.
Marinetto, Michael. 1999. *Studies of the policy process: A case analysis*. London: Prentice Hall Europe.
Marsh, David. 1998. The development of the policy networks approach. In *Comparing policy networks*, ed. David Marsh, 1–17. Buckingham: Open University Press.
Martin, Josh. 2015. *Universal credit to basic income: A politically feasible transition?* Unpublished M.Sc. dissertation. London: London School of Economics.
Marx, Karl. 1938/1875. *Critique of the Gotha programme*. London: Lawrence and Wishart, first published in German in 1875, and in Russian in 1891.
Marx, Karl, and Friedrich Engels. 1967/1888. *The Communist Manifesto*. Trans. Samuel Moore. Harmondsworth: Penguin, first published 1888.
Mau, Steffen. 2003. *The moral economy of welfare states: Britain and Germany compared*. London: Routledge.
McKay, Ailsa. 2013. Crisis, cuts, citizenship and a basic income: A wicked solution to a wicked problem. *Basic Income Studies* 8(1): 93–104.
McLeay, Michael, Amar Radia, and Ryland Thomas. 2014. Money creation in the modern economy. *Quarterly Bulletin*, 1st quarter. London: Bank of England. www.bankofengland.co.uk/publications/Documents/quarterlybulletin/2014/qb14q1prereleasemoneycreation.pdf.
Mead, Lawrence. 1992. *The new politics of poverty: The non-working poor in America*. New York: Harper Collins.
Mead, Lawrence. 2005a. A summary of welfare reform. In *Welfare reform and political theory*, ed. Lawrence Mead and Christopher Beem, 10–33. New York: Russell Sage Foundation.

Mead, Lawrence. 2005b. Welfare reform and citizenship. In *Welfare reform and political theory*, ed. Lawrence Mead and Christopher Beem, 172–199. New York: Russell Sage Foundation.

Mead, Lawrence, and Christopher Beem (eds.). 2005. *Welfare reform and political theory*. New York: Russell Sage Foundation.

Metcalf, David. 1999. *The British national minimum wage*. London: Centre for Economic Performance, London School of Economics.

Methodist Church, Division of Social Responsibility. 1991. *Sects and parties: Christian values and political ideologies*. London: Methodist Church.

Mewes, Jan, and Steffen Mau. 2012. Unraveling working-class welfare chauvinism. In *Contested welfare states: Welfare attitudes in Europe and beyond*, ed. Stefan Svallfors, 119–157. Stanford: Stanford University Press.

Michaeu, Pierre-Carl, and Arthur van Soest. 2008. How did the elimination of the US earnings test above the normal retirement age affect labour supply expectations. *Fiscal Studies* 29(2): 197–231.

Migny, Gabriel. 1982. *The power of minorities*. London: Academic Press.

Miller, Anne. 1986. Poverty and adequacy. *BIRG Bulletin* 6: 13–16.

Minogue, Martin. 1997. Theory and practice in public policy and administration. In *The policy process: A reader*, ed. Michael Hill, 10–29. London/New York: Prentice Hall/Harvester Wheatsheaf.

Mitchell, William, and Martin Watts. 2005. A comparison of the economic consequences of basic income and job guarantee schemes. *Rutgers Journal of Law and Urban Policy* 2(1): 64–90.

Morçöl, Göktuğ. 2012. *A complexity theory for public policy*. New York: Routledge.

Morgan, Patricia. 1995. *Farewell to the family? Public policy and family breakdown in Britain and the USA*. London: Institute of Economic Affairs.

Moscovici, Serge. 1976. *Social influence and social change*. London: Academic Press.

Moscovici, Serge. 1980. Toward a theory of conversion behavior. In *Advances in experimental social psychology*, vol. 13, ed. Leonard Berkowitz, 209–239. New York: Academic Press.

Murakami, Shinji. 2014. The financial feasibility of basic income and the idea of a refundable tax credit in Japan. In *Basic income in Japan: Prospects for a radical idea in a transforming welfare state*, ed. Yannick Vanderborght and Toru Yamamori, 219–245. New York: Palgrave Macmillan.

Murphey, Dwight. 2009. A "classical liberal" rethinks the market system: Invitation to an intellectual odyssey. *The Journal of Social, Political, and Economic Studies* 34(3): 347–355.

Murphey, Dwight. 2011. Capitalism's deepening crisis: The imperative of monetary reconstruction. *The Journal of Social, Political, and Economic Studies* 36(3): 277–300.

Murphy, Jason Burke. 2010. Baby steps: Basic income and the need for incremental organizational development. *Basic Income Studies* 5(2): 1–13.

Murphy, Richard, and Howard Reed. 2013. *Financing the social state: Towards a full employment economy*. London: Centre for Labour and Social Studies.

Murray, Charles. 1984. *Losing ground: American social policy, 1950–1980*. New York: Basic Books.

Murray, Charles. 1996. *Charles Murray and the underclass: The developing debate*. London: Institute of Economic Affairs, contains 'The Emerging British Underclass', first published in 1989, and 'Underclass: The Crisis Deepens', first published in 1994.

Muuri, Ana. 2010. The impact of the use of the social welfare services or social security benefits on attitudes to social welfare policies. *International Journal of Social Welfare* 19(2010): 182–193.

Nemeth, Charlan, Mark Swedlund, and Barbara Kanki. 1974. Patterning of the minority's responses and their influence on the majority. *European Journal of Social Psychology* 4(1): 53–64.

O'Brien, Michael. 2007. *Poverty, policy and the state*. Bristol: Policy Press.

Offe, Claus. 2013. Pathways from here. In *Basic income: An anthology of contemporary research*, ed. Karl Widerquist, José A. Noguera, Yannick Vanderborght, and Jürgen De Wispelaere, 560–563. Chichester: Wiley Blackwell.

Pahl, Jan. 1983. The allocation of money and structuring of inequality within marriage. *Sociological Review* 31(2): 237–262.

Pahl, Jan. 1986. Social security, taxation and family financial arrangements. *BIRG Bulletin* 5, Spring, London: Basic Income Research Group, 2–4.

Parker, Hermione. 1889. *Instead of the dole: An enquiry into integration of the tax and benefit systems*. London: Routledge.

Parker, Hermione. 1994. Citizen's Income. *Citizen's Income Bulletin* 17: 4–12.

Parker, Hermione. 1995. *Taxes, benefits and family life: The seven deadly traps*. London: Institute of Economic Affairs.

Pasquali, Francesca. 2012. *Virtuous imbalance: Political philosophy between desirability and feasibility*. Farnham: Ashgate.

Pateman, Carole. 2005. Another way forward: Welfare, social reproduction, and a basic income. In *Welfare reform and political theory*, ed. Lawrence Mead and Christopher Beem, 34–64. New York: Russell Sage Foundation.

Pech, Wesley J. 2010. Behavioral economics and the basic income guarantee. *Basic Income Studies* 5(2): 1–17.

Pennycook, Matthew. 2012. *What price a living wage? Understanding the impact of a living wage on firm-level wage bills*. London: The Resolution Foundation.

Piketty, Thomas. 2014. *Capital in the twenty-first century*. Cambridge, MA: The Belknap Press of Harvard University.

Plunkett, James, Alex Hurrell, and Conor D'Arcy. 2014. *More than a minimum: The Resolution Foundation review of the future of the national minimum wage: The final report*. London: The Resolution Foundation.

Pond, Chris, and Steve Winyard. 1983. *The case for a national minimum wage*. London: Low Pay Unit.

Presthus, Robert. 1974. *Elites in the policy process.* London: Cambridge University Press.
Purdy, David. 2013. Political strategies for basic income. In *Basic income: An anthology of contemporary research,* ed. Karl Widerquist, José A. Noguera, Yannick Vanderborght, and Jürgen De Wispelaere, 477–484. Chichester: Wiley Blackwell.
Rathbone, Eleanor. 1949. *Family allowances.* London: George Allen and Unwin, a new edition of *The Disinherited Family* with an epilogue by William Beveridge.
Rathbone, Eleanor. 1986/1924. *The disinherited family.* Bristol: Falling Wall Press, first published 1924.
Rhys Williams, Juliet. 1943. *Something to look forward to.* London: MacDonald and Co.
Rhys Williams, Brandon. 1989. *Stepping stones to independence: National Insurance after 1990,* ed. Hermione Parker, foreword by David Howells MP. Aberdeen: Aberdeen University Press for the One Nation Group of Conservative MPs.
Richardson, J.J. 1969. *The policy-making process.* London: Routledge and Kegan Paul.
Richardson, Jeremy. 1999. Interest group, multi-arena politics and policy change. In *The policy process,* ed. Stuart S. Nagel, 65–99. New York: Nova Science Publishers.
Richardson, J.J., and A.G. Jordan. 1979. *Governing under pressure: The policy process in a post-parliamentary democracy.* Oxford: Basil Blackwell.
Richardt, Johannes. 2011. Basic income, low aspiration. *The Sp!ked Review of Books,* issue 41, January 2011. www.spiked-online.com/index.php/site/reviewofbooks_article/10136/. Accessed 21 Jun 2011)
Robson, Paul, Shirley Dex, and Frank Wilkinson. 1997. *The costs of a national statutory minimum wage in Britain.* Cambridge: Judge Institute of Management Studies.
Rose, Richard. 2006. Inheritance before choice in public policy. In *Making policy happen,* ed. Leslie Budd, Julie Charlesworth, and Rob Paton, 51–64. London: Routledge.
Rowlingson, Karen. 2009. "From cradle to grave": Social security and the lifecourse. In *Understanding social security,* 2nd ed, ed. Jane Millar, 133–150. Bristol: Policy Press.
Ryan-Collins, Josh, Tony Greenham, Richard Werner, and Andrew Jackson. 2011. *Where does money come from? A guide to the UK monetary and banking system.* London: New Economics Foundation.
Sargant, William. 1976. *Battle for the mind: A physiology of conversion and brainwashing.* London: Heinemann.
Saunders, Peter, and Maneerat Pinyopusarek. 2001. Popularity and participation: Social security reform in Australia. In *Ethics and social security reform,* ed. Erik Schokkaert, 143–164. Aldershot: Ashgate.

Schwandt, Thomas A. 2005. Moral discourses. Encyclopedia article in Sandra Mathison, *Encyclopedia of evaluation*. Sage. https://srmo.sagepub.com/view/encyclopedia of evaluation/n350.xml.

Shone, Ronald. 1981. *Applications in intermediate microeconomics*. Oxford: Martin Robertson.

Smith, T. Alexander. 1975. *The comparative policy process*. Santa Barbara: Clio Press.

Smith, Adam. 1976. *An inquiry into the nature and causes of the wealth of nations*, ed. Edwin Cannan. Chicago: University of Chicago Press.

Smith, M.J. 1993. Policy networks. In *Pressure, power and policy*, ed. M.J. Smith, 56–65. Hemel Hempstead: Harvester Wheatsheaf, also at pp. 76–86 in Michael Hill (ed.). 1993. *The policy process: A reader*, 2nd ed. Hemel Hempstead: Prentice Hall/Harvester Wheatsheaf.

Smith, D.V.L. and Associates. 1991. *Basic income: A research report*. London: Prepared for Age Concern England.

Smith, Gilbert, and David May. 1997. The artificial debate between rationalist and incrementalist models of decision making. In *The policy process: A reader*, ed. Michael Hill, 163–174. London/New York: Prentice Hall/Harvester Wheatsheaf.

Spicker, Paul. 2011. *How social security works: An introduction to benefits in Britain*. Bristol: Policy Press.

Staerklé, Christian, Tiina Likki, and Régis Scheidegger. 2012. A normative approach to welfare attitudes. In *Contested welfare states: Welfare attitudes in Europe and beyond*, ed. Stefan Svallfors, 81–118. Stanford: Stanford University Press.

Standing, Guy. 2011. *The precariat: The new dangerous class*. London: Bloomsbury.

Standing, Guy. 2012. An anniversary note – BIEN's twenty-fifth. In *Basic income guarantee: International experiences and perspectives on the viability of income guarantee*, ed. Richard Caputo, 55–60. New York: Palgrave Macmillan.

Steiner, Ivan D. 1972. *Group process and productivity*. New York: Academic Press.

Stone, Diane. 1996. *Capturing the political imagination: Think tanks and the policy process*. London: Frank Cass.

Sutherland, Holly. 2001. *The national minimum wage and in-work poverty*. Cambridge: Department of Applied Economics, University of Cambridge.

Svallfors, Stefan. 2012. Welfare states and welfare attitudes. In *Contested welfare states: Welfare attitudes in Europe and beyond*, ed. Stefan Svallfors, 1–24. Stanford, California: Stanford University Press.

Tabatabai, Hamid. 2011. Iran's economic reforms usher in a de facto Citizen's Income. *Citizen's Income Newsletter*, issue 1: 1–2.

Tabatabai, Hamid. 2011. The basic income road to reforming Iran's price subsidies. *Basic Income Studies* 6(1): 1–24.

Tabatabai, Hamid. 2012. Iran: A bumpy road toward basic income. In *Basic income guarantee and politics: International experiences and perspectives on the viability of income guarantee*, ed. Richard Caputo, 285–300. New York: Palgrave Macmillan.

Takamatsu, Rie, and Toshiaki Tachibanaki. 2014. What needs to be considered when introducing a new welfare system: Who supports basic income in Japan? In *Basic income in Japan: Prospects for a radical idea in a transforming welfare state*, ed. Yannick Vanderborght and Toru Yamamori, 197–218. New York: Palgrave Macmillan.

Taylor-Gooby, Peter. 1987. *MPs' attitudes to welfare*. Swindon: Economic and Social Research Council.

Thane, Pat. 1996. *Foundations of the welfare state*, 2nd ed. London: Longman.

Thane, Pat. 2011. The making of National Insurance, 1911. *Journal of Poverty and Social and Justice* 19(3): 211–219.

Thatcher, Margaret. 1987. Interview for *Woman's Own*, October 31. www.margarethatcher.org/document/106689. Accessed 18 Jun 2011.

Tideman, Nicolaus, and Kwok Ping Tsang. 2010. Seigniorage as a source for a basic income guarantee. *Basic Income Studies* 5(2): 1–6.

Titmuss, Richard. 1962. *Income distribution and social change*. London: Allen and Unwin.

Tobin, James. 1978. A proposal for international monetary reform. *Eastern Economic Journal* 4(3–4): 153–159.

Torry, Malcolm. 2009. 'Can unconditional cash transfers work? They can', a report of a seminar. *Citizen's Income Newsletter*, issue 2: 1–3.

Torry, Malcolm. 2013. *Money for everyone: Why we need a Citizen's Income*. Bristol: Policy Press.

Torry, Malcolm. 2014a. A new policy world for the benefits system. *Policy World* Spring: 12–13.

Torry, Malcolm. 2014b. *Research note: A feasible way to implement a Citizen's Income*, Institute for Social and Economic Research EUROMOD working paper EM17/14. Colchester: Institute for Social and Economic Research, University of Essex. www.iser.essex.ac.uk/research/publications/working-papers/euromod/em17-14.

Torry, Malcolm. 2015a. Research note: A feasible way to implement a Citizen's Income. *Citizen's Income Newsletter*, issue 1: 4–9. This article was previously published as *Research note: A feasible way to implement a Citizen's Income*: see above.

Torry, Malcolm. 2015b. *Two feasible ways to implement a revenue neutral Citizen's Income scheme*, Institute for Social and Economic Research EUROMOD working paper EM6/15. Colchester: Institute for Social and Economic Research, University of Essex. www.iser.essex.ac.uk/research/publications/working-papers/euromod/em6-15.

Torry, Malcolm. 2015c. Two feasible ways to implement a revenue neutral Citizen's Income scheme. *Citizen's Income Newsletter*, issue 3: 3–11. This article was

previously published as *Two feasible ways to implement a revenue neutral Citizen's Income scheme*: see above.
Torry, Malcolm. 2015d. *101 Reasons for a Citizen's Income*. Bristol: Policy Press.
Townsend, Peter. 1979. *Poverty in the United Kingdom*. Harmondsworth: Penguin.
Trade Union Congress. 1995. *Arguments for a national minimum wage*. London: Trade Union Congress.
Turner, John C. 1991. *Social influence*. Milton Keynes: Open University Press.
Turquoise Partners. 2014. *Iran investment monthly*. Iran: Turquoise Partners. April 2014.
United Nations. 2009. *Human development report, 2009*. New York: United Nations.
van Avermaet, Eddy. 2001. Social influence in small groups. In *Introduction to social psychology*, 3rd ed, ed. Mike Hewstone and Wolfgang Stroebe, 403–443. Oxford: Blackwell.
van Oorschot, Wim. 2006a. Making the difference in social Europe: Deservingness perceptions among citizens of European welfare states. *Journal of European Social Policy* 16(1): 23–42.
van Oorschot, Wim. 2006b. Welfarism and the multidimensionality of welfare state legitimacy: Evidence from The Netherlands, 2006. *International Journal of Social Welfare* 21: 71–93.
van Oorschot, Wim, and Bart Meuleman. 2012. Welfare performance and welfare support. In *Contested welfare states: Welfare attitudes in Europe and beyond*, ed. Stefan Svallfors, 25–57. Stanford: Stanford University Press.
van Parijs, Philippe. 1995. *Real freedom for all: What (if anything) can justify capitalism?* Oxford: Clarendon Press.
Vanderborght, Yannick. 2005. The basic income guarantee in Europe: The Belgian and Dutch back door strategies. In *The ethics and economics of the basic income guarantee*, ed. Karl Widerquist, Michael Anthony Lewis, and Steven Pressman, 257–281. Aldershot: Ashgate.
Vanderborght, Yannick. 2013. The ambiguities of basic income from a trade union perspective. In *Basic income: An anthology of contemporary research*, ed. Karl Widerquist, José A. Noguera, Yannick Vanderborght, and Jürgen De Wispelaere, 497–508. Chichester: Wiley Blackwell.
Vanderborght, Yannick, and Yuki Sekine. 2014. A comparative look at the feasibility of basic income in the Japanese welfare state. In *Basic income in Japan: Prospects for a radical idea in a transforming welfare state*, ed. Yannick Vanderborght and Toru Yamamori, 15–34. New York: Palgrave Macmillan.
Wagner, Richard E. 2007. *Fiscal sociology and the theory of public finance: An exploratory essay*. London: Edward Elgar.
Walley, John. 1986. Public support for families with children: A study of British politics. *BIRG Bulletin* 5: 8–11.
Watts, Martin. 2010. How should minimum wages be set in Australia. *Journal of Industrial Relations* 52(2): 131–149.

Watts, Martin. 2011. *Income v work guarantees: A reconsideration*. Newcastle: Newcastle University. http://hdl.handle.net/1959.13/934140.
Weber, Cameron. 2013. Taking Leviathan with a basic income. In *Basic income and the free market: Austrian economics and the potential for efficient redistribution*, ed. Guinevere Liberty Nell, 81–96. New York: Palgrave Macmillan.
White, Stuart. 2003. *The civic minimum: On the rights and obligations of economic citizenship*. Oxford: Oxford University Press.
White, Stuart. 2005. Is conditionality illiberal? In *Welfare reform and political theory*, ed. Lawrence Mead and Christopher Beem, 82–109. New York: Russell Sage Foundation.
White, Stuart. 2006. Reconsidering the exploitation objection to basic income. *Basic Income Studies* 1(2): 1–24.
Widerquist, Karl. 2010. Lessons of the Alaska dividend. *Citizen's Income Newsletter*, issue 3: 13–15.
Widerquist, Karl, and Michael Howard. 2012. *Alaska's permanent fund dividend: Examining its suitability as a model*. New York: Palgrave Macmillan.
Widerquist, Karl, and Allan Sheahen. 2012. The United States: The basic income guarantee – Past experience, current proposals. In *Basic income worldwide: Horizons of reform*, ed. Matthew C. Murray and Carole Pateman, 11–32. New York: Palgrave Macmillan.
Wilkinson, Richard, and Kate Pickett. 2010. *The spirit level: Why equality is better for everyone*, 2nd ed. London: Penguin Books.
Wu, Xun, M. Ramesh, Michael Howlett, and Scott Fritzen. 2010. *The public policy primer: Managing the policy process*. London/New York: Routledge.
Yeatman, Anna. 1998. Activism and the policy process. In *Activism and the policy process*, ed. Anna Yeatman, 16–35. St. Leonards: Allen and Unwin.
Zahariadis, Nikolaus. 1999. Ambiguity, time, and multiple streams. In *Theories of the policy process*, ed. Paul A. Sabatier, 73–93. Boulder: Westview Press.
Zelleke, Almaz. 2008. Institutionalizing the universal caretaker through a basic income? *Basic Income Studies* 3(3): 1–9.
Zelleke, Almaz. 2012. Basic income and the Alaska model: Limits of the resource dividend model for the implementation of an Unconditional Basic Income. In *Alaska's permanent fund dividend: Examining its suitability as a model*, ed. Karl Widerquist and Michael Howard, 141–168. New York: Palgrave Macmillan.

Index

A

Abel-Smith, Brian, 33, 208
absenteeism, 212, 213
academic (*n*), 125, 230, 234
   institution (*see* institution, academic)
actors, 135, 169, 196, 197, 226, 239, 243
   diffuse / discrete, 27–9
   political, 28, 167, 178, 180, 199
   self-interested, 199
Adam Smith Institute, xxvii, 236
administration. *See also* government, administration by
   of Citizen's Income (*see* Citizen's Income, administration of)
   government (*see* government, administration by)
   of means-tested benefits (*see* means-tested benefits, administration of)
administrative. *See also* government, administration by
   complexity (*see* complexity, administrative)
   costs, 9–11, 55, 57–9, 65, 79, 81, 86, 152
   feasibility (*see* feasibility, administrative)
affordability, 39, 52, 81, 129, 183. *See also* feasibility, fiscal
age cohort/group, ix, 19, 26, 29, 32, 35, 39, 40, 67, 80, 104–6, 154, 163, 243. *See also* demographic group; year cohort
agency. *See* actors
Alaska's Permanent Fund Dividend, 45, 47, 102, 123, 138
arguments for/against Citizen's Income, 5, 9, 17, 41, 42, 45, 60, 77, 83, 91, 101, 109, 139, 169, 172, 175–9, 187, 203–4, 210–11, 218–20, 222–4, 242
assumptions. *See* embedded assumptions / presuppositions
Atkinson, Tony, 82, 124–5, 138
automatic (payments), vii, 1, 10, 55, 138, 145
automation, 13
autonomy, 174, 176

B

bad jobs. *See* jobs, bad
bank account, 10, 45, 87, 120–2, 131–3, 145, 156
Bank of England, 211
banking, global, 122, 197
Basic Income, v, viii, 83, 106, 172, 178, 181, 216. *See also,* Citizen's Income; Universal Basic Income
Basic Income European / Earth Network (BIEN), xvi
Basic Income Research Group, xv, 217
Basic State Pension, ix, xi, 16, 54–6, 59, 65, 76, 85, 207, 218
behavioural
  change, 47, 98, 144, 162–3, 170
  feasibility (*see* feasibility, behavioural)
benefits (social security), 3, 40–2, 93, 101, 105, 120, 125, 131, 149, 154, 197–8, 204, 205, 237. *See also* administration
  abolition of, 9, 49–50, 54–8, 65, 123–4, 139, 155, 182–3
  advisers, 99
  calculation of, viii, x, 5–11, 48–51, 54, 57, 59, 72, 76, 134, 155, 183, 237 (*see also* benefits, recalculation of)
  child, ix, 7, 10, 17, 19, 32–3, 39, 58, 78, 104–5, 121, 131, 138, 205 (*see also* Family Allowance; Child Benefit; Citizen's Income, Child)
  complexity of, 30, 35, 50, 76, 98, 101, 200, 219
  conditional, 2, 40, 92, 94, 104, 124, 170, 217 (*see also* benefits, conditions; unconditional benefits)
  conditions, vii, ix, x, 1, 6, 17, 125, 138, 203, 205–7, 218
  contingency, x, 93, 221
  contributory (*see* contributory, benefits)
  cost of, 33, 39, 49–59, 70–2, 79, 81, 85–6, 122, 130, 152, 213, 219
  duration of, x, 7
  existing (levels of/reductions in/system of)40, 42–3, 49, 54, 57–60, 67–70, 76, 83, 100, 103, 123, 133, 139, 144, 159–63, 197, 216
  household (*see* household, claimant unit)
  individualized, 103, 138, 243 (*see also* individual claimant unit)
  in-work (*see* means-tested benefits, in-work)
  legislation (*see* legislation, benefits)
  levels of, 40, 42–3, 51, 78, 93, 103, 124
  means-tested (*see* means-tested benefits)
  misnamed, 11, 139, 214
  names of, vii, xi, 139, 208, 217
  National Insurance, xv, 15, 55, 132–4, 139, 159, 207, 215, 217, 224
  nonwithdrawable, vii–ix, 1, 9, 18, 25, 39, 40, 67, 78, 87, 96, 106–8, 124, 131, 197, 203–4, 215–17, 220–3, 238, 244
  out-of-work (*see* means-tested benefits, out-of-work)
  payment intervals/mechanisms, 46–7, 102, 121–3, 132–4, 138, 172
  policy, 11, 196, 200, 240, 244
  rates (*see* benefits, levels of)
  recalculation of, 10, 51, 57, 77, 123–4, 139 (*see also* benefits, calculation of)

regulations (*see* regulations)
renaming of, 16, 208, 217
retention of, 49–51, 56–8, 77, 134, 139, 183, 218
social insurance (*see* social insurance, benefits)
system, vi, xi, xv–xvii, 2, 25–6, 29, 31, 43, 46, 49, 67, 77, 83, 87, 93, 98–100, 105, 119, 129, 144, 148, 159, 179, 202, 207, 215, 221, 226, 238–40
unconditional (*see* unconditional benefits)
universal (*see* universal, benefits)
withdrawal of, 96, 145, 208, 219
Bennett, Natalie, 183
Beveridge Report, 18, 181, 198, 207, 216
Beveridge, William, 16–18, 32, 198, 205–7, 239
borrowing (by government), 42–3
bottlenecks, 122, 238
break-even point, 126
Brittan, Samuel, 173–4
budget
constraint, 157–60
household, 69, 70, 77, 133
statement, 214
bureaucratic control/interference/intrusion, 8, 87, 101, 143, 154, 174
business, 15, 46, 99, 211–13
business cycle, 152

C
Callinicos, Alex, 171–3
Canada, 148–50
capital/capitalism, 148–50, 169, 171–2, 174, 176, 181, 210–11
carbon tax, 69

career, 11, 13, 143, 199
carer/care work, 21, 39, 55, 80, 93, 131–2, 136, 173, 182, 197, 205, 206, 209
case studies, vi, xi, xvi, 15–28, 32–5, 53–60, 74–81, 106–8, 130–8, 154–62, 195, 204–23, 237
casework, 8, 125, 137
Castle, Barbara, 34, 209
Catalonia, 58–60, 77, 83
causal direction, 105, 110, 151. *See also* relationships, causal
central bank, 45
Centre for Research in Social Policy (Loughborough University), 212
Centre for Social Justice, 208
Chancellor of the Exchequer, 89, 111, 131, 176, 214, 220
change
employment market (*see* employment market, change in)
to existing tax and benefits regulations, ix, 17, 26, 30, 42, 49–50, 57–9, 67, 75, 78, 80, 83, 108, 123–4, 131, 144–5, 148, 202, 241
experienced (behavioural/promised/psychological), 26, 28, 47–8, 70, 90, 91, 95, 98, 101–2, 107, 144–7, 154, 156, 170
forced, 144–5
in circumstances, 9, 10, 13, 14, 131, 137, 143
incremental (*see* incremental change)
policy (*see* policy change)
in public opinion, 29, 91, 97–8, 107, 154, 240
social, 35, 90, 96, 101, 146, 222, 240, 244

Child Benefit, ix, xi, 10, 12, 16–17,
    32–5, 54–5, 59, 65, 76, 78–82,
    85–6, 95, 104–5, 107–8, 121,
    131–3, 176, 182, 185–7, 197,
    208–9, 215, 217–22, 225
child/children. *See also* Child Benefit,
    Child Tax Allowance, Child Tax
    Credit; Family Allowance
  allowance, 18, 205–6
  benefits (*see* benefits, child)
  carer of, viii, xi, 3, 39, 80, 105, 125,
    131–2, 147, 153, 197, 205–6,
    209
  dependent, 86, 135–6, 172
  deserving group, 5, 19, 32, 80, 94,
    105, 108, 209, 237
  families with, 14, 71–3, 77, 95, 107,
    136, 146, 148, 207
  poverty, 78–9, 185, 192, 208–9
  tax on, 131, 220
Child Citizen's Income, 10, 17, 19,
    32, 39, 48, 59, 64, 65, 76–83,
    85, 104–5, 122, 128, 131–2,
    160, 162, 217, 237, 243
Child Poverty Action Group, 33–4,
    99, 209
Child Tax Allowance, 33–5, 108, 209
Child Tax Credit, xi, 55, 65, 85, 101,
    208
choices
  new, 133, 145–7, 153, 155, 173
  political, 83–4, 179
Churchill, Winston, 211
citizenship, v, vii–ix, 9, 17, 25, 39, 45,
    67, 89, 100, 103, 107, 120–1,
    130–1, 175, 217, 223
Citizen's Income, *passim*. *See also*
    government, and Citizen's
    Income; government, Citizen's
    Income feasible for
  administration of, 9–11, 26, 77, 87,
    96, 101–4, 119–42, 143, 152,
    155, 203, 216, 218–22, 238
    (*see also* administrative, costs;
    feasibility, administrative)
  child (*see* Child Citizen's Income)
  definition of, vii–ix, 1, 4, 100,
    109–10
  desirability of, v–vi, xiii, 1–19, 29,
    107, 240
  economic case for (*see* economic case
    for Citizen's Income)
  education about (*see* education,
    about Citizen's Income)
  eligibility for/entitlement to,
    120–3, 132, 175, 216
  feasibility of (*see* feasibility)
  funding of, ix, 43–53, 57–60, 67,
    144, 177, 183, 244
  global, xxviii
  implementation of (*see*
    implementation)
  legislation (*see* legislation, Citizen's
    Income)
  levels of, vii, 8, 26, 29, 39–40,
    51–2, 53, 57–60, 64–5, 67, 74,
    76, 85, 139, 172–3, 197
  moral case for (*see* moral case for
    Citizen's Income)
  scheme (*see* Citizen's Income
    scheme)
  Young adult (*see* Young adult
    Citizen's Income)
Citizen's Income scheme, ix, 9, 26–7,
    29–31, 35, 39, 41–3, 49–53,
    56–60, 67–84, 92, 101, 103,
    109, 129, 139, 144, 159, 161,
    178, 183, 237, 242
  administration of (*see* Citizen's
    Income, administration of)
  illustrative, 53, 56, 59, 76, 109,
    160, 162, 182–3
  implementation of (*see*
    implementation)

net cost of, 31, 49–59, 65, 71–2, 79, 81, 85–6
revenue neutral (*see* revenue neutrality)
Citizen's Income Trust, xv, xvii, 53, 183, 186, 217
Citizen's Pension, 17, 39, 55–6, 59, 65, 76, 85, 105, 128, 160, 162, 217
Citizens UK, 212
civic labour/minimum, 93, 101
civil
  liberties, 175
  partnership, 98
  rights, 175
  servant/service, 13, 125, 129, 138, 196–7, 199–203, 206–9, 216, 218–19, 223–4
claimant
  demeaned, 7, 15, 125
  error (*see* error, claimant)
  fraud (*see* fraud)
  unit, individual (*see* individual claimant unit)
classical market. *See* market, classical
climate (-change), 46, 152
coalition (-building), 16, 167, 178–80, 195, 244. *See also* government, coalition
coercion, 74, 88, 215, 219
cohabitation rule/test, x, 7
collective bargaining, 219
collectivism, 151
Commission on Social Justice, 17, 175–6
Commonwealth Fund, 130
community, 68, 92–3, 182, 239–40
  groups, 203
  organizing, 212
  policy (*see* policy, community)
Compass, xxvii
complexity, 10

administrative, 10, 103–4, 143
benefits systems (*see* benefits, complexity of)
labour market, 13
policy process (*see* policy process, complexity of)
tax systems (*see* tax, complexity of)
theory, 196
computer
  -ization, 99, 131–2, 198, 202, 203
  manufacturers, 196, 202
  modelling, 83
  programme, 50–51, 83, 196, 202
  system, 11, 46, 209
conditional benefits. *See* benefits, conditional
conditions, benefits. *See* benefits, conditions
Confederation of British Industry (CBI), 211
conservatism, 149–50, 180
Conservative Party, 12, 99, 176, 180, 208. *See also* government, Conservative
constraint, x, 46, 243
  budget (*see* budget, constraint)
  prospective/retrospective, 27–31, 104
consultation exercise, 47
consumption, 46, 210
  taxes, 42, 44
contact details, 10, 132, 156
context, 26–7, 30–31, 35, 100, 124, 147, 168, 183, 195, 226
  economic, vi, 14, 45, 93, 96, 102, 148, 170, 182, 240
  political, 35, 154
contingency (benefits), x, 3, 41, 93, 133, 207, 221
contracts, 1, 13, 169–70
  zero hour, 13, 21, 144

contributions, social insurance. *See* social insurance, contributions
contributory
  benefits, x, 4, 7, 9–10, 16, 74, 110, 154, 207, 220 (*see also* social insurance, benefits)
  pensions, 9, 10, 16
  principle, 93
  unemployment insurance, 16, 207
convergent mental processes, 97
conversion experience/process, 91, 96–8, 100, 111, 187, 240–1
co-operatives, 171–2
corporate taxes, 42
corporatism, 148–9
cost of living, 106–7
Council Tax (Benefit/Support), xi, 15, 55–9, 64, 76, 134, 155–6, 220, 230, 234
counter-intuitive ideas, 109, 212
couple, viii, 1, 7–8, 70–1, 103, 133, 146
criminalization, 156
crisis, 222
  financial, 45, 90, 187
Crocker, Geoff, 46
culture, 88, 93, 151, 239
currency (exchange/trading/transactions), 43, 197

D

debate, v, vi, 41, 83–4, 102, 105, 109–10, 119, 125, 129, 133, 180, 200, 208, 211, 214–15, 217, 239, 240, 244
debt, 46, 49
decision-making, 7, 39, 60, 109, 125, 137, 146, 174, 185, 196, 200, 204, 205, 208
delivery mechanisms, 123–4, 209
demand, 44, 175, 210
democracy, 1, 3, 121, 144, 147, 171, 174, 181. *See also* social, democracy
demographic group, 64, 80, 108–109, 203–4, 222, 237. *See also* age group; year cohort
Department for Work and Pensions, 58, 133, 182, 208–9, 218, 220, 222
dependency, 170, 174, 181
deserving / undeserving, 17, 19, 80, 93, 105–9, 163, 203–6, 209, 211, 213, 218, 222–4, 237
desirabilities. *See also* Citizen's Income, desirability of; feasibility, desirability and
  contested, 3–6, 110
  differential, 9
  uncontested, 9–12
developed countries, 3, 6, 41–2, 44, 46, 98, 122, 147, 152
developing countries, 99, 122, 148
De Wispelaere, Jürgen, xiii, 27–9, 88, 100, 104, 119, 121–3, 125, 143, 167–8, 178, 183, 187, 195
diffuse actors. *See* actors
disability, xi, 56, 93, 105, 125, 134–5, 172, 207
Disability Living Allowance, xi, 56
disapproval, public, 104, 238
discrete actors. *See* actors
disincentive, 43
  employment, 4, 6, 7, 18, 43, 95–6, 101–2, 160, 170, 172, 215
Disinherited Family, The, 18, 205, 239
disposable income. *See* income, disposable
dividends (of a permanent fund), ix, 43, 46–7, 52, 60, 67, 100, 102, 123, 138
Duncan Smith, Iain, 208

INDEX   271

E
earned income. *See* income, earned
Earned Income Tax Credit, vii, 12, 13, 138
earner, 159
   higher, 12, 15, 21, 34, 148
   low, 11, 15, 34, 77
   second, 208
ecological sustainability/welfare, 169, 182
economic
   activity, 48, 92–4, 153, 169, 218
   arrangements, 93–4, 100–1, 104
   case for Citizen's Income, 175
   context/environment, vi, 35, 94, 148, 197, 240
   growth, 45–6
   handicap, 172
   incentives, 182
   independence/individuation, 152, 169
   opportunity, 174
   planning/management, 176–7, 240
   policy, 173
   problems, 15, 240
   rights, 175
   stability, 152
   success/wellbeing, 94, 153, 169, 174–5
   system, 240
economically active/inactive, 135–7
economies of scale, 7–8, 70, 100
economy, 13, 15, 18, 45–6, 77, 83, 144, 169–70, 241
   change in, 101, 144, 152, 240
   free market, 169–71, 173
   informal, 9
   post-productivist, 182
   real, 43, 45–6
   share, 181
   social/planned, 173, 177

education(-al)
   about Citizen's Income, vi, 19, 98–102, 107, 109, 126, 179–80, 202
   background, 106
   outcomes, 145, 147–8, 153, 177
   as participation criterion, 125
   publicly funded, 11, 42, 102, 170
Education and Training Income (ETI), 221. *See also* Young adult Citizen's Income
elderly people, 5, 16, 19, 39, 48, 94, 105, 108, 125, 128, 135, 218, 237
elections, v, 12, 16, 17, 99, 129, 132, 144, 182, 183, 211, 217, 244
electoral
   assistance/success/threat, 179
   base, 89
   register, 121, 132
Elizabethan Poor Law, 5–6, 96
embedded assumptions / change / presuppositions / public opinion, 5, 29, 89, 96, 108–9, 154, 162, 177, 241
employee/-er, 8–11, 13, 14, 102–3, 126–8, 144, 149, 176, 181, 202, 209, 212–13. *See also* social insurance, contributions; subcontractors
employment. *See also* own account economic activity; unemployment; zero hour contracts
   coerced (*see* coercion)
   formal, 180
   full, 149, 206–7
   full-time, 14, 33, 173
   guaranteed, 48
   incentives/disincentives, viii, 4, 6–7, 15, 18, 33, 54, 95–6, 101–3, 138, 159–61, 170, 172, 176–7, 187, 198, 206, 208, 215, 219 (*see also* motivation)

employment (*cont.*)
  income, 93, 133, 176 (*see also* wage)
  low-paid, 3–4, 156, 174, 210–11
  market (*see* employment market)
  occasional, 219–20
  as participation criterion, 125, 135
  part-time, 13–14, 116, 153, 156–8, 159–60, 173, 180, 220
  patterns of, 5, 9, 14, 28, 137, 143, 146, 156, 177, 219–21
  quality of, 94, 143, 172 (*see also* jobs, bad/good)
  seeking, x–xi, 4, 17, 136, 161
  self-, 9, 13, 49, 116, 125, 135, 137, 147, 153, 179
  status, vii, 64, 143, 206
Employment and Support Allowance (ESA), xi, 55
employment market, xvi, 14, 44, 47, 77, 88–9, 124, 146, 173–4, 177
  change in/effect on, 13, 103–4, 146–8, 153, 210, 212
  efficiency/inefficiency of, 14, 19, 147, 169–70, 177–8, 205
  flexible, 13–14, 26, 80, 101, 116, 143, 173, 179, 220
  incentives (*see* employment, incentives)
entitlement. *See* Citizen's Income, entitlement to
equalities legislation, 29, 37, 98
equality/inequality, 7, 12, 18, 34, 44–7, 78–9, 82, 89, 94, 95, 102, 106, 149–53, 169–73, 174–6, 178, 181–2, 185, 206
errors (in benefits calculations), 9–11, 99, 101, 122, 131–2, 152, 156, 218, 220, 243
Esping-Andersen, Gøsta, 148–50
EUROMOD, xvi, 57, 59, 63–5, 84–6, 192
Europe, v, 89, 98–100, 171, 173, 181, 197
European citizenship, 120
European Union, xxviii, 63, 85, 120
Euroscepticism, 99
evidence, 29, 53, 61, 63, 83, 91, 94, 154, 177, 182, 197, 201, 211, 216, 222, 240–42
  for behavioural feasibility, 28, 146–54, 162–3
expenditure tax. *See* tax, expenditure
experiments, 108, 153, 239
  constructed, 147–8, 153
  global natural, 148–53
  natural, 148, 153
expert, 99
pathway, 238
power, 202

F
Fabian Society, xvi, xvii, 236
family, 5, 105, 136, 170, 175
  with children (*see* child/children, families with)
  larger, 18, 136, 206
  structure, vii, xvi, 146, 219
Family Allowance, 16, 18, 32–5, 108, 198, 205–8, 209, 218, 223–4, 238–9. *See also* Child Benefit
Family Credit, 208, 210
Family Income Supplement, 11, 16, 148, 208–10
Family Resources Survey, 51, 63–5, 85, 192
feasibility, v–vi, xiii, xvi, xxvii, 1–2, 27–8, 35, 168, 226, 237–44
  administrative, xiii, 2, 28, 30–2, 34–5, 84, 104, 119–39, 167, 179, 196, 203, 209, 218, 223–4, 237, 242
  behavioural, xiii, 27–32, 34–5, 47, 84, 105, 143–63, 167, 196, 223, 237–8, 242

in context, 26–7
definition of, 25–6
desirability and, 1–3, 6, 19
financial, xiii, 30–2, 39–60, 67–84, 88, 91, 104, 168, 196, 223–4, 237–8
fiscal, 30–1, 34–5, 39–60, 185, 223, 237
gateway, 31
household financial, 25, 30–1, 34–5, 67–84, 87, 183, 185, 223, 237
institutional, 27–8, 119, 167
policy process, xiii, 28, 30, 31, 34–5, 84, 105, 119, 195–226, 237–8, 242–3
political, xiii, 28, 30–2, 34–5, 68, 84, 105, 167–87, 223, 237–8, 241
psychological, xiii, 27, 29–32, 34–5, 84, 87–111, 162–3, 167, 187, 195–6, 203, 237–8, 242
relationships between feasibilities, 31–2, 35
scheme, 27, 60, 238
strategic, 27–8, 119, 167–8, 195
test, 237
Field, Frank, 33, 209
financial
crisis, 45, 90, 187
feasibility (*see* feasibility, financial)
independence of women, 7, 48, 103, 132, 148, 153, 220
market (*see* market, financial)
transaction tax, 43–4, 69, 124, 197
First World War, 18, 205
fiscal feasibility. *See* feasibility, fiscal
Fitzpatrick, Tony, 124–5, 174
flat tax. *See* tax, flat
flexibility. *See* employment market, flexible; relationships, flexible
flexible consistency, 97
food stamps, 8
framing, 100, 107, 109

France, 11, 43, 149–50, 233
fraud, 9–11, 101, 131, 152, 156, 218
freedom, individual, 87, 98, 101, 145, 173, 177, 198, 200
free market
economy (*see* economy, free market)
in labour, 26, 101, 169–70
free trade. *See* trade, free
Friendly Societies, 16, 207
funding. *See* Citizen's Income, funding of

G
gains and losses, 30, 52, 65, 67–83, 85–6, 183, 185, 218
geographical location, 134, 152, 197
Germany, 7, 94, 149–50
global, 173
Citizen's Income (*see* Citizen's Income, global)
debate, v–vi
factors, 197
financial crisis (*see* financial, crisis)
financial transaction tax (*see* financial, transaction tax)
-ization, 176
market (*see* market, global)
natural experiment (*see* experiment, global natural)
paradigm shift (*see* paradigm shifts)
shift in public opinion (*see* change, in public opinion)
good jobs. *See* jobs, good
goods
consumption of, 46, 48, 156, 210
imported, 69
merit, 152
public, 42, 152
taxed, 44
trade in, 13, 43, 45

government
- administration by, ix, 9–11, 44, 70, 126–9, 136, 238 (*see also* administration; administrative)
- bonds, 45
- borrowing, 42–3
- and Citizen's Income, v, 39–40, 46, 52, 67, 69, 73, 82, 107–9, 128, 139, 144, 154, 177, 214, 217, 238, 244 (*see also* government, Citizen's Income feasible for)
- Citizen's Income feasible for, 1, 30, 39, 67, 73, 82, 139, 238 (*see also* government, and Citizen's Income)
- coalition, 16, 244 (*see also* coalition (-building))
- committee, 17–18, 32, 182, 184, 205–7, 216–17, 239
- Conservative, 16, 129, 180, 210 (*see also* Conservative Party)
- departments (and heads of), xv, 10–11, 13, 58, 129, 133, 198–202, 206, 209, 218, 222
- education by, 19, 108 (*see also* education, about Citizen's Income)
- Labour, 33, 132, 208, 210 (*see also* Labour Party)
- localisation, 64, 134
- minimal, 169
- ministers, 10, 16, 197, 199–200, 202, 219, 242
- national/regional, xxviii
- policy (*see* policy, government)
- and policy process, 27, 34, 83, 98–100, 130, 186, 196–9, 201–3, 209, 217, 238, 241, 243–4
- pressures on, 3, 33, 42–3, 88, 112, 130, 134, 177, 186, 209–10, 241
- and public opinion, 29, 60, 88–9, 94, 98, 106–8, 110, 200, 242 (*see also* public, opinion)
- research, 83, 154, 208 (*see also* research)
- revenue, 30, 33, 39–46, 52, 60, 67, 69–70, 123, 171
- spending, 3, 5, 8, 11, 16, 30, 33, 39, 41–2, 44, 46, 48, 52, 60, 67, 70, 82, 89, 94, 106–7, 110, 123, 134, 148–9, 171, 207

Gramsci, Antonio, 88
Greater London Authority, Living Wage Unit, 212–13, 234
green parties, 178
Green Party (UK), v, xvi, 182–4
Greenwich, xvii, 213, 221
Greenwich Local Labour and Business, 221
Gross Domestic Product, 46, 182
group
- age (*see* age cohort/group)
- identifiable, 17, 27–8, 205
- task (additive, conjunctive, disjunctive), 31, 241

growth, economic, 45–6, 182
guaranteed job. *See* job guarantee

H

health service / healthcare, 12, 17, 48, 89, 94, 102, 106–8, 121, 130–1, 147–9, 153, 170, 198, 200
heating costs, x, 7
hegemonic moral discourse, 88–90, 96, 241. *See also* moral, discourse
Herbison, Margaret, 34
Her Majesty's Revenue and Customs (HMRC), 55, 133, 209
Hill, Michael, 197–9, 222
Hofstede, Geert, 151–2
homeless people, 133

household
  and Citizen's Income, viii, 4, 5, 7–9, 14–15, 25, 28, 30, 48–51, 57–8, 69–77, 79, 81–2, 87, 122, 132–3, 139, 143–7, 151, 153, 155–6, 170, 183, 217–18, 221, 237, 244
  claimant unit, viii, x–xi, 4–5, 8, 9, 15, 21, 49, 51, 57, 64, 70, 75, 103, 107–8, 131, 133–4, 145, 155–6, 176, 187, 208, 218, 237
  complex/diverse, 9, 72, 82, 219
  financial feasibility (*see* feasibility, household financial)
  head of, 48, 123
  income (earned/disposable), 5, 13–15, 26, 30, 41–2, 48, 50, 65, 67–77, 79, 81–3, 85, 86, 101, 133, 144–6, 151, 156, 170, 172, 183, 206–8, 214, 217, 221, 244
  relationships (*see* relationships, household)
  resources (*see* resources, household)
  structure, 6–8, 10, 26, 28, 82
  typical, 71–2, 75
House of Commons, 187
  Treasury and Civil Service Committee Sub-Committee, 216
House of Lords, 187
houses of correction, 6
housing
  costs, xi, 10, 72, 134, 155, 207, 220–1
  stock/supply, 48, 146
  tenure, vii, 71
Housing Benefit, xi, 15, 54, 56–9, 76, 101, 134, 154–6, 221, 230, 234, 239
Hovwells, David, 180–1

I
identity (card/checks/evidence of/fraud), 10, 121, 131, 157
ideology (political), 28, 89, 167–87, 195, 201, 239
illness, x, xi, 3, 4, 9, 135, 207
immigration, 105. *See also* migration
implementation, xiii, xviii, 1, 9, 11, 16–18, 25–35, 41–2, 44, 48, 50–1, 53, 56, 61, 68–71, 73, 76, 82–3, 87–8, 90–2, 100–1, 110, 119–20, 122–4, 129, 134, 143–7, 153–4, 156, 162–3, 167–8, 170, 174, 177–9, 183, 185, 195–206, 208–9, 211–19, 222–4, 226, 237–9, 241–4
  all at once, 26, 81, 109, 139, 223–4
  evolutionary / gradual / phased / sequential, 13, 19, 26, 32, 35, 77–81, 83, 102–6, 109, 144, 162–3, 201, 203–4, 222, 224, 243
  point of, 30, 40, 67–71, 75–6, 79, 81–3, 87, 183, 218
incapacity, 174
Incapacity Benefit, 55–6, 65, 85
Incentive. *See* economic incentives; employment incentive; savings, incentive
income
  additional, xi, 4, 15, 53, 71, 95–6, 103, 124, 127, 132, 138, 145, 218, 220
  decile, 72–4, 76–7, 79, 81–2, 149–50, 152, 185
  disposable, 14, 18–19, 28, 30, 33, 41–2, 50, 65, 68, 72–4, 79, 81–2, 85, 87, 101–2, 139, 143–5, 147, 151, 170, 183, 185, 214

income (*cont.*)
  earned, viii, x, 3–4, 8, 13–15, 33, 40, 42, 44, 46, 48, 54, 57, 68, 71–2, 75, 80, 95, 126, 128–9, 139, 143, 145, 147, 150–1, 156–9, 170, 174, 204, 215, 221 (*see also* wage)
  floor, 101, 180
  household (*see* household, income)
  inequalities, 149–53
  independent, 7, 153
  investment, 54–5, 204
  maintenance, 41–2, 61, 80, 87, 155, 187, 204–5, 208
  net, 33, 53–4, 75, 126, 128–9, 138, 145–6, 149–50, 152, 156, 159–62, 206
  subsistence, 14–15, 173, 179, 182
  tax (*see* income tax)
Income Support, xi, 53, 55–6, 65, 85, 160
Income Tax, vii, ix–xi, 3, 7–8, 14–16, 34, 40–2, 44, 50–2, 54–5, 57, 58, 75, 82, 95, 101, 103, 107, 126–8, 130, 132, 144–5, 154, 159, 181. See *also* Child Tax Allowance; Income Tax Personal Allowance
  allowance (threshold), 40–2, 58, 61, 87, 123–4
  basic rate, 40, 51–2, 54–5, 59, 63, 65, 75, 79, 81, 85, 183
  rates, x, 1, 15, 30, 40–2, 49–54, 58–61, 65, 67–8, 70–1, 74, 75, 78–81, 83, 86, 101, 123–4, 126–8, 139, 155, 177, 185
Income Tax Personal Allowance, vii, 55, 58, 75, 78, 80, 139
incremental change, 98, 196, 201, 203–4, 222, 243–4
India, v, 48–9, 69, 102, 122–3, 133, 147–8, 218–19

indifference curves. *See* utility curves
individual claimant unit, vii–ix, 1, 7, 9–10, 25, 30, 39–42, 45, 48, 51, 64, 67–70, 87, 100, 103, 107, 120, 122, 124–6, 128, 133, 138, 155, 217, 223, 243
inequality. *See* equality/inequality
inflation, 18, 34, 45, 47, 69, 124, 206
informal economy. *See* economy, informal
inheritance, 90, 100, 173
injury, 135
innovation, 110, 196
Institute for Economic Affairs, 241
Institute for Social and Economic Research (University of Essex), xvii, 57, 183
institutional
  feasibility (*see* feasibility, institutional)
  relationships (*see* relationships, institutional)
institutions, 11, 26–8, 35, 89–92, 97, 99, 110, 119, 147, 168, 179, 195–9, 202–4, 226, 239–40, 243
  academic, 83, 202
insurance, 3, 16, 130, 170
  healthcare, 12, 130
  National Insurance (*see* National Insurance)
  social (*see* social insurance, benefits)
intimate details/relationships, 8, 143
intra-household redistribution. *See* redistribution, intra-household
investment income. *See* income, investment
Iran, v, 48–9, 69, 102, 123, 238, 239, 242
issue network, 198, 226

J
James, William, 96
Japan, 52, 103–4, 106–7, 128–9, 149–50
Job Centre, 221
job guarantee, 177–8
jobs
  bad, 15, 143
  casual, 175, 216
  good, 14, 143
  lousy (*see* jobs, bad)
  low-skill, 13
Jobseeker's Allowance, vii, xi, 53, 55, 65, 85, 156, 159. *See also* Unemployment Benefit
Joseph Rowntree Foundation, xvii, 214, 222

K
Keynesian mindset, 240
Kuhn, Thomas, 239

L
labour, 13, 44, 48, 171–2, 174–5, 181
  civic (*see* civic labour)
  free movement of, 197
  marginal product of, 210
  market (*see* employment market)
Labour Exchange, 215
Labour Party, 12, 17, 33–4, 107, 175–6, 187, 211. *See also* government, Labour
Land Value Tax, 44–5
legal residence. *See* citizenship
legislation/legislators, 6, 26, 27, 29, 35, 88, 98, 167, 179, 197–9, 201–2, 228
  anti-discrimination, 98
  anti-smoking, 29
  benefits, 16, 33–4, 209
Citizen's Income, 195, 203, 220
civil partnerships, 98
equalities, 29, 98
minimum wage, 14, 211–14
same sex marriage, 97–8, 108
leisure, 145, 156–61
less eligibility, 5–6, 19
liberal, 174, 176
  democracy, 174
  welfare regime, 149–51
liberalism, 149–50, 168, 173–4
life chances, 175, 180
lifecycle, redistribution across, 93, 116
living costs, x, 14, 212, 214
Living Wage, 205, 212–14, 219, 230, 234. *See also* National Living Wage
Local Authority/councillor, 134, 155, 213
localisation. *See* government, localisation
London, 155, 212–14, 221, 234
  Mayor of, 98, 213
London Citizens, 212
London School of Economics, xvi, 205–6
London Stock Exchange, 43
lone mother/parent, xi, 64
losses. *See* gains and losses
lousy jobs. *See* jobs, bad
Lower Earnings Limit, 57, 59, 65, 85, 139
low pay. *See* employment, low paid
Low Pay Commission, 211–12
Low Pay Unit, 211

M
main carer (of child), 39, 80, 131–2
manifesto, v, 182–3, 211, 238, 244

marginal deduction rate, xi, 15, 30, 53, 71, 82, 87, 101, 103, 134, 138, 148–9, 151, 155
market
  classical, 14
  employment (*see* employment market)
  financial, 45, 172
  free (*see* free market)
  global, 13, 169, 173
marriage, 7, 17, 97–8, 106, 108, 181
Marx, Karl, 171
Maternity, x, 55, 221
means-tested benefits, viii, x–xi, 3–17, 19, 31, 33, 41, 49–51, 53–5, 57–9, 61, 65, 70–2, 75–7, 80, 82, 85, 87, 91, 95, 99–103, 108, 110, 123–5, 133–4, 139, 145–6, 148–9, 151, 153–7, 159, 163, 170, 173, 176–7, 180–3, 186, 207–10, 212, 214, 218–21, 230–2, 234, 237, 240
  administration of, 9–11, 13, 16, 103, 239
  in-work, 11, 13–14, 16, 70, 133, 146, 176, 208–9, 212, 214, 232
  out-of-work, 70, 133, 146, 208–9, 232
  retained (*see* benefits, retained)
  withdrawal of, xi, 4, 11, 53, 70–1, 103, 127, 138, 145, 208, 219, 243
media, the, 89, 96, 99, 162–3, 195, 200–3, 213, 219, 240
Member of Parliament. *See* Parliament, Member of
microsimulation, xvi, 50–1, 57–8, 65, 71–7, 138
migration, 103, 197. *See also* immigration
mindset, 95–8, 101, 107, 239–40. *See also* paradigm shifts
Minimum Income Standards, 57, 64, 185, 212
minimum wage, 14, 174. *See also* National Minimum Wage
minister. *See* government minister
misnaming. *See* benefits, misnamed
modelling, computer, 51, 82–4, 86, 138, 146
monetarism, 240
monetary system, 46
money, creation of, ix, 41, 43, 45–7, 52, 60, 67, 69, 123–4
monitoring. *See* surveillance
moral
  authoritarianism, 169
  case for Citizen's Income, 175
  discourse, 88–90, 94, 96 (*see also* hegemonic moral discourse)
  intuitions, 94
mortgage payments, 41
Moscovici, Serge, 96–7
motivation, 212–13. *See also* employment incentives/disincentives
motives, diverse, 18, 112
multiplier effect, 153
Murray, Charles, 170

N
Namibia, v, 102, 147–8, 218–19
national accounts, 33, 49–50
National Assistance, 207–8, 215, 223–4
national dividend, 100. *See also* social, dividend
National Health Service, 89, 107–8, 130–1, 149, 200
National Insurance
  benefits, 55, 133, 207, 215, 224

Contributions, xv, 15, 65, 139, 160, 207–8, 217
number, 132
National Living Wage, 205, 214, 224
National Minimum Wage, 53–4, 160–2, 177, 205, 209–12, 225, 233. *See also* minimum wage
national statistics, 49–51, 53–7, 71, 134
National Union of Students, 221
natural experiment. *See* experiment, natural
needs, x, 5–6, 9, 14, 18, 101, 107, 155, 170–72, 174–6, 206
Negative Income Tax, vii, ix–x, 103, 126–9, 138–9, 147, 170
Neil, Andrew, 183
neoliberalism, 169, 180
New Right, The, 168–70, 175
New Zealand, 148
Noguera, José Antonio, xiii, 17–9, 178, 183, 187, 195
nonwithdrawable, v, ix, 1, 9, 18, 25, 39, 40, 67, 78, 87, 96, 106–8, 124, 131, 197, 203–4, 215–17, 220, 222–3, 238, 244
definition of, viii

O

obligations, 92, 101, 105, 120, 170, 180, 182, 204
older people. *See* elderly people
One Nation Conservatives, 12, 180–2
one step at a time, 77–84, 102–6, 109, 162, 243
opportunity
economic/employment, 92, 170, 174–5, 180, 216
equality of, 175, 182
ladder of, 173

Organization for Economic Co-operation and Development (OECD), 130, 148, 213
Osborne, George, 89. *See also* Chancellor of the Exchequer
overpayments, 13
own account economic activity, 48

P

paradigm shifts, 239–42
parent(s), 64, 74, 121, 132, 135–6, 146
Parker, Hermione, xv, 125
Parliament, 34, 132, 196, 198, 202–3, 206–8, 222, 224, 239, 244
Member of, 17, 18, 34, 37, 107, 179, 184, 186, 199, 211, 216, 230, 239
parliamentary
champions, 211, 219, 223
committee, 17, 184, 207
enquiry, 53
Participation Income, 82, 86, 103, 124–6, 134–9, 177, 243
path dependency, 196, 224
pay. *See* income, earned
low (*see* employment, low-paid)
Pay As You Earn, 44
payment mechanisms/periods, 121–2, 133–4
Pennycook, Matthew, 213
pension. *See also* Basic State Pension; Pension Credit; Single Tier State Pension
contributions, 40, 51
contributions tax relief, 54–5, 57, 183
contributory, 9–10, 207
Minister for, 16, 217
non-contributory, 16
policy, 218, 222

pension (*cont.*)
  private/public sector, 148–9, 170, 220
  taxation of, 54
  unconditional/universal, 7, 17, 104, 152 (*see also* Citizen's Pension)
Pension Credit, xi, 16–17, 53, 55, 65, 85, 160, 218
Pensions Policy Institute, 218
permanent fund dividends, ix, 45, 47, 52, 60, 67, 102, 123, 138
pilot projects/studies, v, 48, 102, 122, 123, 147–8, 203, 206–7, 211, 218–20, 222–4
policy
  accidents, 35, 238–9, 242
  advisors, 10, 196
  analysis, 83, 120, 204
  change (*see* policy change)
  community, 198–9, 206, 226, 240, 242
  continuity, 206–9, 211, 213, 218–19, 222–4
  economic (*see* economic policy)
  entrepreneurs, 167, 195, 200, 238
  environment, 199
  government, 3, 5, 7–9, 12, 16, 17, 19, 32–3, 39, 41–2, 46, 48, 51–2, 60, 64, 67, 70, 82–3, 89, 94, 98, 106–7, 110, 126, 129, 134–6, 139, 144, 177, 180, 186, 196, 198–9, 200, 201, 203, 207–11, 214, 217, 238, 241–4
  makers / making (*see* policy process)
  monopoly, 240
  network, 195–204, 226
  objectives, 34, 201
  options, 2–3, 83, 168, 199, 201, 203, 209, 238, 243
  problems, 5, 7, 13, 18–19, 30, 35, 36, 70–1, 126, 134, 138, 143, 171, 173, 176, 183, 196, 199–201, 203, 206, 209–11, 216, 219–21, 238–41, 244
  process (*see* policy process)
  proposal, v, vi, viii, ix, 2, 11–12, 16–19, 25, 35, 51, 58, 68, 77, 80, 82, 92, 100, 105, 109, 129, 144, 152, 167–8, 173, 181, 183, 195–9, 201, 203–6, 211–12, 216, 219, 223–4, 242
  window, 238
policy change, 10–11, 17, 34, 35, 47, 49, 77, 87, 91, 96, 98, 105, 108–9, 131, 176, 196, 198–222, 238, 240–1, 243–4
  evolutionary, 35, 103–4, 144, 169, 171, 175, 196, 224
  incremental, 98, 196, 201, 203–4, 222, 243–4
policy-making. *See* policy process
policy process. *See also* feasibility, policy process; government; think tanks; political party; civil servant/service.
  accident, 242 (*see also* political, accident)
  complexity of, 34, 196, 238, 241
  context-specific, 168, 195, 226
  contingencies, 237
  diffuse, 195
  feasibility (*see* policy process, feasibility)
  institutions, 35, 92, 197, 223
  pathways, 238
  political model of, 83, 199–200, 238–9
  predictable / unpredictable elements of, 199, 239
  rational model of, 199–202
political. *See also* feasibility, political; policy press, political model of
  accident, 35, 242 (*see also* policy process, accident)

activist/actor, 18, 27, 28, 106, 167, 174, 178, 180, 187, 195, 199, 210 (*see also* politician)
capital, 178
choices, 83, 185, 204
coalition, 167, 195
context, 35, 154
factors/forces, 199, 201, 204, 239, 241
feasibility (*see* feasibility, political)
ideology, 28, 167–8, 170, 174, 177, 179, 180, 187, 195, 239
institutions, 27
modelling as, 83
party, 27, 99, 168, 179, 187, 201, 202, 217
rights, 175
spectrum, v, 74, 152, 169
sphere, 27, 167
support, 124, 180, 242
will, 46–7
politician, 25, 27, 74, 89, 107, 167, 178, 197, 243. *See also* political activist/actor
Pond, Chris, 210–11
Poor and the Poorest, The, 208
Poor Law/relief, the, 6, 16, 149
Post Office Card accounts, 122, 133–4
post-productivism, 182
poverty, 5, 104, 185, 202–4
  abolition of, 34, 198
  alleviation of, 33–4, 45, 71, 95, 100, 109, 138, 153, 174, 178, 198, 206–7, 211, 213, 215, 217–19, 221–4
  child (*see* child, poverty)
  in-work, 16, 209, 214
  trap, 3–6, 71, 95, 138, 148, 153, 159–60, 173–4, 180, 202, 204, 206–11, 213–19, 221–4
Power Difference Index (PDI), 151–2

prejudice, 6, 200, 241. *See also* embedded assumptions / presuppositions
pre-retired. *See* retired people, retirement
Pre-Retirement Income (PRI), 78, 108, 116, 220–1
press, the. *See* media
pressure groups, 197, 202–3, 217
presuppositions. *See* embedded assumptions / presuppositions
prices, 13, 33, 43–6, 48, 69, 210
Prime Minister, 99, 211, 213, 220
private provision, 149, 170
problems. *See* policy problems
professionals, 99, 197–8, 200, 226
progressive tax system. *See* tax system, progressive
psychological
  feasibility (*see* feasibility, psychological)
  shift, 90–1
psychologies, 26, 90–1
public
  acceptance/approval, 17, 80, 93, 98, 110, 121, 125, 137, 154, 206, 216, 222 (*see also* public, understanding)
  expenditure, 3, 5, 33–4, 50
  goods, 42, 152
  opinion (*see also* change, in public opinion; survey)
  sector, 147, 203
  servants, vi, 7, 8, 10, 11, 13, 15–19, 27, 198, 205, 211, 221 (*see also* civil servant)
  services, 41, 123, 131, 171
  understanding, 17, 19, 98, 100, 102, 104–5, 110, 163, 203, 205, 207, 208, 211, 213, 218–19, 223, 224 (*see also* public acceptance/approval)
Purdy, David, 168, 244

Q

quantitative easing, 45, 123

R

random sample, 48, 50, 94, 239
Rathbone, Eleanor, 18, 205–6, 215, 239
reciprocal agreements, 131
reciprocity, 92–4, 100–101, 175, 241
redistribution, 44, 74, 82, 93, 100, 107, 149–50, 153, 169–70, 173, 175, 181, 184–6, 216
redundancies, 10, 221
referendum, v, 98–9
refugee, 120
regime. *See* welfare state, regimes
regressive tax system. *See* tax system, regressive
regulations, vii, ix, 6, 15, 41, 51, 64, 71–2, 75, 83, 99, 124, 137, 156, 172, 202–3
relationships
  between feasibilities (*see* feasibility, relationships between feasibilities)
  causal, 105, 153 (*see also* causal direction)
  flexible, 14, 71
  household, 9
  institutional, 28, 199, 202, 226, 239
  intimate, 143, 146
  permanent, 7
  personal, 28, 70, 219, 238–9
  social, 5, 11, 182
  test, x
relay race, 31–2, 241
renaming of benefits. *See* benefits, renaming of
rent, 64
  levels, 10, 72
  rebates, 56

rental
  markets, 134
  value, 44
Republic of Ireland, 7, 98
research, xxvii, xxviii, 10, 11, 33–4, 53, 72–3, 83–4, 86, 94, 97, 99, 102, 105, 110, 129, 148, 151, 163, 183, 199, 200, 202, 212–13, 217, 235–6, 238–9, 241, 243–4. *See also* government, research
residency test, 105
Resolution Foundation, The, 213
resources
  common, 100
  household/individual, 6, 153
  limited, 182
  political, 178, 199
  state, 180, 203
  survey (*see* survey)
responsibility
  collective/government, 94, 106, 178
  personal, 94, 169, 175
retired people, retirement (and pre-retired) x, 20, 32, 105, 108, 116, 125, 135–7, 148, 163, 220–1, 237. *See also* Pre-Retirement Income (PRI); state, pension age
return to capital, 210
revenue
  foregone, 33
  neutrality (and strict revenue neutrality), 40–3, 49–60, 70, 74–6, 79, 81–3, 87, 144
Rhys William, Brandon, 17, 180–1, 184, 215–16, 223
Rhys Williams, Juliet, 17, 181, 215–16, 223
rights, 89–90, 100, 120–1, 175, 182
  economic (*see* economic, rights)
Royal Commission, 186–7

Royal Society of Arts, xxvii
running costs (departmental), 54–6, 58

S
safety net, 3, 149, 169, 175, 218
same sex marriage. *See* legislation, same sex marriage
sanctions, 6, 17, 88–9, 92–3, 205
satisficing, 201
savings (personal), 153. *See also* administrative, costs; Citizen's Income scheme, net cost of
 incentive/disincentive, 181, 217
 income, x, 58
 trap, 217–18, 220
scheme, Citizen's Income. *See* Citizen's Income scheme
school (attendance/performance), 11, 12, 43, 48, 132, 136. *See also* education
scroungers, 89, 163. *See also* strivers v. skivers
second earner. *See* earner, second
Second World War, 18, 32, 205–7, 239
secure financial floor. *See* financial floor
self-employment. *See* employment, self-
self-interested actors. *See* actors, self-interested
service provision 13–14, 123
share trading, 43–5, 124
sickness. *See* illness
Sickness Benefit, 9, 207
Single Tier State Pension (STP), 16–18, 78, 108, 217–19, 222, 224–5
skill (-ed), 175. *See also* unskilled
 low-, 13
 new, 4, 15
 semi-, 13, 14
Smith, Adam, xxvii, 169

smoking, 29, 98
social
 acceptance, 88
 cohesion, 11–12, 26, 45–6, 101, 143, 219
 construction, 199
 democracy, 149, 152, 168–9, 174–6
 differentiation, 12, 180
 dividend (*see* national dividend; dividends (of a permanent fund))
 division, 89
 economy (*see* economy, social)
 exclusion/inclusion, 176
 fracture, 11
 insurance benefits (*see* social insurance benefits)
 justice, 174–6
 norm, 90–1, 93
 relationships (*see* relationships, social)
 security benefits, 3, 40–1, 93, 105, 120, 125, 131, 149, 154, 197, 204–5 (*see also* benefits)
 structures, 151–2, 180
 work, 198
social insurance
 benefits, x, 3–5, 10, 18, 33, 87, 91, 93–4, 106, 133, 151, 177, 207, 215 (*see also* contributory, benefits; National Insurance)
 contributions, x–xi, 4–5, 93
Social Insurance and Allied Services, 207, 215
Social Policy Association, xvi, 212, 214
socialism, 149–50, 168, 170–3, 176
software, 196, 202
solidarity, 109, 174
sovereign wealth fund, 43, 47, 60
Soviet Union, 171
spouse, non-earning, 136–7
stability, 13–15, 152, 240

staff turnover, 212, 213
standard of living, acceptable, 205, 212
state
　minimal, 170
　pension (*see* Basic State Pension; Pension Credit; Single Tier State Pension (STP); State Second Pension)
　pension age, 105, 135, 220
State Second Pension, 55–6, 218
stigma, 8–9, 95, 156, 175, 210
Stirton, Lindsay, xiii, 122, 125
stock exchange, 43
Stock Transfer Tax, 43
strategic feasibility. *See* feasibility, strategic
street-level bureaucrats, 8, 125, 202–3
strict revenue neutrality. *See* revenue neutrality
strivers v. skivers, 89. *See also* scroungers
student, 19, 21, 55, 135–7, 220–1
subcontractors, 13
suboptimal solutions, 196
subsidy
　programmes, funding redirected, 48–9, 52, 60, 67, 69, 99, 123
　to wages, benefits as, 176–7, 210
successive limited comparisons, 243
sufficiently fair/just (society as), 92–3
surveillance, 172
survey (opinion/resources), 50, 51, 63–5, 85, 94, 103, 106–7, 110, 128–9, 152, 192
Switzerland, v, 149–50

T

taper rate, xi, 61, 64, 75, 219
targeting, 29, 96, 110, 122, 176, 180–1
tax
　alcohol, 44
　allowances (*see* income tax, allowance; Income Tax Personal Allowance)
　complexity of, 44, 76, 98
　corporate (*see* corporate taxes)
　expenditure (*see* public, expenditure)
　flat, 58
　global, 44
　income (*see* income tax)
　progressive, 44, 58, 68, 82, 96, 102, 170
　rates (*see* income tax, rates)
　reductions, 46
　regressive, 58
　regulations (*see* regulations)
　system, vi, 2, 26, 29, 30, 41–4, 46, 49, 58, 60, 67, 69, 83, 87, 96, 98–9, 103, 108, 119, 127, 129, 144, 148, 152, 159, 187, 220, 226, 238
　thresholds (*see* income tax, allowance)
　tobacco, 44
Tax Credit, vii, ix–xi, 16–17, 103–4, 126–9, 138–9. *See also* Child Tax Credit; Earned Income Tax Credit; Negative Income Tax; Working Tax Credit
taxpayers, 21, 33, 55, 77, 93, 108, 131–2, 176, 187, 220
TELCO (The East London Communities Organization), 212
Thatcher, Margaret, 169
think tanks, v–vi, xvi, 27, 83, 179, 196, 199–202, 206–7, 208–9, 211, 213, 217–18, 223–4, 241
Titmuss, Richard, 33
Tobin, James, 44
Tobin tax. *See* financial transaction tax
Townsend, Peter, 33, 208

trade, free, 43, 169, 173
Trades Boards, 211
trade union, 9, 18, 34, 102–3, 179–80, 196, 202, 206, 208–10, 218–19, 221–4
  women members of (*see* women, trade union members)
Trade Union Congress (TUC), 210
training, 125, 131, 143, 212, 221, 225
transition (from one benefits system to another), 13, 19, 25, 28, 32–5, 40, 47, 68, 78, 80, 82, 88, 98, 103, 108, 119–20, 124, 129, 168, 176, 185, 203, 206–9, 213, 218–21, 223–4
Treasury, The, 211, 216
treaties, 120
trial and error, 49, 52, 65, 85, 243
tug of war, 31, 241

U

uncertainty, 144, 151, 240
unconditional benefits, v, vii, viii, ix, xi, 1, 2, 7–10, 16–18, 25, 32, 39, 40, 48, 67, 78, 87, 91, 94–6, 98, 100–2, 106–8, 110, 121, 123–4, 130–1, 137, 148, 153, 155, 162, 172, 175–8, 197, 203–4, 206, 215–17, 219–23, 238, 243. *See also* universal benefits
uncontested desirabilities. *See* desirabilities, uncontested
undeserving. *See* deserving / undeserving
unemployment, x, xi, 3–6, 9, 16–17, 89, 94, 103, 105–6, 110, 125, 127, 135, 156, 181, 206–7, 210, 213, 215–16
  trap, 3–6, 174, 216

Unemployment Benefit, 16, 206–7. *See also* Jobseeker's Allowance; sanctions
United Kingdom (UK), v–viii, xi, xxi, 5, 7, 11, 12, 15–16, 18, 21, 32–4, 45, 51, 53, 56, 58, 60, 65, 74, 75, 77, 82, 85, 89, 91, 93, 96, 98–9, 101, 107–8, 122, 126, 129, 131–7, 139, 144, 149, 154–63, 175, 180–7, 195, 197, 199–26, 234, 237–9, 241–4
United States of America, xxi, 45, 98, 142, 147–50, 170, 173, 212
universal
  benefits, ix, 3, 7, 19, 91, 96, 106–8, 110, 151–4, 163, 177, 185, 187, 197, 216, 240–1 (*see also* unconditional benefits)
  franchise, 19, 102
Universal Basic Income, 172. *See also* Citizen's Income; Basic Income
Universal Credit, xi, 11, 15, 75, 101, 127, 129, 133, 156, 208–9, 219, 223–4, 239, 242
unskilled, 105, 175. *See also* skill (-ed)
Upper Earnings Limit, 58–9, 65, 78, 80, 85
utility curves (indifference curves), 154–62

V

vested interests, 46
voluntary
  community activity, 93, 125, 135, 137
  organizations, xv, 147, 213
  scheme, 213, 220–1
  sector, 198
voters, 126, 200

W

wage, ix, x, 7, 14–15, 18, 49, 50, 102–3, 143, 157, 172, 176–7, 184, 205–7, 210, 212–16, 221. *See also* employment, income; Living Wage; National Living Wage; National Minimum Wage
  demand, 33–4
  -setting, 210–11
  total value of, 46, 210
Wages Councils, 211
Webb, Steven, 16, 217, 220
welfare
  benefits (*see* benefits)
  chauvinism, 105
welfare state, 109–10, 169, 174, 186
  regimes, 148–53
  residual, 149
  structure, 154
White, Stuart, 92, 100–101
Winter Fuel Allowance, ix, xi, 56, 107
withdrawal, of means-tested benefits. *See* means-tested benefits, withdrawal of
women
  financial independence of (*see* financial, independence of women)
  status of, 17, 48, 122, 181, 215
  trade union members, 18, 34, 206, 209
work. *See* carer/care work; employment; employment market; voluntary, community activity
  ethic, 93, 174, 176
  fares to, 4
  test, x, 87

Work and Pensions Select Committee, 63, 182
workers
  emancipation of, 172
  shift, 21, 89, 144–5
workfare, 6
workhouse, 16
working age adult, x, 14, 19, 39, 52, 53, 55, 57, 59, 72, 76, 80, 105, 108, 116, 127, 139, 160–2, 170, 207, 215, 221–2, 237
Working Age Income, 221–2, 224
working conditions, 143, 210
Working Families Tax Credit, 99, 208
working poor, 211, 213
Working Tax Credit, vii, xi, 11, 15, 55, 65, 75, 85, 99, 101, 156, 159, 183, 208, 230, 232, 234

Y

year cohort, 13. *See also* age cohort/group; demographic group
York, University of, 57
young
  adults, 39, 80–1, 108, 132, 136, 162, 221, 243
  people, viii, ix, 32, 39, 64–5, 78, 85, 98, 105, 121, 128, 177, 237
Young adult Citizen's Income, 64–5, 80–1, 83, 85, 86, 160. *See also* Education and Training Income (ETI)

Z

zero hour contracts, 13, 21, 144